MARRIAGE AND REVOLUTION

Marriage and Revolution

Monsieur and Madame Roland

SIÂN REYNOLDS

OXFORD

UNIVERSITY PRESS

OXFORD
UNIVERSITY PRESS

Great Clarendon Street, Oxford OX2 6DP
United Kingdom

Oxford University Press is a department of the University of Oxford.
It furthers the University's objective of excellence in research, scholarship,
and education by publishing worldwide. Oxford is a registered trade mark of
Oxford University press in the UK and in certain other countries

© Siân Reynolds 2012

First published 2012

Impression: 1

British Library Cataloguing in publication data

Data available

Library of Congress Cataloging in publication data
Reynolds, Siân.
Marriage and revolution : Monsieur and Madame Roland / Siân Reynolds.
p.   cm.
Summary: "A double biography of Jean-Marie Roland and Marie-Jeanne Phlipon, later Madame Roland,
leading figures in the French Revolution"— Provided by publisher.
ISBN 978–0–19–956042–4 (hardback)
1. Roland, Mme (Marie-Jeanne), 1754–1793.   2. Roland de La Platière, Jean-Marie,
1734–1793.   3. France—History—Revolution, 1789–1799—Biography.
4. France—Intellectual life—18th century.   5. Revolutionaries—France—Biography.
6. Intellectuals—France—Biography.   I. Title.
DC146.R7R49   2012
944.04′10922—dc23 [B]   2012006103

Printed in Great Britain
on acid-free paper by
MPG Books Group, Bodmin and King's Lynn

ISBN 978–0–19–956042–4

For Peter France

Contents

PART IV: IN THE THICK OF IT

PART V: A CLOSING TRAP

List of Abbreviations

Actes	*Actes du Tribunal révolutionnaire*, ed. Gérard Walter (1968/1986), Paris: Mercure de France.
AD	Archives départementales
AHRF	*Annales historiques de la Révolution française*
AML	Archives municipales de Lyon
AN	Archives Nationales, Paris
AP	*Archives parlementaires. Recueil complet des débats législatifs et politiques des Chambres françaises, Première série 1787–1799*, ed. J. Madival et E. Laurent, 82 vols (1867–1913).
BML	Bibliothèque municipale de Lyon
BNF MSS, naf	Bibliothèque Nationale de France, Département des Manuscrits, rue de Richelieu, Paris, Nouvelles Acquisitions Françaises [+ number = the Papiers Roland]
Champagneux (1800)	*Oeuvres de J.M.Ph. Roland, femme de l'ex-ministre de l'Intérieur*, 3 vols, ed. L.A. Champagneux (1800), Paris: Bidault [most references are to the *Discours préliminaire*].
Corr.	*Lettres de Mme Roland*, ed. Cl. Perroud (1900–1902), 2 vols. Vol. I: *1780–1787*; Vol. II: *1788–1793*, Paris: Imprimerie Nationale.
Corr., NS.	*Lettres de Mme Roland*, Nouvelle série, ed. Cl. Perroud (1913–1915), 2 vols. Vol. I: 1767–1776; Vol. II, 1777–1780, Paris: Imprimerie Nationale.
DCRF	*Dictionnaire Critique de la Révolution Française*, ed. François Furet and Mona Ozouf (1988), Paris: Flammarion.
Dictionnaire	*Dictionnaire des Manufactures, Arts et Métiers*, ed. J.-M. Roland, 3 vols (1784, 1785, 1790), Paris: Panckoucke [part of the *Encyclopédie Méthodique*].
FH	*French History*
FHS	*French Historical Studies*
Grandchamp	*Souvenirs de Sophie Grandchamp*, in *Mémoires de Mme Roland*, ed. Cl. Perroud (1905), Paris-Plon, II, pp. 461–497.
Jacobins	*La Société des Jacobins*: *Recueil de documents pour l'histoire du club des Jacobin*s, ed. F.A. Aulard, 6 vols, [Paris/New York]: AMS Press (1889–97/1973), facsimile edition.
Lettres d'Italie	*Lettres écrites de Suisse, d'Italie, de Sicile, de Malte par M. *** à Mlle *** à Paris en 1776, 1777 et 1778* [Amsterdam], 6 vols.
Lettres d'Amour	*Roland et Marie Phlipon. Lettres d'amour (1777 à 1780)*, ed. Cl. Perroud (1909), Paris: Picard.

Lettres et pièces	*Lettres et pièces intéressantes pour servir à l'histoire du ministère de Roland, Servan et Clavière*, Chez les directeurs du Cercle social (1792).
Mém.	*Mme Roland: Mémoires*, ed. Paul de Roux (1966/1986) Paris: Mercure de France.
*Mém./*Perroud (1905)	*Mémoires de Mme Roland*, ed. Cl. Perroud (1905), Paris: Plon, 2 vols.
Mémoire des services	J. M. Roland's *Mémoire des services* in BNF MSS, naf 6243 (account of his inspectorship).
Mémoire d'extraction	Genealogical papers of J. M. Roland's family, in BNF MSS naf 6243.
OC	*Oeuvres complètes*
ODNB	*Oxford Dictionary of National Biography* (2004) Oxford: Oxford University Press.

List of Illustrations

Glossary

Pre-metric weights and measures

livre (1) one pound in weight (roughly half a modern kilo) (2) basic monetary unit worth 20 sous (value varies, see examples in text)

écu silver coin worth 6 livres in the reign of Louis XVI (aka *louis d'argent*)

setier unit of measurement for grain, 150–300 litres

French pre-revolutionary and revolutionary terms

abbé usually a courtesy title for all clerics, not an abbot

amis des noirs 'Friends of the blacks': club founded against black slavery and for emancipation

ancien régime the former regime, i.e. before 1789

appel au peuple proposal by some deputies in the Convention during the king's trial, that his fate be decided by referendum

armoire de fer an iron safe discovered in the Tuileries Palace by J.-M. Roland, containing compromising papers about Louis XVI's secret correspondence

assignat originally a government bond, later paper currency assigned against the sale of church land

biens nationaux nationalized property of the church, later extended to cover royal domains and property of émigrés

cahiers de doléance grievance registers drawn up for the Estates General in 1789

ci-devant literally 'before now', referring to pre-revolution aristocracy

commissaires emissaries sent out, usually on propaganda missions, to the provinces or the armies by various bodies (e.g. the Convention)

Commune insurrectionnelle the reconfigured municipal council of Paris after 10 August 1792, involved in the insurrection of that day

Contrôleur-général usu. translated in text as Controller-general, minister of finance under the ancien régime

corvée forced labour under the ancien régime

déchéance deposition [of Louis XVI]

département new administrative division of France formed in 1791, originally 83 in number, and still in force (95 today in metropolitan France, 5 overseas)

échevins approx = 'aldermen' in the ancien regime

émigrés those who left France on political grounds during the Revolution, many of them nobles

Enfants Trouvés foundling home in Paris

fabricants manufacturers, usually on a small scale

fédérés mostly national guardsmen, sent from the provinces to celebrate the Fête de la Fédération on the anniversary of the fall of the Bastille

femmes savantes 'bluestockings', mocking reference to women with claims to learning

Feuillants monarchists previously in the Jacobin club who seceded in summer 1791 after Varennes, and met in the monastery named for this clerical order

gardes-jurés representatives of manufacturers who worked with the inspectors

généralité administrative division, roughly a province, under the ancien régime, overseen by an *intendant*

gabelle salt tax under the ancien régime

Garde nationale usually translated as National Guard: citizens' militias formed early in the Revolution and organized thereafter

Hôtel-Dieu charitable hospice under the ancien régime

intendants administrators of *généralités* under the ancien régime

journée literally 'day'; used of significant popular uprisings, e.g. 10 August

lettres de noblesse grant of nobility on application, ancien régime

levée en masse mass conscription of 1793

loi agraire proposal for expropriation of landowners

manège literally riding school; the building previously attached to the Tuileries Palace, used for the revolutionary assemblies from Autumn 1789 until spring 1793, when they moved into a more suitable chamber

maximum fixed price for nominated foodstuffs

menu peuple 'little', or ordinary, i.e. poor people

Montagne, Montagnards used of the group of radical deputies sitting high up on the left during the Convention

noblesse de robe nobility granted through legal or political office-holding, ancien régime (as distinct from *noblesse d'épee*, by the sword)

octrois local excise duties on a variety of everyday goods

Palais de Justice central law-courts

parlements courts of appeal under the ancien régime; not 'parliaments', but they had certain powers of approval/disapproval of royal measures

patriotes the term used in the early years of the Revolution for 'true revolutionaries' who supported the *patrie* = fatherland, nation

philosophes especially used of the writers most associated with Enlightenment thought (Voltaire, Diderot, Rousseau etc.)

Ponts et chaussées specialized body of engineers responsible for bridges and highways

procureur prosecutor, attorney; in local government after 1790 of municipal officer defending community interest; also used of specialized administrators

rentes income from investments

sans-culottes term popularized in 1792 = 'men who wore trousers instead of knee-breeches, *culottes*', the latter seen as sign of higher-class status. Not to be taken literally, but used of radical popular groups, especially in Paris, during 1792–1794

sections administrative divisions of Paris: there were 48

Thermidor month in the revolutionary calendar, usually referring to 9 Thermidor Year II [27 July 1794], date of the fall of Robespierre

Tiers Etat Third Estate, representatives to the Estates-General who were neither clergy nor nobles (the first two estates) but represented all others entitled to vote

vie chère term for the high cost of living

I sometimes think, as you say, that I was born for some other country; I used to think so when I was fifteen, reading my ancient history, and I used to weep with frustration at not being born during the great days of Sparta and Rome.

But if heaven got the *place* wrong, it made the right choice in the *marriage* it made me contract. When there are two of you who think the same way, it makes you very strong, and that's probably one of the secrets of my courage.

Mme Roland, letter to Jacques-Pierre Brissot
[whom she had not yet met], 16 March 1790

Every marriage enacts most of its important dramas behind closed doors.

Terri Apter, *Times Literary Supplement*,
12 March 2010

Prologue: 4 February 1780

It was a very quiet wedding. On 4 February 1780, a handful of people gathered in the church of Saint-Barthélémy on the Ile de la Cité in Paris. Twenty-five-year-old Marie-Jeanne Phlipon, the daughter of a Parisian engraver, was marrying forty-five-year-old Jean-Marie Roland de la Platière, an inspector of manufactures for the royal administration. There were four witnesses, and the bride's uncle, Nicolas-Pierre Bimont, a canon at Vincennes, blessed the union.

The proper forms were observed, but by ancien régime standards, this marriage was hardly conventional, let alone arranged. Mlle Phlipon had been staying not at her father's house, but at her old convent school. The banns had been read just a week earlier. Lent was approaching, which partly explains the haste—marriages were forbidden during Advent and Lent—but that wasn't all. The short notice, the small attendance (hardly anyone from the groom's family), the convent, are all signs that preparations had not been smooth. No, the bride was not pregnant. But Jean-Marie Roland wrote to a colleague that 'everything has been repaired, agreed, fixed up, in five or six days, and I haven't had time to tell my friends or even my relations'. The bride wrote to her regular confidante Sophie Cannet, to whom the announcement was a complete surprise, that everything had been carried out 'with extreme simplicity'.[1]

Dark-eyed and dark-haired, Marie-Jeanne Phlipon was her widowed father's only child. Sophie described her as 'more beautiful than pretty [. . .] She has a wide mouth, regular features and her nose is rather big; her face is lively; she has a sweet smile, interesting eyes and a humble but open brow.'[2] Later witnesses—including several young men who fell in love with her—agreed that she was attractive and engaging, if not a classical beauty.

Jean-Marie Roland was the ninth of ten children in an old Beaujolais family that had come down in the world, but still owned property and a slender claim to noble status. His branch of the clan had taken the appellation 'de la Platière' in earlier times. His wife later described him as 'quite tall, rather careless of his appearance, with that kind of stiffness which comes from hours in the study; but his manners were simple and easy'. He was thin, rather sallow-complexioned, and his hair was

---

[1] *Corr.*, NS, II, Supplement, p. 433; *Corr.*, I, pp. 1, 6, 16, February 1780; cf. Lebrun (1975), pp. 10 ff. Parish records, Jal (1872); *Mém.*/Perroud (1905), p. 418. (All translations my own, unless otherwise attributed.)
[2] *Corr.*, NS, I, pp. 315–16; *Corr.*, II, Appendix V, on portraits.

already receding, but 'his extremely fine smile and a lively expression transformed his face and made it look quite different when he became animated'.[3]

The *contrat de mariage*, setting out the couple's financial resources, had been signed a week earlier at a notary's office in the Place Dauphine, before ten witnesses.[4] Apart from 'clothes, linen, and personal jewellery', Marie-Jeanne brought to the marriage a notional 840 *livres* income made up of *rentes* on the Ville de Paris, the Compagnie des Indes, etc. Even this meagre amount was largely fictional. The bridegroom contributed a much larger sum—again notional, since it was a loan—60,000 *livres* 'to be taken against the domains and vineyards' of the family farm. His friend François Lanthenas stood proxy for the Beaujolais relatives.[5]

The new couple had scarcely seen each other in the previous six months, and their engagement had been conducted largely by correspondence. The silences and misunderstandings during this courtship by post are not unlike a novel—both partners admired Jean-Jacques Rousseau's best-seller, *La Nouvelle Héloïse* (1760). Marie-Jeanne Phlipon had formally agreed to the marriage only a fortnight before. True, there was a twenty-year age difference, but this was not the chief impediment. Affection had in the end triumphed over obstacles more social than emotional. For in ancien régime terms, even in 1780, this was a *mésalliance*, unequal in terms of status and wealth. It was a love match, opposed or only just tolerated by both families. Their marriage was to be the crucial factor in both partners' lives, with far-reaching consequences, private and public. At the time, it went virtually unnoticed outside the family circle.

---

[3] *Mém.*, p. 322.
[4] BNF MSS, naf 9532.
[5] Ibid., and *Corr.*, NS, I, pp. xix–xx. Most couples had a *contrat de mariage*: 95 per cent in Lyon, 65–75 per cent in Paris, Lebrun (1975), p. 37; Daumard and Furet (1961), p. 74. The Phlipon parents' contract (14 June 1750) had 59 witnesses, *Corr.*, NS, II, pp. xv ff.

Introduction

WHY THE ROLANDS?

This slightly unconventional alliance is the subject of this book. It is a double biography. The two people who married in February 1780 were thrust, a few years later, into the centre of national events. Living near Lyon in 1789, they welcomed the French Revolution with enthusiasm. In March 1792, Jean-Marie Roland was a surprise appointment as minister of the Interior in the so-called 'Brissotin' or 'Girondin' Ministry. Dismissed by Louis XVI in June, he was reinstated as minister after the fall of the monarchy in August, and remained in his post during the early months of the republic. He resigned in January 1793, and both he and his wife died during the Terror later that year. All biographies end badly, but this one has a more tragic ending than most.

We would probably know comparatively little about either of their lives, if the book that became known as 'Madame Roland's memoirs' had not become a publishing success in the late 1790s, as 'An appeal to impartial posterity by Citizeness Roland'. Written from prison, in anger, sorrow, and defiance over the summer of 1793, her manuscripts were smuggled out by friends, and the first version appeared in print eighteen months after her death. The memoirs contain reflections on the Revolution and many of its leaders, followed by a detailed account of her childhood and youth. Running to many editions, this work turned the engraver's daughter, for good or ill, into a 'heroine' of the Revolution: an enthusiastic revolutionary, but better known as a victim of the guillotine, and romantically idolized by such writers as Lamartine and Stendhal. Her famous, if unconfirmed, last words, 'O Liberty! What crimes are committed in thy name,' will be familiar to many people.

They are unlikely to know much about her husband. The aim of this book is to go behind the scenes, so to speak, of Mme Roland's fame—which has inspired many biographies—to explore the workings of a remarkable, but strangely underrecorded partnership. Of Jean-Marie Roland there are no biographies in French and only one in English—a scholarly one by Charles Le Guin (1966), now virtually unobtainable. Even his identity is now shadowy: the Wikipedia article on him (2011) describes him, quite erroneously, as a 'marquis', and the cover of the 1986 edition of his wife's memoirs calls him, equally wrongly, *financier du roi*, or tax-farmer. If Mme Roland has arguably been given too much attention, the posthumous fate of her husband has been to attract too little. His is the curious semi-absence at the heart of many books on his wife. Their daughter, Eudora, who survived the Revolution, regretted that her mother's celebrity had obscured that of her father.[1] The image of 'the Rolands' as a colourless elderly husband with a dominant wife, although not quite how contemporaries saw it, has often been recycled by historians, and is partly explained by the celebrity of Mme Roland's memoirs—which, for reasons to become clear, say little about the years of marriage, and that little misleading. Hilary Mantel's impressive novel *A Place of Greater Safety* imaginatively perpetuates this image.[2] Concentration on conflict in the revolutionary assemblies in modern histories, has obscured a man who could not remotely be described as colourless, and who was in a position of extraordinary potential power during 1792. He was correspondingly both idolized and reviled by his contemporaries as the events of that year—the outbreak of war, the fall of the monarchy, the September massacres, and the king's trial—took their course.

A starting point for this book was the unusual presence at the heart of the Revolution of a couple in which the wife played—or seemed to play—a significant political role. There were not many such for whom we have documentation. The wives of married revolutionaries usually acted as a domestic support system—not negligible, sometimes very important, but seldom visible to the historian. Many of the best known revolutionaries were only in their thirties. Jacques-Pierre Brissot (b. 1754) married Félicité Dupont in the 1770s. Although an observer of politics, she played no special part in them and had three young children to care for. Georges-Jacques Danton (b. 1759), was another family man, neither of whose wives stepped visibly outside a domestic role. Maximilien [de] Robespierre (b. 1758), unmarried, was cared for during 1791–1794 by the Duplay family or by his sister, Charlotte. Louis-Antoine Saint-Just (b. 1767) was unmarried, as was Jean-Paul Marat (b. 1743), although the latter was living maritally at the time of his death. Of the few couples who have been studied, the marquis de Condorcet (b. 1743) had—like Roland—married a much younger and well-educated wife: Sophie de Grouchy (b. 1764), who published books and translations, and entertained visitors. Although highly born, she provides an interesting parallel for Marie-Jeanne Roland, but compared with the latter, she played relatively little part in her husband's political life. The tragic Desmoulins couple, Camille (b. 1760) and Lucile (b. 1770), had not long been married when Camille went to his death alongside Danton: the pretext for Lucile's execution was plotting to rescue her husband, rather than political activity.[3]

The Rolands were different. Married for nine years by 1789, with one child, they were equally and fully committed to the Revolution from the start. Thrust into a prominent position in 1792, they turned out, like many key players on the revolutionary stage, to have both talents and faults, and made judgements one could view as brave or foolhardy, sensible or questionable. Both, in different ways, rose to the occasion, but made enemies in so doing. General histories refer mainly to the last two dramatic years of their lives, 1792–1793. But this book is not

---

[1] 'Nothing in the world [...] is dearer or more sacred to me than the memory of my father,' 24 October 1822, BNF MSS, naf 22424, fo 468.

[2] Mantel (1992), pp. 383, 422–3.

[3] On these couples see Baker (1975); Badinter and Badinter (1990); Schama (1989).

just about the Revolution, it is also about marriage. It aims to look back into the couple's hinterland: to examine the social and cultural baggage they brought to their marriage, and how that combined before and during the Revolution into a partnership that fell apart only at the very end.

Theirs was a marriage contracted under the ancien régime, with the expectations of the time. Until the Revolution, their lives were outwardly unremarkable, spent mostly in the provinces. But the wealth of documents from earlier years gives a virtually unrivalled picture of what came close to being a 'companionate' eighteenth-century marriage, both typical and untypical of French society. It was typical in its everyday concerns, less so in that *both* partners were enthusiasts for Enlightenment thinking, part of the cultural landscape of the immediate pre-revolutionary years. Together, the curiously modern Rolands form part of the 'revolution before the revolution'.[4]

SOURCES AND INTERPRETATIONS

In attempting this biography, I am of course not starting from scratch. The couple is possibly the best documented of the eighteenth century and the problem is more an *embarras de richesses*. Because of Mme Roland's posthumous fame, any papers were carefully preserved by friends, descendants, and memento hunters. The definitive four-volume edition of her correspondence (1900–1902 and 1913–1915) along with a scrupulously researched edition of the memoirs (1905) is a monument to the scholarship of Claude Perroud (1839–1919), to whom all later researchers are deeply indebted.[5] Unlike his wife, Jean-Marie Roland left little autobiographical material, and few of his letters, apart from the courtship correspondence, have been published. Some papers were destroyed by Roland himself or the friends who sheltered him. However, there are plentiful personal and official documents, in the Archives Nationales in Paris, in Lyon, and with his wife's papers in the bulging ledgers in the Manuscript division of the BNF.

Among the many secondary works on the revolutionary period, biographies of Marie-Jeanne Roland vary in range, approach, and the degree to which they include her husband's story. Most rely closely on Mme Roland's version of events in the memoirs; more thorough ones draw on the correspondence and primary material. I think it is fair to say that writers usually focus more on Mme Roland than on her husband, keeping fairly narrowly to her chronological trajectory, and treating her, with critical sympathy and some psychological speculation, as a highly unusual individual. She has long been seen as a kind of exceptional 'woman of the Revolution'.[6]

---

[4] See Pasco (2009).

[5] Perroud in *Corr.*, I, introduction, p. xxii: many letters are lost; what we have are 'the remains of a much fuller correspondence'. The early letters, in private hands, are readable only in Perroud's edition.

[6] In English, the most recent biography—scrupulously based on contemporary sources—is May (1970); in French, cf. Kermina (1976) who does not neglect J.-M. Roland, but infuriatingly, has no footnotes.

By now many interpretations have accumulated of the roles open to women in the Revolution. More scholarly work on women's participation in the events of 1789–1793 appeared in the last thirty years than in the previous hundred. True, individual women, like Mme Roland herself, had long been singled out for attention. The already familiar names of Olympe de Gouges, Théroigne de Méricourt, Etta Palm d'Aelders, Claire Lacombe, Louise Kéralio (Robert), and Lucile Desmoulins were further celebrated in the 1970s, in a determined effort to raise their profile—since after all the Revolution has often been narrated in terms of famous men. Arguably, the sample of women became a little over-familiar: 'continuous retellings of a small band of activists', as it has been called.[7]

Later writers explored the active role of unprivileged women and pioneers of women's rights: the *femmes du peuple* who marched to Versailles in 1789, or women's clubs, like the Société des républicaines révolutionnaires. Empirical archive work, by Dominique Godineau on Paris, but also in provincial studies, has demonstrated evidence of ordinary women's participation in revolutionary events. Olwen Hufton, who pioneered study of the fallout of the Revolution on women, also joined the active debate about citizenship and the question of women's exclusion or otherwise, represented in the work of Joan Scott, Joan Landes, and others. Suzanne Desan has studied the consequences of revolutionary legislation for women, nuancing some of the negative views of the Revolution as 'a bad thing for women'. Cultural history has contributed major new insights, especially in the work of Lynn Hunt. We are now far more aware of gender used symbolically; of the consequences of the Revolution for women; of women as both speaking and spoken about, joining in all kinds of public actions: popular riots, festivities, vociferous attendance in the gallery at Assembly sessions; presenting petitions; speaking up in clubs, whether mixed or single sex; writing journalism; providing support systems for men; joining the armies; emigrating; benefiting from, opposing, or regretting the Revolution. Even Marie-Antoinette has been the subject of a more sympathetic revision.[8] While at first more was written in English than in French on the subject of gender, that has begun to change.[9]

Mme Roland, if not entirely forgotten by feminist historians, has been somewhat sidelined. Their lack of interest stems partly from a view of her as an 'elite' woman—despite her humble origins—who has had her fair share of attention. If you google her name, it will often come up with the term 'salon' attached. This view of her as a *salonnière* (a nineteenth-century neologism) will be examined later, but it sits uncomfortably with a history looking for progressive political engagement. What is more, her references to the proper role for women in society

---

[7] Outram (1987), p.120; Moore (2006) on several famous individuals; for a 'first-person' biography, Cornevin (2002).

[8] See Hufton (1971, 1992); Levy *et al.* (1979); Outram (1989); Godineau (1988); Hunt (1984, 1992); Desan (2004) and her essay in Knott and Taylor (2005). On the citizenship/exclusion debate Reynolds (1985), Landes (1988), Scott (1996). Cf. Offen (1990); Conner (1990), and on the queen, Fraser (2001).

[9] *Les Femmes* […] (1989–1991) had little follow-up, but cf. Godineau (2003), Viénot (2008); special number of AHRF (2006) and Martin (2008) for a recent survey.

are not seen as supporting women's rights—indeed, taking a contrary position, a topic that will also be explored. This neglect or disparagement has been sharply analysed by Dorinda Outram in a study connecting public and private life.[10] In the many books for a wider audience about 'women of the French Revolution', the obligatory chapter on Mme Roland is usually too short to go beyond a summary of familiar points.

In the cultural/gender history of the longer eighteenth century, by contrast, she plays quite an important role, and it is here that the most sophisticated approaches to her life can be found. She is a key witness on women's education, literacy, and self-presentation. Modelled on Rousseau's *Confessions*, the second section of the memoirs is today regarded as a classic of French 'life-writing' with all the ambiguities and contradictions of autobiography. Marie-Jeanne Phlipon's youthful correspondence with Sophie Cannet has been a particularly valuable source. This literature offers detailed analysis of her early years, when she was an obscure, but retrospectively unusual 'Enlightenment woman'. But these writers are less concerned with her later career, or with the Revolution—rarely examining her marriage or husband.[11]

If one turns to modern, mainstream, revolutionary history, posterity has been far from impartial towards the Rolands. While Jean-Marie Roland's name rates plenty of index references, little serious work has been devoted to him. Le Guin's thorough biography remains an isolated exception. The many brief mentions of him in general works tend to be disparaging. 'Le vertueux Roland', as he was known by his supporters and (ironically) by his enemies, attracted extravagant praise and blame in 1792–1793, but the blame is what has mostly survived. Over breakfast at a recent conference, a distinguished French historian said to me, on hearing about this book: 'Mais Monsieur Roland est odieux!'

The disparagement is partly explained by his closeness to the politicians known as Brissotins or Girondins, for whom few modern historians have a good word.[12] In France, much scholarly work has been under the aegis of the active Société des études robespierristes, and generally more sympathetic to the Jacobins. But whatever their position on the Jacobins or the Terror, historians tend to be sparing in their praise and liberal with their censure for the Girondins, and that goes for the 'revisionists' in the wake of François Furet, as well as for much recent work in English. It also applies to the single work in French devoted to Roland's career, Edith Bernardin's thesis on the ministry of the Interior. That book, however, is a mine of information and one of the very few close studies of a revolutionary ministry. An extra reason for Jean-Marie Roland's historical obscurity is historians' concentration on the politics of the revolutionary assemblies and their orators, and a comparative lack of studies of ministerial power.[13]

---

[10] Outram (1989), chapters 8 and 9; cf. also Dalton's perceptive article (2001).
[11] See in particular Goodman (2009a), Trouille (1997).
[12] On the Gironde, Sydenham (1961); Patrick (1972); Mathiez, ed. (1930); Soboul, ed. (1980); Furet and Ozouf (1991), and articles in the bibliography by M. Dorigny.
[13] With Bernardin, recent exceptions are Brown (1995) and Howe (2008).

As for his wife, extravagantly admired by nineteenth-century pro-Girondin writers, Mme Roland is no heroine to political historians. Her writings are widely used as source material, but her career is regarded as more questionable. It is not unusual to find her described as an 'Egeria of the Girondins', in terms sometimes amounting to caricature. A gendered subtext suggests that, as a woman, she was a 'meddler' in politics where she had no business, invariably 'ambitious', and that her 'illicit' influence 'round the dinner table' or in her 'salon', was unfortunate, especially on young politicians who fell for her 'Circe-like' charms. Such images draw on the hostile attacks on her by talented, but vitriolic contemporary journalists: Marat, Desmoulins, Jacques-René Hébert, all bitter enemies of her husband and the Brissotins. In prison she wrote, 'the people who have said the worst things about me have never met me'. In particular, she has been accused of encouraging the destructive factionalism of Year I (1792–1793), with the perhaps unintended effect of making her seem a real—if malign—power in revolutionary politics. One extreme formulation is that by Gérald Walter as late as 1968: 'It is painful and disappointing to have to state that the rancour of an ambitious and vindictive woman *lies at the origin* of the terrible conflict which would plunge the young republic into blood and mud.'[14]

Faced with such strong opinions, any historian must feel the urge to probe the myth. Does one unavoidably end up writing a brief for the defence? When studying lives close up, the biographer surely experiences moments of sympathy with the subject—and equally moments of exasperation. Is *tout comprendre*—even if it were possible—really *tout pardonner*? Should one approach it with hostile enthusiasm or sympathetic criticism?

In some quarters, biography will always be suspect as a form of special pleading. As one historian puts it, 'even biography which meets the requirements of modern scholarship is not without its critics... The problem of bias cannot be lightly disposed of. [It] encourages a simplified linear interpretation of events.'[15] It could be answered that a linear narrative has certain advantages when exploring events such as the French Revolution, in which one could 'live ten years in a day', as Marie-Jeanne Roland wrote. The fine chronology is the enemy of the quick generalization. I have found this a sobering experience myself, and have tried to be as scrupulous about dating as the records allow, because it can expose inadvertent errors in general narratives. Quoting from contemporary letters means knowing exactly what the context was when they were written. Events between 1789 and 1793 were often unpredictable: general causes can be argued about when looking down the tunnel of years. Individuals had to take one day at a time, without knowing what tomorrow would bring.

Another objection is that tackling the lives of already famous public figures requires some justification—new material or a new approach. It is perhaps more pressing to write the lives of people who have been hidden from history, as some recent biographies have done, and as many feminist historians have chosen to do. Here, the subject is the intertwined lives of two people, each with claims on our

---

[14] *Actes*, pp. 350–1. My italics.   [15] Tosh (2000), pp. 75–6.

historical attention. One is, yes, famous, the other should be well known, but isn't. While writing this book, I have usually drawn blank looks when asking even well-informed friends if they have ever heard of 'Monsieur Roland'. Studying them together makes a difference to how we look at each of them and at their time. Double or multiple biographies are one way of avoiding the intense linearity of the single life-story.[16] In this case, it also allows a privileged combination of public and private. Whether the subject is male or female, we are less inclined than in the past to see these spheres as rigorously separate.

Public figures have often written their own stories, but their biographers regard autobiography and memoirs with suspicion: they certainly can't be seen as incontrovertibly and transparently telling 'the truth', but are always a form of self-presentation or performance, with which the biographer has to live—that is very much the case with Mme Roland's famous text. Private letters and diaries have stronger claims to help construct a record. Letters, too, are constructed texts—they don't necessarily tell us 'how it really was', but they can offer us sharp-edged fragments with which to puncture memory or carve twists in a story. It was from reading Mme Roland's remarkable letters and comparing them with her memoirs that this book took shape. Because of the circumstances of their deaths, the papers of many well-known French revolutionaries have been lost. We know comparatively little about their private lives before 1789, so their public lives dominate their biographies. The Rolands, however, left an exceptional record of their domestic life. The 'biographical pact' ought to entail considering all aspects of life, dramatic or mundane, as worth enquiring about, and all evidence as deserving critical consideration.

At the same time, no biography is contextually neutral—we can't help writing from within our own time. The present time is one of scepticism about the reliability of attempts to tell a story. Most modern biographers argue at least for greater self-reflexivity, and awareness of the interconnectedness of subject and author. They are also more inclined to stress the fractures, discontinuities, and unknowns in any individual life. Virginia Woolf, as so often, was there already:

> You have overheard scraps of talk that filled you with amazement. You have gone to bed at night bewildered by the complexity of your feelings. In one day thousands of ideas have coursed through your brain; thousands of emotions have met, collided and disappeared in astonishing disorder. Nevertheless you allow the writers to palm off upon you a version of all this, an image of Mrs Brown which has no likeness to that surprising apparition whatsoever.[17]

Revolutionary biographies offer instructive examples of how various 'the writers' versions' can be. Norman Hampson, who wrote an enjoyably cynical, but sympathetic biography of Danton in his own voice, felt he could only approach

---

[16] Cf. Félix (2006) on Louis XVI and Marie-Antoinette; Wiewiorka (2010) on Maurice Thorez and Jeannette Vermeersch.

[17] Woolf (1966); cf. Margadant (2000), p. 7: 'the subject of biography is no longer the coherent self but rather a self that is performed to create an impression of coherence, or an individual with multiple selves [reflecting] the passage of time, the demands and options of different settings [etc.]'.

Robespierre's story by having a sort of running debate between people of different political views. In her recent biography of Robespierre, Ruth Scurr said she had 'tried to be his friend and to see things from his point of view', but added, cunningly, that friends have 'opportunities for betrayal that enemies only dream of'.[18]

The biographer always has an agenda. Even when doing his or her level best not to conceal any material, however awkward, the result is a narrative that we have contrived to justify to ourselves—what Pierre Bourdieu called the 'biographical illusion'. In this book, by concentrating on the marriage, and trying to avoid repeating in detail too much well-known material, I have aimed to explore areas of the Rolands' lives which have remained most hidden—often hardly mentioned in the famous memoirs. Some of these are private: family relations, bringing up their daughter, love affairs, and plans for a utopian community. Some are more public—Jean-Marie Roland's radical role in local politics in Lyon during the early years of the Revolution, how he ran the ministry of the Interior. I have also tried to probe some sensitive and controversial topics around which accretions of questionable information have gathered—the early acquaintance then breach with Robespierre, the fortuitous, but long-lasting links with Brissot—one of Marisa Linton's 'fatal friendships';[19] the extent to which Mme Roland really 'intervened' in politics; Roland's reaction to the September massacres; the much-mentioned 'salon' and the ministerial dinner parties; and what lay behind the notorious *bureau d'esprit public*.

But while asking questions, the biographer is always going to tell a story with a beginning, middle, and end (if not necessarily in that order). The outline of this book is broadly chronological, with thematic interludes, but it is essentially the record of a marriage. It looks at the lives of the two principals before they met; at their courtship and early life together; the joint projects on which they collaborated in the 1780s; and then their partnership during the Revolution. In any marriage, there is more than one power relationship at work. Contemporaries made crude guesses at what went on inside this one, but their judgements about domination, inequality, or betrayal were not necessarily correct, which has not stopped them being repeated down the ages. I have tried to bring documentary evidence to bear on some of the more hasty judgements of 'impartial posterity'.

---

[18] Hampson (1978/1988) and (1974/1988); Scurr (2007), p. 7. Peter McPhee's *Robespierre: a revolutionary life* (2012) was published when the present book was in the press.
[19] Linton (2008).

PART I

GETTING MARRIED:
BEFORE 1780

1

The Bride's Story (1)
The Child Manon

On 31 December 1772, Marie-Jeanne Phlipon wrote in a notebook:

> Already the earth has made me go eighteen times round the sun. If it were not to carry me much further, what more could I see of it? [...] Placed in a situation where it is easier to think than to act, my time must be employed in acquiring knowledge [...] shaping myself into a more enlightened and better-intentioned member [of society]. If no more, at least I shall have done as much as possible, [...] I shall have lived. To say you have done so without reproach must be happiness![1]

This eighteen-year-old turned into one of the best-read women in France—surprisingly, given her humble origins, lack of formal education, and a not-very-bookish environment. Nor was she just a bookworm—she thought about the major ideas of her time. Her notebooks throb with extracts and comments: 'I take pleasure in writing and reasoning: it's necessary to me, it's my daily bread [...] Nobody feels a more lively pleasure in thinking, or has a greater taste for reflection.'[2] She was as committed to what we think of as Enlightenment thought as many of her male contemporaries. This chapter explores her early life. How exceptional was the little girl raised in an engraver's workshop? Do some elements in her background explain her intellectual and moral trajectory?

A frustrating question for her biographers had better be raised at once: what to call her. In her memoirs, Mme Roland explained that her pet name within the family was 'Manon'. Her schoolfriends, Sophie and Henriette, had more distinguished names: 'Yes, they called me Manon; I'm sorry to have to say so, to people who like novels, it's not a noble name, not one for a heroine in the grand manner, but it was mine, and I'm writing a history.'[3] (Oddly enough, Manon *is* the name of the heroine of a notorious novel, *Manon Lescaut* by the Abbé Prévost (1731). Was she distancing herself from the morally dubious title character?) Some biographers, call her familiarly 'Manon' throughout, but the sentence is in the past tense—it suggests she wasn't called Manon after childhood. Was she later called 'Marie', 'Jeanne', or 'Marie-Jeanne'? Certainly not Jeanne-Marie—as not a few historians call her. Letters are unhelpfully signed with her surname: 'Phlipon', which she used all her life: aged twenty-five, she wrote to 'my Sophie': 'are you expecting a letter from your prompt Phlipon?'[4] After marriage, her signature varies: 'de la Platière', 'DLP', or 'Roland de la Platière'. During the Revolution,

---

[1] Quoted Champagneux (1800), p.iij, 'with the document sitting in front of [me].'
[2] To Sophie Cannet, 24 July 1774, *Corr.*, NS, I, p. 211.
[3] *Mém.*, p. 205.   [4] 15 July 1779, *Corr.*, NS, II, p. 390.

the would-be-aristocratic suffix was dropped, and she usually signed 'Roland née Phlipon'. In letters, she and her husband addressed each other simply as *mon ami*, *mon amie*, or by the pet name 'Loup' [Wolf]. Not once does the name Manon appear. I will call her 'Manon' when referring to her early childhood, and Marie-Jeanne, Mlle Phlipon, or Mme Roland thereafter.[5]

THE CHILD MANON

An obvious obstacle to becoming an eighteenth-century 'intellectual' was to be born a girl. It wasn't insuperable. Many women of this generation were well-read; women writers were not rare in late eighteenth-century France,[6] but most recorded examples were well-born, with resources to match. The education of an artisan's daughter was usually confined to literacy and household matters. Still, the child born on 17 March 1754 on the Ile de la Cité had one advantage.[7] She was starting her life in the right place. Paris was where to be, if you wanted to keep up with advanced thought. French intellectual life—bookshops, the university, libraries, the Academy—centred on the capital. From her home overlooking the Pont-Neuf, she could in theory walk anywhere in the city centre, appropriately chaperoned as a rule. As Louis-Sébastien Mercier (born nearby) wrote in his *Tableau de Paris*:

> The Pont-Neuf is to the city what the heart is to the human body: the centre of move-ment and circulation. The ebb and flow of local residents and foreigners is so striking on this passageway that if you are looking for someone, you only have to walk around there for an hour every day.[8]

Manon was also born at a critical time. Her date of birth puts her in the same generation, give or take a few years, as many leading revolutionaries: Robespierre (b. 1758), Danton (b. 1759), Desmoulins (b. 1760), Talleyrand (b. 1754), Brissot (b. 1754), Pétion (b. 1756), Buzot (b. 1760), Vergniaud (b. 1754). These young men, generally well-educated, would all have read Voltaire (1694–1778), Rousseau (1712–1778), and Diderot (1713–1784)—philosophers living in Paris or visiting it, when she was a girl.

But for Manon Phlipon, her sex and family background meant that she had nothing like their start in life. Her father, Pierre-Gatien Phlipon (1724–1789) was an engraver, governed by the institutions and practices of the trade guilds. He handled not pictures, but metal objects: coats of arms, swords and scabbards, snuff-boxes, matrices, and punches for seals used in legal documents. That was why he lived near the Palais de Justice, the law courts, where like trades were

---

[5] During courtship she was sometimes 'Amanda', Dauban (1867), p. xvi. May (1970) p. 124, quotes Jean-Marie: 'Are you determined to keep my Manon much longer?' However, the original (*Corr.*, I, p. 399) has *ma moitié*, 'my other half'. Cf. Kermina (1976), p. 40; *Corr.*, II, pp. 454n., 696, monogram 'MJP'. During the Revolution she was referred to as Citoyenne Roland, 'la femme Roland', but most often 'Mme Roland'.

[6] Hesse (2001); Goodman (1994, 2009a).

[7] Baptismal certificate, church of Sainte-Croix, 18 March 1754, *Mém.*/Perroud, p. 418.

[8] Mercier (1982), I, p. 56.

concentrated—goldsmiths (on the quai des Orfèvres) and jewellers.[9] His immediate forebears had been *marchands de vins*, wine sellers, a trade his daughter chose not to mention in her memoirs. Her grandfather Phlipon sold wine in the Latin quarter; her grandmother, Marie-Geneviève Rotisset (1696–1784) came from a family of *marchands de vins* in the same street.[10] Marie-Jeanne's mother, Marie-Marguerite Bimont (1723–1775), the daughter of a haberdasher in the rue de la Pelleterie, belonged to a rather higher class of shopkeepers. Her maternal grandmother, Marie-Marguerite Trude, came from a family of mirror- and glassmakers to the aristocracy. Apart from one priest and one steward, the immediate family came from the milieu of artisans and shopkeepers in central Paris.[11]

Without an engraver father, Phlipon must (unusually) have broken into his trade, perhaps with financial help, serving an apprenticeship of several years, producing a 'masterpiece', and paying a fee to the corporation. Unlike engraving paintings, his work did not call for a large space or much capital,[12] and he made good. The household included several journeymen and apprentices throughout his daughter's youth. His wife worked on the accounts, as well as running the household. Her marriage contract stipulated that she was to train as a midwife, but this never happened, and her own childbearing history was unhappy. The Phlipons were not rich, but they were not exactly 'le peuple' either. They employed one live-in servant, a soldier's widow, Marie Renard, known as 'Mignonne'. Her married name was Montmignon, but it is also an affectionate diminutive—she was effectively one of the family. As David Garrioch points out, many Parisian artisans and even unskilled workers employed a maidservant so that wives could work alongside their husbands.[13]

The Phlipons lived in reasonable comfort, in a second-floor apartment, rented for 950 *livres* on the quai de l'Horloge—not the pink-brick house bearing a plaque today, but (probably) the next to the left, partly rebuilt in the 1770s. Manon was born round the corner in the rue de la Lanterne, but the family moved to the quai in about 1756.[14] Notarial records unearthed in the twentieth century describe the flat as roomy and well-furnished. A detailed inventory from July 1777, when Marie-Jeanne and her father moved out for the rebuilding, mentions two staircases, one to the quai, one to the Place Dauphine. An antechamber doubled up as a dining-room for the family and apprentices. The maidservant had a folding bed in the kitchen. Looking north across the Seine were the workshop (*c.* 5 metres square),

[9] On the Phlipon-Bimont family, *Corr.*, II, Appendix B, pp. 555–60; *Corr.*, NS, I, 'Notices sommaires', pp. xl–l.; ibid., I, p. x, for Phlipon's death (20 January 1789).
[10] On *marchands de vins* (*not* wine-merchants), Garrioch (1986), pp. 25–6.
[11] On Jacques-Louis Trude and his wife, the beloved 'Mme Trude' of the memoirs, *Corr.*, NS, I, pp. xxi–xxii.
[12] Garrioch (2002), p. 68; Savary des Bruslons (1726 edn): *graveurs en métail*, p. 127; Sonenscher (1989), chapters 1 and 7.
[13] Calemard (1929), p. 10; *Mém.* p. 307. Cf. Garrioch (2002), p. 36, quoting Mercier, *Tableau*: 'Servants were part of the family.'
[14] Baptismal certificate, note 8 above; Perroud (1909); *Corr.* NS, I, p. xxvii; Calemard (1929), p.19: different views on the exact house. Cf. Carbonnier (2006).

with the 'salle' next to it. There were two bedrooms. The *salle* had a parquet floor, walnut chairs with cane seats, and several other pieces of good furniture. Decorations included family portraits and mirrors—unusual features perhaps, until one remembers that M. Phlipon knew several painters, and that Mme Phlipon's relatives owned a mirror shop. Manon later had her own bedroom overlooking the river, a little annexe walled off by her father from the *salle*.[15]

One two-edged advantage emerged over time. Marie-Jeanne was her parents' only surviving child. Her memoirs contain a surprisingly casual reference to her five or six dead siblings, although it may not signify indifference. She remarks simply that her mother described her as the 'only child who had given her no trouble'. Baptismal records for central Paris were lost in the fires of 1871, but Auguste Jal's earlier research records that the firstborn in 1752, Marie-Marguerite, died almost immediately. Marie-Jeanne, born in March 1754, was the second. She was sent to a wet-nurse in Arpajon, 30 kilometres south-west of Paris, where she spent her first two years. In her absence, another girl was born and died in 1755. In 1758, when Marie-Jeanne was four years old, a boy was born, but did not survive; in 1761—she was seven—another boy died at birth, and in 1763, when she was nine, a final child was stillborn.[16] An observant child, she must have registered her mother's three last pregnancies and the deaths of the children, and knew of the others, but nowhere else does she mention them. Only when she was a mother herself did extreme anxiety about her baby daughter's survival reflect a distress that may have been implanted in early childhood. It was not a unique childbearing history in eighteenth-century France, although the family was particularly unlucky.

Mme Phlipon paid the Arpajon wet-nurse for two years—the normal interval for weaning.[17] The child's comparatively well-off great-aunt and uncle, who took an interest in her, knew the district well. Marie-Louise Besnard (1705–1794) was Gatien Phlipon's aunt, and her husband, Jean-Baptiste, was steward for tax-farmer André Haudry's chateau of Soucy, Fontenay-les-Briis, near Arpajon. In Paris, the Besnards lived in the rue Platrière, the street where Jean-Jacques Rousseau lived after 1770.[18]

Although we know almost nothing about the wet-nurse's household, Manon survived and grew up healthy, perhaps because her great-aunt 'supervised me'. The (unnamed) nurse, who had a 'brutal husband', another element passed over quickly in the memoirs, was recalled with affection, and regularly visited the family. It is pointless to speculate further, since wet-nursing applied to so many urban children of the period—including Manon's future husband—but we now know how strongly early experience affects future emotional development, and two years is a long time. The grown-up Mme Roland merely remarked with misleading cheerfulness

---

[15] Calemard, pp. 19 ff.; cf. descriptions in Pardailhe-Galabrun (1988).

[16] Jal (1872), entry 'Roland'; *Mém.*, pp. 203–4, note. Mme Roland says seven, Jal records six.

[17] Sussman (1982), pp. 67 ff., quoting Lenoir, *lieutenant de police*: in 1780—after Rousseau!—of 21,000 Parisian children, only 5 per cent were fed by their mothers; 70 per cent were wet-nursed, 25 per cent were foundlings.

[18] *Corr.*, NS, II, 29 May 1778, p. 275; ibid,. I, p. ix, 'Notices sommaires'. (The Trude cousins' glass shop was nearby.)

that she had acquired rural habits and was surprised to learn what chamber pots were for, on her return to town. But she also mentions an emotional encounter in adulthood with her former wet-nurse, who hastened to Paris when Marie-Jeanne's mother died, but whose arrival further increased her distress. This may hint at some conflict of feelings about her biological and her surrogate mother.[19]

Whatever traumas lay beneath the record of stillbirths, sibling deaths, and a two-year separation from her birth parents, being an only child brought material and intellectual benefits. Throughout her childhood, Manon was a cherished daughter whom her parents, although strict, indulged a good deal. She showed early signs of strong will and rebellion. One episode is recalled in the memoirs: her father whipped her, not for the first time, when she resolutely refused a dose of medicine. Having swallowed the potion under protest, she vomited and became even sicker, so, she says with some satisfaction, he abandoned the idea of physically forcing her to do anything. For her, this became a scene, often replayed in her head, which she literally compared with being prepared to go to the scaffold. Her mother, who she claimed to adore, took a different line, and when calling her to order had only to say sharply 'mademoiselle', instead of the gentler *ma fille*, or her pet name 'Manon'.[20]

Her later strained relations with her father are reflected in the memoirs by the attempt she makes to be objective about him. Her parents' marriage was not ideally happy: her 'sensitive' mother would have been better suited to someone more 'déli-cat' than her 'robust, irascible', over-ambitious, and to his daughter's mind, rather vulgar father. 'He loved his wife and appearances [...] nobody could call him a virtuous man, but he had a great deal of what is known as honour: he might have accepted higher payment for something than it was worth, but he would have killed himself rather than fail to pay the price of something he had bought.'[21]

The little girl was made much of. For walking on Sundays in the Tuileries gardens, her mother made her miniature versions of fashionable silk dresses. Her hair was curled, and passers-by would have thought she had 'stepped out of a carriage', although for every-day wear, she ran about in a 'plain linen shift', and was sent downstairs alone to buy 'parsley or lettuce'. Marie-Jeanne later developed strong views on dress, favouring respectable simplicity, but a touch of nostalgia is readable into her account of the brocade dresses of her childhood. All this attention could only bolster her view of herself from an early age as someone special.[22]

Gatien Phlipon's status was modest. His daughter described it as 'médiocre', not because he was unskilled, but because his trade was not as well-paid as others nearby (goldsmiths for instance), nor was he of high artistic talent. He had acquaintances in the fine arts—and sometimes took his daughter to visit the *Salons*, annual exhibitions in the Louvre. Among artists visiting the workshop were Jollain

[19] Ibid., p. 204; Sussman (1982), p. 79.
[20] *Mém.*, note, pp. 209–10, 'scaffold', another echo of Rousseau's *Confessions*.
[21] Ibid., p. 203; cf. letter of 26 December 1778, *Corr.*, NS, II, pp. 345–6. for mixed feelings— affection and mortification—for her father.
[22] *Mém.*, p. 216, cf. Roche (1987), p. 74.

and Falconet junior, and Manon once met Greuze.[23] But the household was a site of manual work, rather than connoisseurship. One of Marie-Jeanne's letters describes the 'gold-washers' visiting:

> … the tapestries are shaken out, the furniture, kitchen utensils, masters and mistresses are stirred, shaken and pushed about, not because we are moving house, for although everything changes place, nothing is taken away. Add to this upset the loud presence of the gold-washers. They are kindly fellows, as black as devils, and as dirty as coachmen, who arrive with big buckets and two mills. They spend several days putting the ashes of our sweepings through the mills with quicksilver, to separate out any gold that might be mixed up in the dust (which we have been collecting all year). This may make you laugh, but their search is better rewarded than that for the philosophers' stone.[24]

The workshop was embedded inside the family home, so the child's earliest outside acquaintances were the apprentices, adolescent boys who entered the household. Up to half a dozen shared the family's meals, and at times lived in. The memoirs say that her father 'employed quite a large number of journeymen'. Teenage youths had far greater freedom than girls to roam the streets, watching public events or street performers, and generally assumed to be up to no good.[25] The presence of boys was an obvious hazard for the family daughter. In her memoirs, Mme Roland relates an incident that she concealed even from her husband. When she was about ten, one apprentice, to whom she had become quite attached, twice assaulted her sexually. His actions were not exactly violent—exhibitionism the first time, then more seriously masturbating while holding on to the little girl—but they were quite frightening enough to distress her, and to cause panic in her parents. Thereafter, a closer watch was kept on both the child and the boys.[26]

What could a girl like Manon expect in the way of education? She could read by the age of five and showed early intelligence. Part of the family budget was devoted to her accomplishments, which would have been unlikely if her siblings had survived. As the eldest sister, she would have had to help her mother care for them, and more money would normally be spent on any brothers. On the other hand, if she had survived as an only *son*, she would have received more formal education, but with a technical bent. A boy would have been destined to become the chief apprentice and learn his father's trade. Access to the guild of master artisans was largely through kinship networks—journeymen rarely managed it. It wasn't unthinkable for a girl. The earliest women painters were often artists' daughters, familiar from childhood with the tools of the trade. Manon's father also taught her draughtsmanship. She was competent with the burin, and took her grandparents drawings, or a copperplate on which 'I had engraved a bunch of flowers and a compliment'. Much later, she even considered carrying on the workshop (technically possible for a woman after the edict of August 1776). Her mother, while alive, was not keen: 'I don't want her to become a painter: she would have to study in

---

[23] *Corr.*, NS, I, p. 335, 31 October 1775; *Mém.*, p. 270.
[24] *Corr.*, NS., I, p. 104, 18 Mai 1772.
[25] Cf. Darnton (1984).
[26] *Mém.*, pp. 217–21; see Chapter 7 below; cf. Garrioch (2002), p. 138.

common with others and make acquaintances we can do without.' Not being a boy meant not having this choice forced on her.[27]

However, her slightly privileged education did not take her as far as a boy's might have done. A training in plain household management came first. She boasted that by age eight she was used to making an omelette, preparing vegetables, and skimming the pot. 'I am at home anywhere and can make my own soup' as she put it.[28] She helped nurse servants, apprentices, and family members when they were sick. But her parents also hired masters who taught her some accomplishments—handwriting, playing guitar and viol, and dancing. Music would always play a great part in her life, rather rarely for someone of her status.[29] A bright child who soaked up learning like blotting paper, she learned a little history and geography, but had no serious access to the classics. Her uncle, the priest, taught her some Latin, but inconsistently, and she had no Greek. It was reading that made her a passionate lover of the ancient world.

Above all, as a girl she was subject to much closer supervision than a boy. Running errands was one thing, but from an early age, 'girls began to observe taboos on their movement and to form ties [only] within a restricted neighbourhood, in whose affairs they were as women to play a central role.'[30] The teenage Marie-Jeanne was obliged to have Mignonne accompany her on longer walks. Revealingly, when she was twenty-two, she 'escaped' only by borrowing clothes from the servant and 'running like a peasant girl, pushing everyone who got in my way, walking through gutters, splashing through the mud, being jostled by people who would have made way for me if they had seen me in my better clothes'—another clue to the status of an artisan's family.[31]

One public place girls did frequent was church. Brought up in an atmosphere of traditional piety, Manon accompanied Mme Phlipon to mass every morning. Church attendance was something she continued most of her life, for the sake of propriety—long after she had lost her faith. Catechism classes were her first formal lessons.[32] With this upbringing and her determined character, she went through a phase of religious enthusiasm, which took her parents by surprise. She pleaded to go to a convent to prepare for her first communion—even entertaining thoughts of becoming a nun, something strongly discouraged at home. Since they could afford it, the Phlipons found a convent school, Notre-Dame de la Congrégation, in south-east Paris, dominated by the great Abbaye Saint-Victor. Despite dread at leaving her mother, Manon insisted on the move, and the date was engraved on her mind: '7 May 1765: I was eleven years and two months old.'[33]

---

[27] *Mém.*, p. 215. Garrioch (1986), p. 113 on obstacles to women other than widows taking over a workshop, cf. Horn (2006), p. 28, on edict.

[28] *Mém.*, p. 216.

[29] Cf. Pardailhe-Galabrun (1988) p. 190: only 4 per cent of wills included a musical instrument.

[30] Garrioch (1986), p. 59.

[31] *Corr.*, NS, II, pp. 14–15, 14 January 1777, cf. Garrioch (2002), p. 286. She went to the Porte Saint-Denis ('I had never been so far on my own before'), to check on her father's mistress, a 'working girl'.

[32] *Mém.*, p. 207.   [33] Ibid., p. 223.

The convent and gardens stood on the rue Neuve Saint-Etienne-du-Mont (later excavated to uncover the Roman amphitheatre, the Arènes de Lutèce.)[34] During her year there, Marie-Jeanne experienced long moments of religious exaltation and even ecstasy, recalled with striking fervour in her memoirs. Her lifelong desire for the absolute found expression in the rituals of the convent, in her first communion, and in solitary walks in the gardens. Even when, as an adult, philosophy had 'dissipated the illusions of a vain belief', she remained sensitive to the mass, if it was 'carried out with gravity' and especially if there was music. She returned to her confessor at Saint-Victor for the next three years, because of his sense of the sublime.[35]

Educationally, a year or so with the sisters was hardly an advantage. There was one class for all boarders from age six to eighteen: 'brought up as I had been, it was not surprising that I was better educated than my companions'. Manon received a little individual tuition in handwriting, spelling, and grammar. But the school brought her the benefits of emotional development and female friendship. She was popular with her teachers—one of the lay-sisters (*soeurs converses*), Soeur Sainte-Agathe (Angélique Boufflers, *c.*1741–1797) virtually adopted her, and remained in touch with her to the end of her life.[36] Most of her schoolmates were from higher-status families, but less serious-minded. She later wrote: 'I was in a convent with about forty young girls who just wanted to play about [*folâtrer*].'[37] However, one friendship indirectly changed the course of her life. The Cannet sisters from Amiens became lifelong friends. From a wealthier background than 'little Phlipon', neither was in her league intellectually. Henriette (*c.*1747–1838) was older; Marie-Sophie-Caroline (1751–1795), known as Sophie, was closer in age and they became bosom companions.[38]

Manon was still far from writing perfect French after a year at the convent,[39] but her precocious literacy was encouraged by a stay with her paternal grandmother. The widow of the *marchand de vins* was also former governess to the noble Boismorel family. The twelve-year-old went to live with her (and aunt Angélique) on the Ile Saint-Louis, because her father had become an official in his guild: her mother was fully occupied running the shop.[40] Manon perfected her style and

---

[34] Buildings visible on the 1739 Plan Turgot, see Fierro and Sarazin (2005); *Corr.*, NS, I, p. xxviii; some rooms were for 'dames pensionnaires' cf. prologue.

[35] *Mém.*, pp. 222–7; *Corr.*, NS, I, pp. xxvii–xxix; Goodman (2009a), pp. 74–5: in 1769, a Paris almanac listed 38 convent boarding-schools; fees 150 to 600 *livres*; most girls spent only a year there.

[36] Eight nuns are mentioned by name in the memoirs. On Angélique Boufflers (*c.*1741–1797) *Corr.*, II, pp. 785–7; *Corr.*, NS, II, 16 November 1779; 16 January 1780; 8 April 1784, 20 July 1790, etc.

[37] To Louis Bosc, 10 June 1783, *Corr.*, I, p. 255.

[38] Goodman (2009a), p. 79, on convent connections. On the Cannet family, *Corr.*, NS, II, Appendix A, pp. 549–54, and NS, I, pp. xxiii–xxvii. Their father (d.1766) was a lawyer.

[39] See *Corr.*, II, pp. 419–20: examples: 'ji serai encor trois semaines'; 'je ne toublie pas'. On the stay in the Ile Saint-Louis, *Mém.*, pp. 232–3, 238–43.

[40] *Corr.*, NS, I, p. 2, 15 April 1767: cf. Brouard-Arends and Plagnol-Dieval (2007).

spelling, and later recalled her time there as one of intellectual exploration, warm affection, and calm walks on the quayside with her aunt.

Even so, by the age of fourteen, except for music lessons, her formal schooling was over. It was nothing like that of her educated male contemporaries: Robespierre for example, from an impoverished legal family in Arras, was a scholarship boy at the Collège Louis-le-Grand in Paris, where his close friend was Camille Demoulins. Both boys did solid classical studies from the age of eleven to their early twenties, going on to read law.[41] Many of the men she would frequently meet after her marriage—with the notable exception of her husband—had had much more formal education than Mlle Phlipon. Like her hero, Jean-Jacques Rousseau, she would always be a virtual autodidact.

A strong-willed child, with a religious upbringing, a smattering of polite accomplishments, and the undivided attention of parents, grandparents, aunts, and uncles, Marie-Jeanne was the centre of her little world. Socially, her parents rarely left the neighbourhood. She occasionally went with her mother to musical evenings held by a cultured Italian woman, Mme L'Epine, and with her father to art exhibitions, but until her twenties, she met few people who might be regarded as having a superior education, let alone one attuned to the more advanced authors of the day.[42]

The hidden advantages mentioned above help to explain why this girl might fashion some education for herself from what came to hand. But nothing yet suggested that she would have a destiny other than her mother's: to marry a local shopkeeper, preferably a well-off jeweller, and devote herself to husband and children. If she did so, as she wrote aged seventeen:

> I shall find myself burdened with all the duties and troubles of a married woman and mother of a family, but also of a shopkeeper, sitting all day behind a counter, dealing with the trade in precious stones or silver, as well as the household. It's not that I feel strongly for or against commerce [. . .] thinking it to be the one for which Providence has destined me, I will carry out these duties [. . . but] if I followed my own inclination for tranquillity, and thought about what happens in marriage, I would never enter into it.[43]

[41] Scurr (2007), chapter 1 for details. [42] *Mém.*, pp. 270, 279.
[43] *Corr.*, NS, II, 8 November 1771, cf. Goodman (2009b).

2

The Bride's Story (2)
Becoming an Enlightenment Woman

Marie-Jeanne

The mass of contrary ideas besieging me teaches me to be content not to know. Without being discouraged by these contradictions, I will settle quietly for a doubt I cannot resolve, waiting for further enlightenment [*plus de lumières*].

Marie-Jeanne Phlipon, notebook, 20 May 1776[1]

When, contrary to expectations, Mlle Phlipon remained single until her mid-twenties, the energy that might have gone into domestic life went instead into developing her intellect.

Back home from her grandmother's, she went on behaving like a dutiful daughter: making routine visits to church, to relations and acquaintances, cooking, sewing. However, she also embarked on a reading programme—disjointed, governed by chance, by the generosity of acquaintances, and by whatever she could lay hands on, but pursued with dedication and formidable extract-making. 'First thing in the morning, I would set down on paper what had struck me the previous evening, then take up the book [...] to copy out a passage I wanted to possess in its entirety. This taste became a habit, a need, and a passion.'[2] The notebooks, in which she also wrote philosophical essays and copied out mathematical equations, give a remarkable record of an intellect struggling to form itself.

Although unusual, given her background, she was not necessarily unique. Nicole Pellegrin, considering records from six or seven women from the same period, but in rather better-off households, concluded that 'quite a few female readers wanted to convert themselves into true scholars, capable of reproducing, by going over them, books they had read, pen in hand'. Marie-Jeanne exactly fits or may have inspired Pellegrin's description of these self-educators: 'having a domestic training, often parallel to the apprenticeship in masculine trades, and a certain autodidacticism', ending up with 'a rather haphazard education, supervised by a mixed but attentive entourage'.[3]

---

[1] BNF MSS, naf 6244, fos 290–6, quoted *Corr.*, NS, I, pp. li–lvii.
[2] *Mém.*, p. 245.
[3] Pellegrin (2003), pp. 115–16; early writings BNF MSS, naf 6244, 9533; cf. Goodman (2009) p. 153, on extracting, with a letter from 1776 as an example.

One advantage was having a best friend to write to. 'It is sad to be always talking to oneself, one needs another support, a second oneself' (20 February 1774). Several historians have explored eighteenth-century epistolarity—letter-writing—among women, and Dena Goodman provides an insightful case-study of Mlle Phlipon.[4] She was lucky, and so are we, that Sophie Cannet lived in Amiens. The girls saw each other only rarely in the 1770s. For over ten years, she had a confidante to whom she could—at length!—express her feelings, describe her reading, and record her everyday life. The letters, over 250 of them, reached a peak in 1776–1778. Sophie could not always reply in kind, but was a sympathetic listener. From the start, Marie-Jeanne's side of the exchange was serious. A page picked at random from 9 February 1771—she was almost seventeen—was concerned with self-love. The list of nouns there, almost all abstract, gives some sense of it:

state/slavery/vessel/winds/reefs/reason/pilot/efforts/chains/blindfold/light/Faith/reflexions/happiness/feeling/liberty/thoughts/motives/Providence/situation/crowd/profit/*retreat*/veil/eyes/truth/reflections/leisure/lessons/goal/change/gaze/future/peace/heart/joy/price/paper/thoughts/heart/multiplicity/extent/portrait/people. Arguments/judgements/decrees/history/events/doctrine/men/instruments/will/rules/wisdom/inconstancy/instability/things/reflections/necessity.[5]

Marie-Jeanne consciously used her correspondence as a sounding board for her thoughts, to 'reason and describe, consequently to observe and reflect'.[6] The letters are as striking for their protestations of affection as for their intellectual content. One contains, like little girls draw today, a heart over her signature (11 September 1770); another says: 'You're right: we are like Orestes and Pylades, only women.'[7]

Her parents' affection for their odd, bookish child made this retreat into books and letter-writing materially possible. The confined 'cellule' [= cell] they constructed for her was her version of Virginia Woolf's 'room of one's own', a private space, from the mid-1760s to 1778. Facing north over the river, it had just room for a bed, 'on to which I had to climb from the end', a chair, bookshelves and a 'tablette' to write on. In 1778, her father made her a second version, with which she was even better pleased: 'my study (*cabinet*) is especially pretty; I have organized it to suit me, my books and papers are well shelved: it's a sanctuary dedicated to Minerva and friendship: my temple and my refuge'.[8] As well as books, she obtained writing materials: goose-quill pens, paper, ink, sealing wax, a little desk. On 20 March 1772, she wrote that she had made sure not to run out of paper; 'as for pens, I am never without them, though they are not always the best'. In her teens she was often up at 5 a.m., or stayed up until past midnight, so she must have been allowed a candle or lamp. Her contemporary, Geneviève Randon, aged sixteen,

---

[4] Goodman (2009) *passim*, esp. introduction, and p. 3 on letter-writing as offering 'relational autonomy' for women; Diaz (1999, 2002, and 2006); Grassi (1994).

[5] *Corr.*, NS, I p. 28: 'retreat' refers to her *cellule*.

[6] *Corr.*, NS I, p. 279, 31 March 1775.

[7] 11 June 1772, *Corr.*, NS, I, p. 112; on self-discovery, ibid, p.80, February 1772: and p. 112, 11 June 1772. Perroud's 1915 edition gives a date-table. Hardly any of Sophie's letters survive.

[8] *Corr.*, NS, II, p. 340, 12 December 1778; the 1777 inventory describes the titles as 'mostly religious'.

wrote to a friend 'You are lucky to be allowed to read in bed, my governess takes [my lamp] away with her.'[9] Françoise Kermina writes perceptively that Marie-Jeanne must have 'loved the paper, the scratching of her pen, the flow of words, the pile of pages, the table holding them, and [...] the enclosing walls'.[10]

On her reading between ages fourteen and twenty-five, much has been written. Roger Chartier warns us not to trust first-person accounts of early reading—we all make a conscious or unconscious selection.[11] In her memoirs, Mme Roland goes into remarkable detail about the authors and titles she read. The letters to Sophie confirm much of this. Even so, she may have exaggerated her precociousness: biographers sometimes unquestioningly quote the books in the order they occur in her memoirs. Certainly, she was a determined and voracious reader: 'I devour everything: history, mathematics, poetry, legislation, agriculture, I like everything.' The sheer volume of information, however, puts us in some danger of making Marie-Jeanne *too* exceptional. The same books were read by other girls of her age, although usually those of higher status.

The Phlipon household's basic 'little library' was soon exhausted: an odd assortment, including lives of the Saints, Scarron's *Roman comique*, works on heraldry. At her grandmother Rotisset-Phlipon's house, she had read St François de Sales and St Augustine (her religious faith still being strong), but also, with enthusiasm, the letters of Mme de Sévigné.[12] Marie-Jeanne confesses to abstracting books from the locker of one apprentice, who was 'trying to improve himself'—Fénelon's *Télémaque*, and Plutarch's *Lives*. As well as a threateningly masculine presence, these wide-awake Parisian adolescents were a source of outside ideas reaching the household, specifically bringing in books. In her mid-teens, she also had the run of the library of the Abbé Le Jay, uncle Bimont's *vicaire*, during Sunday games of backgammon ('tric-trac'). They were a mixture of the sacred (several Jesuit authors) and the secular: travel writing and history. The same titles occur in the correspondence of women studied by Pellegrin and Martine Sonnet: the Abbé Vertot's Roman history (1727); Buffon's natural history, and Mézeray's *Histoire de France*, although he was 'the driest of writers'.[13]

Marie-Jeanne's father borrowed books for her from lending libraries—hence, the need to copy out passages. He brought among others 'Montesquieu, Locke, Burlamaqui, and our leading playwrights [...] I had no plan or aim, except to educate myself [...] I usually had several books on the go at once, some for work, some for pleasure, histories being read out aloud' in the evenings with her mother.[14]

[9] Sonnet (2003) p. 140; on Randon, and the physical apparatus of writing letters cf. Goodman (2009, chapters 5 and 6); on the *cellule*, *Mém.*, p. 212; *Corr.*, NS, I, pp. 88, 145, etc.
[10] Kermina (1976), p. 52.
[11] *Pratique de la lecture*, quoted Diaconoff (2005), p.62. Cf. May (1970), Goodman (2009), Godineau (2003).
[12] *Mém.*, pp. 239 ff. Goodman (2009) pp. 149–510: a 1774 letter in imitation of Mme de Sévigné: an 'in-joke' between girls. Cf. Pardailhe-Galabrun (1988), pp. 174 ff., similar titles in the average urban household.
[13] *Mém.*, p. 246; Pellegrin (2003), p.120; Sonnet in Brouard-Arends (2003), pp. 131–42.
[14] *Mém.*, p. 249.

She started wrestling with her first religious doubts—concealed from Mme Phlipon—during her teens: both heart and reason rebelled against official doctrine, beginning with the unacceptable idea that all non-Catholics—even from pre-Christian ages or in other religions—were damned. Then she began to feel 'the absurdity of infallibility'. Her beloved confessor, M. Lallement, died when she was fifteen. Her next confessor, on hearing of her doubts, lent her books by Christian apologists such as Bossuet; however, these writings, by suggesting the case could be argued, sent her straight to the opposition: Voltaire, Diderot, D'Alembert, Helvetius, Holbach, and Raynal.[15]

Marie-Jeanne certainly read Voltaire in her youth. 'One day as I was reading *Candide*,' she remembered, a lady visitor expressed astonished disapproval. Although some commentators have dated this very early, from its place in the memoirs, it would be surprising if she read *Candide* before the age of twelve: within the first few pages, the reader is plunged into caricatural accounts of sex, rape, and torture. It was banned by the Paris Parlement when it appeared in 1759, both as immoral and for its religious scepticism. Since Marie-Jeanne was going through her most religious phase between about eleven and fourteen, the incident—which surely took place, so vividly is it recalled—is more likely to have happened after about 1768. In her 1773 notebook, she wrote of religion: 'one doesn't think at eighteen the same way one thinks at fourteen', but still believes in God. *Candide* could have come from the apprentice's locker. Apprentice boys were said to run round the streets quoting 'Mangeons du jésuite' ('Let's eat Jesuit!') when it appeared. Its mention in the memoirs is—whatever the date—a marker of precociousness and braving *les bienséances*.[16]

An even more important example is Plutarch's *Lives* (of Greek and Roman heroes). Mme Roland is famous for her love of Plutarch. She claimed she took her copy to church instead of her missal 'during Lent 1763 [...] I was nine years old'. We have to take her word for this. Certainly Plutarch touched a nerve more than anything else she had ever read—or perhaps would ever read. It is not impossible that she read some Plutarch at nine, and had a small volume tucked into her skirts, perhaps a selection suitable for young people. Longer editions ran to thirteen volumes, and to say one has 'read Plutarch' is more a statement of intent than a record of actual reading.[17] But the Greek author still remained in her mind years later, since she was reading him in prison. We don't know the real age at which she read some of these books, but decoding the prison memoirs means looking through the prism of her models, Plutarch and Jean-Jacques Rousseau—heroism and sensibility—who would supercede Voltaire in her mind after the age of twenty. The section of the memoirs describing her childhood is transparently inspired by Rousseau's *Confessions* (see Chapter 27) and, significantly, Rousseau says that *he* read Plutarch at the age of nine. Plutarch was surely the inspiration behind this French girl

---

[15] *Mém.*, pp. 211, 212, 213, 239, 245, 246, 248, 249; Perroud (1905), II, pp. 91 ff., thought she actually read these books a little later.

[16] *Mém.*, p. 213.

[17] Few references in *Corr.*, but see NS, I, 8 May 1772; II, p. 62; II, pp. 271 and 321.

wishing many times that she had been born in Greece, Rome, or Sparta—or that she had been born a man.

If Marie-Jeanne had been entirely self-taught, her reading might have been as haphazard throughout her youth as during her early years. Her pious mother was ever-watchful, even reading letters from Sophie (though, surprisingly, she did not ban *Candide*), but her sudden death from a stroke in May 1775, although a dreadful shock to her grieving daughter, probably liberated Marie-Jeanne from maternal censorship. Thereafter, she had an unusual experience for a young woman of her age and station—a succession of much older, well-educated men, who became her literary advisers. Had her mother lived, things might have been different.

Thanks to these men, her reading after 1775 expanded to take in recent works of the *philosophes* and especially Jean-Jacques Rousseau. The new mentors started turning up at the house when her widowed father, previously regarded with affection and kept in line by her mother, was a changed character—irritable, spendthrift, speculating in precious stones, and taking a mistress. The procession of elderly male friends were more substitute father-figures than suitors, although there was some ambiguity at times. Their role was, above all, to open doors to the wider world—through their personal travels, their contact with well-known writers, or in terms of books and thought.[18]

Monsieur Moré (first name unknown), a sixty-year-old watchmaker from Geneva, had the glory of being an acquaintance of Jean-Jacques Rousseau. A valued family friend during the 1770s, he presented Mlle Phlipon with Rousseau's complete works for New Year 1778.[19] A greater intellectual influence was that of Robergé de Boismorel (*c.*1730–1776), a married nobleman in his forties. Son of the disdainful aristocratic family to whom Marie-Jeanne's grandmother had been governess, he described himself as 'your grandmother's *Emile*',[20] and had known Marie-Jeanne in her childhood. She called him 'the Sage of Bercy', where his house had a garden running down to the river. That summer of 1775, after her mother's death, he opened his library to her, and took her with her father on an expedition to Rousseau's 'hermitage' at Montmorency. Boismorel seems to have embarked on an *amitié amoureuse* with the young woman. Both his caste-conscious mother and his wife disapproved of his lending her works by Bayle (and perhaps of his visits). His sudden death, in September 1776, affected Mlle Phlipon deeply.[21]

Older again was sixty-year-old Joseph-Charles de Sainte-Lette (1717–1777), a friend of the writer Helvétius. A Louisiana veteran, on leave from the French India service, he visited Gatien Phlipon 'three or four times a week' in 1776. This 'atheistic old bachelor' promised to bring Marie-Jeanne a book by Locke. In their discussions—with and without her father in the room—Sainte-Lette helped dispel what remained of her Christian beliefs. He seems to have been cherished in

[18] Perroud (1905), introduction, p. 12.
[19] *Corr.*, NS, II, p. 179; on Moré, ibid., I, pp. xli–xlii.
[20] BNF MSS, naf 6241, letter from Boismorel, 17 September 1775, one of six; cf. *Corr.*, NS, I, pp. xxxv–xxxvii; *Mém.*, pp. 309–14.
[21] 5 December 1775: Raynal and Bayle. She wrote at his request an anonymous letter of advice to his wayward son.

a genuinely filial way, but returned to Pondicherry in November, dying there a year later.[22] Before leaving, Sainte-Lette had prompted a more questionable relationship with his friend Firmin Sévelinges d'Espagny, a tobacco tax-farmer in Soissons, outside Paris. Aged fifty-six, and recently widowed, Sévelinges was well-read and up-to-date with philosophical thought. It was to him that Mlle Phlipon sent her first attempt at 'public writing'.

Those who read a lot usually end up wanting to write. Marie-Jeanne wrote copiously—but privately. For all the protestations against *femmes savantes* that punctuate her correspondence, she already had a repressed ambition to send her words outside the little cell. In January 1777, she confided to Sophie that she had 'begun an academic discourse: ahem!'—no small thing. The Académie de Besançon had set a prize essay competition, on 'How the education of women could contribute to make men better.' 'I was struck, I got to thinking, I wrote it amid all the little mental distractions which were perpetually troubling me, I penned this little discourse and without showing it to a soul, I sent it off in April, anonymously, as befitted me.' In July she sent it to Sévelinges for comment: 'I ought to have done this before stupidly sending it off [...] his criticism was wise, delicate, enlightened and sincere...' Her views on women's education repeated a certain number of received ideas, but she accurately remembered that she had said good laws would be a better way of 'making men better'. She was mortified when no prize was awarded—although she was in good company: Bernardin de Saint Pierre was also 'commended'.[23]

Literary criticism was not all that Sévelinges was interested in. When her father queried their correspondence, Mlle Phlipon asked Sévelinges to send letters secretly, via her uncle in Vincennes. Then in 1778, she received an unconventional offer from the tax-farmer: that she come and live in a *pavillon* in the grounds of his estate, so that they could 'philosophize together'. Although Marie-Jeanne saw the impropriety of such a proposal, she hinted that she might accept a 'mariage blanc' or platonic settlement. The relationship eventually cooled, ending with a firm note from her in April 1779, but it had been serious enough for her to show Jean-Marie Roland the correspondence before they married, as earnest that it had been quite innocent, at least on her side.[24]

The older men who climbed the Phlipons' stairs were emissaries from the grown-up male milieu of the *philosophes*. They had seen the world. Sainte-Lette faced a barrage of queries about whether the colonies were really like the accounts by Marie-Jeanne's favourite travel-writer, De Pauwe.[25] Sévelinges showed her a letter he had received from the *Encyclopédie* editor, D'Alembert. Boismorel took her to

[22] *Corr.*, NS, I, pp. xxxvii–xxxviii; ibid., p. 84, re Locke; *Mém./*Perroud (1905), II, p. 91, concludes that by late 1775 she was 'a thorough non-believer'.

[23] *Corr.*, NS, II, pp. 84 and 97; ibid., I, p. xxxix; cf. *Mém.*, p. 327; see Roland (1964), noting pp. 157–81 (strictures on *femmes savantes*) and *Corr.*, NS, I, p. 444 on Thomas's *Essai sur les femmes*; cf. Trouille (1997), pp. 163–93.

[24] On Sévelinges, *Corr.*, NS, I, pp. xxxviii–xli; II, p. vi, and *Mém.* pp. 326–8.

[25] *Recherches philosophiques sur les Américains, les Egyptiens et les Chinois*, 1774; de Pauwe was the uncle of her subsequent enemy, Anacharsis Cloots, see *Mém./*Perroud (1905), II, p. 195.

the annual session of the Académie française, where she heard D'Alembert in person (he had a 'squeaky voice'). The Abbé Bexon, whom she met in 1778 because he lodged with her mirror-making cousins, was one of Buffon's contributors.[26] Despite her sheltered life then, she had some threads connecting her to the advanced thought of her day. Intellectual Paris was after all a small world, whose tentacles could reach into modest households—but none of her mentors was a woman, which will have reinforced her sense of her own oddity.

So it is wrong to think of her as entirely without guidance. The seriousness and individual nature of her responses to what she read are striking though. A couple of examples. In 1775, she read *De l'Esprit* by Helvétius, published in 1758 and condemned by the Paris Parlement.[27] Its argument was that the vices and virtues derived from physical sensations, from a human desire to maximize pleasure and minimize pain. Good government would seek to create a balance, rather than appeal to moral authority. Marie-Jeanne's teenage comments have a priggish tone, which she later mocked herself:

> It would have been more desirable for the author of *De l'Esprit* [...] if the vivacity of his genius, the energy of his expressions had been employed to depict the certainty of the principles on which morality is founded, and the beauty and advantages of virtue, rather than being ingeniously employed in combatting both of these. Then one would not find oneself saying to him: 'if the degree of esteem which the public grants people of sharp intellect [*de l'esprit*] is proportional to the usefulness which it derives from them, what degree of esteem would *you* claim to deserve, monsieur?'

Underneath, at some later date, she has written: 'The time has come when this criticism makes me laugh.'[28] In another passage, she had been reading Diderot's *Entretiens sur le fils naturel* (1757) and gives a sort of film of herself reading:

> I found [there] something which struck home so strongly that, delighted to find I thought the same way as a distinguished writer (*un homme de mérite*), I threw the book down on the table and rising to my feet involuntarily, I made an exclamation and gestures which would have made me look crazy if there had been anyone about.[29]

It was Diderot's *sensibilité* that most attracted her, and the same reason inspired a more long-lasting passion for Jean-Jacques Rousseau. While she sampled many writings of the *philosophes*, she later repeatedly referred to her trinity of heroes: 'I had chosen Rousseau for my breviary, Plutarch as my master, Montaigne as my friend'.[30] Plutarch made her a republican, Madame Roland claimed (whatever she meant by this), but Rousseau showed her the possibility of living a fulfilled life.

Rousseau burst upon her intellectual and emotional horizon at a vulnerable moment. She was still distressed at her mother's death in 1775 when the Abbé

---

[26] *Corr.*, NS, II, p. 670, Appendix K; D'Alembert, *Mém.*, p. 311.

[27] First mention in *Corr.*, NS, II, is May 1775.

[28] BNF MSS, naf 6244 (Manuscrits de jeunesse).

[29] To Boismorel, 28 May 1776, *Corr.*, NS, I, p. 419. Cf. 15 March 1775, ibid., pp. 273–5, portrait of her days: mornings: work, read, mass; frugal meal in cellule; then 'writing, studying, dreaming, extracting, commenting', before lighter things: music and visits.

[30] *Corr.*, NS, II, p. 271.

Legrand, a friend of uncle Bimont, brought her a copy of Rousseau's *La Nouvelle Héloïse* (1761), a book that became a talisman for her and which she read several times (if not 'every year' as she sometimes claimed).[31] She already knew his *Emile*: a Rousseau-inspired conversation with her mother about breastfeeding, remembered in the memoirs, must date from before 1775. But *La Nouvelle Héloïse* turned Rousseau into her favourite author. Of this best-selling novel she wrote, 'The woman who has read this book and does not find herself a better person, or at least desire to be, has a soul of mud; she will never rise above the commonplace.'[32] By December, she was calling him 'le divin Jean-Jacques', and had set out to read as many of his works as she could. While *La Nouvelle Héloïse* touched the hearts of many readers, especially women, in the mid-eighteenth century, Mlle Phlipon applied herself intellectually to his other writings more than most people. In spring 1776 she could write:

> His *Discourse on Inequality* is as deeply thought as it is strongly written; this production alone would have earned him the title of a leading philosopher. His *Discourse on the Sciences and Arts*, strange though the principles advanced there may be, is better supported by proof than everything that has been written against it. His *Social Contract* is wisely argued, his *Letters from the Mountain* contain a thousand truths relative to government and his *Letter on the Theatre* [...] sparkles with a thousand beauties. In short, in everything he has done one recognises not only the man of genius but the *honnête homme* and the citizen, His probity and uprightness everywhere appear; if he is unusual, it is for his frankness. Telling the truth (or at any rate what he believes it to be) is his chief concern: to make people love the good is his purpose. All the personal faults with which he is reproached can be reduced to the vague accusation of being difficult to live with [*insociable*]...A thoughtful, applied and deep writer is not the sort of being to shine at social gatherings [*cercles*].[33]

Just a week or two earlier, on 29 February 1776, Marie-Jeanne had made a famous, but unsuccessful, attempt to meet Rousseau. His fellow-Genevan, Moré, generously provided her with an excuse: a musical commission, for Rousseau to compose a few songs. Guessing that she might be turned away, she wrote a careful letter first, hoping to pick up the reply in person. She told the whole story to Sophie: how she hauled off Mignonne as chaperone and climbed the stairs in the rue Platrière—she had served behind the counter at her cousin's mirror shop round the corner. She described the dialogue with Mme Rousseau (Thérèse Levasseur) who effectively guarded the door. The caller had to be content to hear that Rousseau had read her letter, apparently believing it was written by a man. 'The writing alone indicates it was in a man's hand,' as Thérèse told her. Marie-Jeanne reflected honestly—and no doubt accurately—that 'he must have thought all I wrote was just a cunning pretext, to enable me to get to see him by a pointless visit'.[34]

[31] Ibid., NS, I, p. 95.
[32] Ibid., NS, I, p. 392.
[33] *Corr.* NS, I, pp. 392–3, 21 March 1776. Few private libraries had the *Contrat social*, Linton (2001) p. 143; cf. *DCRF*, pp. 872–86. On Rousseau, May (1964) and (1970).
[34] *Mém.*, p. 307; *Corr.*, NS, I, p. xxi: the Besnards and the Trude family lived nearby, *Corr.*, NS, II, p. 78.

Moré's gift of Rousseau's collected works overwhelmed her, inspiring passionate letters to Sophie. What influence did Rousseau have on this strange and isolated young woman? Gita May's view is that she recognized in him a tone of voice, that of the outsider, uncomfortable, depressed, and discriminated against, who has nevertheless the right to be heard. When she said he showed her how a life could be happy and fulfilled, she was referring to the vision of both passionate love and companionate marriage in the figures of Julie, Saint-Preux, and Wolmar in *La Nouvelle Héloïse*. She shared his love of simplicity and dislike of luxury, and took seriously his cult of truth and sincerity.

Her loss of faith had already begun long before she read Rousseau—she later wrote that she had been successively 'Jansenist, Cartesian, Stoic and Deist'. But her mother's death no doubt liberated her from a feeling of religious constraint, which was always very strong during Mme Phlipon's lifetime. Conversations with her older mentors and reading in particular the *Profession de foi* in Rousseau's *Emile* sent her towards a position that, with some variation, she maintained to the end, of a kind of deism. She continued to view the Catholic Church as an institution requiring unacceptable total submission: 'that's the basis of [the priests'] empire; it is destroyed the moment one begins to reason'.[35]

Politically, Rousseau may also have brought into focus her precociously-sensed anger and resentment at the arrogance of the 'well-born' or wealthy. Two incidents are recalled in the memoirs as particularly stinging. The first was a visit with her grandmother to the aristocratic Boismorel house in the Marais. She had been discomfited by hearing her respectable grandmother referred to as 'Mademoiselle', and found the whole visit humiliating. The second was with her great-aunt and uncle Besnard in the Soucy chateau: expecting to sit down to dinner with the family of their employer, she found herself in the servants' hall. On the broader questions of politics, there is evidence that Rousseau had already inspired some radicalism in her thinking, although this was in isolation from anyone else, except possibly her future husband.[36]

Overall, this was a sheltered background: 'for me [to go out alone] is as rare as for a young Spanish girl' (11 January 1775). By the time she married, Marie-Jeanne had seldom left Paris and its immediate surroundings. The family sometimes went by boat down the Seine to Meudon and other suburbs, or spent some summer weeks with the Besnards at countrified Fontenay. The furthest expedition from home was to the market town of Etampes in 1778. In 1774, she visited the palace of Versailles (and was not impressed) and her uncle's apartment in the grounds at the chateau of Vincennes became a regular refuge after her mother's death, 1775–1779. If one adds up all the people whose paths crossed hers, however, simply through visiting the house, or being met at the houses of her relatives and family friends, it includes quite a cross-section of middling French society—artists, engineers, doctors, clerics, ladies of various rank as well as tradesmen.

Was she very unusual for her time? It is not so much that we are in the presence of a genius or a unique mind, but Marie-Jeanne Phlipon was a particularly earnest

---

[35] *Mém.*, pp. 250–2.   [36] *Mém.*, pp. 240–3, 274–5.

and dedicated example of a not large, but growing generation of young women amassing some modest cultural capital. Her reading was haphazard (in one sentence she might mention the history of Siam, Pluche's account of manufactures, Plutarch, physics, and Descartes). Without yet seriously challenging the dominant discourse about women, bolstered further by reading Rousseau, she expressed discontent and frustration at having been born a girl, wistfully imagining that in Roman society she might have been a heroine of her own story.[37] In theory, though, a domestic future was still mapped out for her.

[37] See, for example, *Corr.*, NS., 1, pp. 374–5, many other examples.

3

The Groom's Story (1)
Odd Man Out

Cooper, wheelwright, joiner, engineer, mason, stonecutter, gardener—were all there [...] And I, who could never see a work-tool without wanting to pick it up, could follow all the trades in a day [...] Everywhere, I found the workman's eye was infinitely more precious, mechanical practices more solid in execution, and a hundred times quicker than all our calculations and wearisome theories...I soon realised that these uncultured men were not the ignorant ones: I was the one who was learning the most, by watching them at work and listening to what they said.

J.-M. Roland, 1769[1]

A BEAUJOLAIS CHILDHOOD

Jean-Marie Roland de la Platière, still a bachelor at thirty-five, wrote this on returning home to the Beaujolais during the wine-harvest, after fifteen years away. He had been putting himself through courses in 'theory'—mathematics and chemistry—to make up for his poor initial schooling, but all his life, unlike most of his family, he was fascinated with physical materials and manual work.

His early years could not have been more different from his future wife's. Whereas she was brought up literally in a workshop, and found her escape from it by reading literature, history, and philosophy, he came from a privileged, though not rich background, where none of his immediate forefathers had worked with their hands—then spent most of his adult life in workshops and factories. While she stayed in the family home, or close by, always under watchful eyes, he left home and his large and stifling family as soon as he could, and threw himself into travelling the length and breadth of western Europe. Marie-Jeanne Phlipon had a small, but stable number of relatives and friends, including servants, whom she saw regularly. She formed close if sometimes oppressive bonds with them, but was the centre of an adoring circle. Jean-Marie Roland was probably the centre of nobody's attention as a child, and spent his middle years living alone in hotels or temporary lodgings. While Mlle Phlipon took advantage of her modest, but exploitable circumstances and ended up making a 'good' marriage, becoming materially

---

[1] J.-M. Roland (Perroud, 1769/1913), p. 56.

better-off than her parents, Jean-Marie's trajectory illustrates, to some degree, the downward mobility that was always possible in the ancien régime.

*

We know a good deal about his family, little about his childhood. The Roland clan, long-established in the Beaujolais, had several branches. The customary name 'de la Platière' had been attached by an earlier generation to the family manor. (*Platière* = limestone pavement; it was on the site of a bleaching-ground.) Jean-Marie used the handle under the ancien regime—he is referred to as 'Monsieur de la Platière' in official papers—but dropped it, as a good revolutionary, after the 1790 decree. His father—also Jean-Marie (1692–1747)—was a lawyer, *conseiller du roi*, alderman of Villefranche, and in the 1730s *recteur* of the charitable Hôtel-Dieu. The family once owned three properties: a three-storey house in Villefranche, a historic town with a population of about 5000, twenty miles north of Lyon; the manor of La Platière, in Thizy, ten miles out of Villefranche; and a smaller wine-growing domain, a glorified farm really, called Le Clos, in the parish of Theizé, five miles away. Jean-Marie's mother, Thérèse Bessye de Montozan (1699–1790), was the daughter of Laurent Bessye, sieur de Montozan, *avocat au Parlement* and *conseiller du roi*: she came from authentic *noblesse de robe* (and one was not allowed to forget it). Her husband's claim was less sure: the paternal line included royal office-holders, but their titles were not hereditary.

An efficient administrator, Jean-Marie *père* was either careless or preoccupied when handling his private affairs, and his wife had extravagant habits. At his death, his oldest son Dominique (1722–93) became, by Beaujolais [written] law, the 'universal inheritor', receiving half the estate plus a share of the rest. The holdings were dilapidated, and Dominique had to sell property to pay debts. By 1752, the Thizy manor had gone: the name 'de la Platière' was transferred to Le Clos.[2]

All the children were born at Thizy. After Dominique in 1722, came Anne, Antoinette, and Antoine. Laurent followed in 1728, Jacques-Marie in 1731, Pierre in 1732. Jean-Marie *fils* was born on 18 February 1734: Anne, aged eleven, and Antoine, aged eight, presented him at the font for his baptism next day. Antoine died in childhood, another daughter, Marie-Thérèse (1735), did not survive, and a boy had been stillborn in 1729. So, although to a lesser extent than the Phlipons, this was a family marked by infant deaths and those, too, of older children. Five brothers and Anne survived to adulthood. The closely-spaced pregnancies of their mother suggest—again—that the children were all sent out to wet-nurses, a common practice for town-dwelling families of means.

Jean-Marie would have been aware of this history by hearsay. He was probably with his wet-nurse in 1735, when nine-year-old Antoine and the infant sister died. Anne died, aged twenty-eight, in the 1760s, after he left home; he never mentions her. Jean-Marie remained the baby of the family, and was always closest to his

---

[2] The name is sometimes written 'Rolland' and 'Laplatière', plus or minus *de*; it appears as 'DLP' on envelopes and signatures, *Mémoire d'extraction* BNF MSS, naf 6243, and Perroud (1896). Cf. Appendix C in *Corr.*, II, pp. 561 ff., plus family tree: no ancestors were in finance or commerce; all were described as bourgeois or nobles, 'and the title "bourgeois" never had in [Beaujolais]…any other meaning than that of a man living nobly', quoted Le Guin (1966), p. 8: material usefully summarized in English.

brother Pierre. Dominique was so much older as to seem like an uncle, and the gulf was not only one of age: they clashed often in later years.[3]

All four older brothers took orders and went into the church. Their choice may have combined vocation and economic pressure—lack of means after their father's death was probably the clincher. Dominique, already a canon of the cathedral in Villefranche, succeeded his father at the Hôtel-Dieu; Laurent lived at home in the Villefranche house. Jacques-Marie entered the Cluniac (Benedictine) order, and became prior of Crépy-en-Valois outside Paris: between themselves, the Rolands later called him 'le Crépyssois'. Pierre went to the Cluniac order's college in Paris's Latin Quarter, before being sent to the suburb of Longpont, 'the poorest parish in Christendom', and was correspondingly nicknamed 'le Longponien'.[4]

Jean-Marie must have received some early education at home:

> My tender age meant I was neglected for a while. I wanted to make a better go of my studies, which I had started badly, [we don't know what this means] so I was sent to the Jesuit college in Roanne, in the Forez, and I confess that had it not been for an illness which meant I returned home, I would have been a ready prey for that order—so supple and insinuating when it wanted something, so arrogant and insolent when it had [cause] to fear.[5]

The illness kept him off school for a year, at about age fifteen. In later life, as the comment suggests, he was outspokenly anticlerical, while remaining on reasonably good terms with his brothers. It seems, from his taste for all things Greek, that he acquired some elements of the classics from the Jesuits. Despite clear and confident handwriting, his spelling was sometimes erratic and his French not always correct. His early education may have been at the hands of his mother, an aristocrat of an earlier age whose literacy might be patchy, and a couple of years at college had not improved things much. By his own admission, he spent a year convalescing, and another year idling at home.[6] So despite having some formal schooling, Jean-Marie Roland was not, in his youth, much better educated than his future wife. His later considerable knowledge was mostly acquired as an adult student, so he was also something of an autodidact. He had a law degree—like many future revolutionaries—but it was acquired quickly by private study, and he never practised.

Of Jean-Marie's childhood relations with his parents, little is known. Perroud suggests that his father was hardworking and irascible (which could equally apply to his youngest son). Thérèse Bessye, who survived until 1790, was described by her daughter-in-law, who knew her only in old age, as selfish, extravagant, and domineering. The correspondence mentions her high-handedness and love of

---

[3] J.-M. Roland (1769/1913), p. 63 on Dominique, p. 91 on Pierre: 'I hide absolutely nothing from him; he doesn't agree with me, but I can talk to him about anything, because he tolerates it all'.

[4] BNF MSS, naf 22422, letter of November 1777; Laurent died in 1782; Pierre in 1789; Dominique was guillotined during the Terror. Only Jacques-Marie survived the Revolution, as joint inheritor with Eudora Roland of the remains of the estate.

[5] Pinet (1990), p. 115, quoting Roland (Perroud, 1769/1913).

[6] Ibid. Desmoulins repeated the charge that Roland was a poor writer. From his manuscripts, his hand is fluent but his style more blunt than elegant. On aristocratic mothers, Goodman (2009), p. 116.

succulent entertaining. Jean-Marie remarked that she seemed pleased to see him on his return, but soon lost interest. There is little sign of true affection. He avoided scenes by leaving without farewells. Pointedly, he put as great a distance as possible between himself and his family, once he was old enough, rarely returning to see them before his marriage.[7]

His first move was to Lyon, in 1752, 'to try a calling for which he felt little enthusiasm', as an apprentice or junior clerk to a silk-merchant named Dupont, whom he left in disgust: 'the cheating and malpractice I saw among the people where I had unwisely been placed would have made the most enthusiastic person turn away in horror [...] I was eighteen or nineteen'.[8] His aversion to merchants was life-long. Still, in Lyon he acquired some expertise to support his later specialization in textiles.

An energetic rebel against his background, Jean-Marie criticized his stay-at-home brother Laurent for allowing himself to be 'tyrannized' and he was never tempted by a clerical life ('the smallpox of the spirit').[9] Unsupported by his family, he made his way to Nantes, aged nineteen, on foot and alone, but never reached his likely destination, the French West Indies.[10] Once more, illness changed his plans. As he was seriously ill at intervals all his life, either his constitution was not strong, or he had acquired some recurrent problem. In Nantes, he coughed blood, and reconsidered the prospect of a long sea voyage. Instead, he turned to a family connection in northern France. A distant cousin, Mlle Thomé de Saint-Cire, had married Pierre Godinot, *inspecteur de manufactures* in Rouen. Not disdaining some help this time, in August 1754 Jean-Marie Roland became a 'supernumerary' *élève-inspecteur*, in other words a trainee on a very low allowance, under Godinot's patronage.[11]

TRAINEE INSPECTOR AND PERPETUAL STUDENT

The service of *inspecteurs des manufactures* was created in the seventeenth century by Jean-Baptiste Colbert (son of a master draper himself). Their primary role was not to inspect working conditions, as a modern factory inspectorate would, but to guarantee quality control, so that consumers would be confident in getting what they paid for—and French trade would prosper. Over three-quarters of inspectors were primarily concerned with textiles, especially woollen cloth. When Jean-Marie Roland entered the profession, production was subject to a mass of regulations covering the quality of raw material, closeness of weave, dimensions of pieces or bolts of cloth, dyestuffs, perfection of finish, and so on.[12] To certify that the finished

---

[7] *Corr.*, I, pp. 505–7, 539–40, 556–9.

[8] J.-M. Roland (Perroud, 1769/1913*)*, p. 62.

[9] Ibid., p. 61.

[10] Guadeloupe, Martinique or Saint-Domingue (present-day Haiti) were the options. Cf. Pinet (1990), p.116; *Mém.*, pp. 329–30; *Mémoire des services*, BNF MSS, naf 6243.

[11] See Minard (1988), p. 139 on the Godinot 'dynasty'.

[12] The 1780s regulations are set out in Roland's reference work, the *Dictionnaire des Manufactures* (hereafter referred to as *Dictionnaire*) in Panckoucke's *Encyclopédie méthodique,*1784, 1785, 1790 (article 'Règlements' and supplements). See Parker (1979) pp. 17 ff.

product met all the regulations, it was tagged with a *plomb*, a piece of lead, by the *gardes-jurés*, representing the manufacturers. Their judgement was checked by the state inspector, who regularly toured his district. One senior inspector was attached to each ancien régime *généralité*, with *sous-inspecteurs* under him. In the mid-century, there were about 50 senior inspectors in post (64 by 1791). Most of them stayed in post for life—it was a very stable profession, if not (to most people) an exciting one.[13]

The factory inspectorate's recruitment and training was haphazard, and dependent on patronage—unlike that of the elite corps of road and bridge-building engineers in Ponts et Chaussées, who had an entry competition, technical training, career structure, and pensions. Inspectors of manufactures learnt on the job, and were not always over-competent. They were appointed by the Bureau de commerce, under the authority of the Controller-General, the king's minister of finance, commerce, agriculture, and industry. Who you knew was more important than what you knew, and a word at court for a relative always helped.[14] Roland himself protested against 'these positions lobbied for by the grand, and given to their hangers-on, often filled by persons who knew nothing about manufacturing [...] who had no idea about competition in any branch of industry, or the law [...] They could talk a blue streak, but they never got much done.'[15]

The inspectors' pay came out of the industrial tax budget. In other words, the people they inspected paid for the service—another reason they weren't universally popular. Their salaries were modest, but intended to allow a dignified way of life; they could claim additional 'expenses' for travel and accommodation. A horse in stables was essential for patrolling their district. An *élève* received only about 500 *livres* a year; a *sous-inspecteur* earned about 1200, a full inspector usually 3000 +. It was no way to get rich. Even at the end of his career in 1791, Roland was only earning 5000 *livres* basic pay. To judge how little this was, in 1766, Turgot said that with an income of 6000 *livres* per annum, one was moderately comfortable but not rich: to be well-off, one needed 12,000 in the provinces, 15,000 in Paris.[16] Roland did receive several bonus payments, summarized in 1778 when he applied for compensation for a journey to Italy: roughly about 1000 *livres* in each of seven of the ten previous years.[17] But the pay was often in arrears, and he had to borrow to survive. After his marriage, needing more money, Roland hoped to supplement his income from his writings and the somewhat irregular proceeds from the farm at Le Clos.[18]

He remained an inspector most of his life. Before his marriage, he had three postings—Rouen, Clermont-de-Lodève in the Languedoc, and Amiens, ending his career back in Lyon, before the inspectorate was abolished under the Revolution in

---

[13] Minard (1988), p. 66. Cf. Bacquié (1927), *passim*.
[14] Under Controller-General Desmaretz in 1708, an inspector's post was promised to 'a relative of Mme de Maintenon's lady-in waiting', quoted Lenoble (1908).
[15] *Dictionnaire*, II, 1784, supplement, p. 73.
[16] Quoted Showalter (2004), p. 102.
[17] *Mémoire présenté à M. Necker*, BNF MSS, naf 6242, fos 106 ff., quoted Le Guin (1966), p. 39.
[18] Roland's pay in the 1770s is described in detail, ibid. He received 3000 *livres* compensation for his Italian trip, plus 2000 *livres* extra.

1791. He also travelled widely, officially to gather information, but perhaps to escape the harassment by which the life of a conscientious inspector was plagued, and which his combative character positively invited. He studied to make up for his early lack of education. In the years before his marriage, he developed ideas, qualifications, and expertise that made him a very different kind of 'Enlightenment man' from his younger contemporaries in the revolutionary years, who mostly had a conventional classical education followed by law. Political economy, and especially first-hand technical knowledge of industry, was his primary interest, and he became well-known in certain circles, for technical reports, learned publications, and contributions to proceedings of academies.

To progress to *sous-inspecteur* and finally full inspector meant chasing preferment, through highly-placed patrons or by pleasing your superiors. Without connections at court, Roland had to take the latter route—not always successfully, since he was far from docile or tactful when he thought he was in the right. He remained an *élève* in Rouen for nearly ten years, not unusual, given the competition for posts, but disappointing. Hoping to enter the better-paid Ponts et Chaussées, he followed a course in 'differential calculus and conics' run by the Académie de Rouen in 1759. Twenty years later, the Rouen pharmacist Baillière de Laisement (1729–1800) wrote of him:

> M. Roland spent the best years of his life here with us. He applied himself to his work with a zeal and intelligence which made him generally respected. He also took up science and very soon carried off prizes in our School for mathematics. He cultivated drawing [design] with the same ardour; he studied natural history, chemistry, botany, and anatomy.[19]

Baillière was one of a group of contemporaries whom the trainee inspector met in Rouen in the late 1750s and early 1760s. For all his prickliness, he must have had a facility for making friends, to whom he remained devoted, and they to him, throughout his life. The Rouen circle was the first and the most congenial circle he moved in. As a perpetual self-improver, Roland met other young people interested in applied science and industry, but also fond of literary and philosophical discussions. They were too junior at this stage to join any academies, as some did later on.

The group contained a dozen men and at least three women. The friends gave each other Greek names: Roland was 'Thales' after the philosopher. In later years he referred to Rouen as 'Athens', while Picardy was the uncivilized 'Boeotia'. As well as Baillière, the group included the Abbés Athanase Auger, 'Demosthenes' (1734–92), a translator of Greek, and J.B. Cotton-Deshoussayes (1727–83)—teachers at the college de Rouen; the chemist Louis-Guillaume de la Follie (1739–1780); the literary scholar M. Dornay (1729–1834); F.A. Descroizilles (1746–1825), later professor of chemistry; Anicet-Charles-Gabriel Lemonnier (1743–1824), artist, later prix de Rome. They were all in their twenties or thirties. Two 'corresponding'

---

[19] Quoted Le Guin (1966), p. 11; *Corr.*, II, Appendix M. He also took a course of chemistry in Paris with Demachy.

members lived in Dieppe: the Cousin brothers, Michel and Louis, known as Cousin-Despréaux. Roland collaborated on the latter's *History of Ancient Greece* (1770), sending notes from his travels in Sicily. The group met at the Malortie household in the rue aux Ours. The Malorties, a large, well-educated, but not well-off family, included three daughters, Aimée, Charlotte, and Marie-Magdeleine, to whom Roland was for a while engaged (see Chapter 5).[20]

These were Roland's formative years. Although on the bottom rung of the ladder and earning very little money, he regarded this period as one of the happiest times of his life. He spent ten years (1754–1764) in 'the most delightful friendship, cultivating philosophy and the arts by choice'; he had been 'aimé et chéri'. Far from what is sometimes called a salon, this was an egalitarian and unpretentious group of young people, a mixed 'circle', who liked talking about intellectual topics. For Jean-Marie Roland, it operated as a substitute family, replacing the one he had more or less rejected. However, his career would take him away from Rouen for many years.[21]

---

[20] Le Guin (1966), pp. 11–13; on the Malorties, Le Corbeiller (1909).

[21] '*Aimé et chéri*', quoted Thomson (1982) p. 444; *Corr.*, II, pp. 578–81; the links and threads connecting these people in later life were strong, e.g. Descroizilles got Aimée Malortie out of prison in 1794; Auger was a member of the Cercle social, Kates (1985), p. 109.

4

The Groom's Story (2)
A Disciple of Turgot

Jean-Marie Roland was not only from an older generation than most revolution-aries, but well-acquainted with the French industrial economy and unusually well-travelled. He had explored many regions of France, and been on fact-finding missions to several European countries. Sharing the ideas of his patrons, the Trudaines and Turgot, he was torn between his contractual obligation to enforce the regulations in textile manufacture, and his growing belief that, at least within France, there should be a freer and less restricted market. His early years in his job provide clues to his later policies, but also reveal the aspects of his character which most struck his contemporaries.

The trainee inspector's first reports came to the attention of Charles-Daniel Trudaine (1703–1769), Intendant des Finances and unofficial 'minister of com-merce'. Roland became Trudaine's protégé, and later that of his son, Jean-Charles Philibert (Trudaine de Montigny, 1733–1777). Both Trudaines were 'steadily favourable to pragmatic reform from 1751 to 1777'.[1] Trudaine senior wrote in 1760: 'I like and esteem M. de la Platière, you may assure him. I will show him evidence of this when occasion arises.'[2] The occasion did not soon arise, but Roland's reports distinguished him from colleagues who owed their positions to relations at court. A memo on Normandy wool (1754) won him a bonus. His commission as *élève-inspecteur* followed in May 1755, and he was sent in 1756 to the pays de Caux to investigate bleaching and dying cotton. Over the next decade, he became an expert on textiles. More papers shot off to Paris, and in 1760 the Rouen chamber of commerce even signed a petition for him to be promoted. Promises of 'the first vacant place', including 'something in Ponts-et-Chaussées', came to nothing. Finally, in 1764, Trudaine found him a job in south-west France: *sous-inspecteur* in Cler-mont-de-Lodève (today Clermont-L'Hérault) in the Languedoc. His patron was grooming him for higher things. Roland's immediate reaction was distress at being sent so far from his Rouen friends, but he accepted the post.[3]

---

[1] Kaplan (1976), I, p. 148, and note: there is little on the Trudaines in English or French, but see Horn (2006) and Gillispie (1980). On Turgot, Poirier (1999).

[2] Parker (1979), p. 26 ff; Le Guin, (1966) p. 10; Roland's *mémoire des services* (CV), records dates and places (BNF MSS, naf 6243) and is the basis of Perroud's appendices D and E, *Corr.*, II, pp. 574 ff. The Controllers-General with whom Roland had most to do with were Turgot. (1774–1776), Necker (1776–1781), and Calonne (1783–1787). See Poirier (1999), p. 167, and on freedom and competition, p. 63; cf. Horn (2006), pp. 52–5.

[3] Le Guin (1966), p. 19, following Perroud, *Corr.*, II, Appendices D and E.

Since Clermont-en-Lodève has been thoroughly studied by James Thomson, we know something of this obscure period in Roland's life. His stay in Languedoc was short, but revealing of the conflict of interests between government inspectors and local producers, as well as of Roland's intransigence, which had not been greatly tested in Rouen. Languedoc was the main southern centre for French woollen cloth exports, via Marseille to the Levant. A recent relaxation of the rules had allowed manufacturers to get away with a decline in standards, and to off-load poorer-quality cloth, with repercussions in foreign markets. Previous inspectors had been either lax or bought off.[4]

The zealous thirty-year-old arrived in Clermont in July 1764 and was soon writing to Trudaine in horror:

> You have sent me among a people of ferocious beasts. Never were honest folk so dominated in their opinions [*opionés*] by rascals [*la canaille*] as they are here. Either you did not know about it, or you wanted to make me experience all the disgust and bitterness that may come the way of someone with little fortune of his own [...] No sentiment, honour, or justice will re-invigorate the perfidy [*bassesse*] of their souls; they are inaccessible to all that is honest, no, nothing can be expected of people like this.[5]

On arrival, he had asked to see past registers of inspection. Unused to such rigour, local cloth-manufacturers concluded that he was, in every way, bad news. They wrote a four-page letter to Trudaine, complaining that 'he speaks by theory, we act by practice'. Cloth production was too important to be held up by the formalities of time-wasting inspection visits.[6] Roland did not hesitate to take them on, and boldly (or foolishly) told an audience of *fabricants*:

> The disorder I see here has made me more than once detest the calling I have embraced. It is because probity has always seemed to me to merit the protection of the government and the largesse of those who hold its reins, that the low self-interest which cheapens the soul, leading it to the most odious fraud and manoeuvres, appears to me to be punishable with the utmost rigour.

Some manufacturers tempted him with 'fine partridges, to make me of more pacific humour'; others whispered that he could increase his meagre 1200 *livres* salary if he played his cards right. Finding these suggestions beneath contempt, he refused to 'go and eat their soup'.

Within weeks, he was asking for a transfer. To the *intendant* of Languedoc, vicomte Jean-Emmanuel de Saint-Priest—who was sympathetic—he wrote suggesting that some other inspector might find 'associating with these monsters to be less atrocious. I have never felt the weight of misfortune as cruelly as since I got here. I will ask all my relatives, friends, and acquaintances who have access to M. Trudaine to help me to diminish the horror by transferring me.'[7]

---

[4] All 'ineffective or corruptible, with the notable exception of Roland de la Platière', Thomson (1982), pp. 399–400.

[5] AD, Hérault, C 2213, 13 September (quoted from Thomson's manuscript notes with thanks).

[6] AN, F¹² 557, 8 July 1764; presumably the registers were 'lost' or incomplete.

[7] 23 October 1764, AD, Hérault, C2212, Thomson's notes.

At times he went in fear for his life. After his happy years in Rouen:

> What a sight now to see me [...] forced at every instant to detest the day when the terrible idea came to me to enter this accursed calling! Judge of my situation, Monsieur, when I can't put a book by Racine in one pocket without putting a pistol in the other; if I want to pull out a Plutarch or a Newton or a Rousseau, my hand finds a firearm, and instead of being able to relax with the charms of study, I am obliged to have ideas of bloodshed.[8]

He had a 'long and violent struggle' (Thomson) with one influential clothier, Jean Martin, who had built up an empire under the previous dispensation, leading the trend towards poorer-quality cloth. After shouting the inspector down at a meeting, Martin had publicly told his dyer 'that he had only to keep a vat of boiling water and throw us into it, myself and the *gardes-jurés*, the first time we showed our noses there'. When Roland received the call to leave Languedoc, the Martins claimed they had driven him out.[9]

AMIENS

Roland was delighted to get away, even if not to the coveted Rouen post. Trudaine appointed him full inspector at Amiens in Picardy, a major textile centre with over 30,000 inhabitants. It was another woollen-producing area, with 11,000 looms in all, (about 5500 in Amiens itself), but also produced linen, knitted goods (*bonneterie*) and was starting to work cotton.[10] Roland would spend many years in this northern city, of which he was never over-fond. He regarded it as uncivilized: 'no philosophy, taste for the fine arts, not an idea of the higher sciences, not a shadow of literature'.[11]

The first signs, though, were good. Roland arrived there in November 1766. A difficult situation awaited him: Amiens was riven by rivalries, especially between the town's leading *fabricants* and producers of cloth in the countryside, recently authorized by Trudaine's liberal policy. Roland had to negotiate between local manufacturers and his free-trade overlord in Paris. Not without difficulty, he achieved some compromises. The current opinion, which he still shared, was that French textiles were doing badly in foreign markets because of their poor quality, so some rules remained necessary. His proposal was to allow freedom in choice of material, dye and design, but to impose some regulations (length, breadth, and quality, i.e. closeness of weave). He favoured small-scale enterprise, free from guild oversight—so he had no objection to rural manufacture, but insisted that this, too,

---

[8] ibid., quoted Thomson (1982) p. 444: his choice of reading parallels that of Mlle Phlipon.

[9] AD, Hérault C 2213, 13 April 1766, quoted Thomson (1982), p. 401 (Martin was eventually disciplined); *mémoire des services; Dictionnaire*, Errata, Vol II, p. 92, for Roland's claim that others regretted his departure.

[10] Hubscher (1986), esp. chapter by C. Engrand. Business peaked *c.*1765–1766 just before Roland got there, before a collapse in the 1780s, ibid. pp. 147–50: in the 1770s, only 10 per cent of *fabricants* had over 10 looms; cf. Hunt (1984/2004), esp. pp. 160–2, 192 ff.

[11] Le Guin (1966), p. 15.

should have some quality control. Never one to underestimate his own role, he reported that:

> I arrived, I listened, I reasoned, I calmed things down; there were no more summons or arrests, seizures, or fines. I banned the intervention (sometimes interested) of lawyers. [...] I did in Picardy the same as in Languedoc: made pleas and requests. [...] I did what an inspector should always do, be the adviser, advocate, and protector of the manufacturers.[12]

This seems to have been a fair summary of his initial handling of his task, but Roland, who always favoured manufacturers over merchants, soon ran into trouble in Amiens where merchants and manufacturers were often the same people, dominating the chamber of commerce and the town council. He forever distrusted the commercial sector, as being interested only in short-term profit:

> The spirit of trade [*le commerce*] which is to disseminate knowledge, to broaden minds, and increase work for labourers, is always and everywhere contrary to that of the merchant [*le commerçant*] who gains pleasure only from the privations of others and whose desire to amass profit, in private and even in secret if possible, rules out any generous [sentiment regarding] the common good.[13]

In his *mémoire des services*, Roland summarized his first ten years in Amiens (1766–1776) as follows: he sought to enable French-made goods to compete with the foreign, i.e. British textiles flooding into the country, often illegally. He aimed for both quantity ('double or triple the number of workshops') and quality: perfected spinning methods, weaving and dyeing; greater consistency. So he encouraged innovations: a bleaching works, a new fulling mill, and different textiles (silk ribbon, gauze). He went out of his way to get funding for local inventors, and lobbied for the introduction of a prize for developing new dyestuffs, such as indigo.[14] All this went well beyond the pedestrian remit of the inspector, and none of it happened easily. There was obstruction from the local nobility, and from the Cathedral canons who controlled the only fulling mill in Amiens. Roland's long-term aim was to get Picardy on the industrial map of Europe, by imitating English fabrics, and possibly bringing over English machines, know-how, or experts. In this he was paralleled by—and unfortunately at odds with—John Holker of Rouen.

Holker (1719–1786) was a remarkable man, an English Jacobite exiled in France after the '45, who introduced British technology to French textile manufacture. Intelligent, enterprising, and ambitious, he, too, was encouraged by the Trudaines: he owned a large factory in Rouen, but was also an inspector general—promoted, naturalized, and even granted letters of nobility in France for his services to French manufacture.[15] Holker is rightly the central figure in J. R. Harris's book on industrial espionage (1998). He and Roland should have had plenty in common, but

---

[12] *Corr.*, II, Appendix E, p.596; Le Guin (1966), p. 16.
[13] *Corr.*, II, p. 609.
[14] Engrand, in Hubscher (1986) pp. 155–6.
[15] On Holker, see *ODNB*: 'intelligent, brilliant', 'favoured and respected adviser of both the Trudaines'; cf. Rémond (1946) *passim*; Chassagne (1991); Parker (1979); *Corr.*, I, p. 543, 19 November 1785.

their relationship deteriorated in 1773, apparently because Holker used his privileged position as both manufacturer and inspector to try to discover industrial secrets. An Amiens cloth-maker, Flesselles, friendly with Roland, had collaborated with an Englishman, Price, over new finishing processes for woollens, which were giving English products an edge in the markets. They refused Holker admission to their factory, claiming 'the Inspector-Manufacturer sought to see for his own profit, not for that of the public'.[16] Rightly or wrongly, Roland took Price and Flesselles's side, and remained bitterly critical of Holker for trying to spy on others, while being unwilling to share his own secrets—a conflict of commercial interest which Roland's upright, or inflexible, nature abhorred. Their quarrel would deepen in the 1780s.[17]

Holker was not his only enemy. Roland had campaigned to get the 'newcomer' manufacturers admitted to the chamber of commerce. With Trudaine's support he succeeded, but made himself thoroughly unpopular with the magnates. Next, he found himself fighting his one-time allies, the manufacturers, over workers' conditions, notably whether employers had the right to stop any worker leaving their employment. During a case of poaching labour, Roland took the view that the workers should be free to change master, if better pay was offered elsewhere. There is also evidence of his concern for independent weavers, and for workers in manufacturing shops, although strictly speaking this was not his job. He complained to a colleague about 'the disorder of our factories and the situation of our unhappy weavers [...] the wages for skilled labour are at the lowest possible level'.[18]

Roland's constant belief that he was in the right, and his habit of firing off irascible letters of complaint to his hierarchical superiors, did not endear him to his immediate line-managers, the *intendant* of Picardy, D'Agay, and the *intendants de commerce*, Jean-François Tolozan (b. 1722) and Antoine-Louis Blondel (b.1747), both in Paris.[19] The *intendant* who really wanted him was Saint Priest, in Languedoc, but Roland had no wish to return south.[20]

Things weren't entirely black. He made a few friends in Amiens, whose names crop up regularly in his papers: local lawyers, and scientists, bibliophiles, and professional contacts, such as Flesselles. Nothing like the Rouen group was recreated, although the same people did form a 'Museum' in the later 1780s, after Roland had left.[21] In particular, he met the Cannet family during the 1770s. They were not as cultured as the Malortie sisters, but they held convivial evenings.

---

[16] Le Guin (1966) pp. 18–19, 48–9, based on Perroud, *Corr.*, II, Appendix E, pp. 631–41. Cf. ibid. Appendix I, pp. 656 ff.

[17] Ibid. Roland *claimed* to have brought back from England the secret of [Arkwright's] cotton-spinning jenny (possibly the water-frame), *Corr.*, II, p. 656, Appendix I, on Flesselles; Rémond (1946) for Holker's perspective (hostile to Roland; see Chapter 7 below).

[18] January 1768, cf. Le Guin (1966), p. 21; *Corr.*, II, pp. 606–7 (1775).

[19] *Corr.*, II, pp. 617–24; BNF MSS, naf 6242; Le Guin (1966), pp. 15–28; AD, Somme C286, quoted Minard (1988), p. 94.

[20] BNF MSS, naf 6242, 9 May 1767. The salary was higher in Picardy, but even in Amiens, it was irregularly paid, Le Guin (1966), p. 23.

[21] He stayed in touch, *Corr.*, II, pp. 656–61, and Le Guin (1966), p. 29.

TRAVELS

Out of frustration, or to please Trudaine, Jean-Marie Roland undertook a series of fact-finding journeys, summarized in his *mémoire des services*. He always lived extremely frugally, and this equivalent of Europe on $5 a day bred in him habits of thrift. What his colleagues made of his frequent absences is not known, but his voyages were driven by a perpetual hunger for information. As he once wrote to Marie-Jeanne Phlipon: 'On my travels, I have no other ambition except to learn. For me it's not unlike the craving of the drunkard who increases his thirst by drinking'.[22]

In August–October 1768, he was in Flanders and Holland, exploring linen and lace manufacture, porcelain, diamond-cutting, and iron foundries. 1769 found him in Switzerland, looking at foundries, mines, and factories, ending up with a visit to Voltaire's house near Geneva, armed with a letter of introduction from M. de Cideville, a former schoolfriend of the Sage of Ferney.[23] In 1771, he went to England, an important journey of which no record survives, but he undertook some industrial imitation, if not espionage, à la Holker.[24] In 1772, he was in north-west France, from Brittany to the Loire. In 1773, he travelled to Switzerland, southern France, and Catalonia. His sixth journey, to Germany, Austria, and Bohemia in 1775, lasted five months. He visited Frankfurt, Mainz, Leipzig, Nuremberg, Vienna, Berlin, and Hanover, collecting samples and making copious notes for Trudaine de Montigny, who replied:

> I read with pleasure, Monsieur, the summary of your observations on German trade. I have often thought, like you, that industry of all types in France has been held back by the regulations [. . .]. I have long considered that while strict instructions may be useful in countries where industry is not yet established, more detailed and minute instructions are correspondingly harmful in a country where industry is starting to become vigorous and prosperous. I can only applaud your intention to get [our *fabricants*] to imitate the fabrics you have seen in Germany. You could accomplish no action more useful to the State and I will make every effort to help you.[25]

With this support in high places, Roland's views seemed to fit the prevailing ideology of those at the top, notably Turgot, who was appointed Controller-General in 1774.

The inspector set off on his Italian journey in the summer of 1776, with the latter's blessing, confident that he would soon be promoted to *inspecteur général*. His trip followed his usual pattern, investigating manufactures and conscientiously sight-seeing. An unsympathetic, but possibly not inaccurate description of him was left by a young travelling companion, named Bruyard. His portrait of Roland suggests an intelligent and well-read individual, who never let you forget it; who

---

[22] *Lettres d'amour*, 17 September 1777, p. 37.

[23] *Lettres d'Italie*, I, pp. 130 ff; Roland was treated to a tour of the grounds, several lectures, and dinner: 'we were just five at table', though Voltaire asked permission to open letters during the meal.

[24] *Corr.*, II, p. 598; a report to the *conseil* may be in AN, F[12] 1771 (not visible on my visits to the Archives).

[25] *Mémoire des services*. See Kaplan (1976), I, p. 149: 'Trudaine regarded the battle for liberalization as his greatest challenge'.

took economy to great lengths (no handkerchiefs), since he had sold everything, including his clothes, to make the voyage; who regarded everyone as his equal, including the Pope; but who asked to be called by the Greek name of 'Bias' (one of the seven sages), and who confessed—interestingly—that he would really like to be governor of a desert island: 'he felt he had been born to make laws which would be recognized throughout the world for their equity'.[26]

Roland himself summarized the journey melodramatically as follows:

> I travelled throughout Italy, crossing the Alps three times, and the Apennines three times, visiting cities and country regions, and going as far as Malta; I took ship nine times, three times I was in the greatest danger and likely to die; I spent thirty nights on deck, and eighty without being able to undress, once twenty-two days on end, barring two or three changes of clothing. I endured great fatigue, making haste, observing things by day, going without necessaries to do so, and writing down my observations at night. My ardour and passion to see and learn kept me going. When I got home, I collapsed and remained for several months between life and death.[27]

This was written in the autumn of 1777. As much as by the journey, his illness was precipitated by despair at the loss of his patron. Turgot had been dismissed in 1776, after the disastrous 'Flour Wars' over his experiment in free grain trade. When Jacques Necker was appointed finance minister in June 1777, he abolished the six posts of *intendant des finances*: Trudaine de Montigny, who was one of them, retired to his family estate, dying there in August, his health compromised and 'his spirit nearly broken by his efforts to liberalize trade'.[28] Necker placed the inspectors of manufactures under the aegis of the *intendants du commerce*, who were hostile to ideas of economic freedom. The men and the policies of mid-century went into eclipse. In fact, Necker's administration was not unkind to Roland, compensating him generously for back pay and expenses. But the upper echelon of the administration was out of sympathy with his trade philosophy.

The 'missions' continued though. In 1778, Roland went to the Boulogne region to study English-type sheep-farming and crossed the Channel again to see the real thing. His English journey was rendered hazardous by the outbreak of war in June, when France supported American independence, but he met no personal hostility. He visited sheep farms, watched shearing, took samples of raw and spun wool, chatted with farmers, and may have gone as far north as Manchester.[29]

WHAT SHOULD A PROGRESSIVE INSPECTOR BE DOING?

Roland's quarrels with the Languedoc clothiers of the 1760s might make him look like a fussy bureaucrat, but he was working out a broader view of how—or

---

[26] Dauban (1867), I, pp. xiv–xv.   [27] *Mémoire des services*, BNF MSS, naf 6243.
[28] Kaplan (1976) II, p. 149.
[29] Minard (1988) p. 234; Roland's memo on sheep appeared in the *Journal de physique* (1779); *Corr.*, II, p. 611.

whether—industry ought to be regulated and encouraged. He admired his former patrons for their courage and farsightedness.[30] The inspector's official job might be to check quality and punish cheating, but his higher function was to be the agent of progress, the policy Roland tried to follow in Amiens:

> [He] is the man sent by the council into the provinces to examine the state of [manufacturing] and trade, observing any cause of slow progress [...]; to search for and indicate the proper ways of extending them and bringing them to the perfection of which they are capable. It concerns the public good, and this confidence ought to raise his spirit.

He should give advice on agricultural and industrial practice. 'Are people being vexed by undue charges, arbitrary [levies], acts of violence or scorn, by which the weak are often oppressed?' The inspector would find out by entering factories, farms and cowsheds. Above all, the system of obtaining royal privileges to set up a manufacture, effectively a local or national monopoly, was cramping French progress: it reduced enterprise and was often corruptly obtained. The inspector's constant concern, by contrast, should be France's ability to become a major industrial and commercial power—like England. Regulation was only useful if it was integrated into enterprising development.

Over the years, Roland became thoroughly disillusioned by the very regulations he was appointed to enforce. In a famous reply written in 1778 to Necker's survey, he wrote:

> I have seen 80, 90, or 100 lengths of cloth cut to pieces in a single morning; I've seen them burnt in the marketplace[...] I saw all that in Rouen, and all because of the rules, or ordered by the ministry, and why? Because there was some irregularity, some fault in the weaving or some other defect, and because they were making the kind of *pannes de laine* that the English were making. I have looked in vain for the kind of manufacturing rules that we should leave in place for the good of the trade; I've read them all, I have always meditated on this cold and heavy compilation, I've envisaged the effects, and followed up their consequences. I think they should all be abolished.[31]

The only point of the administrative apparatus, he came to think, was to provide a central record, so that the government could know when to intervene to make 'particular interests' coalesce, in a Rousseauist ideal, directed towards the common good. The inspectorate, whose raison d'être all this thinking undermined, ought to conform to this idealistic view:

> [The ideal inspector] should have received a vigorous manly education, and his frugal and hard-working life will be the result: his manners must be urbane [...] and the

---

[30] *Corr.*, II, p. 594, quoting *Dictionnaire*, III, preface, p. lxi: Turgot had 'the probity of Aristide, the disinterest of Phocion, the devotion of Brutus and the firmness of Cato'; his edict of February 1776 'granting liberty to industry and the arts [= manufactures] made his fame immortal'. Of Trudaine, Roland wrote ibid. that he had to overcome intrigues, cabals and the 'cries of all the manufacturers and merchants' to allow printed cottons in France.
[31] *Dictionnaire*, I, p. 291; cf. Horn (2006) pp. 30–3, 52, 55 on Roland; AN, F[12] 661 Parker (1979) pp. 31–3, 57, 86; Rémond (1946).

most absolute disinterestedness must characterize it. His outward demeanour will be modest, his soul sensitive and humane. Inspired by the love of the good, he will have no other object in view.[32]

I think we can guess who this description is intended to describe.

The corps of inspectors has been described as a 'dominated fraction of the ruling class'.[33] Roland was a natural meritocrat, conscious of his outsider status. In the right circumstances, he got on well with his equals—modestly privileged circles in provincial cities. With his superiors, he was prickly, and often at odds. Perpetually defensive, he resented the effortless prominence of men who in his view (and Beaumarchais's) had done no more than be born in the right place. Personally, he lived a life of enforced frugality, practising thrift to a fault. Yet under a severe appearance, he concealed a passionate and sensitive nature: tears often figure in his private letters. Among his intellectual influences, was his heartfelt veneration for ancient Greece, which seems to underlie his attachment to moral uprightness—some would say stiffness—and constant references to virtue. He also read his modern philosophers, including Voltaire and Rousseau, and from them had absorbed both a boost to his long-held anticlericalism, and a certain idealism about how society could be better ordered (the common good). His later writings display some of the qualities and faults of the autodidact: an immense thirst for information, with a corresponding tendency to get over-involved in detail, not to say nit-picking. But he was attuned to the economic thinking of the day and he seems to have had genuine sympathy with manual workers. He was familiar with their everyday existence and their struggle to make ends meet. For him unemployment rather than poverty was the supreme evil.

From his first forty-plus years, we can see that Roland was well-equipped to be a member of the awkward squad. His dream of administering a desert island does not necessarily indicate his desire to be a leader of men—rather it reflects an ideal vision of a *tabula rasa* instead of the messy, everyday reality of ancien régime France, with its multiple weights and measures, local tolls, obstructive officials, restrictive guilds, profiteering merchants, and above all the system of privileges emanating from the court of Versailles. Despite his combative professional stance, he must have had a degree of charm: no doubt that transforming smile was kept for social encounters. At any rate, the Cannet family thought well enough of him to give him an introduction to their dear Paris friend, Mlle Phlipon in 1776. At the relatively advanced age of forty-two, was it too late to think of marriage?

---

[32] *Dictionnaire*, II, Supplément (1790), p. 148.   [33] Thépot (1985) pp. 12–13.

5

Who to Marry? Suitors and Fiancées

I don't mind where I live with you, log cabin or temple.

Marie-Jeanne Phlipon to Jean-Marie Roland, 1779.

Marriage in eighteenth-century France, for anyone with even modest wealth, had a lot to do with property: a husband needed an income or prospects; a wife should have a minimal dowry. Inheritance laws aimed to keep estates within the family. In wealthy or noble families, arranged marriages were virtually de rigueur. For the propertyless working population, there was 'relatively greater independence for children', but 'in better-off artisanal and merchant circles, [such as the Phlipons] parents spoke as if the decision was entirely theirs'.[1] Matches were suggested or arranged by family or friends. By the age of Enlightenment, admittedly, the rules were often bent or broken in favour of love matches. Novels and plays had long made the unhappiness of arranged marriages their subject.[2] As for the *philosophes*, 'the crusade for companionate marriage [...] was one of the central campaigns of the Enlightenment against tradition and patriarchal authority'.[3] Advisers on the subject—usually the young person's parents—saw common sense and compatibility as a firmer foundation for a happy marriage than passion, but affection was still essential, wrote the author of a *Catéchisme de la morale à l'usage de la jeunesse* (1785):

> the sacred knot of marriage makes it the strict duty of the two spouses to love each other. What a torment is the life of two disunited people! To live in happiness under the married yoke, do not embark upon it unless you are loved...A marriage contracted without tenderness is a form of rape.[4]

For neither of the Rolands, when they finally made it to the altar that February morning in 1780, was this the first time marriage had been on the agenda. Both families had tried to find a more suitable match elsewhere, by conventional methods. When they did begin courting seriously, considerations of wealth and status put obstacles in their way. Mme Roland had her own motives, years later, for suggesting that it had been a marriage of reason. Reason was actually the last thing either party had in mind at the time and they had both had previous entanglements.

---

[1] Garrioch (1986), p. 69; Desan and Merrick (2009), chapter 1.
[2] See Daumas (2004), Pasco (2009), p. 180.
[3] Goodman (2009), p. 275.   [4] Quoted Godineau, (2003), p. 173.

TURNING DOWN SUITORS: A WOMAN'S PRIVILEGE

While a man could propose, a woman could refuse. The strong-minded Mlle Phlipon did refuse—again, and again, and again. For someone whose resources were shrinking alarmingly, this was unwise. Good-looking, healthy, and well-trained in domestic management, Marie-Jeanne originally had a respectable endowment. Her protected upbringing, only child status, and attractive dowry made her a tempting catch for any merchant or master-artisan. Both parents soon realized however that they would be unable to force a choice on her.

In her memoirs, Mme Roland described the 'swarm' of suitors,[5] listing up to ten serious proposals, starting when she was seventeen. Some biographers describe this inventory as 'complacent' and boastful, but her largely accurate list, confirmed by contemporary documents, was a common-sense appraisal of what the only daughter of an artisan might attract. Indeed, Claude Perroud unearthed a further ten offers.[6]

The suitors were a mixed bunch, from her music tutors—sent on their way with concealed giggles—to local tradesmen, or their sons, who wrote to Mlle Phlipon's father, politely requesting an interview. Those who made no further progress included her parents' butcher, who sent good cuts of meat; a widowed diamond merchant; a dry goods merchant; a *limonadier*; one or two older shopkeepers, and at least one lawyer. Monsieur Phlipon was unimpressed by lawyers—he thought they had pretentions and debts. His daughter, however, was not anxious to marry a shopkeeper. While she could hardly object to a husband in trade, she told her father that she could not marry a man with whom she would have nothing in common.[7]

Some proposals were taken more seriously. When in 1773, advanced negotiations with a Provençal doctor, Joseph-Jacques Gardanne, fell through, the prospect of 'leaving behind a kind of independence' crossed Marie-Jeanne's mind for the first time.[8] A melancholy conversation with her mother about marriage followed. Sooner or later, Mme Phlipon warned, the offers would stop. She urged her daughter to accept 'an honest jeweller', who realized that mademoiselle was no ordinary girl; he would even countenance maternal breastfeeding (an interesting sidelight on Marie-Jeanne's infancy). She would be able to bend him to her will. But her daughter replied that she 'wouldn't want a man who commanded me: he would only teach me to resist; but nor would I want to rule my husband'. In the first case she would rebel, in the second she would have no respect for him. She wanted mutual esteem, which meant honouring each other's wishes—what today's historians would call a 'companionate marriage'.[9]

One suitor did seriously touch her affections. She became infatuated with a young man from an old family. 'Small, dark, and rather ugly', Mammès-Claude Pahin de la Blancherie (the last bit added by himself), came to pay his respects in

---

[5] *Mém.*, pp. 283 ff.　　[6] *Corr.*, NS, I, pp. xlvi–xlviii, lists them all.

[7] *Mém.*, pp. 285–6.

[8] *Mém.*, pp. 288–92; *Corr.*, NS, I, pp. xxxiv–xxxv on Gardanne (1739–1789). Her dowry then was a handsome 20,000 *livres*.

[9] *Mém.*, p. 293.

autumn 1773, aged twenty.[10] Marie-Jeanne's father remarked tartly that he would prefer him not to be a gentleman and to have 40,000 *écus* instead. La Blancherie made an interesting proposition: he would study law, using his wife's dowry, plus whatever he could inherit, to set up in practice, while the young couple lodged with the Phlipons. Despite this impudent plan, the attraction Mlle Phlipon felt for this man of literary and philosophical tastes persuaded her father to accept a provisional commitment. Pahin went off to law school in Orleans. When her father ruled that there was no economic future in this project, Marie-Jeanne rashly wrote a passionate love letter to Pahin: since they could not marry, she would never think of anyone else. Her covering letter, to Sophie Cannet, exclaimed: 'My soul burns to confess itself. I think I must, to save the life of one dear to me. [...] *O Dieux*! How I am suffering [...] Love has conquered me.'[11] Eventually she lost her illusions. Not only was Pahin's travel book 'not very good', she discovered that she had not been the sole object of his advances: he was a mere fortune-hunter. To cap it all, she had seen him foppishly parading around the Luxembourg Gardens 'with a plume in his hat'. The feather was the last straw.[12]

While losing her heart to this young hopeful, Marie-Jeanne was conversing with that procession of older men, with an occasional thought of matrimony in the background. Their attentions help explain why she warmed to Jean-Marie Roland. In his forties, he was nothing like as old as some other admirers. Marriage was supposedly her destiny, but by 1776, her circumstances had changed for the worse. After her mother's sudden death, her father went downhill, losing money and custom. His speculation in jewels was unwise, and the offstage presence of his young mistress raised the worrying thought that he might remarry. Little would soon be left of the all-important dowry. Offers from local suitors dried up in the face of discouragement, and none of the older mentors had really been attractive or willing to take the step. Marie-Jeanne saw her chances of marriage disappearing. She contemplated the convent again or taking over the workshop. Although marriage without love or intellectual equality did not tempt her, she had periods of depression, as she glimpsed a future as 'une vieille fille'.[13]

JEAN-MARIE ROLAND DE LA PLATIÈRE: A FOOTLOOSE YOUNGER SON

Jean-Marie was the Roland family's only hope of producing descendants, his brothers being celibate priests. His widowed mother had a strong sense of her aristocratic birth, and the family hoped he would make an appropriate marriage in terms of status, preferably to a well-dowried bride. But he had turned forty without any serious

---

[10] *Corr.*, NS, I, pp. xxx–xxxiv; *Mém.*, pp. 282, 287–8, etc.

[11] 11 January 1776, *Corr.*, NS, I, pp. 355–6.

[12] *Corr.*, NS, I, 25 June 1776, pp. 428, and 536, 27 August 1785; *Mém.*, pp. 324–5; Pahin later founded the *Salon de la correspondance*, 'to instruct savants, men of letters, artisans and amateurs', cf. Lyon (2006) pp. 76–80. He became a bit of a joke between the Rolands ('your old flame').

[13] Cf. Pardailhe-Galabru (1988) p. 69.

sign of this happening. He was certainly interested in the opposite sex: his travel writings hint at love affairs, tantalizingly briefly. On his visit home in 1769, he revisited the scene of some adolescent passion—or passions: 'The temple where my young heart made innocent and intoxicated sacrifices to love; altar where my first incense burned and where the kindly god permitted so many others—you still exist!'[14]

During his Italian journey in the late 1770s, he had at least one serious flirtation, of which he made no secret. He met a 'deliciously' attractive widow in Livorno: she spoke four languages, played the harpsichord and mandolin, sang with passion, read poets and philosophers, danced 'like a nymph', and had beautiful eyes. 'I did not leave Livorno; I was torn away.'[15] A curious letter survives, dated 22 August 1778, from another woman, Catherine Mutone or Mentone, hinting at intimacy: 'I opened my heart to you before knowing your feelings for me...I have no strength to write more, etc.'.[16] Some of his past relationships were no doubt sexual, but Jean-Marie kept them in a different compartment from any marriage plans. (The 'delicious nymph' turned up later as a neighbour in Lyon, married to someone else.)[17] But there were at least two more formal episodes in his past.

In Rouen, the youngest Malortie sister, Marie-Magdeleine, was known in the Philhellene circle as 'Cléobuline', after a Greek poet. Roland proposed marriage in the early 1760s. Since his income was modest, his immediate prospects unclear, and the Malortie family was also poor, a long engagement was on the cards, and he did not inform his family.[18] He later referred to 'three delightful years' of engagement, but they languished away to nothing, partly because of Roland's posting to Languedoc in 1764, partly because of the continuing lack of money, but there must have been some waning of enthusiasm, on either his part—or hers. From November 1766, he was in Amiens, only about a day's journey away, and in 1767, he made overtures to Villefranche about his inheritance, possibly with a view to marriage, but nothing happened. Cléobuline's health was fragile and she developed tuberculosis. Nevertheless, there was a long gap before she called for him on her deathbed in 1773. They took a tragic farewell in each others' arms. Greatly affected, Roland composed a long document in her praise, and—surprisingly in the circumstances—remained on friendly terms with the family thereafter.[19]

When he encountered the marriageable Cannet sisters in Amiens, their brother apparently suggested a match with Henriette, but the timing was wrong—the inspector was about to leave for Italy. He had also just met Marie-Jeanne Phlipon—through an introduction from the Cannets themselves. Perhaps the new acquaintance gave

---

[14] *Lettres d'Italie*, VI, p. 432.

[15] Ibid., VI, p. 350; he discussed with her the libertine question: 'Is seduction of a married woman more reprehensible than of one who is unattached?'

[16] BNF MSS, naf 22422.

[17] *Lettres d'amour*, pp. 44–5 on the incident; cf. *Corr.*, I, 18 August 1786, and index references to Mme Chevandier.

[18] Le Corbeiller (1909).

[19] *Corr.*, II, p. 583; Roland's 'Eloge de Cléobuline', July 1773, BNF MSS, naf 9532, fos 348–54: she had said: 'Come and kiss your tender friend...she will love you until the grave.' There are hints later that it was she who broke off the engagement. Cf. Le Corbeiller (1909); Charlotte (b. 1730) and Aimée Malortie (b. 1737) remained in the family home, BNF MSS, naf 22422.

him pause for thought. Perhaps he was simply too settled in his lonely—or untram-
meled—life, to think of marriage. Nothing was decided.

His own family was, however, increasingly keen to marry him off, preferably to
an heiress. During the Italian trip, his brother Pierre thought he had found a suitable bride, and wrote early in 1777: 'I've found you a wife, yes, a wife! [...] who has
all the qualities that a wise and honest husband could ask [...]. It is time to stop
travelling and playing Don Quixote, to become in short a citizen who provides his
contingent towards the mass of population.' The unnamed young woman was
twenty-three, a lawyer's daughter, slim, healthy, dark-haired, well-educated. With
her 'Roman profile, and a large mouth, she's not exactly beautiful or striking, but
looks as if she will age very well.' Importantly, she had been brought up 'under the
gaze of a watchful mother'. Petty nobles with red heels on their shoes did *not* frequent the house. Explaining that she was the second of four daughters (her family
was keen to have her settled), Pierre got to the point: 'Let's talk dowries: not as
much as I could wish, but you can't have everything. 25,000 *livres* the day of the
contract, more after the death of the father.' Timothy Tackett estimates that the
average dowry of brides of Third Estate deputies of 1789, many of whom married
in the 1770s or 1780s, was similar: 26,000 *livres*.[20] Further letters were encouraging:
'she's the kind of woman Rousseau would approve of, for a husband's tranquillity'.
Pierre gave assurances about his brother: 'I told them you were thrifty and clean.'
Villefranche was written to. Jean-Marie's duty was to become useful to his fatherland and his family, by providing his unmarried brothers 'with some nephews.'[21]

The correspondence about this possible match offers a detailed example of
marriage-arranging in the eighteenth century. Jean-Marie's destiny, no less than
Marie-Jeanne's, was assumed by his family to be marriage and children. His 'fiancées'
were all young women of good family, fenced round with watchful relations, but of
varied fortune. Marie-Magdeleine Malortie had very little; Henriette Cannet was
better off, and the anonymous bride found by his brother was encouragingly well-
provided for. Family members had twice made the running, but Jean-Marie preferred
not to walk into an arrangement, and felt hard done by by his own relations. He
wrote exasperatedly to Pierre on his forty-third birthday, in February 1777: how
could he marry and expose a widow and children to poverty, since his family would
allow him no property: 'I expect nothing from them, I don't give a toss for them' ['je
me f*** d'eux'].[22] Perhaps, during the negotiations, he was thinking of the young
woman he had met a few times in Paris. She, in turn, was thinking about him.

FIRST MEETING

In January 1776, Marie-Jeanne Phlipon had received an unannounced visit from a
'Monsieur Roland', bringing letters from the Cannet sisters. He was curious to see
the schoolfriend of whom they spoke so warmly. Embarrassed at being caught

[20] Tackett (1996), pp. 40–1 and Appendix I.
[21] BNF MSS, naf 6241, fo 212, 31 January and 19 February 1777.   [22] ibid.

off-guard, she told Henriette and Sophie, she had a cold in the head, and was wearing a bonnet and a housecoat over a plain white *camisole*, her usual dress when not expecting guests. In the polite chat that quickly turned to philosophical matters (Raynal and Jean-Jacques Rousseau) she felt she hadn't done herself justice in front of the serious visitor. In her memoirs, she gives the downbeat, though not unfair portrait of her future husband, quoted earlier.[23]

Later portraits of Roland do not contradict her. Always a sober dresser, he never wore a powdered wig; his 'severe but finely chiseled' features were framed simply by his long, straight hair. People remarked on his resemblance to Benjamin Franklin, which he cultivated by keeping this hairstyle (and later wearing spectacles). His wife's pen-portrait in the memoirs may have projected an older image on to that first appearance. Perhaps the younger Jean-Marie looked less austere.[24]

For the young woman he saw, one source is her self-portrait in the memoirs. At fourteen, she was already five feet tall—average height for a woman. Her figure was good, with a 'superbly-equipped bust' and 'well-shaped legs':

> My features [are] not striking except for their freshness and a gentle expression; none of them is regular, yet all in all they are pleasing. My mouth is rather large, there are prettier ones everywhere, none with such a tender and attractive smile. My eyes are not big, grey-brown; but they have an open, frank, lively and gentle gaze and are crowned with eyebrows as brown as my hair [. . .] My nose used to trouble me, I thought it was too big at the end, but overall and especially in profile, it doesn't harm the rest.

Her features included a wide brow, a 'voluptuous' chin, a highly-coloured complexion—she blushed easily—and 'good regular teeth'.[25]

That first call was repeated, but Marie-Jeanne was still obsessed with La Blancherie. Roland re-appeared during May–June 1776 and their philosophical conversations were not always chaperoned, M. Phlipon judging the visitor respectable enough to be trusted. An intellectual friendship was kindled, but they did not meet again until February 1778. It was their love of books and philosophy that had brought them together. Henriette could hardly compete in this respect. When Roland left for Italy in June 1776, he paid Marie-Jeanne the compliment of leaving her his travel manuscripts. A fragment of her journal, dated June 1777, reveals that she liked his 'imaginative' and lively remarks about London and his comments on Switzerland:

> This man has a strong and noble soul, an active and penetrating enthusiasm [*feu*] which animate and enliven his writings; his philosophical eye, his simple and true taste recognises the beautiful [. . .] I am always singularly touched when I meet people who are like me in some respect; so many people say they are sensitive, and so few really are! What a pleasure it is to find the latter.

[23] *Mém.*, p. 322, cf. May (1970) p. 82.
[24] See *Corr.*, II, Appendix V, p. 788: several portraits exist by Pierre Pasquier, one by Bonneville, one by Colibert, all *c.*1792.
[25] *Mém.*, p. 254. Family tradition was that she was plump and not very tall, cf. Kermina (1976), p. 47: *Corr.*, NS, I, pp. 315–16, *c.* August 1775, note on portraits.

But she also expressed anxiety: 'the dangers of a long voyage, an absence of ten months, no news for four, all that exhausts my imagination'.[26]

Roland had unexpectedly asked permission to kiss her farewell in company before leaving, but Mlle Phlipon heard from him only occasionally, usually through his brother. It is not surprising, given his family pressures, that Jean-Marie avoided too close a connection with the impoverished and bookish young woman in Paris. Understandably piqued at his long silences, she thought herself forgotten, and consoled herself in conversations with Sainte-Lette and Sévelinges. In September 1777, Roland wrote directly, but her prompt reply remained unanswered—because he was severely ill.[27] When his brother reported this to her, Marie-Jeanne's response was surprisingly emotional, given their supposedly 'friendly' relationship, and her habitual self-control:

> I want to write to you, but in truth, I find no words or expressions. If I were trans-ported to be beside you this moment, my interest and sympathy [*attendrissement*] for your situation would leave me no other language but silence [...] In the name of friendship, take care of yourself, do not torment us, wait for strength [...] I cannot bear to think of you travelling in this season, being so weak. [...] the last three weeks have been an eternity. [...] I wish to see you again. I don't know what I want, nor what I'm writing [and so on].[28]

This rather wild letter exists, oddly, only in Pierre Roland's hand—he copied and forwarded it on 12 November. By then, he had met Marie-Jeanne in person, and was favourably impressed, becoming a potential ally.

A SECRET ENGAGEMENT

Absence made Roland's heart grow fonder. In December 1777, his new friend François Lanthenas, whom he had met in Italy, signed a document allowing him to act as proxy for the family for a settlement in any future wedding plans. When Roland returned to Paris in February 1778, he proposed marriage to Mlle Phlipon—only to be refused. Prompted by a sense that their stations were too far apart, her decision caused Marie-Jeanne some distress: she assumed his family would oppose a penniless bride. Moreover, the Cannets still seemed to think Roland was committed to Henriette, as Sophie confided during a visit to Paris.[29]

So Roland vanished again during the summer, on missions to northern France and England, and to sit his 'quickie' law exams in Reims:

> I arrived on 30 July, had my enrolment registered, picked up some law books, studied day and night, defended my thesis on canon law and civil law on 3 [August] and was

---

[26] Mme Roland, 'Unpublished diary' ed. Bright (1872).

[27] *Lettres d'amour*, pp. 35–9, 39–42. Most quotations in this chapter are from this edition: originals in BNF MSS, naf 6238 and 6240.

[28] *Corr.*, NS, II, supplement, p. 431, 9 or 10 November 1777.

[29] Cf. *Mém*, p. 330, pride at her self-sacrifice; *Lettres d'amour*, pp. 46–7, 24 February 1778, and p. 81, 24 June 1779.

received bachelor; got some more books the same day, and defended my thesis on the 5, and was received licenciate at the same time. Left the same night at 8 o'clock.[30]

No letters survive for several months—the affair seems to have been put on ice. Roland broke the silence on 30 December 1778, a new year greeting stressing that there was no question of marriage with Henriette (who lived to an old age, and married three times).[31]

By now it was clear to Marie-Jeanne Phlipon that she could not hope to marry Roland—or anyone else—unless she stemmed the dwindling of her resources. In March 1779, she reached the age of majority—twenty-five under the ancien régime. She could marry without her father's consent, although that would be unusual. She even reconsidered taking over the engraving business, before deciding she was not well enough qualified. Instead, she made the bold move now open to her: claiming a *partage des biens*, a division of assets, from her father, to rescue what remained of her mother's property.

Her initiative was encouraged by Roland's persistence. Back in Paris in spring, staying in the rue de la Licorne, he courted the Phlipons with ducks—'deux canards d'Amiens dans leur terrine'.[32] One marker of intimacy in French correspondence is *tutoiement*—the use of the familiar second-person singular. Even between spouses, 'the move from *vous* to *tu* is incontestably the passage from the language of convention to the language of the soul'.[33] Its first use between the two hesitant lovers appears in Italian, the day before her twenty-fifth birthday: '*Che fa tu adesso, mio amico? Pensi tu a me che t'amo che te scrivo.*'[34] By April they were using *tutoiement* regularly, and did so for the rest of their lives. However, Marie-Jeanne suddenly took refuge with her uncle in Vincennes and the letters reached a peak of intensity. Why? Because Roland had 'stolen a kiss'—or two. It hints at her fear of being seduced and abandoned:

> The delirium into which we might fall, seemed terrifying to me [...] I had promised myself, [...] not to permit the slightest of favours except to the man to whom I would be tied by the most sacred of bonds. That first sweet kiss [*questo primo dolcissimo bacio*] impetuously seized, gave me atrocious pain. The repetitition of this lapse, too feebly avoided, increased my turmoil and regrets. [...] I will never be anyone's plaything. I am not skilful enough to turn love into a game. For me it is a terrible passion that seizes my whole being.[35]

Roland had to protest he was no 'vile seducer', but by the end of the month, he had made another, absolutely clear proposal of marriage:

> I have no metaphysics to show off, no antithesis to parade, I simply have a heart, which is no longer free to offer. It is frank, excessively sensitive [*sensible*]; it loves you. That's all I'm worth. You have conquered [...] I demand, by all the rights of friendship, to ask and obtain an answer: yes or no.

---

[30] To Cousin-Despréaux, 7 August 1778, ibid.
[31] *Lettres d'amour*, 30 December 1778: '*il fratello a fatto a detto qualche cose che facevano veder che si pensava ancora e ella seppe ben che… niente, niente. Niente.*'
[32] Ibid., p. 66.   [33] Grassi (1994), pp. 176, 178.
[34] *Lettres d'amour*, p. 69, 16 March 1779.   [35] Ibid., p. 88, 29 April 1779.

Marie-Jeanne replied equally unambiguously on 6 May: 'I fling myself on your breast, I am yours. If you don't understand this "yes", what more do you want?'[36]

But this was just the beginning of their troubles. Anticipating opposition from the Roland family, they kept the engagement secret. Clandestine engagements while not unknown were the exception: normally, the two families would contact one another. Secrecy soon became a burden. Jean-Marie explained later that he meant to present his mother and brothers with a *fait accompli*. He even rented a house in Amiens (given his lack of experience, it turned out rather unsuitable) and hatched the daring plan that they would marry that summer, and tell his family afterwards.

PRIDE AND PREJUDICE

Marie-Jeanne went ahead and separated her property from her father's without telling him why. By 9 June, she could report that she was 'the owner of [a measly] 530 *livres* income, clear and distinct'.[37]

Then, for virtually the entire time from proposal to wedding (May 1779–January 1780) the betrothed did not set eyes on each other: Jean-Marie was in Amiens, Marie-Jeanne in Paris. Both sides of their courtship by letter, in its lengthy, troubled, and indeed wearisome complexity, were published by Claude Perroud (1912). There was plentiful scope for misunderstandings and cross-purposes. Letters took between 24 and 48 hours to travel between Paris and Amiens, often crossed, and both parties used highly-strung and allusive language. Missives had to be received secretly ('I go down to meet the postman', 11 May) or sent via a cousin, Mlle Desportes, to avoid arousing suspicion; the possibility of third parties reading them explains why they are sometimes hard to follow.[38] Inescapably, one is reminded of the *La Nouvelle Héloïse*, which both correspondents quoted. William Reddy uses some of their letters to illustrate what he calls 'sentimentalism': emotional rhetoric as a refuge from codes of honour.[39]

The early ones radiate hope and happiness ('I don't mind where I live with you, log cabin or temple', Marie-Jeanne, 17 May), and calculations about setting up house,[40] but both writers were quick to take offence, and Roland had a lifelong tendency to depression: 'I felt black and melancholy beyond anything I can say' (19 May, no letter had arrived). Hasty remarks were magnified into quarrels. 'Let's write to each other differently, or let's stop writing at all.' 'If only we could just talk for a few hours' (Marie-Jeanne, 29 August).

The real trouble was not so much these lovers' tiffs—they went on protesting undying affection in increasingly desperate terms—as circumstances. Some obstacles arose from the time-consuming realities of everyday life. Roland was a lifelong workaholic, something not yet appreciated by Marie-Jeanne. He was

---

[36] *Lettres d'amour*, 30 April and 6 May 1779, pp. 95–9.   [37] Ibid., pp. 154, 246.
[38] Ibid., p. 23; *Corr.*, N.S., II, p. 559.   [39] Reddy (2001), p. 146.
[40] *Lettres d'amour*, pp. 130–1, 137 ff.

hoping for promotion, while preparing his travel writings, under ancien régime restrictions calculated to vex someone of his temperament.

Mlle Phlipon had to deal with her father's moods, and the illness and death of the family servant, Mignonne. Then she had to fend off the puppy-love of an apprentice, who simultaneously developed measles and a crush on his master's daughter. With jealousy's sharp eyes, he threatened to kill his rival, 'the tall *monsieu* [sic] who came with papers under his arm'—a threat Roland took seriously.[41] Marie-Jeanne also made a Rousseau-esque clean breast of her contacts with Sévelinges—to which Roland's reaction was stupefaction: 'my jaw dropped. You were taken in by an uncertain, weak, and inconsequential mind.' Keeping the secret from the Cannets was painful. She drip-fed them information, but deceived them about the engagement, and their friendship was affected.

Still the greatest obstacle was parental consent and disparity of fortune. The project almost foundered on the twin reefs of pride and prejudice. Holding out no longer, in June Marie-Jeanne told her father she was engaged—it wasn't hard to guess to whom. Relief and a family reconciliation followed. The scene, she wrote, was 'Diderotian': tears were shed. 'Kiss my letter, tremble with joy. My father is happy, he esteems you, he loves me, we shall all be happy.'[42] Roland's reaction was not as wholehearted as she hoped. He would have to inform his family before he was ready. In fact, he and Gatien Phlipon now contrived to irritate each other so seriously by letter that in early September it looked as if it was time to call the whole thing off.[43] Marie-Jeanne herself wrote to do so:

> You seem only to be keeping to our plan out of consideration for me, and because you gave your word, and with the sweetness of reminiscence rather than the attraction of hope. [...] I will never accept a title offered out of anxiety and fear... only one given by attachment and confidence. I leave you all the freedom that a declaration like this by me adds to that which you naturally possess.[44]

If this was pride, Roland gave way to prejudice. His mother's consent, as Dena Goodman perceptively remarks, meant a lot to him. Marrying out of his class was 'the hardest and scariest thing he had ever done'.[45] Among other worries was his anger at his prospective father-in-law taking a mistress (the *grisette,* the lovers called her). He returned repeatedly to this 'dishonour'. Marie-Jeanne defended her father, but by mid-autumn, although they went on corresponding, marriage plans had receded into an uncertain future.[46]

Marie Jeanne Phlipon now took a decision that biographers have usually treated as a calculated strategy. With her limited room for manoeuvre, it was certainly an inspired choice. A face-to-face meeting was desperately needed, but Roland could hardly meet her father without hypocrisy or a quarrel. If the marriage fell through,

---

[41] *Corr.*, NS, II, p. 417; *Lettres d'amour*, 21 July 1779, p. 214.

[42] Ibid., 27 June 1779, pp. 182 ff.

[43] Her father asked to see their correspondence. Cf. Roland's letter of 5 September, ibid., p. 268.

[44] Perroud calls it her letter 'de rupture', though it is somewhat ambiguous. In the memoirs, she states more firmly that she 'asked him to abandon his plans', *Mém.*, p. 331.

[45] Goodman (2009), p. 301.   [46] *Lettres d'amour*, pp. 300 ff.

she would have to think seriously about her future. On 2 October (this took some gall), she asked Sophie Cannet for a loan: '300 or 400 *livres* would permit me to take a step which will influence the rest of my life'.[47] It would enable her to return to the convent—not to take the veil: the convent had rooms for laywomen. But it wasn't a cheap option. On 1 November, Marie-Jeanne told Sophie that she had rented a room for 20 *écus*, and with her 530 *livres* income would be able to survive with care. To Roland she sent her address: 'Write when you have a moment.' Her days would be spent quietly: reading, sewing, music, talking to the other 'ladies who lodged', and seeing her father twice a week—indeed she handled his laundry and mending, but received 'very few visitors'.

Her future plan as (not entirely sincerely) disclosed to Sophie, was to support herself by teaching 'geography and guitar' to respectable girls. Neither her baffled father nor the irascible Roland was sympathetic.[48] The correspondence took a melodramatic turn:

I have left my father, am far from my family, under a foreign roof, living in a cloister which will probably be my last home. (Marie-Jeanne)

Even if you didn't have a penny, you would be above all riches for me, [...] the one I love more than I can say. [But!] the idea of your father makes me tremble for myself, my relatives, and more still for any future [children]. (Jean-Marie)

Since our time on earth is so short [...], better have an instant of rest before being plunged into eternal night. (Jean-Marie)

Your letters tear me to pieces, but I kiss them and drench them with tears. (Marie-Jeanne)

Come and see your friend, [...] Tear the veil that absence, and the inconvenience of a written correspondence, [...] have put between us. I am dying [*je meurs*] to see you. (Marie-Jeanne)[49]

THE DÉNOUEMENT

Finally, Roland's Paris trip was fixed. He took the coach from Amiens on 27 December, to stay with Pierre, promising to visit his fiancée. He appeared at the convent grille on Wednesday afternoon, 12 January. Seeing her in person, in this affecting and somewhat romantic situation, broke down all his reserve. He wrote next day: 'Triumph in your retreat, my friend! [*amie* = 'beloved'] What is the secret of your empire, and what a state you have thrown me into!'[50]

Pierre Roland arrived a week later, to confirm the marriage offer. Jean-Marie could write with assurance: 'Know once and for all and positively, that my relatives love me, they want me to be happy; their only fear is that I will not work efficaciously enough to achieve it.' Mlle Phlipon's reply, a formal and much-quoted letter, is so coolly phrased that it has led most biographers to adopt the 'marriage of convenience' theory:

---

[47] *Corr.*, NS, II, p. 399.   [48] *Lettres d'amour*, p. 346, on the 'grisette'.
[49] Ibid., letters of November–December 1779.   [50] *Lettres d'amour*, p. 386.

Yes, I trust you, I believe you to be sincere and constant, I have faith in your upright-ness and tenderness; I have no less faith in myself, I feel myself to be true, attached, faithful; I am no more than this [*je ne suis que cela*] but I am certain of being so, and since your honest soul appreciates this enough to expect your happiness from it, I have no reason to refuse it. [...] Since the esteem which won my avowal [of love] in the past has not diminished, there was no obstacle at all to my reiterating it. If circum-stances since that first avowal have authorized me to add some 'buts' to the second, it is to you alone that I would wish to address them [...] I look forward to Sunday [23] to be able to speak with you in the outpourings of my heart. [...] *Adieu mon ami*, the world stage is very changeable.[51]

It is possible to read this as a formal missive, readable by outsiders if necessary, and showing maidenly reserve, but it contains a strong reproof. A further official accept-ance ('the choice with which you honour me') followed the visit to the convent by Roland's grand, but sympathetic relative, Mlle de Belouze.[52]

Matters moved with striking speed. As we saw, the approach of Lent was a com-pelling motive. Both parties perhaps felt—as may the reader—that if they did not marry at once, it might never happen. Once the contract was signed, on Thursday 27 January, Marie-Jeanne wrote to Sophie Cannet, in remorseful and embarrassed terms. Can Sophie ever forgive her lack of openness? Her excuse is the difficult time she has been through, before becoming 'the cherished wife of a man whom I respect and love [...] in a word, I am marrying Monsieur Roland. The contract has been signed, the banns will be read on Sunday, and before Lent, I shall be his.' She is about to leave the convent, and will return the 350 *livres* to Henriette, to whom she will now 'open my heart'.[53]

So in the four years before their wedding on 4 February, Jean-Marie and Marie-Jeanne had been in the same city, Paris, for about perhaps fifteen months. For six months before their reconciliation, they met not at all. In this match, questions of status, propriety, and property weighed heavily. Their courtship by correspondence is sometimes harshly judged—one biographer writes, not unfairly, that 'Roland is imperious, hesitant, and self-pitying; Manon sentimental, calculating and extremely verbose'.[54] In her memoirs, Mme Roland gave a foreshortened and not over-accurate description of events in 1779, in particular the secret engagement, her self-denying letter in September, and her decision to go to the convent. In 1793, she had reasons for insisting that she had married 'in all the seriousness of reason', and downplaying her own pressing letters to Roland, urging him to come to Paris.[55]

A correspondence has its own momentum, an element of performance and dis-play. This unique set of letters, when read closely, contains elements of many moral qualities and failings—selfishness and altruism, affection and irritation, despair

---

[51] Friday 21 January 1780, *Corr.*, NS, II, supplement, p. 424.
[52] Mlle de Belouze, daughter of a *parlementaire*, later retired to a convent, *Corr.*, II, p. 567.
[53] This letter from the Alfred Morrison Collection (V, pp. 309–10) is not in the collected Corres-pondence but is in *Lettres d'amour*.
[54] Le Guin (1966), p. 45.
[55] *Mém.*, pp. 330–2. These are perhaps the pages most clearly written for someone else's benefit (see chapter 27).

and desire for conciliation, and certainly some calculation on both sides. But it has to be read within the constraints on what was seen by the outside world as a *mésalliance*. The one thing it is hard to call it is, by any stretch, a marriage of convenience. On the contrary, it had caused maximum *inconvenience* to all concerned, with virtually everything against it, aggravated by the touchy sensibility of the two principals. However, for almost all its duration, the marriage turned out to be surprisingly solid and affectionate. As Roland wrote to a close friend: 'This marriage happened just as I was overwhelmed with work. [But] I looked for happiness, and I believe I have found it.'[56]

[56] To Cousin-Despréaux, February 1780, *Corr.*, NS, II, Supplement, p. 433. Earlier in September he had written 'I believed in happiness but it is an illusion', *Lettres d'amour*, p. 319.

PART II

MARRIED LIFE: 1780–1789

6

Bonjour Loup! Living Together

Bonjour Loup! Hullo Wolf! I'm well, and I love you. Great news! The Necker is Controller-general! I kiss you and kiss you again, eternally. Look after yourself and save yourself for me, who love you.

Marie-Jeanne to Jean-Marie, 26 August 1788.[1]

Reader, she married him, but did she love him? It's important, since their marriage is the centre of this book, but a vexed question, as the evidence is not straightforward. Charles Le Guin asserts firmly that 'it was *of course* a marriage without great emotional involvement, an archetypal *mariage de raison*'.[2] Other historians, largely on the evidence of Mme Roland's memoirs, have assumed something similar. How accurate is that description?

As we saw, it was not a *mariage de raison* as the ancien régime understood it. For months before the wedding, Mlle Phlipon was capable of declarations of passionate love. But later biographers have, not unreasonably, tended to dismiss these as sex in the head, like her passion for Pahin de La Blancherie, brought on by overheated letter-writing and too much Rousseau. They can also rightly point to that lukewarm sentence from her letter agreeing to marry Roland, in January 1780: 'je me sens vraie, attachée, fidèle. Je ne suis que cela, mais je suis sure de l'être'. Above all, in her memoirs, Mme Roland goes to some lengths to convey the impression of a sober partnership. She tells of her constant support for her husband's writing and public role, but only dutiful affection in private. 'His gravity, his morals, his habits, all dedicated to work, made me think of him as a person *without a sex, as it were*, or as a philosopher who existed only through his reason.'[3] Her retrospective matter-of-fact account of her decision to marry him goes as follows:

I thought deeply about what I ought to do. I did not disguise from myself [the thought] that a man aged under forty-five would not have waited several months before setting out to change my mind, and I confess that this had cooled my feelings to a measured state which held no illusions. [. . . But] was it not better to exercise my faculties and my courage in this honorable task [i.e. marriage] than in the isolation in which I then lived?[4]

---

[1] Original in BNF MSS, naf 9533. *Corr.*, II, p. 25.
[2] Le Guin (1966), p. 55, my italics: Their personalities 'made a truly warm and affectionate union impossible'.
[3] *Mém.* p. 330, my italics; this passage refers to their early meetings.   [4] *Mém.* p. 332.

Elsewhere in her memoirs, she makes some much-quoted references to the wedding night as less than idyllic. These can't be ignored, but can perhaps be contextualized. In 1793, Mme Roland was writing as a long-married woman. Even so, she was surprisingly frank about sexual matters—some passages were cut or censored by her early editors. She is one of very few women to refer to the onset of menstruation: 'at the age of fourteen, [nature] like a fresh and lively rose flowered suddenly'. More surprisingly still, she refers to 'accidents nocturnes' which seem to be masturbation ('an extraordinary ferment [*bouillonnement*] worked on my senses in the warmth of my place of rest') for which she felt guilty at the time, and 'overcame', but nevertheless chose to disclose in her memoirs.[5]

Most striking of all—deplored by Sainte-Beuve—is her account in graphic detail of the assault by the apprentice boy, mentioned earlier: how he held her tightly on his lap, 'putting a bold hand where nothing else ever went', while masturbating to orgasm: 'I was horrified: his eyes seemed to be popping out of his head, his nostrils were enlarged, I nearly fainted.' In distress, she told her mother, who panicked. After Mme Phlipon's frantic and intrusive questions, the little girl developed feelings of anxiety and was frozen into a sexual fear lasting many years. She had never told anyone about the apprentice incident, 'not even my husband, from whom I conceal very little'. The whole passage in the memoirs is a conscious evocation of what was earlier firmly repressed.[6]

It is in this context, on the same page, that she writes the famous sentence, explaining that because of her fear of anything sexual, she found 'the events of the first night after my wedding as surprising as they were disagreeable'.[7] Elsewhere, she refers to her wedding night as painful:

> My little experiences [of pain] had convinced me I could bear greater sufferings without crying out. A first night of marriage was enough to overturn the illusions I had kept until then; it is true that surprise was an element, and that a Stoical novice should be able to withstand better a pain foreseen than one which strikes suddenly when she was expecting the contrary.[8]

Gita May, like most other biographers, concludes from this that she was a dutiful, rather than loving wife, or as she puts it: 'Mme Roland was a full-blooded, lusciously-developed young woman and there is no doubt that she would have overcome her maidenly modesty with greater ease had she been physically attracted to Roland.' Dena Goodman, who writes perceptively about the young Marie-Jeanne Phlipon and love, also accepts her version of the marriage in the memoirs as applying from the start, making it an example of an unhappy union.[9]

---

[5] *Mém.* pp. 251, 280.
[6] *Mém.* pp. 217–21. See also Outram (1989), chapters 8 and 9. Mme Roland compares her avowal to Rousseau's confession about the stolen ribbon—even as a victim she felt guilty, and found it hard to set down in writing.
[7] *Mém.* p. 221.
[8] *Mém.* p. 256.
[9] May (1970), p. 102; cf. Goodman (2009a), pp. 300–1, and esp. (2009b) *passim*; cf. Pasco (2009), p. 66, on the rarity of love in marriage.

It is hardly surprising if the early days were difficult. Marie-Jeanne would not be the only woman of her time to be ignorant of sex until marriage, although possibly less so than she admits: she is disingenuous in the memoirs, for example, failing to report that La Blancherie's 'travel' book, which she 'read and re-read' was largely concerned with the perils of masturbation.[10] Mme Phlipon seems not to have spoken even cautiously to her daughter about what she could expect from marital relations.[11]

But there were complex motives behind references in the memoirs to her marriage. By 1793, Marie-Jeanne had fallen passionately in love with someone else. Perhaps sincerely, she may have projected her present feelings back over the past. Arguably she was writing for her new love (who might, after all, read this text), assuring him of a heart previously untouched by passion. She was by then acutely conscious of the age difference: at nearly sixty, Roland was an old man in eighteenth-century terms. She went out of her way to contrast filial affection with love: 'I honor and cherish my husband as a sensitive daughter adores a virtuous father, to whom she would even sacrifice her lover; but I have found the man who might be that lover.' Like many writers of confessions, she found it difficult to recapture sincerely an emotion now lost. It is easy to allow that the feelings expressed in the memoirs reflect something real, the recall perhaps of a clumsy and painful sexual initiation, intimidation at being married suddenly to a man so much older, of higher status, and whom she had not seen for months; and no doubt too, her chafing at Roland's assumption of intellectual superiority.[12]

But the many letters exchanged (and kept) by the Rolands *after* their marriage, tell a different story: that it was marked on both sides by strong affection, quite compatible with sexual love. There is little written evidence from the first year, since the couple were together in Paris or in Beaujolais almost all the time. However, Marie-Jeanne's first surviving letter to her husband after marriage is an affectionate note in Italian, when they were separated for a few days:

> Sogno a te; me spiace d'essere allontanata mi carissimo amico. Che fai? che pensi? Oime! come stai?...Ho sopra il cuor questa lontananza, elle mi fa male...ti bacio teneramente [I am thinking of you. I am sorry to be a long way from you, my dearest friend. What are you doing? What are you thinking? Alas! How are you? My heart is troubled by this distance, it pains me. I kiss you tenderly].[13]

Plentiful references in the letters over the next few years indicate more than dutiful affection:

> I shut myself in to read your letter, I read you, re-read you, shed tears, God knows! I kiss your letter, you touched it, this paper where you set out what is in your heart, a

---

[10] See Dauban (1867), vol II, p. 444, this book, *Extraits du journal de mes voyages*, was quite explicit about what went on in boys' colleges, 'mauvaises habitudes', and hardly the kind of present for a fiancée.

[11] Some retrospectively unpleasant gossip from, of all people, Marat, Kermina (1976), pp. 86–7.

[12] See *Mém.* pp. 332–3, reflections on his intellectual domination, and his 'caractère dominateur', not the usual image of the marriage.

[13] *Corr.*, I, pp. 14–15, June or July 1780.

heart so tender and honest, where I take refuge and the only place I want to be (etc.).
(1781)[14]

'I love you with all my heart and certainly much more than the first time I told you this and that was not a little' (1781); 'You'll find me in much better health now, and loving you more than my life' (1782); *'amico carissimo, ti bacio per tutto, di cuore ardente e devotissimo'*; *'ti bacio sulli occhi ed anche la bocca'*.[15] In a (rather indiscreet) letter to their friend Louis Bosc, Marie-Jeanne explained that the pet name of 'Loup' [= wolf] 'which seems so terrible to you, is an endearment, an affectionate, and charming name, which I acquired not from time immemorial, but the day after a certain 4 February, three years ago. I don't know how or why, but I'm "wolf" to someone, as perhaps you are "my beautiful friend" for someone you don't talk about' (1784).[16] Physical endearments punctuate the correspondence right up to the Revolution: 'Adieu, gros loup! Je te mange tout entier.'[17]

Quite beyond doubt is Jean-Marie Roland's passionate devotion to his wife, which endured to the end. One of the first surviving letters (February 1781) deserves quoting at length for what it conveys about their relationship, and about Roland's private morality. He had recently learnt that his wife suspected she was pregnant: she was in Rouen, staying with his old friends:

Three days and no letter from you! Oh *mon amie*, how long it seems! Is it as long for you as it is for me? Will I have to see a fourth go by? I shall be anxious until midday. [...] What are you doing? What are you thinking about? What plans are you making? Tell me, *mon amie, ma tendre amie*, have you received my letter? [...] I've got the roofer, masons, carpenters, upholsterer, and mattress-maker here, all these men are driving me mad, but I think everything would tax me when you're away. [...]

I wrote to Paris [...] about the material for your bed. I think it has sunk to the bottom of the Rhône. [...] All I can see is that you'll never be as comfortable as I would wish you to be [...] Today I read something that drew many tears from me; all the time, I had you before my eyes [...] It was the continuation of *Emile* [when Sophie forsakes Emile]. Oh *mon amie*, how touching and penetrating this section is! [Rousseau] didn't complete this work, but I have completed it in my head: I see virtue triumphing over all the horrors of fate, I see [Sophie] remaining with the one who loves her, and always replacing the rest of the world for him. Come to my arms, *ma tendre amie*, you will never be guilty, or I should die. Your virtue has all its youthful force, and we will taste the sweetness of innocence, without any need for remorse, ever. Perhaps, alas, you find this virtue that I idolize rather harsh, too inclined to get irritated and indignant. As you know, I've lived a great deal of my life alone, and I don't

---

[14] *Corr.*, I, 8 February 1781, p. 34 and note. She suspected pregnancy at the time. Sequences of letters: Mme Roland was in Rouen, January–February 1781; Roland was in Paris winter of 1781 82; again in January 1783; in 1784, Mme Roland was in Paris mid-March to late May. When apart, the couple wrote almost every day.

[15] *Corr.*, I, pp. 33, 218, 446, 461, etc.

[16] Cf 'Adieu loup-loup, reviens bien vite', 25 July 1781, *Corr.*, I., p. 50. 'Bonjour Loup!' ibid. II, p. 25, 26 August 1788; 'Adieu gros loup', *Corr.*, I, p. 683, 1787. See Grassi (1994) on formulae of affection, e.g. 'je vous embrasse de tout mon coeur' their usual signing-off, to close friends, or to each other, cf. 'Je t'embrasse avec une tendresse inexprimable,' 24 January (1783).

[17] Many other examples, especially in Italian: *Corr.*, I, p. 24, 3 January 1781; BNF MSS, naf 6238, 28 January 1781; and 9533 fos 69–70: 19 August 1783; *Corr.* I, p. 602, 21 May 1786.

regret it; it makes my heart more worthy of you; you will never find another more lovable, because you will never find another so loving.[18]

One could set alongside this letter one dating from much later (1787) from his wife, again inspired by Rousseau, and reflecting a conversation we know they often had:

> [Being unwell] I sat by the fireside and read Rousseau. *Mon ami*, I shall read this author all my life, and if ever we are in that position we have often amused ourselves imagining, you old and blind, and making bootlaces, while I work with the needle, it will be enough to have kept as our books the works of J.J. [*sic*]. Reading them will make us weep delicious tears and revive feelings which will make us happy in spite of fate.[19]

When Roland wrote from Paris that he would rather be 'in your bed than in Paris, with snow on the roof', she replied 'I too would rather you were where you said, than where you are.' In 1786, Roland wrote from a northern trip that 'riding alone across an empty landscape, if I didn't think I would be seeing you soon, my heart would have broken'.[20] Over time the sexual element in the marriage may indeed have given way to what ended up as companionate partnership, then during the revolutionary years, to a real marriage of (political) minds. However, the contemporary evidence is that in the early years, this marriage was one of fondness and physical intimacy, and that several years on, strong affection remained.

STATUS: M. AND MME DE LA PLATIÈRE

The Rolands did not immediately move to Amiens in 1780. Their first year was mostly spent in Paris. Because of his foreign experience, Jean-Marie had been summoned to headquarters—the Hôtel du Contrôle Général in the rue Neuve-des-Petits-Champs—by the Necker administration, to help re-draft the rules for manufactures. It was a frustrating experience, since he was unconvinced of their value, but had little success persuading anyone else. 'He fought against the rules with all his might, on account of the principles of liberty which he everywhere supported,' as his wife later wrote.[21]

The post kept the new 'Monsieur et Madame de la Platière', as they were known, in temporary lodgings. For both, marriage brought changed status. Roland was no longer a restless bachelor, dodging between addresses: he had a presentable wife, devoted to his physical and intellectual well-being. For the former Mlle Phlipon, the change was greater, and on balance positive. A married woman, with a husband of higher status than her father, she could go on living in Paris with greater freedom

---

[18] To 'Madame de la Platière, chez Mlle Malortie, rue aux Ours, Rouen' from Amiens, 13 February 1781, BNF, MSS, naf 22422 and 6240 (copy). Cf. his letter from Amiens, 3 June 1786, ibid.

[19] *Corr.*, I, p. 695, 18 November 1787.

[20] *Corr.*, I, p. 151, 18 January 1782; BNF MSS, naf 6238, 3 June 1786.

[21] *Mém.* p. 333. The *mémoire des services* says he also offered a plan for the reorganization of the corps of inspectors; BNF MSS, naf 6243, fos 31–43; cf. Reddy (1984), p. 44 on these meetings.

Figure 1. Marie-Jeanne Roland, image in profile. Engraving by C. Dien after an original in private hands. Note the 'jockey' hairstyle she usually favoured. Reproduced from Mrs Pope-Hennessy (Una Birch) *Madame Roland, a Study in Revolution* (London, Nisbet & Co., 1917). Photo from the author's collection.

than before. She acquired a constant companion, a new family, and her *entrée* to their property in the Beaujolais. Learning to live with someone else twenty-four hours a day could be a strain, and they were not rich, but on the whole the year worked out well.

For the first few weeks, they stayed with Marie-Jeanne's father (however awkward that must have been). Roland told a friend to address letters 'chez M. Phlipon, rue de Harlay près le Palais, Paris'. There were a few days 'honeymoon' at Vincennes with her uncle.[22] However, soon afterwards, they moved to Roland's usual lodging, the Hôtel de Lyon in the rue Saint-Jacques. François-Xavier Lanthenas occupied a cheaper room in the attics there.[23]

This is the place to say more about Lanthenas, the witness to their wedding who attached himself, limpet-like, to the couple for the next ten years or more. There were three people in this marriage from the start. Lanthenas was the same age as Marie-Jeanne: born in Le Puy in central France on 18 April 1754, he was the

---

[22] To Sophie, *Corr.*, I, p. 6, 16 February 1780. By the time she wrote again on 22 April, they were in the hotel, to avoid the 'little harassments' of living with her father, ibid. I, p. 10.
[23] See *Corr.*, II, Appendix L, pp. 688 ff.

youngest of three surviving children of a well-off wax-merchant. His younger son status, like Jean-Marie's, was a critical factor in his attitude to life. He thought primogeniture profoundly unfair. He too made a couple of false starts: he too was apprenticed to a Lyon merchant, and stayed four years. In Italy in summer 1777, on a quest to find markets for silks, Lanthenas first met Roland. Disliking commerce, the younger man eventually persuaded his father to let him study medicine, and 1780 found him at medical school in Paris. Roland wrote of him: 'The friend is up to his neck in cadavers'.[24]

That first year, the three of them saw a great deal of one another. In 1784, Lanthenas qualified as a doctor in Reims—famous as a place where one could buy degrees; he might have found it too difficult in Paris. From then on, he divided his time between Paris, Le Puy, where he chafed against his dependent status, and occasional stays with his friends. Strong affection united them, and the Rolands regarded him as a young protégé in need of friendship and protection from his unsympathetic (but allowance-giving) family. He ended up with a reasonable enough settlement, but was later almost certainly behind some of the Revolution's legislation on inheritance.[25]

We know from subsequent events that Lanthenas had conceived an unrequited passion for Marie-Jeanne Roland. However, she resolutely treated him as a younger brother (*il fratello*)—he called her '*sorella*'—and she was apparently never tempted to go beyond this sisterly relationship. Many of her surviving letters and those of her husband are addressed to him (many more are lost). His 'irresolute nature' (Cl. Perroud) meant that he found it hard to settle to anything and appears to have become emotionally dependent on the Rolands and some of their other friends. But he was restlessly available as an acquaintance of many people in Paris in the late 1780s—Creuzé-Latouche, Bancal des Issarts, and Brissot among them—and was destined to be the link between the Rolands and these men, a key figure in their Paris network. In these early days, they were inseparable. Madame Roland later explained their fondness for him by his sweet nature: 'before the revolution he was occupied in interesting and solid studies: gentle in his habits and human with affection'.[26]

The couple made another, even younger friend, Louis-Augustin-Guillaume Bosc (or Bosc d'Antic [Dantic] as he is sometimes called).[27] The hard-up son of a doctor-scientist from a Protestant family in the Cévennes, Bosc was born in 1759. After school in Dijon, he entered the postal service in Paris at nineteen, received early patronage and rose to the responsible position of *secrétaire de l'Intendant des postes* by the early 1780s. He lived nearby in the rue des Prouvaires. The day job left him time to engage in his real passion, botany, and he attended lectures at the Jardin du Roi (later Jardin des Plantes) given by A.L. de Jussieu, of the scientific dynasty, and

---

[24] *Corr.*, II, Appendix L, p. 690.

[25] See *Corr.*, I, p. 546: Lanthenas and Roland often joked about being younger sons.

[26] *Corr.*, II, pp. 535–6, 27 October 1793, to Mentelle ('Jany'); Lanthenas helped care for the sick in the villages round Le Clos. A ferocious judgement on him, *Mém*, p. 334.

[27] Often referred to as 'Dantic' in correspondence; see Appendix K, *Corr.*, II, pp. 666, ff. There are two biographies, Rey (1882) and (1901).

natural history demonstrations by L.J.M. Daubenton, head of collections. He also knew the hospitable family of the garden supervisor and botanist André Thouin (1747–1824), who lived inside the Jardin. Bosc enjoyed regular field-trips, especially to the countryside round Montmorency, with its Rousseauist associations. Being in touch with several scientists, he almost went on the ill-fated La Pérouse expedition of 1785.[28]

It was in the lecture hall that Bosc, just twenty-one, met the Rolands. They were regular visitors in 1780, because of Roland's research on plants and dyestuffs. Marie-Jeanne became, like Bosc, a keen 'herborizer' (specimen collector). She already knew the Jardin from her walks there with her father. The attraction seems to have been immediate, and Bosc—despite his denials, several other liaisons, and an illegitimate child—also became over-attached to the young Mme de la Platière, again apparently provoking only sisterly affection. His friendship—as a scientific informant to Roland, but extending well beyond that into close everyday intimacy—proved, despite some tearful quarrels, faithful, and longlasting. There were many undercurrents in this relationship: Mme Roland may have encouraged him to think of her daughter as a potential wife. As Perroud remarks, the fact that the Rolands used his post office privileges to send each other unsealed letters shows how thoroughly they trusted him.[29] Another acquaintance who became a long-distance friend was Albert Gosse from Geneva (1753–1816), studying chemistry in Paris in 1779–1781.[30]

Mlle Phlipon was now occupied being Mme de la Platière, although her household tasks were lighter than in the past or the future. She was free to move around, attending lectures and cultural meetings, as well as visiting relatives. On the other hand, she started helping her husband prepare his writings for publication, no small undertaking. Her time was fully taken, she told Sophie Cannet. Only a few letters reached Amiens that year.

In September, Roland took his new wife to meet his family. They embarked on the five-day journey to Lyon by coach and 'water-diligence', then on to Villefranche, and later the farm at Le Clos. The stay lasted three months, and despite the pre-marriage scares, was a successful, even a happy one. The new Mme de la Platière did her best to be accepted, and the 'penniless engraver's daughter' turned out to be far less vulgar than Jean-Marie's relations may have expected. Reading between the lines, one senses mutual feelings of relief in Villefranche. The mother-in-law was described as gracious, and Dominique was obviously charmed.[31] The Villefranche Rolands lived in their town house with gardens, on the Grande Rue and the corner of the rue Sainte-Claire, near the church. Built before the sixteenth century, it still stands [today 181 rue Nationale], with its courtyard galleries, and elegant ironwork and staircases. It had come down in the female line, being sold in 1592 to a 'Laurent Bessie' (the family name of Roland's mother). It passed as a marriage dowry to a

[28] Perl-Rosenthal (2011), chapter 6, explores in detail the scholarly network of the 1780s of which Bosc and the Rolands were members, using the Roland papers in the BNF MSS collection.
[29] *Corr.*, II, p. 672. See Lyon (2006), p. 74 ff, on the Museum as a less exclusive venue than academies or salons; cf. Peiffer in Haase-Dubosc and Viénot (1991).
[30] They kept in touch, see *Corr.*, NS, II, supplement, p. 474 note.
[31] *Corr.*, I, pp. 17–18, to Sophie, 28 September 1780.

Jean-Baptiste Roland de la Platière in 1686.[32] The ground floor was let out to a local functionary; Mme de la Platière senior and Dominique lived on the first floor; the younger couple, then and later, lodged on the second floor.

The farm at Le Clos was always at its best during the wine-harvest. Since it was assumed it would be theirs if they came to live in the south, they naturally took an interest in it. Jean-Marie described it in 1769, as 'not well placed', almost 1000 feet up, looking on to the densely-forested slopes of the Beaujolais hills, 'surrounded by vines, and blocked at the back by a very high slope entirely devoted to them. Other people might think it gloomy, but I quite like it.'[33] Marie-Jeanne had her first sight of the estate, and described it to friends, then and later, in enthusiastic terms:

It's an ancient inheritance, the remains of a once sizeable fortune [...] in the midst of hills covered with vines, not far from some wilder peaks; for a view we have a vast extent of oakwoods; the blue range of the Dauphiné mountains bound the horizon in the distance; and the frozen and shining white summit of Mont Blanc is our prospect.[34]

To Sophie she wrote: 'the sky is beautiful, the air healthy, the evenings delicious. Never was nature more laughing, more beautiful, more fertile and better cultivated [...] than in the rich hills of the Beaujolais.' Le Clos survives today, an unmarked low building surrounded by walls, near the village of Theizé, on what is to modern eyes a picturesque hillside covered with vines. In the 1780s, it was a working farm, with a full complement of outbuildings, cellars, wine stores, and winepresses, stables and so on, as well as rooms for the family to stay in. Four local winegrowers worked the land as sharecroppers, under the local system known as *vigneronnage*, though the property did not apparently bring in much surplus.[35]

*

The prolonged honeymoon was a prelude to a more settled life. The couple returned to Paris in December. In January 1781, with Roland's official work completed and a publishing contract just signed with Panckoucke, he went ahead to prepare the rented Amiens house. Marie-Jeanne meanwhile visited the loyal Malortie sisters in Rouen, to oversee the editing of Roland's Italian travelogue, before beginning housekeeping in earnest. Some of her biographers have regarded the next few years, first in Amiens then in the Beaujolais, as not worth much comment: Roland had his duties and writings, his wife was homemaking, tending the garden, and caring for their daughter: 'a retreat into domesticity' as Gita May describes it. But in the history of the marriage of Jean-Marie and Marie-Jeanne, these years are critical. The next chapters look at the 1780s from three different perspectives: the couple's approach to parenthood; their shared academic endeavours; their move south, and their everyday life, of which there are many glimpses in their correspondence between 1781 and 1788.

[32] Personal knowledge; Rhône-Alpes region website, section of www.culture.fr for Villefranche: 'Immeuble Maison Roland'. Cf. *Corr.*, II, p. 710; *Colloque Roland* (1990), pp. 101–14.
[33] J.-M. Roland (Perroud, 1769/1912), p. 77.
[34] To Lavater, 7 July 1788, *Corr.*, II, pp. 21–2. 'It's not picturesque...or brilliant'.
[35] 28 September 1780, *Corr.*, I, p. 16–18; on Le Clos: *Corr.*, II, Appendix M, p. 710 ff. Both houses are described with photographs in *Colloque Roland* (1990), pp. 101–11.

7

Educating Eudora
Parenthood Together

The chick would make you crazy about her if you weren't so already. Mercy! [*Miséricorde*!] The little wolf-cub is climbing on my chair to see what I'm writing to you.

Marie-Jeanne to Jean-Marie Roland, January 1787.[1]

The Rolands' only child, their daughter Eudora, was born in Amiens on 4 October 1781. Jean-Marie Roland was absent on a mission to Sens all of December 1780 and January 1781, returning to Paris only briefly to celebrate New Year, and to sign a contract with the publisher, Panckoucke, on 31 December (see Chapter 8). The baby must have been conceived then. The pregnancy was suspected immediately, suggesting that it had been much wished-for. A letter of 13 February 1781 was written at night, since Marie-Jeanne was 'vomiting every morning on waking'. By 16 February 1781, Jean-Marie Roland was writing enthusiastically, assuming a son was on the way:

> If it's really true [...] do you think it can have happened so quickly? Look after yourself and believe me, I shall have great pleasure seeing him run here and there: brought up by you, educated by me; I'll be able to die in your arms and leave him with you for consolation, loving and respecting you, and proving in your old age the sweetness of the confidence and friendship I enjoy with you.[2]

By July, his wife wrote: 'your little one is kicking five or six times and punching me: a bold rascal, like his father'.[3] An accident in mid-August could have been serious, when she fell in the staircase, but the pregnancy was unaffected.[4] Mme Roland described her experience of childbirth and breastfeeding in a forty-page essay addressed to her six-month-old daughter.[5] According to her blow-by-blow account, labour lasted eleven hours, and she eventually delivered the baby standing up. She does not minimize the pains of labour: the first ones were accompanied by a 'terrible tearing feeling, sending the whole machine into convulsions, quite nullifying

---

[1] *Corr.*, I, p. 663.   [2] BNF MSS, naf 6240.   [3] *Corr.*, I, p. 45.
[4] Ibid.; cf. p. 471, and BNF MSS, naf 6241, fo 282, letter from Justamont, 20 August 1781 about the fall.
[5] 'Avis à ma fille en âge et dans le cas de devenir mère', in Champagneux (1800), I, pp. 301–44.

any force of spirit', while the later ones were 'less acute but deeper, and spur on one's courage and develop it into resistance'. She also gives graphic details of familiar post-natal problems: constipation, cystitis, and breast abcesses, with hints how to avoid them, in which enemas (*lavements*) figure largely—as they do in most accounts of ill-health in her correspondence. Eudora's father-in-law, Luc-Antoine Champagneux, published the essay in his edition of her mother's memoirs, so Eudora may well have read this off-putting document before giving birth to her first child in 1798, aged only sixteen.

THE BABY

Both parents assumed the child would be a boy—the hoped-for heir to the dilapidated Roland estate. After the birth, her mother wrote in mock-apology to Dominique: 'Well, my dear brother, it is only a girl! I offer you my humblest apologies but [...] I promise that this little niece will love you so much that you will forgive her for having put her nose into the world.' This came with an undertaking 'to do better next time'.[6] There never was a next time—there are one or two hints at miscarriage in later correspondence ('No, Eudora will not have a brother,' 1785), but nothing conclusive.[7] The baby was baptized Marie-Thérèse, after her paternal grandmother, and Eudora, the name she would be known by, in the parish church of Saint-Michel on 5 October: her godparents by proxy were Dominique Roland and Mme Roland senior. The unusual, Greek-influenced name Eudora means 'good gift': a fancy perhaps of her Hellenophile father.[8]

Her parents had read Rousseau, that paradoxical expert on child-rearing. So there was never any doubt that the baby would be breastfed by her mother—Mlle Phlipon had already made up her mind about that. *Emile* was one of her bedside books. Rousseau was not alone in advocating maternal feeding. By the 1770s, there was a chorus of voices: it became briefly fashionable to keep a child at home with its mother. Statistically, as people must have known, many children sent to wet-nurses did not survive—the Phlipon family history was not encouraging. However, mothers in middle-class Amiens rarely chose to breastfeed. Shortly after Eudora's birth, Mme Roland wrote disapprovingly about her friends:

> Mme D'Eu had her baby at midday, a daughter. [...] The poor baby was sucking its fingers and drinking cows' milk, in a room far from her mother, while waiting for the mercenary [nurse] who was going to suckle her. The father was in a hurry to get the baptism ceremony over, and send the poor little mite off to the village. [...] I respect them both a little less since I have witnessed their indifference.[9]

---

[6] BNF MSS, naf 6238: from Amiens, November 1781; *Corr.* I, p. 55.

[7] *Corr.*, I, p. 486, 20 January 1785: 'the little minx realises that, and is more mischievous than ever', cf. ibid., p. 140.

[8] *Corr.*, I, p. 23. The church, now demolished, was near the cathedral.

[9] Ibid., I, p. 53, November 1781. The nursing saga is perceptively analysed in Outram (1989) and Sussman (1982). Cf. Brockliss and Jones (1997), p. 469.

One reason for the father's haste may have been that nursing mothers were supposed not to have sexual relations, which might harm the milk. (Jean-Marie would have had to agree to the arrangement, so possibly the couple abstained from sex most of the next two years.)

Breastfeeding Eudora turned into something of a marathon—'a drama of heroic proportions' (Outram), recounted in a string of letters to Jean-Marie in Paris. Marie-Jeanne first suffered from engorged breasts and sent for another baby to help suckle. This was harder to find than the other way round: the baby's mother came too, to help out. The other child was five months old, 'healthy, strong, and certified free of disease', although 'strange-looking and covered in spots'. Marie-Jeanne fed the children together for three weeks, without a moment's rest. Unsurprisingly, her milk dried up—a major catastrophe. Everyone advised her not to continue, but she persevered through various expedients: a temporary wet-nurse, a breast pump, and even getting a local woman to suckle her three times a day. Eventually, rewarding this remarkable willpower, the milk returned. Eudora was still being breastfed at two years old. In between, there had been many alarms and substitutes for mother's milk: rice water, diluted cows' milk; a sedative of some kind; honey; and cooked apple.[10]

Several biographers comment that the effort put by Mme Roland into breastfeeding, about which these intimate details have survived, has a frantic, ideological, and self-validating aspect—it mattered desperately for her self-esteem that she should succeed. Reading the correspondence and the *Avis*, this is fair comment. She was a determined woman. It is only a short jump (often taken) to assuming that this was effectively all motherhood was about for her, and that it explains her later disappointment at Eudora's development. Françoise Kermina, a perceptive, if unsympathetic biographer, suggests that 'well before her child's birth, she saw motherhood as a philosophical system, and no doubt she exhausted all its juices in her extravagant efforts to apply the first article of the system: breastfeeding'.[11] Such comments are prompted by a much-quoted passage in the prison memoirs, which does sound unusually cold:

> I have a young daughter [aged eleven] who is amiable, but whom nature has made cool and indolent; I breastfed her myself, brought her up with the enthusiasm and the cares of maternity; I gave her examples which one does not forget at her age, and she will be a good woman, with some talents. But her phlegmatic spirit and her less than agile mind will not give my heart the sweet pleasures I had promised myself. Her education can be completed without me; her existence will bring consolation to her father. She will experience neither my strong feelings nor my sorrows or pleasures.[12]

This is, indeed, a self-absorbed and revealing passage, although the context is that of prison, possible death, and the need to steel herself not to see her child again. Undeniably, from many allusions in the correspondence, Eudora's mother became frustrated in her hopes for her daughter's intellectual development. That does not

---

[10] 'Avis à ma fille'; and letters from November 1781, in *Corr.*, I.
[11] Kermina (1976), p. 308.
[12] *Mém.*, p. 42. The passage goes on to be even more egocentric.

mean, however, that she had always felt the same way, or that she did not, at the same time, feel affection for her. What the quotation does confirm is her strong belief that maternal feeding was of the utmost importance in forging a bond with the child, and that how it was handled would determine the child's development.

More interesting, in my view, are the accounts written by Eudora's parents throughout her childhood. From several detailed and confessional letters that her mother wrote to Bosc, one has a running commentary on how this couple tried, perhaps *over*-conscientiously, to bring up their child while leading busy lives. One or other was sometimes absent—most often her father—but whichever parent was at home spent much time with the little girl, usually helped by Marie-Marguerite Fleury, their long-standing *bonne*. The Rolands regarded Eudora as a joint 'project', Rousseau-fashion, and both of them vacillated in their behaviour towards her, from tender affection to exasperated punishment. Principled inconsistency, rather than lack of love is probably the best description of her upbringing.

Her father, often omitted from this part of the story, became deeply attached to the child, and equally obsessed with her welfare. In the early weeks, both parents, knowing the high rate of infant mortality, were mainly concerned with keeping her alive. Trying to help at a distance, when artificial feeding became necessary, Jean-Marie Roland went to visit the home in Paris for abandoned children, the *Enfants Trouvés*. The nun in charge had advised him as follows: the best substitute for mothers' milk is 'boiled cow's milk with a little *bouillon gras*' (= fatty soup!).

> Take a little glass bottle about three inches high, such as you will find in the attic. You fit it with a very clean fine sponge, which goes into the bottleneck and projects from it the same length. The child takes hold of the outside section, warm and drenched with milk, you hold it at an angle and press it, and the child will suck it. [Incidentally] all the babies here lie on their sides, not on their back, and they are kept very warm.[13]

There is something touching about the middle-aged inspector going to the wards of the *Enfants trouvés* to find out what worked best, but then he was a practical man. He did not approve of his wife's 'on demand' feeding schedule. She had written to him when the baby was a month old, from a situation modern mothers might recognize: 'You will find this very scribbly, I only have one free hand and can only look at the paper sideways, my little one is on my knees, where I have to keep her half the day. She is on the breast two hours at a stretch, dropping off for little naps then waking up to suck. If I take it away, she cries and gnaws her fingers.'[14]

Jean-Marie had his doubts:

> Above all, don't make your daughter a spoilt brat, for I should hate the day she was born if she resembled most women I know; the more of them I see, the less I dissent from the maréchal de Saxe, who said he did not know a single man whose father he would like to be, nor a single woman whose husband he would be.[15]

---

[13] BNF MSS, naf 6240.   [14] *Corr.*, I, p. 57.
[15] 24 January 1782, BNF MSS, naf 6240.

His wife tried to leave the baby crying, even if it meant walking up and down, biting her nails: 'I would rather lose my daughter than let her acquire an imperiousness which will bring her misfortune [...] but I am also a mother and these stresses, apparently minor, cause me great pain.' She deplored the servants' habits of feeding the child extras when she was away or asleep.[16]

Eudora did go on to be, if not spoilt, at least the centre of her parents' affection as a baby and toddler. Anxiety surrounded her, as she continued an only child. Whenever Roland was away, a stream of letters reported on the baby's progress. Once, aged two, she chewed a piece of rope and vomited: her mother lost sleep and couldn't eat for fright. At three, Eudora fell downstairs (the Amiens staircase had always been dangerous): 'I thought she was dead. And nearly died myself.'[17] When a local child perished from a viper's bite on the Beaujolais farm, Mme Roland panicked: 'When I think it could have been Eudora, I hate Le Clos!'[18] Her childhood illnesses are reported in detail (worms were frequent visitors).

To have these reports from her mother is not so unexpected, but Eudora had a close relationship with her father. Unusually for the age, he found himself looking after her from time to time. When Mme Roland was in Paris for two months in the spring of 1784, (see Chapter 9) she took Fleury, but left Roland and the cook in charge at home. Roland's letters contain a series of snapshots of Eudora, now two and a half, and known as *le poussin* (the chick) or *le lutin* (the pixie), twisting her father round her little finger:

We play a lot, and 'still my *maman* and my *bonne* are in Paris' [...] Eudora chatted to me about an egg she wanted for her supper, which I promised, and she had it. They came to tear her from my arms to go and eat it. [...] Next morning before 6 o'clock: 'Papa, look at me, come on papa, look at me!'; so I had to look at her, get out of bed myself, and then get her up.

Once the chick was dressed she asked for some 'biner' [for 'dîner']; I gave her dry bread, while we waited for breakfast at nine... I have organized a routine for her, both moral and physical. She is well, always coming and going, running up and down, singing, babbling baby talk, shouting very little, and no longer crying. She says "Maman is in 'Pazi' with my *bonne*".

Last night [...] Mlle Eudora decided to have a long conversation; two or three times, I ended it with 'Eudora, bye-bye, time to sleep now' [...] so of course she was still asleep at eight-thirty in the morning. She wished me good morning in the prettiest way. I picked her up [...] Now she is cutting up paper by the fire and I'm writing to you [..] but she doesn't think too much about the absent ones, [...] ah, but just now, this minute, she's babbling about her *bonne* again and seeing me turn the page, she got up and said 'Is that for *maman*, is that for *maman*?'.[19]

---

[16] Cf. *Corr.*, pp. 154–5: 20 January 1782'; cf. ibid., pp. 31–4, also quoted in Sussman (1982), p. 84.

[17] *Corr.*, I, p. 443, 7 June 1784, and p. 451.

[18] Ibid., p. 529, August 1785: NB this quotation ('je hais Le Clos') is sometimes taken out of context to suggest that Mme Roland was bored with the countryside. Not so in 1785.

[19] BNF MSS, naf 6240, various letters.

Roland's main method of babysitting appears to have been to let the child cut up papers while he worked, so perhaps it was not surprising to find her cutting other things as well.

> I must tell you about a bone I have to pick with your little monster, Eudora; don't laugh: she cut my [red] garters to ribbons and did this fine job while sitting on the ground beside me in my study![20]

These reports had the desired effect of touching Eudora's mother. When a relative asked after her daughter, 'I was surprised to find my eyes so full of tears that I couldn't stop them falling: the idea of her little voice often calling for me and her *bonne* strikes my heart and I become just a *maman* with all the weaknesses of a *maman*'. After a two-month absence, 'poor Eudora did not recognize her mother', who burst into tears and thought, 'I am like those women who did not feed their children themselves'. Revealingly, Mme Roland wrote, 'I wish she still needed milk and that I had it to give her'.[21]

THE CHILD

But once Eudora *was* weaned, her mother began to expect a great deal from her, especially that she learn her letters. The pressure started when she was three: 'playing at my feet she has learned some of the alphabet; she wants to look in my book'. However, 'although she learned the letters quickly by playing, putting them together makes her yawn so hugely at every word, that she makes me feel pity'.[22] Despite the example of her parents, 'whom she sees reading and writing', Eudora continued to yawn over her books. Perhaps pushed to read too early, she started to see papers as her enemy. 'Just now she made a pretty little face and came to try and kiss us, after having had a tap from her papa on her fingers because she came and disturbed the papers on our desks.'[23] Not until after her fourth birthday did she show any interest. 'Thirty-six hours ago, Eudora seemed to take an interest in reading, or at least to combine it with greed, having a sweetmeat when she has learnt her lesson well.' When the little girl met the astronomer Lalande on the stairs in Villefranche, she told him, '*Maman* loves me now, because I read well.'[24]

However, children do not always turn out exactly as their parents expect. No doubt her mother was expecting a replica of herself—an eager early reader, gifted at music, composed, and obedient to her mother's wishes, if capable of great determination. Eudora, with her 'blonde curls falling to her shoulders', turned out to be fonder of dolls than books. By the time she was six, 'my daughter is driving me crazy' her mother wrote to Bosc:

---

[20] BNF MSS, naf 6240, fos 217–18; Lanthenas picked the letter up in Paris and everyone had a good laugh.
[21] Letter to Bosc, 7 June 1784, *Corr.*, I, p. 443.   [22] *Corr.*, I, p. 479.
[23] Ibid., p. 494, 9 February 1785.   [24] *Corr.,* I., 25 November 1785, p. 552.

She likes writing and dancing, because these exercises do not tax her brain [...]. Reading amuses her when she has nothing better to do, which is not often, and she only likes stories that are finished in half-an-hour; she is still a thousand miles from Robinson [Crusoe]. The harpsichord makes her yawn [...] She likes wearing a white dress because it makes her look pretty [...] but she would prefer even more to run and jump in the countryside than to stand stiff and white in company.[25]

Eudora was turning out very self-willed (now there's a surprise). This was glossed by Mme Roland as: 'she has something of the temperament of her father', whom 'she reveres [...] to the point where she begs me to kindly conceal her follies from him'. Indeed, she had heard from Jean-Marie's brother, she told him, 'that you were just like her in your childhood, just as careless and cheeky, so I feel more reassured about the future'.[26] Certainly, many quotations show that Eudora was very fond of her father, and had worked out that he was more indulgent. Her mother reported one conversation:

The wolf-cub told me yesterday that she loved you more than me.
'Oh, why?'
'I just do.'
'But there must be a reason why you love papa more?'
'Yes, because he always forgives me and he gives me more kisses.'
'But he corrects you too?'
'Oh *he* always forgives me every day, and sometimes when I have been naughty *you* remember it, and you don't let me kiss you.'[27]

Many years later the family found in a drawer 'a heart embroidered white on white with the legend: "Dear Papa, I do not know how to write but I will say I love you in embroidery"'.[28] As the extract above shows, her mother tried hard to maintain discipline. When Eudora was seven, Mme Roland wrote to her new acquaintance, Johann Kaspar Lavater, complaining of Eudora's 'waywardness, inconstancy, and opposition':

How I wish my daughter was more like yours of the same age! She would not try my mother's heart so, and I am often obliged to hide my tenderness under a mask of coldness and severity. Teach me how to guide a disobedient character, a careless nature, on which neither caresses nor punishments and firmness seem to have much effect.[29]

There are plenty of letters in this vein. Rather late in the day, the Rolands realized that the education of childen was not as easy as they had thought.[30] As working parents, often at their desks, they had put their own wishes first. A revealing letter from Marie-Jeanne to her husband in December 1787 contains some clear-sighted self-criticism about their odd situation for the time, as an 'academic couple':

---

[25] To Bosc, 6 April 1788, a long letter, *Corr.*, II, pp. 6–8.
[26] 21 May 1786, *Corr.*, I p. 696; several letters that spring mention Eudora missing her father. Cf. also 19 August 1783, 7 November 1784, I, p. 464; 21 April 1785, p. 515.
[27] *Corr.*, I, p. 659, 9 January 1787.   [28] Kermina (1976), p. 101.
[29] *Corr.*, II, p. 22, 7 July 1788.   [30] Cf. Jean-Marie, 30 May 1786, BNF MSS, naf 6240.

I re-read Julie's plan [in *La Nouvelle Héloïse*] and I found we have got too far away from it. [...] We have been paying too much or too little attention to our child. Being extremely busy, in the kind of work that requires peace and quiet, we have expected her to do lessons without taking the time to allow her to develop a taste for them [...]. Then if there is a tantrum, we do everything to obtain silence, because without it we can't get on with our work. What makes children whine, Julie says, is the attention one pays to them [...] but if one takes no notice, they soon stop [crying], because nobody likes to go to a lot of effort for no result.

That is why, my dear friend, we haven't a good conscience about this. [...] We impose constraints, the child reacts against them [...] We should not hide it from ourselves, our little one is decidedly wilful; but she lacks sensibility and taste as yet; this must partly be our own fault [...] I have resolved in future:

1. Never to lose my temper, and to remain cool and calm, in equity, when the child needs correction.

2. Never to use the whip, slaps, or any gesture or tone of voice indicating impatience. Any physical blow seems to me odious and calculated to harden, cheapen and close for ever the gateway to feeling. We have a few *mea culpas* to make in this respect. When the child was small, we thought a little smack on the naughty hand would produce the best effect. But the little smack led to the whip, the child became mischievous, and we were upset; the little smack was a mistake, we must backtrack, and there isn't a moment to lose.

3. We must organize things so that the child is happier with us than with anyone else [...]. That might not be so difficult where a mother doing needlework would gently watch her child [...]. But in a study, between two desks, where serious work is going on in absolute silence, the child simply gets bored; especially if we forbid her to sing or babble to herself because she has no one to talk to; so we drive her into doing something [naughty] to get our attention.

Such are the contradictions of our way of life. People who write treatises on education never consider the scholar or any other profession; they just talk about the father and the mother, and consider them in that role, subordinating anything else to that. You have research to do; and I am happy to help you, because I am a wife as well as a mother, and was the one before the other. So let's find a way to stay at our desks, and for the child to be happy alongside us [...]. If nature has not made her for great knowledge, don't let us force instruction on her, but educate her character, and hope the rest will come through inspiration, not compulsion.[31]

This is a surprisingly modern letter. It also indicates that Mme Roland was not lacking in affection for her daughter, but was disconcertingly clear-eyed about her development.

In these early years, Eudora was still central to the Rolands' view of themselves as a family unit. The coming of the Revolution would disrupt much more violently the attention both parents had previously given her. At various times, she was sent to friends or to a convent when they were occupied elsewhere, although it was clearly a wrench. In October 1790 for instance, Mme Roland wrote to a friend:

---

[31] 1 December 1787, *Corr.*, I, p. 716; evidently 'research', even if a bit boring, was more to Marie-Jeanne's taste than constant child-minding.

Tomorrow I will be taking my dear E[udora] to the little town [to the Dames de la Visitation]. This new separation reminds me bitterly of all the reasons which have obliged me to do it, and my heart is torn in two. Must one know the charms and duties of motherhood only to be deprived of the sweetest task [i.e. education]. What is the care of nursing one's child in comparison with that of forming her heart?[32]

---

[32] To Bancal, *Corr.*, II, p. 187, 28 October 1790.

8

Essays and Academies
Writing Together

What could be more touching than domestic life rendered happy by the close union of its heads, whose tastes and wisdom are identical and lead them to act in concert?

> J.M. Roland, reception speech for the Académie de Lyon, 1785.

If Eudora sought attention by disturbing the papers on the desk, that was because her parents worked closely together on various writing projects. Jean-Marie Roland had given up hope of promotion—his ideas about French industry would not succeed through the usual channels.[1] But authorship could provide extra income, at the price of sitting up late. It might raise him from an overworked *fonctionnaire* to the coveted status of man of letters. His wife, through a combination of tragedy and talent, became known as a major writer of the age, for her memoirs. Her correspondence, never intended for publication, has also been preserved. By considering some of the writings that *were* meant to be published, we can eavesdrop on aspects of Enlightenment thought, while exploring how much Mme Roland contributed to her husband's works, a question which has exercised her biographers.

Roland went into print in 1780. Mme Roland later wrote rather acidly of this period:

> The first year of my marriage was entirely spent in Paris. [My husband] was publishing his *Arts* for the Academy, and putting finishing touches to his Italian manuscripts. He made me his copyist and proof-corrector. I carried out this task with a humility I cannot now recall without laughing, and which seems almost irreconcilable with a mind as well-exercised as mine; but it proceeded from my heart. I respected my husband so completely that I easily imagined that he could see things better than I, and I was so afraid of his frown, and he was so firm in his opinions, that it took me a long time to acquire the confidence to contradict him.[2]

Allowing for retrospective irritation and the overall intention of depicting her marriage as one of respect, rather than love, this picture rings true. As a young wife, Marie-Jeanne was probably in awe of her husband and Roland's writings were always opinionated, even if only reports to head office.

---

[1] See Horn (2006), pp. 32, 46 ff.; Minard (1998), pp. 325–6; Brose (1998); Jacob (1997).
[2] *Mém.*, p. 333. Three months of the year were, in fact, spent in the Beaujolais.

He had high hopes for his travel journals. His friends, the Cousins, handled the printing and (anonymous) publication of his Italian–Swiss notes of 1776–1777. Things did not go smoothly. The editors made changes without his say-so and his wife was dispatched to Rouen to resolve matters. The Italian letters finally appeared in 1781 in six volumes. Even such 'an inoffensive work' needed approval from the ministry of Foreign Affairs. The censor insisted on the fiction that they had been printed abroad; copies were sent to Neuchâtel and reimported, carrying the misleading imprint 'Amsterdam 1780'. All this cost money, but sales and reception were disappointing. Roland later wrote that the letters:

> were written on the road and pitilessly cut, [...]. Language was not always respected, and even geography received a few affronts. All this in the depths of the provinces, forty leagues from the author. [...] But the facts therein were truly observed, and the comments made after due reflection. I presume to think that this journey into Italy and Switzerland, [...] may have seemed novel in some respects, and still think so today.[3]

The *Letters* do not seem to have made much impact: their disparate elements, not uninteresting individually, are odd in combination: sightseeing and visits to famous men (Voltaire and Pope Pius VI); reports on textile production and marketing; forward-looking reflections on trade exhibitions; a section on the role of the inspector of manufactures; and scattered items of autobiography. It is not clear to whom this combination would appeal: the books were remaindered at a Left Bank bookshop within a few years. Mme Roland commented that they had not impressed his superiors in head office, probably because of her husband's usual strictures on regulation, so they did him little good at work either.[4]

His first signed imprints were his technical 'Arts': three essays from the mid-1770s recycled for the Paris Académie des Sciences, which commissioned a series of short treatises. The first two, on woollen fabrics and 'velours de coton', appeared in 1780. The third, on peat extraction, came out in 1783, again under the Académie's patronage.[5]

These might seem uncontroversial subjects, and Roland knew what he was talking about, but the essay on cotton velvet revived his previous quarrel with John Holker. Holker had the chief royal privilege to produce 'cotton velvet', or velveteen, a fabric pioneered in England, made of cotton but looking like (silk) velvet. His factory at Saint-Sever in Rouen was exempt from visits by *gardes-jurés*, and could be checked only by a special inspector. Roland's preface referred insultingly to the 'calender-operator from Manchester' who had made one 'of the most astonishing fortunes in France', by his monopoly of the fabric, and by keeping prices 'artificially high'. As a result, France was being 'flooded by cheap, contraband,

---

[3] *Dictionnaire*, II, supplement (1790), p. 91. The letters were dressed up as being to 'Mademoiselle ***', which in a sense they were.

[4] Le Guin (1966), pp. 33–4, 51, 54: 'badly received by critics'; on the censor see *Dictionnaire.*, I, p. 625; *Lettres d'Italie*, IV., p. 320; *Corr.*, II, Appendix D, pp. 588 ff.; Roche (1988), pp. 29–46.

[5] *Corr.*, II, p. 627: an *Art du Toilier* [linen] and a study of aquatic plants of the Amiens region never appeared.

English-made cotton velvet'. Had it not been for this unnamed—but easily identifiable—manufacturer, he argued, France would have thousands of workers making this desirable fabric. A more open internal market in France would have rendered French-made textiles competitive, benefiting 'the public interest'. This *ad hominem* attack diverted a (perhaps) reasonable argument into a full-blown quarrel.[6]

Holker complained officially, the Académie obliged Roland to withdraw his preface, and a furious exchange of pamphlets by hired guns followed. Roland's mouthpiece described Holker offensively as a person of low degree, who had

Figure 2. Jean-Marie Roland. Terracotta bust by Joseph Chinard, Musée des Beaux-Arts, Lyon. Photo Wikimedia (attribution to Stouf mistaken).

---

[6] Roland's preface is included in BM, Lyon, Fonds Coste 353440, 'Lettre d'un citoyen de Villefranche', pp. 41–6, reproduced in part in Le Guin (1966), pp. 48–9. See Chassagne (1991), esp pp. 45–50, for a full description of Holker's operation. Perroud's version of the quarrel, *Corr.*, II, Appendix G, pp. 626 ff., is followed by Le Guin. Both Rémond (1946), pp. 100, 128 and note, and Harris (1998) pp. 145–60, are more favourable to Holker and very hostile to Roland, whom Harris describes as 'ambitious', 'embittered', and 'lazy'. While it was probably not Roland's finest hour, it seems there were rights and wrongs on both sides. Harris (Conclusion) provides persuasive explanations for England's advance in textile manufacture.

misrepresented his own history and that of textiles in France.[7] Holker's pamph-leteer, the inspector Brown, claimed, apparently inaccurately, that the Englishman had protected the ungrateful Roland when he was a 'lowly worm of an *élève-inspec-teur*' in Rouen.[8] The dispute, which lasted until Holker's death, is partly explained by Roland's allergic reaction to profiteering, something that colours his attitude towards subsistence policy during the Revolution, and his angry responses when challenged. Meantime, this bitter quarrel divided two people who were both ener-getically concerned to make French textiles competitive.[9]

Still there was a silver lining (sort of). Roland's treatises on textiles had appeared at an auspicious moment, attracting the attention of Charles-Joseph Panckoucke (1736–1798), one of the eighteenth century's most enterprising publishers. In June 1780, Panckoucke acquired the privilege to produce a revised version of the *Encyclopédie* of Diderot and D'Alembert, one that would be 'easier, more portable, more accessible to the new generation'. The original was in alphabetical order: the new version, *L'Encyclopédie méthodique,* would be divided into volumes by subject, each a dictionary of a branch of knowledge. Publication, by fascicle, originally set at 57 volumes, eventually ran under Panckoucke's son-in-law, Henri Agasse, to 166, completed in 1832.[10]

On 31 December 1780, Roland signed a contract with Panckoucke for the *Dic-tionnaire des Arts et Métiers*: two in-4 volumes on 'manufactures'. They would cover every kind of textile production—hemp, linen, cotton, wool, silk, lace, hosiery. The pay was modest: 24 *livres* per folio, or 3 *livres* a page, still a useful addition to the household income. In 1785, Roland contracted for a third volume, leather goods and dyestuffs –better paid, at 72 *livres* per folio.[11]

The *Encyclopédie méthodique* forms a transitional phase between the original version and the presentation of knowledge in later centuries. It has attracted less attention than its famous predecessor, but is the subject of an illuminating chapter in Robert Darnton's *The Business of Enlightenment.* Roland's contribution is not exactly typical, but its complexity illustrates what was new about the enterprise. In February 1781, he sent the publisher an ambitious plan, divided into fifteen dis-sertations and twelve treatises.[12] This appeared, after a historical-geographical pref-ace, in Volume I, plus a pull-out table to illustrate the overall conception. In an afterword, Roland described the plan as his own invention:

---

[7] BML, Fonds Coste, 353442, 'Lettres imprimées à Rouen' (October 1781).

[8] BML, Fonds Coste 353440, 'Lettre d'un citoyen de Villefranche', p. 29., which elicited the 'Réponse à la lettre', ibid. Roland riposted that the only contact he had with Holker back then was in claiming back pay that was due him, rather than patronage.

[9] *Corr.*, II, Appendix G, pp. 627–41; Le Guin (1966), pp. 18–19, 48–9, 56. The practical intro-ducers of the 'mull-jenny' according to Roland, were his friends Martin and Flesselles: patent *arrêt* of 18 Mai 1784, *Dictionnaire*, II, part 2, p. 137.

[10] On Panckoucke, *Corr.*, II, Appendix H; Tucoo-Chala (1977), p. 327. Watts (1958), pp. 362–5; Gillispie (1980), p. 357; Darnton (1979).

[11] Perroud, in *Corr.*, II, Appendix H, p. 642, estimated the first volume as paying 2376 *livres*: total pay for two: 4000–5000 *livres*.

[12] In *Dictionnaire*, III, p. lxiiij, Roland noted that the Academy considered his plan too ambitious. *Corr.*, I, p. 258, and for Marie-Jeanne's input, ibid, p. 273, 26 August 1783: 'I've been working on the plan for three days.'

I didn't find the idea in any book, nor was it inspired by any person. This plan looks simple [well, not very!] but it was not as easy to compose as one might think; as far as I know, few attempts have been made to consider manufactures in their reciprocal dependance and their mutual relationships.[13]

Such relationships were abstract—but the dictionary was of course alphabetical and perfectly easy to consult—beginning with A for *At[t]elier* [= workshop] and running to T for *Toile* [= lighter fabrics, linen, hemp, and cotton].

The intellectual plan was an invisible substructure, common in encyclopedias of the time, surfacing with certain keywords such as *Filature* [= spinning], which all reappeared in the *sommaire*, an alphabetical table. The *plan* was for people who wanted to read with a 'philosophical spirit', the *sommaire* for those 'less concerned with the subject as a whole'. As the reader will guess, all these para-texts, extra items surrounding the actual dictionary, were starting to be considerable. And it didn't stop there. Because the work was published in instalments, Roland wrote a supplement to the first two volumes, containing updates, extra notes, and asking for comments from readers.[14] The 145-page supplement (October 1790) contains one of the most useful elements of the enterprise, a glossary of terms used.

It was a Sisyphean undertaking. The first two volumes (693 and 523 pages) were published in 1784–1785. The author's distress at updating shows through at many points: 'I am ageing ten years every day,' he wrote in a frantic last minute addendum during the early days of the Revolution.[15] Volume III was not printed until January 1792, shortly before the author's life changed radically, and he never finished the sections on dyestuffs. (A version by two new authors appeared only in 1828.)[16]

The *Dictionnaire* is packed with concrete detail, but apt to engage in digressions of all kinds. Roland was a well-informed, but not overly well-organized contributor. Advice from a wide range of acquaintances is punctiliously acknowledged, and he and his wife did much research themselves. 'I turned myself into a workman,' he claimed.[17] Speculative remarks are sometimes based on the experience of a moment. One example—about whether insects have a sense of smell, not entirely relevant to his subject, offers a vivid picture of him in the family house in Villefranche:

One day when it was hot out of doors and there was an agreeable coolness in the study [...] I was working, in silence, and the only air coming in was through the fireplace, on the mantelpiece of which was a vessel full of orange-blossom, just picked and giving off an exquisite scent. I heard buzzing, looked round and saw a fly [*mouche*] which I thought at first was a wasp [...]. I got up quickly to kill it, then I saw another join it from the chimney, then a third, a fourth, twelve, twenty, zoomed in and made straight for the orange-blossom. They were honey bees [*mouches à miel*]. I opened the

[13] *Dictionnaire.*, II, 2, 314–15, 'Avertissement'.
[14] Ibid., p. 490.
[15] Ibid., Supplément, p. 1, 'Avis de l'auteur'.
[16] All references here are to the three bound volumes in the National Library of Scotland. Confusingly, Volume I is dated 1785, and Volume II 1784. See III, p. 493, for the explanation for delay.
[17] 'Tableau', p. 48–9, quoted Darnton (1979), p. 445.

windows and got rid of the bees [*abeilles*] by moving the flowers. [So they *must* have a sense of smell, he concluded.][18]

As this extract suggests, for a reference work it is very personal, full of asides and snorts of indignation, typical of Roland. Under 'Inspecteurs', he wrote: 'The author of this article in the [Grande] *Encyclopédie* gave of the word and the thing a definition and idea equally ridiculous and false'.[19] Into the same article, he inserted bitter comments on merchants:

> Irredeemably ignorant or mendacious, merchants will always tremble for their own interest [...]. If the outcry of the Amiens, Reims or Beauvais merchants had been listened to, where no one had ever seen cotton being spun, no attempt would ever have been made in France to manufacture cotton fabrics; [...] Is there a man today foolish enough to say that the manufacture of printed cottons [*indiennes*] has not delivered in France a prodigious amount of work for people engaged on preparation and spinning of raw materials, weaving, printing, and bleaching of these cottons?

In his article on commerce, he deplored the Anglo-French free trade treaty of 1786, since French production still lagged behind England's. The purpose of trade was to provide a living for the farmer and the worker—without whom 'we should be a band of wolves soon devouring each other'. He repeated this view in his dinner conversation with Arthur Young in December 1789—the only point on which they disagreed.[20] Roland's dictionary not only produced a reference work, but took every opportunity to urge the need for French textile manufacture to compete with the English, just then embarking on the industrial revolution. A free internal market within France, allowing the best products to flourish, was essential.[21]

Given the complex history of Panckoucke's project, and the intervention of the Revolution, it is hard to say what impact these volumes had. Roland himself cites (and argues with) both critics and admirers of his work, their stance usually determined by their position on internal free trade. One significant reader wrote to congratulate the author, beginning an association which continued for years before the parties met. In the late 1780s, Jacques-Pierre Brissot—then known as Brissot de Warville—and his Genevan banker friend Etienne Clavière quoted both the *Letters from Italy* and the *Dictionnaire des Manufactures* in their book comparing France and the United States (1787).[22] They spoke of the author as an 'upright man opposed to abuses'. Despite his 'style rèche' [= inelegant style] they wished other volumes in the *Encyclopédie méthodique* had been written with 'the energy and enlightenment which shine in those written by M. de la Platière'. Predictably,

---

[18] *Dictionnaire.*, III, p. 618 (still a matter of some debate: odour versus bee-dance).

[19] 'To have any truth, clarity and precision on this subject', his reader is referred to his *Lettres d'Italie*, of which a long extract follows. *Dictionnaire*, I, pp. 62 ff.

[20] *Dictionnaire*. II, Supplement, p. 68. Cf. Young (1890), p. 284.

[21] Parker (1979), p. 9, notes that in the Supplement to Vol II, p. ix, when the Revolution had just begun, Roland wrote: 'the day is coming when the nation, recovering its rights, will take over a new character, when the name of *la patrie*, and sentiments of the citizen will no longer be vain fantasies': a sentence that could not have been written under the old regime.

[22] Note to 'Commerce', *Dictionnaire*, II, supplement, p. 70, for a disclaimer that Brissot, ['M. de Varville'], who praised the work, was known to him.

Roland took umbrage at the term 'rèche', even pompously wondering if they meant 'riche' (!), but the friendship by correspondence—which had fateful consequences during the Revolution—survived this contretemps.[23]

From the start, the new Mme de la Platière had been drawn into helping, as she says. The manuscripts contain copies of sections, or annotations in her handwriting, and it is clear that she was at the very least Jean-Marie's amanuensis. One file contains sheets of samples of *indiennes* (printed cottons) from Beaujolais, all painstakingly and rather touchingly pasted in and labelled by Marie-Jeanne Roland, for forwarding to Paris.[24] In retrospect, she obviously resented it, though such resentment was mildly expressed, if at all, at the time.[25] Was she in any sense a joint author? Her correspondence contains constant references to the *Dictionnaire*, but few details, except about dealings with the publisher. In 1784, Mme Roland visited Panckoucke's offices and printing house—where she was more successful than her irascible husband. She certainly did proof-reading, pursued topics about which he knew little, such as embroidery,[26] and pestered Bosc for books and advice. Given the idiosyncratic style, and the massive technical know-how of these volumes, however, it is a safe bet that their composition was largely Jean-Marie's own work. His wife's role was to help by copying texts with minor improvements to style and spelling, proof-reading, extracting, translating works from English and Italian—effectively acting as a secretary and research assistant, as many academic wives have done since.

It is easier to find her intellectual influence surfacing in a different kind of text—the papers Jean-Marie read to provincial academies.[27] In her memoirs, she rather loftily claims credit both for style and (even) content of his writings:

> For twelve years of my life, I worked with my husband as I ate my meals, because one was as natural as the other. If someone quoted a passage from his works in which a more graceful style appeared, or welcomed some academic trifle which he was pleased to send to the learned societies of which he was a member, I rejoiced in his satisfaction, without trying to notice whether it was something I had written; and he often ended up persuading himself that really he had been on good form when he had written this or that passage which had come from my pen.[28]

ACADEMIES

On the title page of Volume III of his *Dictionnaire*, Roland described himself as follows (it requires no translation):

---

[23] Quoted *Corr.*, II, Appendix P, p. 729.

[24] AN, F^{12} 677, dossier 3.

[25] Le Guin (1966), p. 63 quotes Taylor (1911), p. 154: 'How greatly I am to be pitied: the work I do [on the *Dictionnaire*] disgusts and exhausts me'. This is much later hearsay from Sophie Grandchamp, see Chapter 16 below: possibly an exaggeration, but plausible.

[26] *Corr.*, I, p. 253; on visits to Panckoucke, see ibid., March–May 1784.

[27] "I'm sending you a first paragraph' of a paper for the Académie de Lyon, *Corr.*, I, p. 553, 25 November 1785.

[28] *Mém.*, p. 304.

M. Roland de la Platière; avocat au Parlement de Paris; Inspecteur général des manufactures du Lyonnais, Forez et Beaujolais; correspondant de l'Académie Royale des Sciences de Paris et de celle de Turin; Honoraire des Sociétés Economiques de Berne, Littéraire et Philosophique de Manchester, d'Agriculture de cette dernière ville, et de celle de Bath; Associé de l'Institut et Académie des Sciences de Bologne et de celles de Rouen, Dijon, Marseille, Montpellier, Bordeaux, Villefranche, Bourg etc. Titulaire de l'Académie et de la Société d'Agriculture de Lyon et l'un des Administrateurs de l'Ecole Royale gratuite, pour le progrès des Arts et celui des Manufactures de cette ville.

Le Guin rightly characterizes this list as a sign of Roland's perpetual and insecure quest for recognition. However, he wasn't alone. Daniel Roche comments that while famous writers could take or leave academy memberships, for 'the larger class of would-be intellectuals', it was worth accumulating evidence of one's standing. Roche uses Roland's case to make his point. 'He is incontestably a good example of the way academic titles could consolidate a social and scholarly position.'[29]

The functions of eighteenth-century academies varied widely, depending on city: elected members held meetings where papers were read, and offered essay prizes—the Dijon academy's prize had launched Jean-Jacques Rousseau's career. They sponsored enquiries into scientific inventions, or founded philanthropic institutions.[30] The grades of membership, *académicien, titulaire, associé, correspondant*, and so on, partly depended on whether one was resident. Membership was an excellent means of exchanging ideas and making contacts in the world of letters and sciences.

Of Roland's foreign memberships, little note need be taken: they resulted partly from travels or contacts, but were not actively followed up.[31] As Perroud remarks, the Académie des Sciences in Paris was 'the most serious item in all his academic baggage'. His links with Montpellier probably resulted from his stay in Languedoc in the 1760s; the presence of Rouen in the list is explained by his many Normandy friends—and the conspicuous absence of Amiens by his enemies in Picardy.[32] Membership was less significant than activity. For obvious reasons, Roland had most to do with his local academies after 1784: Villefranche, Bourg-en-Bresse, above all Lyon, where he became a full academician once he had a residence qualification, and where the academy played a significant role in the region's intellectual life.

Perroud lists fourteen occasions between 1785 and 1791 when Roland reported in person, read papers, or took part in some deliberation for the Académie de Lyon. Its archives hold twelve of his manuscripts. In his admission speech in January 1785 on 'The influence of learning in the provinces compared with its influence in

---

[29] Roche (1978), p. 304, based on information from Le Guin.
[30] See ibid., pp. 114 ff., 'Le rôle des académies' and statistics for provincial academies.
[31] *Corr.*, I, p. 474, note; *Corr.*, II, Appendix, on academies, and pp. 725–8 on Frossard (1754–1830) as contact for England; on Berlin (not elected) see BNF MSS, naf 6243, fo 59; *Corr.*, II, pp. 646–7, December 1781.
[32] *Corr.*, II, p. 265 and note, and Appendix H; Le Guin (1966) pp. 60–5; he did become a corresponding member of his friends 'Musée' in Amiens as compensation.

the Capitals,' he attacked the corruption of Paris. More curiously—one wonders how it was received—he argued that in the provinces 'because you get bored seeing the same faces every day', the need for literature is greater: 'the educated man is never alone'. He fiercely criticized gaming (including card games) as a scourge of provincial life, and ended with a passage about the need for women in particular to avoid such frivolity, and to receive education: 'we are no longer in the days when women's ignorance was a guardian of their virtue and the guarantee of their good behaviour [*sagesse*]'. The paper's conclusion is a plea for unity of thought between husband and wife: 'what could be more touching than domestic life rendered happy by the close union of its heads, whose tastes and wisdom are identical and lead them to act in concert'. The paterfamilias's repose depends on a 'wise, feeling, and modest wife and a tender and enlightened mother'.[33]

Both Rolands shared these Rousseau-esque opinions at the time, and the turns of phrase are reminiscent of Marie-Jeanne's style. She wrote to her husband on 12 December 1784 that she had been entirely taken up with domestic cares, without 'a moment of inspiration for the poor little discourse', which suggests he had asked her to help.[34] She may also have had some input to his paper on Plutarch: on 22 December 1786, she wrote: 'I like your notice on Plutarch; it is written from the heart; so the style is more flowing than in your dissertations on the Arts. I have revised it and copied it, since that will be a burden avoided for you if you accept my *slight changes*, and an easier way to correct me if you don't.' This suggests tactful editing and improved wording, rather than any new ideas.[35]

One of her husband's most distinctive papers was on a 'universal language'.[36] In reply to Antoine de Rivarol, the journalist who argued that French should be that language, Roland's paper to the Society of Emulation of Bourg-en-Bresse took the unusual (and prophetic) view that English would be better qualified, on the grounds that it should reflect state and nation and was the language of the two countries he most admired: England and the United States. We also have Mme Roland's ideas on it, since in 1789 she wrote to the agronomist Varenne de Fenille, who quarrelled with Roland's choice. She eloquently backed up her husband's paper with her own, more literary views—another example of her not-quite-public method of being an author: 'I know, Monsieur, that silence is the ornament of women,' she begins, but launches into a long reply, rejecting the excuse that English is hard to prononce, or hard to learn; that it is not sufficiently the language of culture ('you haven't read Shakespeare?'). As for novels, no one yields to her in admiration for Rousseau, but the author of *Julie* 'acknowledged Richardson as his master'. Her praise is based on the pleasures of English literature, but she also refers to the United States as offering a practical reason to learn English. This letter, of

---

[33] BM Lyon, Fonds Coste 353455, pp. 11, 35, also quoted Le Guin (1966), p. 63.
[34] 12 December 1784, *Corr.*, I, p. 475, Perroud notes this must refer to the *discours de réception*.
[35] *Corr.*, I, pp. 649–50, my italics.
[36] 'Aperçu des causes qui peuvent rendre une langue universelle, et observations sur celle des langues vivantes qui tend les plus à le devenir,' Académie de Lyon, manuscript, MS 151. Thanks to the curator for finding the manuscript for me.

which the copy is in Roland's hand, carries an ironic and mocking—but perhaps affectionate (?)—joke at his expense:

> Despite my taste for languages and my passion for literature, I love my husband better than all that, and since he writes about *Arts* [techniques] above all, I haven't been able to study, see or hear anything but *Arts* for a few years; so it is only for recreation, and always together, that we sneak away [from work] and have little escapes into this beautiful domain of literature, to which I hope to return and forget all the *Arts* in the world.[37]

Perhaps this is a suitably ambiguous conclusion to the question of Marie-Jeanne's collaboration with his husband's publications. During the 1780s, she moved from being an obedient research assistant, without much knowledge of the matters she was copy-editing, to a more active role. Both Rolands spent many hours writing; hers was by the mid-1780s the more elegant style. But they really did agree on most subjects, as their correspondence and the manuscripts in both handwritings prove. We have glimpses of their working conditions from the letters, and in the inventories of both Beaujolais houses carried out during the Terror: there was a small 'cabinet' or study in each, and many reference books including Diderot's and Panckoucke's encyclopedias, the works of Voltaire, Rousseau, and Buffon, dictionaries, law books, and travel literature.[38]

Madame Roland's writings were, of course, not confined to joint endeavours, but her name never appeared in print. Her letters between 1780 and 1789, which her editor describes as 'the debris of a much greater collection', make up a huge corpus. Her reports from Paris and Versailles in 1784 give a thorough account of lobbying under the ancien régime. And she also penned occasional pieces such as the *Advice to my daughter*, or the accounts of her two journeys abroad, the visit to England in summer 1784, and the journey through Switzerland in 1787. Written with her usual quickness and forthright comments, these are not without interest. Of the two, the English travel journal, addressed to her three-year-old daughter, is the more interesting to English-speaking readers, but as both are helpfully paraphrased at some length in Gita May's biography, I will comment on them only briefly.[39]

The Rolands stayed in London and its suburbs, and apart from some sightseeing, mainly met French expatriates. There is no mention of the radical circles with which their future friend Brissot was familiar. Roland was received by Sir Joseph Banks, President of the Royal Society, and probably met other scientists. At the House of Commons, they heard a debate between Pitt and Fox over the India Bill. Most of Mme Roland's attention, however, went to what struck her as a remarkable difference between London and Paris—the separate lives of men and women. 'Their morals are the better for it and the happiness of families is ensured.' She was also—rarely for her—moved to talk about dress. Little girls had no powder on

---

[37] *Corr.*, II, p. 49, 21 March 1789.
[38] *Colloque Roland* (1990), pp. 108–9.
[39] See May (1970), chapter 9, 'A journey to England', and pp. 150–3 on the Swiss trip.

their hair, but let their curls fall naturally (she would later imitate this style with Eudora) and wore low-heeled slippers with white frocks. She liked the 'great simplicity' of men's costume, and admired the very beautiful white muslin dresses of women, 'exactly like the ones we have borrowed from them, but tucked up around the hem. They all wear [cotton] bonnets [= kerchiefs] under their hats.' Her Swiss journal of 1786 (Geneva, Bern, Zurich) *was* published by a Lyon friend, Delandine, but she insisted it should be anonymous. While having an irresistible urge to put pen to paper that never left her, she was still adamant that her name should not appear: 'Since I have reached the age of reason, I have always said that if I ever had the fancy of publishing anything of any kind, it would be under another name, or at any rate without mine attached.'[40]

What emerges from these years, and would become more relevant during the Revolution, is that despite her insistence on anonymity, Mme Roland was gaining confidence in her writing, often sending it to third parties, not only family friends. She was also writing familiarly to their small Paris 'circle': Bosc, Lanthenas, and before long Brissot. Her husband learned to accept her as an intellectual equal (even in some respects superior) and theirs can be seen as a partnership—and an apprenticeship—unusual for the ancien régime. It explains why some of his more dramatic interventions during the Revolution showed signs of her help. And it is all the more striking since Roland was not an admirer of *femmes savantes* as a general rule: in his academy paper 'Sur les femmes', he wrote (surely not his wife's view?): 'To judge the manners, character, mind, and taste of a woman, it is sufficient to know the men whose particular company she keeps and her cherished relations.'(!)[41]

[40] De Beer (1787/1937), cf. May 1788, to Mme Delandine, *Corr.* II, p. 11.
[41] August 1786, 'Sur les femmes', *Corr.*, II, Appendix H, p. 651, note. Even Perroud adds two exclamation marks.

9

Leaving the North
To the Beaujolais Together

> You couldn't have a better chancellor. All the gentlemen of the administration
> think that you could not have chosen a better wife. Indeed, she is amazing.
>
> Roland's cousin Mlle de Belouze, on seeing his
> wife lobbying for him in Paris.[1]

In autumn 1784, the family left Amiens and moved back to Roland's family home
in the Beaujolais—the unintended result of a request that had the potential to
become controversial during the Revolution: Jean-Marie Roland's application to
acquire *lettres de noblesse*.

There were two ways to acquire noble status under the ancien régime (apart
from buying it): to have a lapsed claim recognized (*la reconnaissance*) or to merit it
by service to the crown (*l'annoblissement*). Roland tried both. As noted earlier, he
had office-holding ancestors, and some of them had married wives from authen-
tically noble families (like Jean-Marie's own mother).[2] This created precedents of a
sort, and the family originally possessed, as Mme Roland explained in a defensive
passage in her memoirs, a coat of arms, a chapel, a fief, etc.:

> The wealth vanished; it was followed by an honest state of modest fortune [*une médi-
> ocrité honnête*] and Roland had the prospect of ending his days in a property, the only
> one left to the family, which still belongs to his older brother. Having become a father,
> he thought that he had the right, through his own work, to safeguard for his descend-
> ants an advantage his ancestors had enjoyed, but which he would have scorned to
> buy.[3]

In this respect, her husband was rather like many of the Third Estate deputies
surveyed by Timothy Tackett: of whom 'a substantial number', about one
twelfth, were 'on the very fringes of nobility' or who had recently acquired
noble status.[4]

Roland was neither by income, situation, or birth, as well-off or high-ranking as
most of the 'prosperous and successful men' of the 1789 assembly. 'Honourable

---

[1] *Corr.*, I, p. 401.
[2] See BNF MSS, naf 6243, *Mémoire d'extraction*. Cf. Le Guin (1966), chapter 1.
[3] *Mém.*, p. 337. Cf. Descimon and Haddad (2010) on ennoblement.
[4] Tackett, (1996) p. 44.

mediocrity' meant worrying about debts. His resentment at noble privileges ran deep, like that of many in his position. He was particularly scathing about those who purchased it:

> France is full of *banqueroutiers*, and other public thieves—from trade, finance, ex-valets and various low stations (*gens de rien*)—who, by throwing money around, have bought the right (shame and execration of our government) to do nothing, to pay nothing, to contribute nothing to the public charges, to despise and look down on other men, to be harsh, haughty, insolent, in a word to be nobles.[5]

But it had never crossed his mind before to apply for privileges; only when he married and seemed likely to produce an heir was the issue raised, probably by his family. To be fair, he was never keen on the idea nor energetic in pursuing it himself. Apart from officially sanctioning the name 'de la Platière', it was, of course, a matter of financial self-interest. It would bring dispensation from some taxes on the family property, which might make the difference between preserving it for descendants and being forced to sell.

Accordingly, once the baby was on the way, in 1781, Dominique Roland sent from Villefranche some genealogical notes, which Marie-Jeanne worked up into the *mémoire d'extraction* with the aim of recognition as noble. In November, perhaps since the child was a girl, making things less urgent, Roland reported from Paris that he was feeling discouraged: 'nothing doing for recognition: you have to have titles as clear as the day', and even when you are not buying them, it could cost 'two thousand *écus* at least for the expenses, the seals, the verification, and the registration. It's rather a dampener.'[6]

His wife replied that she would sooner have milk for her baby than all the *lettres de noblesse* in the world: 'I hope one day she will find a husband like you! She will be quite happy enough and won't think anything missing in her life.'[7]

By 1784, however, they decided to think again. Why? Mme Roland was certainly not pregnant, since she wrote wryly to Roland that she tried to give the impression that she was. At any rate, in March, she set out for Paris, carrying all the required papers: the *mémoire d'extraction* and the *mémoire des services* listing Roland's posts and publications. Lanthenas was still at the Hôtel de Lyon, where she took two rooms, and Bosc was often in attendance. Marie-Jeanne wrote to Roland almost daily, as she indefatigably besieged offices in Paris and Versailles (incidentally conveying a portrait of the three 'young people' eating together or going on outings). This dense correspondence gives a vivid picture of lobbying for favours from the crown or ministers, via officialdom or through unofficial channels at court.[8]

This time the couple had decided to try the route via meritorious service. Mme Roland's original plan was to go over the heads of the bureau directly to the

[5] *Dictionnaire*, II, supplement, p.148 and III, p. 452.
[6] BNF MSS, naf 22422: 23 February 1782.
[7] *Corr.*, NS, II supplement, p. 442, 26 December 1781, consistent with her remarks about the genealogy-obsessed Mlle de Hannaches, *Mém.* pp. 246, 257.
[8] See *Corr.*, II, March–May 1784, a total of 48 letters. Roland's side of the correspondence is unpublished and mostly in BNF MSS, naf 6240.

Controller-General, Vergennes. When that proved impossible, she had to face Roland's immediate superiors, but Roland was not just unpopular with the post-Trudaine hierarchy, he was notorious for his non-cooperation. His reports from Picardy covered everything except what was asked of him: observation of the new regulations. There had been calls for him to be *révoqué* (dismissed) or at any rate disciplined, but things never got that far. Someone resignedly scribbled '*Rien à faire*', 'nothing to be done', against one of his reports.[9] In particular, he had written a letter deemed insulting and insubordinate to *intendant* Blondel.[10]

So, turning up in Tolozan's office on 19 April, Mme Roland was greeted with an 'outburst of which you can have no idea'. Her husband was accused to her face (not entirely inaccurately) of 'pedantry, insupportable pride, desire for *gloire* [= reputation], pretentions of every kind, an ungovernable character; [of being a] perpetual contradictor, bad writer and bad politician, wanting to run everything himself and incapable of subordination'—all of which she reported back to Amiens, before engaging 'a battle long and hard.'[11] Tolozan gradually softened under Mme Roland's tactics. When he said 'all the inspectors will be wanting nobility soon', she argued Roland's family's status. When officials criticized her husband, she let it be thought he would retire with the grant of *lettres de noblesse* and leave them in peace. She let them think she was 'expecting an heir in a few months; they watch me walking and I laugh in my sleeve'. She 'ruined [her]self in cabs', travelling to Versailles, writing letters, distributing Roland's books and CV, and activating any contacts at court she could raise through relations. Although she ended up charming the 'bear' (Tolozan) and the 'cat' (Blondel), she was being strung along. Roland's case was well down the agenda of the king's council, which would have to approve the grant; recognition of title required far more collateral evidence of family nobility than could be proved. Calonne had been persuaded to write a letter of recommendation,[12] but this was deemed not extravagant enough to do the trick.

In the end, Mme Roland's quick mind found another solution. When she heard that a new rank of 'ambulant super-inspectors' was being created, and that one of them was Brisson from Lyon, she realized that a vacancy might be created in Roland's own region. Although it was normally frowned on to send an inspector to his home city, where he might not be neutral, she moved quickly with her request, which was granted—perhaps because it would take her husband a long way from Paris. By persistent lobbying, she ensured that he would also receive the 4000 *livres* salary his predecessor had enjoyed; that he would take to Lyon his 1000 *livres* bonus; that the city of Lyon would owe him 500 *livres* for accommodation; and that they could even fit in their projected trip to England.[13] The family would live cheaply at Villefranche, provided he contrived to be in Lyon from time to time. He would be able to carry out his duties 'in your slippers', and they could leave Amiens,

    [9] AN, F[12] 677 A (on northern France). His report on Picardy in July–August 1781 was not approved. See Parker (1993), pp. 33–5: describing Roland as 'fiercely outspoken, and tactless', and 'a self-righteous fanatic', but 'intelligent'.
    [10] *Corr.*, I, p. 287, 20 March 1784; ibid., p. 292, 21 March 1784.
    [11] *Corr.*, I, p. 347, 19 April 1784.   [12] Ibid., p. 361, 25 April 1984 for Calonne's note.
    [13] Ibid., pp. 417–21, May 1784.

where neither was happy. There was no time to consult him, but Roland agreed immediately.[14]

Mme Roland was understandably defensive in her memoirs about this episode (later unearthed at the Jacobin Club, to derision): 'This was at the beginning of 1784, and I don't know of any man at that time, and in his situation, who would have thought it contrary to wise management [*sagesse*] to do otherwise,' she wrote. As an eighteenth-century public servant, by no means well-paid, Roland tried, like most people, to use leverage to become a little better off. His wife had had her doubts about the claim: 'we are as happy as we can be in this world, with a little land where we can lay our heads and say goodbye to the vanities. If heaven preserves our Eudora, I desire nothing more on earth'.[15] However, she later commented: 'of course if we had 15,000 *livres* [a year] and lived in Paris, and I devoted myself to negotiating, I almost said intriguing', she felt she might go far—indicating that she had discovered an unsuspected flair for negotiations.[16] Other people expressed astonishment at her skill. Both Lanthenas and Bosc sent regular bulletins to Roland, and his cousin Mlle de Belouze told him that 'you could not have a better chancellor. All the gentlemen of the administration think that you could not have chosen a better wife. Indeed, she is amazing.'[17]

As she reached the age of thirty, this experience helped bring out in Marie-Jeanne Roland something beyond the self-absorbed intelligence of the bookish girl, and the anxiety of the inexperienced wife and mother: a new confidence and a talent for social intercourse and influence. It also incidentally revealed a taste for enjoying herself—fairly innocently—in young men's company, something not lost on her husband. After writing some admonishing letters, he finally hurried to Paris to fetch her home.[18]

The episode had ironic sequels during the Revolution. Not only did both Tolozan and Blondel come under Roland's orders when he became minister of the Interior; one of his own actions in the summer of 1792 was to order the destruction of documents from the Royal Library's department of genealogies, including applications for *lettres de noblesse* (see Chapter 21). Some time before that, in accordance with new nomenclature rules, 'de la Platière' disappeared from both of the Rolands' signatures.[19]

---

[14] Flesselles would be the 'only person I would regret in Amiens', apart from the family doctor, Hervillez, ibid., p. 424, 21 May 1784.

[15] Ibid., p. 308, 27 March 1784.

[16] Ibid., p. 401, 14 May 1784.

[17] Ibid., p. 665.

[18] To Bosc: 'Send her home. She has made this old man [*ce bonhomme*] used to her and it's difficult to do without her', BNF MSS, naf 6240; cf. *Corr.*, II, Appendix J, pp. 665 ff.

[19] They were not alone in this, cf. Bosc D'Antic, Brissot de Warville, Bancal des Issarts, etc.

10

The Calm Before The Storm
Housekeeping Together

An elegant sufficiency, content,
Retirement, rural quiet, friendship, books,
Ease and alternate labour, useful life,
Progressive virtue and approving Heaven
These are the matchless joys of virtuous love.

James Thomson, *The Seasons,* given to Marie-Jeanne
by Jean-Marie, January 1787.[1]

The Roland family were three years in Amiens, then five in the Beaujolais, before the Revolution burst upon their lives. The 1780s, apart from Mme Roland's Paris visit in 1784, and their English and Swiss tours, was a time of family life, house-keeping, and academic work. In retrospect, Mme Roland thought how unexciting it had been. For us, it is a chance to reflect on provincial life in France in the decade before 1789. Academic work and raising Eudora were accompanied by the con-crete rituals of everyday life. The contrast is striking between Marie-Jeanne's letters to Sophie before her marriage, full of abstraction, and her correspondence after marriage. Probably under Roland's influence, her letters thereafter, especially to him, are forthright and earthy, full of intimate, physical detail.

For Jean-Marie Roland, despite his forebodings, marriage had been the most rewarding thing he had ever done, bringing him a beloved wife and child, and a partner in his writing ambition. He could continue everything he wanted to do, with a better support system at home. Any frustration at work was balanced by domestic comfort and affection: at last someone was looking after him. It is true that he acquired a father-in-law who required rescuing financially, but he rarely had to meet him after the early days.[2]

For his wife it was more complicated. Marie-Jeanne Roland's existence in Amiens or Beaujolais could be seen as satisfying, frustrating, dissembling, or a mixture of these, especially since Roland was out of the house in the daytime, and absent for days or weeks on end on business. As we have seen, he sometimes shared childcare,

---

[1] *Corr.*, II, pp. 668–9.
[2] Although estranged, the Rolands continued to help Gatien Phlipon out. When in October 1787 he had trouble paying his rent, Mme Roland asked Lanthenas to draw on Roland's account, *Corr.*, I, pp. 688–9; she worried that her father was unwell and being cheated. He died of bronchitis in January 1789.

but ordering of the household was his wife's responsibility. Although not rich, they could afford at least two servants, whom she had to instruct at first. Marriage meant a rise in status, but provincial life, after the prolonged honeymoon, brought the loss of the independence she had once taken for granted—a retreat to her childhood 'cellule' to read and think. Now more visible to the outside world, she had to behave accordingly—visiting acquaintances, giving instructions to servants, being more like 'a provincial wife and mother'. In Picardy, the family attended church 'to get frozen feet on Sundays for the edification of the neighbours and the salvation of my soul'.[3]

The Amiens house (it no longer exists) was not a particularly comfortable place to arrive at in January 1781. It was on the rue du Collège near the cloister of Saint-Denis, which contained a cemetery—the family could watch gravediggers from the back window. The buildings formed a rectangle round a muddy courtyard with a *porte cochère* and a stable. The rather cheerless house had stood empty for some time, explaining why the rent was low (500 *livres*). Rats were seen, and Mme Roland kept a pistol by the bed to chase them away. Amiens is cold in winter, and ordering wood for the fires was a priority. Since Roland regularly went to Paris every January to report to head office, exchanges of marital letters (1781–1784) usually date from this month, and are often concerned with keeping warm and well: 'I have gone straight from my bed to the fireplace, where I'm writing bundled up in scarves'. Irregular or inadequate deliveries of wood were critical: 'You will have plenty of opportunity for exercise in the woodshed, and the sooner the better: the first wagon load seemed so small when it was sawn in three that I divided the next lot in two [...] there's no hornbeam, the beech is all kindling, and the oak is debarked and useless.'[4]

There was little furniture. The letter quoted in Chapter 6 shows Roland still occupied in getting the matrimonial bed sorted out—as well as making the building good structurally. During their courtship, he had explained that because of his vagabond life, he had hardly any moveable goods:

> Some table linen, household linen, and enough body linen for myself for a couple of years. I have eight place settings, two serving spoons, and that's all. I will have to buy the principal piece of furniture [i.e. the bed] and all the rest. In general, of all the indispensable items, I own nothing.

He was also acutely aware that his wife would need to look respectable: 'You will need dresses... nothing fancy, nothing out of the way, but you must be the same as everyone else [of similar status]: bonnets, coiffes, etc.'[5] Marie-Jeanne tried to rise to the occasion by laying down the minimum she could manage with:

> I too can survive without buying any more linen for two years, [...] but I shall need three dresses, one for winter, one for autumn and spring, and a third, very simple. [...]

---

[3] *Corr.*, I, p. 173, 28 January 1782. All these buildings have been demolished to form the Square S. Denis; the street is now rue Porte-de-Paris.
[4] *Corr.*, NS, II, supplement, p. 447, 22 January 1782.
[5] *Lettres d'amour*, pp. 130–1, 19 May 1779.

As for sleeves, fichus and bonnets, which it's normal to have made of lace, that will mean another 12 to 14 *louis*, keeping to what is respectable without trying to be elegant, but without overdoing an affected simplicity. I have some of my mother's lace, which I should like to use, but since there are no complete sets and the design is old-fashioned, it may be difficult to adapt, or to avoid looking rather thrown together. I will try to do without [shoe] buckles which I don't want, and am delighted to see that our taste coincides on this.[6]

She could do without clothes, but not without music, her constant companion. In August 1783, she asked her husband to bring the music for Guillaume Lasceux's quartet for forte piano, 2 violins, and cello (1775) so that she could play the violin part. She had no keyboard, but borrowed a harpsichord from the local Salle du Concert [17 April 1784]. There was one in Villefranche (which Eudora didn't like) and Marie-Jeanne later bought her own fortepiano with her savings.[7]

The first months in Amiens, pregnant, in an inconvenient house, and a stranger to the town, cannot have been easy.[8] There was a brisk turnover of servants at first. The household required a cook, a maid, and a manservant to accompany Roland on his rounds, look after the horse and so on. Fortunately, the Rolands found a reliable housemaid, Marie-Marguerite Fleury, who was to stay with them for the rest of their lives. Marie-Jeanne appears to have been on good terms with her regular servants, and with those of her mother-in-law. Champagneux described her as an excellent housekeeper: 'order, economy, and foresight' marked her household. 'She did not command the people who served her, as other women do; she did not come down to their level but raised them to hers. So their service was more like the price paid by respect and attachment than the pay she gave them.'[9]

The main household concerns were cooking and washing clothes. Laundry was a major undertaking: in January 1782, for example, mistress and servants were doing washing until three a.m., to take advantage of a drying wind. In June 1784, 'I have been stuck with [...] all the worry of washday, which is a huge household affair in the provinces.' In the south, major washdays were held at Le Clos. When Fleury was summoned to Paris in 1792, she had to leave half her clothes behind 'because it was the week for doing the washing'. Mme Roland had been brought up to do her own sewing, and went on mending and perhaps making her own clothes. (Kermina reports that her husband, contrary to his usual thrift, ordered dozens of cotton hose for their daughter, because he couldn't bear to see his wife knitting).[10]

As for cooking, although she could manage the basics, she had never learnt patisserie, so the cook had to show her how to make tarts. In Amiens, the family diet was simple: the occasional glimpses we have suggest that breakfast consisted of

    [6] Ibid., p. 137, 23 May 1779. Until literally his dying day, Roland tied his shoes with ribbons, not silver buckles.
    [7] See, for example, *Corr.*, I, p. 211 on learning to play the *clavecin* (harpsichord), from a tutor-book of chords, January 1783.
    [8] Roland, 3 February [?1781] from Paris; BNF MSS, naf 6240, fos 100–1, 84–5, 86–7, 88–9, *Corr.*, II, letters of February 1781.
    [9] Champagneux (1800), p. lxxvij.
    [10] *Corr.* I, p. 108; ibid., 17 June 1784; Fleury, BNF MSS, naf 22424; Kermina (1976), p. 90, but no source given.

panade (bread and milk) accompanied by chocolate or coffee; at midday, a meat soup or fish; at five in the afternoon, more soup or stew, and supper might mean rice with milk and vegetables. A glass or two of 'small beer', quinquina or wine might be taken. (They bottled wine for their cellar from a supplier.) Since Amiens was not far from the coast, there was sometimes seafood: grilled plaice and on one occasion to settle her stomach (!) a dozen oysters. The main meat in this sheep-farming area was lamb. The small garden provided vegetables and pot-herbs.[11]

The move to the Beaujolais meant eating rather better. Mme Roland wrote to Bosc that 'the most modest bourgeois house here [Villefranche], if it is slightly above average, serves more luxurious meals than the richest houses in Amiens or than plenty of very well-off houses in Paris'.[12] Even when the streets shocked her by having open sewers, she noted that the meals were always *recherché*. The family received produce from Le Clos: 'every Thursday one of the winegrowers brings us eggs, butter, and vegetables from the country'. On one occasion, when guests were expected—possibly on behalf of her mother-in-law, since we know that Mme Roland senior liked to keep a good table—Marie-Jeanne asked Roland to send a list of provisions from Lyon: a good hare for a terrine; an eel weighing at least two pounds, or two smaller ones, a dozen snipe for the second terrine; three fat pigeons or a wild duck. She would also like some crayfish for the entremets, and how much do truffles cost? He carried out his instructions to the letter, and his wife apologized: she had ordered far too much, which suggests this kind of luxury was unusual for her.[13] In 1786, Flesselles sent them by stagecoach a 'paté' from Amiens, made with 'a turkey, two ducks and two partridges'.[14]

Remarks about diet almost always accompany references to ill health—often digestive troubles, described in graphic terms in the letters: constipation, diarrhoea, vomiting, etc. (Perroud as editor has cut one letter, with the comment 'trop c'est trop'—too much information.)[15] A range of everyday remedies was available, some of which had to be made up by the apothecary. The Roland family knew several doctors, and consulted others by letter. Mme Roland also put a lot of faith in reference books. She certainly read Mme Le Rebours's *Avis aux mères*, 'whose wisdom & exactitude I cannot praise enough'.[16] She also tended to run to Diderot's *Encyclopédie*, of which they had a copy: for Eudora's health she looked up entries on *children, nurse,* and *illnesses of early years*, but found Mme Le Rebours a better guide.[17]

As a rule, the family relied on traditional methods: purging, emetics and—especially—enemas (*lavements*). There are literally scores of obsessive references to bowel movements in the correspondence. Marie-Jeanne described to her husband

---

[11] 3 and 11 January 1782, *Corr.*, I, pp. 104 ff., many letters.
[12] 22 April 1785 to Bosc, ibid., p. 517.
[13] 6 March 1785, ibid., p. 496.
[14] Ibid., p. 571.
[15] 14 January 1783, *Corr.*, NS, II, supplement p. 453. (Several letters from January 1783 are published here.)
[16] But calls her 'Mme Le Reboul'. Cf. Brockliss and Jones (1997), p. 450.
[17] *Corr.*, I, pp. 100, 168–9, 132–3.

how their family consultant Ancelin had caused a sensation at the Amiens academy, by demonstrating 'an ingenious tool' operating like a forceps to relieve constipation, 'soothing the unfortunate people who couldn't shit [*chier*]'.[18] Worms
were a perpetual scourge (probably from meat) and were tackled with various
preparations.[19]

Other common remedies were bleeding (for liver complaints) and cupping—
Roland was subjected to *vesicatoires* on his legs for his recurrent ulcers and erysipi-
las. There were Epsom salts for indigestion, quinine for headaches and fever, and
rhubarb for the stomach. 'Cataplasms', i.e. linseed poultices, were common for
chest complaints and not just the chest: Marie-Jeanne wrote from Paris: 'I embrace
you with all my heart. Don't forget the poultice for your backside, I implore you,
it's very important.'[20]

Certain medicines worked well. Bread and garlic settled Eudora's stomach—
only 'I almost faint every time she kisses me!'[21] One night, Mme Roland reported,
'I slept well thanks to the opium ordered by the doctor. Three grains were used to
make me four pills.' She took a 'calming bowl' every night after that. 'I can't tell
you what a lovely feeling that was. After increasing the dose of opium, it was reduced so that finally I could do without it [...] I am no longer surprised at the
common use of opium by a people enervated by ease, idleness and boredom,' she
concluded.[22]

Traditional remedies were not always enough. The 1780s was a time of hesita-
tion over smallpox inoculation. The safer method of vaccination had yet to become
established, and the preventive measure of the day meant injecting smallpox from
a lesion. The Rolands agonized over it for Eudora:

> We are trying to decide whether to have her inoculated. [...] If it was for a stranger,
> I would be in favour, since it seems the probability lies that way, but I would never
> forgive myself if my child was to be one of the exceptions. If she were to be a victim,
> I would prefer it was the effect of a natural cause than my doing.

Evidently they decided against; Eudora caught smallpox in her teens, and was
quite badly disfigured.[23]

Another fashionable topic was Mesmerism, the craze sweeping through France.[24]
It was based on the idea that the cosmos was bathed in a universal fluid of electric-
ity and animal magnetism. Mesmer himself was in Paris when Mme Roland visited
in 1784.[25] Their family doctor in Amiens, d'Hervillez, was an enthusiast, and held
sessions of the *baquet magnétique* attended by Roland, a fan despite his usual

---

[18] Ibid., 25 August 1783.
[19] Vermifuges were often based on wormwood. Cf. *Corr.*, II, p. 15, 11 June 1788, to Bosc: 'Please
send *huile empyreumatique* against worms'; cf. *Corr.*, I, p. 172; Brockliss and Jones (1997), pp. 565 ff.
[20] *Corr.*, I, pp. 300–1, 25 March 1784.
[21] *Corr.*, I, p. 602, 21 May 1786.
[22] *Avis*, 1782; cf. *Corr.*, I, p. 82, 23 December 1781.
[23] *Corr.*, II, 6 April 1788; Brockliss and Jones (1997), pp. 471 ff. The king and queen had their
children inoculated in the 1770s.
[24] Brockliss and Jones (1997), pp. 784 ff.; See Gillispie (1980), pp. 280 ff., 788.
[25] *Corr.*, I, p. 336: 'people are talking a lot about M. Mesmer'.

scepticism. 'Has the magnetism helped you digest better and get to sleep?' his wife inquired.[26] Lanthenas even wondered about buying 'the secret' for 25 *louis* but thought better of it.[27]

In short, this was an ordinary, moderately-enlightened, health-conscious family, touched by the major controversies of the time, yet doing like most people—calling the doctor when they were worried, trusting to traditional medicine, but expressing scepticism when it didn't work.

QUIET LIFE, COUNTRY LIFE

After their move to the Beaujolais in 1784, the Rolands settled into a pattern of life apparently lacking in ambition. There was no prospect of career change, since Roland had no protectors in Paris, and regarded himself as in 'semi-disgrace'. Pipe-dreams of going to America, a sort of promised land, were ruled out by his age. He travelled on his rounds, and his intellectual interests were satisfied by his membership of the Académie de Lyon, the dictionary, and correspondence. The family paid occasional visits to Roland's *pied-à-terre* in Lyon, a flat in the city centre.[28] They were usually at Le Clos for the wine and fruit harvest, but much of their time was spent in Villefranche, with the increasingly difficult Mme de la Platière senior, and the intermittently amiable Dominique. Mme Roland gave Bosc a picture of her daily round:

> These days I am being a housewife above all […] My brother-in-law wanted me to take over running the household, since his mother has not done so for many years now, and he is tired of doing it himself or leaving it to the servants. First thing on rising, I see to my child and my husband. I hear the child read, and make breakfast for them both. Then I leave them together in the study or if the *papa* is away, I leave the child there with the maid, and I go to check everything in the house from the cellar to the attic: fruit, wine, linen, and other details all require some attention daily. If I have time before *le dîner*—note that we dine at midday and one must look a bit presentable, because there might be visitors, since *Maman* likes to entertain—I spend it in the study working on the research I have always shared with my *bon ami*.
>
> After dinner we spend time all together, and I usually stay with my mother-in-law until she has other company. I do some sewing. […] As soon as I am free I go back to the study to start or continue some writing; but in the evening the good brother [Dominique] arrives. We read [aloud] the papers or something better; sometimes some gentlemen come round; if I am not doing the reading, I sew modestly while listening. […] I pay outside visits only when absolutely necessary, and have been out very little lately, just walking with my husband and child after dinner.[29]

As this suggests, life in Villefranche could feel rather stifling. On the other hand, the family base helped them keep their expenses within their modest

---

[26] *Corr.*, I, pp. 328 and 352, Mme Roland seems to have tried it too: ibid., p. 427, 21 May 1784.
[27] *Corr.*, II, p. 690.
[28] Maison Collomb, place de la Charité, where they all stayed in 1785; in 17, he moved to the quai Monsieur—today quai de la Charité, *Corr.*, I, p. 654.
[29] 23 March 1785, *Corr.*, I, p. 505.

income. Mme Roland calculated that living in Lyon would have cost a fortune.[30]

As for the farm, when the couple started to take responsibility for Le Clos, from the mid-1780s, they embarked enthusiastically on a way of life new to both of them: that of country landowners, albeit of a very small estate and for a few months a year. The farmhouse was rather basic and they carried out some alterations. Roland ordered stones for a terrace and planted an avenue of mulberry trees in 1788 (his brother had chopped down almost all the other trees). The vineyards were farmed by tenants, but the owners supervised the wine harvest in autumn. Marie-Jeanne kept chickens and rabbits, grew and bottled fruit. It was very different from the small town garden in Amiens. In October 1785, she wrote to Bosc:

> I haven't held a pen for month. I am making dried pears (*poires tapées*) which will be delicious, and we are drying raisins and prunes; we're doing a big wash, and dealing with the linen; we eat lunch accompanied by white wine; then we have a siesta lying on the grass; we walk round following the grape-pickers, stopping in the woods or in the fields; we pull down walnuts, and all the winter fruits which we have spread out in the barns, and after eating, we will all go out to pick the almonds.[31]

Figure 3. Le Clos la Platière: the Rolands' farm in the Beaujolais. Reproduced from Mrs Pope-Hennessy (Una Birch) *Madame Roland, a Study in Revolution* (London, Nisbet & Co., 1917). Photo from the author's collection.

---

[30] See *Corr.*, I, p. 664, letter of 13 January 1787, for a full set of accounts, original in BNF MSS 6239.
[31] *Corr.*, I, p. 539, 12 October 1785; Kermina (1976), pp. 99 ff., describes the inside of the house.

Autumn letters in later years repeated the scene with variations. In the Beaujolais, both the Rolands were out and about locally. We don't often think of them as on horseback, but Roland had for years been obliged to travel on country roads, with a horse as the only possible transport. To reach Le Clos, one had to ride either a horse or a donkey, so Mme Roland had to get used to it. Jean-Marie described to Bosc in September 1786, an accident that could have been worse, on the way from Villefranche:

> Mother and daughter were tied together on a donkey, and almost broke their necks. The animal bolted, the child panicked, and they all fell in the stream that our caravan was travelling along. I was on horseback behind them: I leapt down, but it took time to lift them upright, untie the sodden silk ribbon which was tightly knotted, while the child was screaming her head off. The mother has sprained her wrist and was bruised all over and wet through: there were big stones in the stream bed and about a foot of water.

Luckily, villagers came to their aid, Marie-Jeanne, wrapped in her husband's overcoat, was helped to a fireside, and they recovered there before going on.[32]

Mme Roland at first ventured only to ride a donkey, but later took to horseback, and told her husband, 'I find it very pleasant and good for me', but, she added, the time must be well-chosen, for 'in the eight to ten days before my periods, it is out of bounds, because it hastens their return and makes them more abundant, which is exhausting'.[33] Nevertheless, during the Revolution, she rode out alone to Le Clos during the Great Fear (see Chapter 11), and the following year rode alone on horseback from Villefranche to Lyon (about five hours each way), to check on the political situation. She also went about the countryside, applying herbal remedies as 'the apothecary of the neighbourhood', sometimes taking Lanthenas, who was called upon to give his medical services gratis to local villagers.[34]

By 1788, the Rolands seemed resigned to a future of cultivating their garden, like Candide and his companions: Marie-Jeanne wrote, sincerely or not, to their Swiss friend Lavater, that in Le Clos:

> We occupy ourselves fixing up the property for our child; we supervise the agricultural work here, which is so pleasant for healthy souls, and we maintain our very simple tastes. Since both of us have been fashioned by bad experiences in the past [...], we find in this modest and honorable existence, Horace's *aura mediocritas,* and we compensate by warmth of feeling for anything we might be missing. When you live in the country, especially in these wine-growing areas where the people are so poor, you think of yourself as having too much comfort, yet not enough means [to help] these people who need so much.[35]

Paris seemed a long way off.

---

[32] See Perroud, *Corr.,* II, p. 151, note. Cf. ibid., I, p. 597, for a similar journey with Eudora in the basket on the donkey, and oxen for baggage, 12 May 1786.

[33] *Corr.,* II, p. 97, 20 November 1790.

[34] Cf. Brockliss and Jones (1997), p. 550, and Sussman (1982), p. 82.

[35] *Corr.,* II, p. 22, 7 July 1788. An 'elegant sufficiency', to quote Thomson.

PART III

REVOLUTION:
BLISS TO BE ALIVE
1789–1791

11

1789: Watching from Lyon

I kept company with you Monsieur, in your journeying in America; my Crèvecoeur in my hand, I often envied your circumstances. How many times did I cry out, 'if I were twenty years younger, that's where I would be too!' but when one is as near the age of sixty as I [he was just fifty-five] the flesh is not as willing as the spirit. I do, it is true, see a revolution brewing here among us; but I also see intrigue getting the upper hand, the cabal winning, and the nation soon under the thumb of men who will dishonour it and whom she despises.

Jean-Marie Roland to Brissot, 30 March 1789.[1]

If my excellent *ami* had been a few years younger, America would already have received us. We regret this promised land less, now that we can hope for a *patrie* [= fatherland worth loving]. The Revolution, imperfect though it is, has changed the face of France. It is developing a character for the country, where we had none, it is offering to truth a free passage, from which the lovers of truth can benefit.

Marie-Jeanne Roland to Brissot, 16 March 1790.[2]

For this provincial couple, the Revolution of 1789 came as a breathtaking surprise. When considering the background of future revolutionaries, biographers wonder whether signs of their political views could be detected earlier. Roger Chartier has argued that, in a sense, the Revolution created the Enlightenment retrospectively, rather than the other way round.[3] From all that has gone before, we can see that the Rolands had links to a range of different (sometimes contradictory) intellectual trends and circles: non-belief in revealed religion, freemasonry, Mesmerism, provincial academies, Parisian scientists, the Panckoucke publishing circle. Their reading was eclectic, but included Montesquieu, Voltaire, and Rousseau. Jean-Marie Roland was an enthusiastic admirer of the Trudaines and Turgot. This puts them squarely into a category of educated people in the late ancien régime, in touch with ideas of reform—economic, scientific, and philosophical. They did not expect political change in their lifetimes, but they were

---

[1] Quoted Brissot (1912), I, p. 220. Crèvecoeur's *Lettres d'un cultivateur américain* (1784, 2nd edn 1787) was an 'Arcadian description of life in the United States', *Corr.*, II, p. 34, note.
[2] 16 March 1790, *Corr.*, II, p. 80. Full text AN, 446 AP, 8/75, quoted in *Colloque Roland* (1990), pp. 65–6.
[3] Chartier (1990) esp. postface.

aware of inequalities and hardships. What was more, they were closely connected—and these links grew stronger over time, mutating into political ties—
with a circle of people who exchanged ideas and information on scientific and
scholarly topics. Nathan Perl-Rosenthal's recent path-breaking thesis has revealed
the origins of their later networks in their correspondence in the 1780s.[4]

We have a window into the couple's more intimate feelings through their private
letters. From these—and Jean-Marie Roland's public writings—we can sense a general political consciousness, reflected in contempt for the royal court, resentment at
privilege, and genuine concern for fellow-beings who were worse off than themselves—feelings without much outlet except for good works around Le Clos. Materially, all things considered, they were not badly off. But they had occasion to feel
undervalued, towards the end of Roland's chequered career in public service, and
always remained 'outsiders' in Villefranche.[5] In Lyon, as Maurice Garden writes:

> Doctors, artists, public servants, such as Roland de la Platière, an inspector of manufac-
> tures, entrepreneurs of urban renewal [...] despite all being members of the Académie des
> Sciences, Belles-Lettres and Arts, were in a sense marginal to real society, [...] removed
> from what constituted the economic power of the Lyonnais metropolis. This breach
> between intellectual elites and the merchant bourgeoisie [was] often remarked on.[6]

Roland had not even studied at the Jesuit college in Lyon, like his fellow-
academicians.

Although Marie-Jeanne had promised he could carry out his work 'in your slippers', Roland was hyperactive at first, regularly commuting to Lyon. In the early
days, he toured the surrounding region on horseback. (His wife worried about
wolves.) In 1786, he also made a trip to northern France, via Paris, Amiens, Rouen,
and Dieppe. In 1787, he visited the Dauphiné Alps with his brother Pierre, then
all four of them: Pierre, Marie-Jeanne, Eudora, and Jean-Marie Roland, made the
month-long trip to Switzerland.[7] Whenever he was at home, Roland—and his
wife—worked on the dictionary or on academy topics.

A full member of the Académie de Lyon by 1785, the following year, he organ-
ized its competition for innovation in printing on silk.[8] He also joined a Masonic
Lodge, and the Société d'agriculture, where he knew some of the members better.[9]
Lyon offered more like-minded people than Villefranche. One contact was Luc-
Antoine Donin [Rosière] de Champagneux (1744–1807), the lawyer from Bour-
going who played a large part in the Rolands' life, and had moved to Lyon in 1785.[10]

---

[4] Perl-Rosenthal (2011) chapter 6: Bosc, Lanthenas, Bancal, and Brissot were all linked in the late 1780s.
[5] Le Guin (1966), p. 62, quotes a hostile source, Guillon de Montléon (1824).
[6] Garden (1972), p. 543, Chartier (1969).
[7] July–August 1787, Geneva, Berne, Lucerne, Zurich, Basle, etc.
[8] Chartier (1969), pp. 236–7; in 1786, Roland expressed hostility to the guild system, ibid., pp. 245–6.
[9] Ibid., pp. 178 ff.
[10] On Champagneux, Feuga (1991); *Colloque Roland* (1990), pp. 123–64: as mayor of Bourgoing in 1777, Champagneux witnessed Jean-Jacques Rousseau's 'wedding', ibid., p. 126, cf. *Corr.*, NS, II, p. 60, 1777.

Through the Société philanthropique, the Rolands met Pierre-Charles Blot, a friend of Brissot.[11] Then there was Benjamin Frossard, the Protestant pastor, to whose family they entrusted Eudora for weeks on end, and through whom they met Arthur Young in December 1789. Young valued meeting Roland ('somewhat advanced in life, he has a very young and beautiful wife') and they discussed manufacturing, agriculture, and commerce, differing only about the Anglo-French trade treaty.[12] Another contact was Antoine-François Delandine—later a deputy for the Third Estate for the Forez—as we know from the brief contretemps over Mme Roland's Swiss travel journal.[13]

Although unsympathetic to Lyon's hierarchical economic structures, Roland was thoroughly familiar with them. In 1780, Lyon was the second largest city in France with a population of 150,000. Its economic life was dominated by silk, since it had held the exclusive privilege for centuries. Manufacture was concentrated in the institution collectively known as the Grande Fabrique, employing thousands of workers.[14] The silk industry was tightly regulated and controlled by about 400 super-rich merchants, the *marchands-fabricants*. It cost a high fee to join the governing body, which could dictate terms to the master-weavers. There was effectively a gulf between the leading merchants on one hand, and all the artisans on the other—whether masters with their own workshops, journeymen, or apprentices. But even the merchants were not at the pinnacle of the social hierarchy, which was dominated by the ruling Consulat or local council, 'drawn from a narrow stratum of established and exceptional wealth'.[15] From this class—in practice, an oligarchy of 'about twelve families'—were elected the *échevins,* rich city councillors ennobled after two years' *échevinage.* Their origins and wealth lay in commerce, but they aimed to distinguish themselves from the commercial class: 'the profits of trade have multiplied in our walls new nobles, the privileged, the rich, or those who hope to become so', as Mme Roland wrote to a friend, unburdening 'my poor heart about what you have to suffer in this town'.[16]

During the 1780s, Lyon's manufacturing went into crisis. Its multiple causes included the collapse of the French luxury market as English cotton fabrics were imported to suit the new 'simple' tastes at Marie-Antoinette's court. Silk went out of fashion, as French women of means adopted fine lawn dresses, and their husbands lighter jackets. In 1786, a strike movement, beginning with Lyon's hatters and spreading to weavers, resulted in violent disturbances and reprisals—the 'two-sous revolt'.[17] 1787 and 1788 were 'the worst years so far', with looms out of action and thousands out of work. The 1789 *cahiers* of the Third Estate claimed that

[11] Pierre-Charles Blot (1754–?) controller of the *marc d'or et d'argent* in Lyon; *Corr.*, II, pp. 2 note and 120; Feuga (1991), p. 58.

[12] Young (1890), p. 284; *Corr.*, II, p. 224, note, and 726, Appendix O.

[13] Ibid., pp. 10–12 and 235, letters in *Corr.*, NS, II, pp. 504 ff.

[14] Wahl (1894), p. 5: 14,777 looms, 58,500 workers. *Maîtres-marchands* owned most of the real estate in the city too, ibid., p. 7.

[15] Garden (1972), p. 283.

[16] To Mme Delandine, 27 December 1789, *Corr.*, NS, II, supplement, p. 520; see Wahl (1894) p. 17, Edmonds (1990) pp. 9–17, Hanson (2003).

[17] Benoît (1999), pp. 24 ff.; Garden (1972), p. 590; Francesco (1994).

Lyon's industries were 'threatened with total ruin'.[18] While the richest merchants did not suffer personally, unemployed workers depended on charity, the only relief available under the ancien régime.

In March 1787, Roland read a paper to the Académie outlining his remedies for the city's woes. Entitled *Des causes de la décadence du commerce et de la dépopulation de la ville de Lyon*, this won him no friends in commercial circles.[19] Predictably, the disciple of Trudaine and Turgot argued for relaxation of the tight regulation of the Grande Fabrique. Yes, the market had collapsed for valuable silk fabrics, but Lyon had failed to diversify into other kinds of textile production. He criticized rules controlling entry to the artisan class—high admission fees, exclusive recruitment, nepotism, restrictions on apprentices, the ban until recently on women's work, refusal to allow rural looms. In short:

> absurd laws, prejudiced and self-interested authorities, management vitiated by its nature and vexatious in its effects, which has enriched private men, impoverished the people, instituted enormous luxury and untrammeled debauchery, created a rentier class, and ruined manufacturing. It has forced those who could just squeeze a living to remain unmarried, while those with nothing, the workers, who live by their hands' daily labour, have had to leave the city. Over the last thirty years the Lyon population has lost 30,000 from this class.[20]

As appears from this rhetoric, Roland's approach to what would today be called 'economic liberalism' was, in his mind at least, associated with rescuing the workers from destitution. The greatest burden on the workers' cost of living, he declared, was the *octrois*—excise duties on essential goods entering the city, such as firewood, coal, and foodstuffs. These should be reduced, so that people could live here as cheaply as in the countryside. He well knew, of course, that the city's finance depended on these taxes. To compensate, 'place a levy on luxury goods: horses, carriages, lackeys and coachmen'. If this drove the rich into the countryside, all the better: 'those who own the land have deserted it'. Furthermore, Lyon had many fine houses, let at exorbitant rents—a tax on these would be only fair. The fortunes of many landlords had originally come from silk, so they should repay some of this wealth to restore the city's industry. To those who claimed that they gave to charity, Roland's response was that charity was not enough—receiving pay for not working made the worker lose his skills and the will to work. Better to provide the conditions for artisans to earn their living. (In practice, however, he organized the Société philanthropique in Villefranche, and subscribed to the Lyon equivalent, run by Champagneux among others in 1789, to relieve distress.)[21]

---

[18] Edmonds (1990), p. 14; 'the caprices of fashion have devastated our manufactures: a large and interesting class of useful workmen is experiencing the horrors of poverty and must rely on public charity', Lyon *cahiers de doléance*, quoted Benoît (1999) p. 27.

[19] Manuscript in Mme Roland's writing, kindly located by the librarian of the Académie de Lyon; cf. Edmonds (1990), p. 27.

[20] ibid., p. 25.

[21] Cf. Mme Roland to Mme Delandine, 27 December 1789, on philanthropy: people do it for the wrong motives, but 'the poor are helped, and that's the main thing'. *Corr.*, NS, II, supplement, p. 520.

Roland's hard-hitting analysis, expressed with his usual bluntness, marked him out as a would-be economic and social reformer. Counter-pamphlets circulated in Lyon, defending the merchant class, and accusing him of personal ambition. As distinct from his economic views, we have little evidence about the Rolands' political views before 1788. The few letters between the couple in the late 1780s suggest that they regarded Paris and the king's ministers primarily as the source of power over Jean-Marie's career. When in spring 1787, Trudaine's nephew was a stop-gap appointment between Calonne and Brienne, Roland even hoped to influence policy on manufacturing. However, Brienne almost immediately ordered a reorganization of the inspection service, and the signs were that the corps would soon be abolished—as, indeed, it was during the Revolution.[22]

But Jean-Marie Roland corresponds, at least in part, to the male bourgeois 'revolutionary elite' during the late 1780s, described by David Garrioch: men who owed their position to work, rather than inheritance, and who favoured the opening up of trade, the suppression of outdated rules, greater help for the poor, combined with a cultural revulsion against the court, corruption, and inherited privilege. Their views often translated into a kind of puritanism of daily life, with the stress on simplicity, modesty of dress and lifestyle, and a strong feeling of moral superiority. We can easily fit Roland into this identikit portrait, but events in Lyon would show that, as a sharp-tongued and enthusiastic supporter of the Third Estate, he went much further in public than most 'respectable' reformers wanted, particularly in his support for 'the people' and the workers in Lyon. He was becoming identified as a dangerous and outspoken radical. His wife, who was also affected by the poverty she had seen in the Beaujolais villages, shared his views about the glaring class division of the city.

Many of Jean-Marie's letters from this time appear to have been lost.[23] Some survive from his wife, but in 1788 she was taking only sporadic interest in national events, such as the recall of Necker in August ('the Necker is Controller-General!'), although she expressed initial support for the *parlements*. Domestic matters like the grape-harvest and bottling fruit still preoccupied her in September, while Roland was preparing Volume III for the press. However, when the Paris Parlement disappointingly recommended using the traditional 1614 form for recalling the Estates General, she found time to write, in terminology inspired by Montesquieu:

The *parlements* are acting in an astonishing way. Should the friends of order and liberty who wanted them restored now be reduced to regretting it? We seem to have the choice simply between vegetating sadly under the rule of a single despot, or groaning under the iron rod of several despots together . . . if the abasement [*avilissement*] of the nation is less general under an aristocracy than under the despotism of an unfettered monarch, the condition of the people is sometimes harsher, and that's how it would be

---

[22] See *Corr.*, I, p. 673, note; p.713, note; BNF MSS, naf 9534, fol 197–8; cf. *Dictionnaire*, II, errata and supplement, pp. 143–4, glossary, pp. 131–2.; *Corr.*, II, p. 4, to Bosc, 2 March 1788, on Brienne.
[23] The Alfred Morrison collection once held 124 letters by Roland, 80 by Mme Roland. Jean-Marie's letters to Bosc were as enthusiastic as his wife's, Perroud (*Corr.*, II, p. 675).

with us, where the people with privileges are everything and where the most numerous class is accounted almost nothing ['*presque zéro*'].[24]

As late as November, she was still wistfully referring to America, and enquiring with interest about the 'society for the emancipation of the negroes', i.e. the Société des amis des noirs, in which Brissot, Bosc, and Lanthenas were all active. Lanthenas was, even at this stage, thinking of crossing the Atlantic.[25]

Early in 1789, Roland, as a member of the Société d'agriculture, had some input as an adviser into the *cahier de doléances* of the Third Estate in Lyon (it reflects many of his views), but in March he was still seeing his glossary through the printers.[26] Then, in June, he was struck down by a serious illness, perhaps pneumonia, described as a 'fluxion de poitrine et fièvre bilieuse putride', and for three weeks was in a desperate state, nursed through it by his wife. He was unwell for weeks afterwards.[27]

As a result, both Rolands were preoccupied with domestic troubles when the Revolution broke out. Were they in Lyon in early July, for the first riots against the *octroi*, and an attack on the 'local Bastille', Pierre-Scize, when several Swiss soldiers were killed? No comment survives. The incidents led to the formation of a bourgeois *corps volontaire* to defend property, and marked out the *octroi* as a future bone of contention.[28] From Lyon, Villefranche, or Le Clos, the Rolands followed events in Versailles and Paris—the sessions of the Estates General, the fall of Necker, the storming of the Bastille—but only at a remove, through the newspapers and letters from their friends. Yet from this time on, the tenor of all the surviving correspondence changes dramatically—what Timothy Tackett has referred to as the 'Revolution of the mind' of summer 1789. Nathan Perl-Rosenthal comments that the correspondence of the Roland circle underwent a 'transformation such that one would be hard-pressed, given only the text of the letters, to say that they were written by the same people'.[29]

Mme Roland later wrote: 'Both of us having strong feelings, being proud and active, Roland and I could not stop talking about the reform of the abuses which had so often enraged us, we devised projects, planned campaigns and predicted events'.[30] A new, determined tone appears in the letters almost overnight, as they bombarded their Paris friends with requests for news (the latter had witnessed some of the most dramatic episodes and were quickly becoming politicized themselves).[31] Roland complained vehemently to Bosc about Villefranche: 'this rotten

[24] To Bosc, 8 October 1788, *Corr.*, II, p. 30.

[25] Ibid., pp. 33–4, note: Roland to Bosc, 14 November 1788, original in Morrison Collection.

[26] To Brissot; PS by Mme Roland: if she was in 'Orange County' she would be 'spinning or weaving, instead of taking an interest in my husband's politics', Brissot (1912), p. 223.

[27] *Corr.*, II, p. 52, to Bosc, 9 June 1789.

[28] Edmonds (1990), p. 44; Benoît, (1999) pp. 27–8.

[29] Cf. Tackett (1996), p. 307 and conclusion. On 'revolutionary mentality', Lilti (2005), Hunt (2007); Perl-Rosenthal (2011) draft chapter 6.

[30] *Mém.*, p. 336.

[31] Bosc joined the Club des amis de la loi, meeting at the house of Théroigne de Méricourt, mentioned briefly as '*l'étrangère*', *Corr.*, II, pp. 83, 675, and he was one of the first Jacobins, December 1790.

hole, where I have had more lances to break, hydra heads and monsters to face than in Lyon, the vainest and most disgusting city in France for aristocratic rule'.[32]

The family suffered several bereavements during 1789: Marie-Jeanne's father died in January, from bronchitis; in September, uncle Bimont died in Vincennes. Her favourite brother-in-law, Pierre, also died that autumn. Though not unaffected by these blows, Mme Roland wrote to her friends that she had set mourning aside: it was idle to allow domestic cares to take precedence when the country was going through such turmoil. Several of her letters are lost, since a postscript to Bosc comments on assumed interference with the mails: 'I write to you by every post. [...] If this letter never reaches you, let the cowards who read it blush to learn it is from a woman, and tremble to think that she can inspire a hundred enthusiasts, who will convert millions of others' [26 July]. It would not be surprising if her missives were impounded, since she specifically referred to the royal house in the strongest terms: 'if the National Assembly does not put two illustrious heads on trial, or if some fearless Decius does not strike them down, you are all f...ed'.[33]

This was written in late July, as the Great Fear in the countryside began. With Roland still unwell, Madame Roland, as a modest property-owner, rode out to Le Clos, and wrote defiantly to Brissot:

> Everyone urges me to come and stay in town, but I have no intention of that. I have done no wrong to anyone; I don't have any feudal charts or titles; I do nothing but good for my neighbours. If they were to become ungrateful, well, *tant pis*: I would be paying for the advantages which my situation has given me over them. But I will not insult them by imagining something before it happens, and even if I should be the victim of brigands, I would not lose hope in public affairs, like those cowards who think the sky is falling in, just because a few houses have been burnt down.[34]

This was the first of a number of strongly-worded dispatches from Lyon and the Beaujolais to be published in *Le Patriote français*, the daily newspaper recently started in Paris by the Rolands' penfriend, Brissot. He described the above as written by 'a very enlightened woman, of truly energetic character, writing from Villefranche'.[35] From merely being readers, the couple now became involved in the world of revolutionary journalism, in Paris through Brissot, and in Lyon through Champagneux, who had started his own newspaper *Le Courier* [*sic*] *de Lyon* in September 1789, as a rival to the conservative *Journal de Lyon*. Its sub-title was *Résumé général des Révolutions de la France*.[36] Brissot's *Patriote* would appear continuously from 1789 until spring 1793. His friendship with the Rolands, starting back in 1787 [Chapter 6], had become warm through exchange of letters, without

---

[32] BNF MSS, naf 6241, fo 3, 16 October 1789.

[33] *Corr.* II, p. 53, to Bosc, 26 July 1789 ('*tous f...*').

[34] Ibid., II, pp. 54–5, 3 August 1789, to Brissot, *Le Patriote français*, 12 August, attributed to Mme Roland by Perroud. The Rolands thought the panic was started by brigands paid by reactionary aristocrats, *Corr.*, I., p. 54, note.

[35] 3 August, published *Le Patriote*, 12 August 1789.

[36] Wahl (1894) p. 117; Feuga (1991) pp.54 ff.: profits to the Société philanthropique; it reviewed Roland's dictionary favourably, 15 February 1790.

any physical meeting (as such relations do by email today). Their Paris friends reported that he was 'a philosopher whose simple life, sound morals, and amiable character were in no contradiction with his writing'.[37]

Brissot's life before the Revolution has been thoroughly explored by historians, without all its obscurities entirely resolved. Qualified in law, this native of Chartres, born in 1754 like Marie-Jeanne Roland, had become a journalist, an employee of the duc d'Orléans, and participant in various enterprises. Robert Darnton regarded him as a typical denizen of Grub Street, and apparently a police informer, although this view has been modified by recent research. Certainly Brissot was chronically short of money, and remained so all his life. He had spent some years in England, where he met like-minded radicals, and in the United States, where he went on business for his friend the Genevan financier Etienne Clavière.[38] He was even imprisoned in the Bastille on what were probably false charges of slandering Marie-Antoinette in an English scandal-sheet.[39]

Mme Roland later described her writing for the *Patriote* as follows:

> Brissot wrote many articles at that time which were sent to us, and he began his newspaper; we communicated all our ideas to him. Since *I was usually the one* who handled this correspondence, I found the task all the more enjoyable in the circumstances. My letters, written with passion, quite pleased Brissot, who often inserted extracts from them in his paper, where I rediscovered them with pleasure. These contacts, becoming frequent, created friendship between us; over eighteen months went by and we treated each other as old friends, without ever having met.[40]

Marie-Jeanne Roland, so opposed to publishing even an innocuous travel journal under her own name, effectively became, for a while, part of a constellation of journalists linked by a common cause. Neither of the Rolands signed articles for Brissot's paper, but the editor made it clear that some were from a woman who can only be Mme Roland—referring to her occasionally as 'a Roman woman', which must have pleased her. She also contributed to Champagneux's *Courier*: her revolutionary journalism puts her among the very few women who had such opportunities to publish.

Her private letters suggest that she was mentally reconstructing herself as a staunch Roman (or Spartan) matron, urging resolution on her 'sons' or younger 'brothers', Bosc and Lanthenas. One letter of 26 July 1789 to Bosc specifically says '*Vous n'êtes que des enfants* = You are mere children'. Another remarkable letter, not printed at the time, was written in early October 1789 approximately (after her uncle's death in September, and before news reached her of the women's march on Versailles). It included a set of recommendations: the Constituent Assembly should form a national fund, so that the court did not have all the resources; establish a

---

[37] *Mém.*, pp. 62 ff.

[38] Cf. Whatmore (1996).

[39] Brissot remains elusive, partly because of difficult access to his papers. See Darnton (1982); Burrows (2003) for a recent re-assessment; Gueniffey (1991), pp. 444–5, notes that judgements on Brissot during the Revolution often hark back to the pre-revolutionary period. Cf. Ellery (1970), Huart (1986), Loft (2002).

[40] *Mém.*, p. 62, my italics. Her letters to Brissot, AN, 446 AP, not all in *Corr.*

subsistence committee; have the provinces send supplies to Paris; stop the court bringing in foreign troops; mobilize volunteers; and 'you'—presumably the people—should go to fetch the deputies from Versailles and bring them to Paris. She signed off with: 'long live the people and death to tyrants!' Evidently, she was thinking along the same lines as the *dames des Halles*, the market women of Paris, who forced the royal family (and thus the Assembly) back to Paris, and whose immediate concern was the price of bread.[41]

Perroud's scrutiny of *Le Patriote* positively identified only five articles by Mme Roland,[42] but reports from Lyon could have been written by either of the Rolands, Champagneux, or Blot. He concluded that between July 1789 and March 1792, over a hundred articles were written by or concerned the Rolands and their 'circle', including Lanthenas, Bosc, and Bancal in Paris. The published versions accompanied a two-way traffic of unpublished correspondence between all these people. The Rolands were thus in touch, by post, with political observers and participants in Paris, some of whom they had never met face-to-face. Jean-Henri Bancal [des Issarts](1750–1826), for instance, mentioned earlier, did not meet the Rolands until the summer of 1790, but would soon be drawn into their orbit. A well-to-do lawyer from Clermont-Ferrand, actively involved in the events of 14 July in Paris, he knew Brissot and Lanthenas through the Société des amis des noirs, 'Friends of Black People'. All the Paris-based members of the circle met frequently in late 1789, and Bosc, Creuzé-Latouche, and Bancal had cemented their friendship by botanical expeditions out to Montmorency.[43]

Brissot himself reported in *Le Patriote* on Jean-Marie Roland's activities as pamphleteer and speaker in Lyon (on salt tax, tithes, local elections, his agenda for the town council, etc.). He referred to Roland's public role in glowing terms: 'A courageous writer who spoke the language of truth under the regime of ministerial despotism'; 'firm and virtuous character'; 'this valuable man' and 'enlightened citizen'; someone of 'talents, energy and reputation', and so on.[44] Parisian readers would therefore have had their attention drawn to the 'celebrated and ardent M. Roland' of Lyon, although they probably did not realize from the descriptions that he was rather advanced in years. Lyon elites did know him: his writings were seen as divisive, and Brissot's recommendations were two-edged when, in the winter of 1789–1790, Roland became involved in the municipal politics that were to dominate his life for the next two years. From observers and commentators, but still essentially onlookers, the Rolands were to be drawn into more practical participation.

---

[41] *Corr.*, II, pp. 65–8.

[42] Perroud (1898): Feuga (1991), p. 57.

[43] On Bancal, Mège (1888); *Corr.*, II, Appendix Q, pp. 736 ff. Bancal was instrumental in the creation of Puy-de-Dôme *département*, and joined the Jacobin Club. Perl-Rosenthal (2011), chapters 6 and 7.

[44] *Le Patriote français*, 25 February, 24 May, 26 August, 25 November 1790, etc.

12

1790: Joining the Municipal Revolution

> Our luck has turned: today there is hope that the party with good citizens
> ['will triumph?' word lost] over all manoeuvres and make a wise and patriotic
> choice, ensuring the tranquillity of this fine city and the happiness of its many
> inhabitants.
>
> Marie-Jeanne Roland, undated fragment, 1790.

In 1790, Jean-Marie Roland was—or was perceived as—a prominent actor in Lyon city politics, so much so that the municipal council came later to be referred to as 'Rolandin'. This chapter traces his emergence as a key player. Marie-Jeanne could only watch, but was concerned with every twist and turn of local matters. The Rolands' horizon, despite correspondence with their Parisian friends, remained resolutely local: they hoped even unpromising Lyon could be 'regenerated' for the new age. However, the old *consulat* had been maintained at first—there was no immediate 'municipal revolution'. *Patriotes,* as reformers were known, were in the minority and already detecting (not without reason) forces of counter-revolution. Lyon was the pinpointed location for two projected royalist plots in 1789–1790, linked to the presence of the king's brothers in Piedmont. Neither came to anything, but they were straws in the wind.[1]

When, late in 1789, the Constituent Assembly sent instructions for municipal councils to be elected by active citizens, Lyon set a high property qualification both for eligibility and the suffrage: three *livres* tax liability for voters, ten for candidates.[2] It did not go unchallenged. This issue, plus confrontation over the *corps volontaire,* led to a popular uprising on 7 February 1790, a *journée* that 'defeated the efforts that the propertied classes had been making since 1789 to maintain a monopoly of armed force'.[3] Lyon's 'municipal revolution' had arrived. The authorities surrendered, allowing the national guard to replace the *corps*; the mayor, Imbert, was forced to flee; and the suffrage was broadened by reducing the qualification on 17 February, an apparent victory for the patriots. We can perhaps date to this week that fragment of Mme Roland's, expressing optimism and pleasure: 'our luck has turned'.[4]

---

[1] Wahl (1894); Edmonds (1990). On Roland as municipal councillor, Le Guin (1966), pp. 62–71.

[2] Wahl (1894), pp. 123–5.

[3] Edmonds (1990), p. 51; Wahl (1894), p. 17.

[4] Brissot papers, AN, 446 AP (8), 12/79, dating tentative.

But *patriotes* like Roland would now be marked men. As Edmonds puts it: 'No matter how much and how sincerely the *patriotes* protested their horror at the *jour funeste du 7 février*, the logic of their position as supporters of the Revolution made them its main beneficiaries, and in some eyes guilty by association with the objectives of the insurgents, [... isolating them] from the rest of the propertied classes.'[5] From everything we know about Roland up to this point, we can identify him as an enthusiastic supporter of the Revolution, convinced that he was both morally and materially right. But he was an unlikely leader of men, let alone a firebrand, and none of his *published* writings had ever endorsed civil disorder, or approved it retrospectively. He was certainly no great public speaker. Undermined by a weak chest, he later had to have his speeches read for him. He said himself that 'with a not very strong voice and with eyes that need artificial help', i.e. spectacles, he had no aptitude for a public career.

In January 1790, he had produced a pamphlet with the not-so-modest title: 'The Lyon municipal council: a glimpse of the work that should be done'. This declared notably:

> I'm not afraid to say so, Lyon needs a total regeneration of its behaviour [*les mœurs*]; and only with the help of a large number of zealous people, will she achieve this [...] The revolution has happened. It is irrevocable: and the good of all, even of those persons who are not inclined to approve of it, requires that everyone should help to further its good consequences.

Among his recommendations was a call for openness. A clear statement of public accounts should be prepared, to educate the people as taxpayers. 'Mystery is favourable only to abuse.' He repeated his remarks about inequality between rich and poor, outlined six committees that would be necessary to divide up the city's responsibilities, and called for freedom of industry, the abolition of the *octroi*, a reduction in excise duties on wine (!); and for council sessions to be public, like the National Assembly.[6]

Was this a bid for election? Roland later said that he was persuaded into office by people spontaneously proposing his name. The couple was in Lyon from February to early April 1790, leaving Eudora in the convent of Notre Dame de la Visitation in Villefranche.[7] The imminent elections must have been one reason, although Roland claimed other concerns: 'I have been much employed these recent days by the Société philanthropique: assemblies, committees, addresses to the king and queen, etc.'[8] He had addressed the Society just *before* 7 February, in terms that could hardly be called incendiary: arguing that the solution to social conflict lay in 'enlightened self-interest expressed through philanthropy on the

---

[5] Edmonds (1990), p. 2.

[6] Roland, *Municipalité de Lyon* (1790); Wahl (1894), p. 141: opinions expressed, 'as if deliberately offending his readers' sensibilities'.

[7] Where she had already been, 'among young companions whose example is useful for her', *Corr.*, II, p. 78.

[8] *Corr.*, II, p. 84, note, Roland to Bosc.

part of the rich, and submission to the law and economic necessity by the poor'.[9]

Brissot praised Roland extravagantly in the *Patriote* (18 February), appearing to call for his election to 'a distinguished place in that city', which needed 'men who understand trade and manufacture'.[10] This puff did more harm than good, provoking a flurry of anti-Roland pamphlets. Rumours circulated that Brissot—that inflammatory Parisian journalist—was Mme Roland's brother.[11] The Rolands reacted hastily, explaining that this unwanted publicity had resulted in their first taste of 'calumny', a word to be come very familiar. Some of these early attacks were *ad hominem*. One of the milder ones mocked Roland's intellectual pretentions: 'Quite the walking encyclopedia, aren't you? When you're on the town council, they'll be able to sell off the library, since you're the equivalent of all the books.' It unkindly mentioned his 'skinny legs still bearing the marks of bleeding', glimpsed when he was on guard on Mardi Gras. However, its main thrust was to challenge his views on the city's merchant elite, and support for 'illiterate journeymen'.[12]

Perhaps Roland genuinely intended to stay on the sidelines. Mme Roland, while hoping the people would be 'just and sensible and choose good administrators', also claimed: 'we wish to have no part in the nominations' to local office.[13] Her husband certainly did not campaign 'in the taverns', as his enemies maliciously said. However, given his determination via his pamphlet to have some input to the council's work, it's not impossible he was hoping for a surge in his favour. In March, in Champagneux's *Courier*, he ostentatiously defended both *le peuple* and the rule of law:

> The people want only justice; the centuries have proved how long they will wait for it. It is also necessary that they have peace, which is today the means of establishing and vindicating laws from which will come the people's happiness; troubles are only advantageous to the people's enemies…Law speaks for the people; it stretches its shield over them.[14]

LYON'S ELECTIONS

The local elections proceeded by stages, first for the mayor. A local politician of moderate views, Palerne de Savy (a distant connection of the Roland family) won with a huge majority in early March. Then began the laborious process in a series of local assemblies ('un travail de Pénélope'—Mme Roland, 20 March) of

---

[9] Edmonds (1990), p. 56, address printed in *Courier de Lyon*, 6 February 1790, Cf. Roland to Bosc (previous note) and Mme Roland's letter of 20 March 1790.
[10] *Le Patriote français*, 18 February 1790; Roland asked him not to continue.
[11] Mme Roland, 16 March to Brissot, AN 446 AP, 8/75: 'they do me the honour of believing me your sister'.
[12] BM Lyon, Fonds Coste 352348, dated 5 April: Lettre à M. R. de la P. sur sa brochure on the municipalité, p. 7.
[13] Mme Roland to Bosc, fragment in *Corr.*, II, p. 83, 18 February 1790; 4 March to Lanthenas; Brissot papers, AN 446 AP 8 (unpublished).
[14] 6 March, printed as brochure, quoted Le Guin (1966), p. 70.

electing the rest of the council: three statutory officials, 25 regular councillors and 42 'notables' who would only attend a few meetings a year.[15] In this first experiment in broader-based local democracy, there were no candidatures or lists.[16] To his surprise (?) Roland received some 650 votes for *procureur de la commune*, one of the three officials. It wasn't enough to be elected, but it led to further accusations of ambition and rabble-rousing, snobbishly expressed: '*Procureur*? What? An *inspector of linen* occupying a rank like that? Someone who is out of his league must float in a sea of uncertainty.'[17] The 'inspector of linen' didn't take this lying down:

> They say my observations on the workers menace public tranquillity by exciting them to revolt. This claim, which I wish to reject as an error, is injurious as well as being false. Never have the people been more tranquil, because they have never been so near the possibility of hope for the reform of so many abuses.[18]

Le Patriote printed his riposte: 'My great crime was that I didn't paint the city in favourable colours...but is that my fault? The city of Lyon is immensely rich and excessively indebted, while the workers are dependent on alms.'[19]

Roland was finally elected, but as a 'notable'—patriots were more plentiful among the 42 *notables* than among the councillors. As Mme Roland put it: 'the hopes of the public are entirely with the *notables*, who have been much better chosen in terms of patriotism and values', although the restricted council was 'trying to gag them'.[20] Progressive *notables* included Bret, Vitet, and one 'new man' who was to have a powerful, indeed devastating influence on the politics of Lyon, Joseph Chalier.

Paul Hanson draws an interesting parallel between Chalier and Roland, calling them both 'outsiders' in the sense used by Lynn Hunt: Chalier (1757–1793), from a well-off background, trained with a silk-merchant, but was radicalized in Paris by participating in the storming of the Bastille and meeting Robespierre. Like Roland, he knew the silk trade well, and both men at this stage agreed that the enemy was the entrenched conservative caucus, hanging on to municipal power. The future was to see them deeply divided.[21]

The new council met in ceremony on 12 April, and organized its committees as Roland had suggested, though he had already left for Villefranche and Le Clos on 3 April, to see to the farm. The couple's divided allegiance was described by Mme Roland to Bosc:

---

[15] Wahl (1894), pp. 130–8, on the 14 December 1789 electoral law. Of nearly 16,000 active citizens, between a third and a quarter voted.

[16] Crook (1996) and Gueniffey (1993), esp. chapter 7, 'Les procédures électorales'.

[17] Anon. (1790b), *Réponse...par un citoyen patriote* = probably a merchant who detested government inspectors ('overpaid busybodies'). Possible reply to letter over his signature, *Le Patriote*, no 215, 11 March 1790, cf. AN, 446/87 AP.

[18] Le Guin (1966), pp. 69–70, see note 14 above.

[19] *Le Patriote français*, 11 March 1790.

[20] Mme Roland to Brissot, 23 April 1790, AN, 446 AP 9/76 (unpublished). Cf. Edmonds (1990), p. 53.

[21] Hanson (2003), pp. 141–2; Edmonds (1990), p. 54; *Courier*, 6 February 1790; Chalier described Lyon as an 'infâme ville', *Révolutions de Paris*, 6 February 1790.

Enough of politics! The weather is delicious…I could forget public affairs and these disputes among men, and be content to get the manor in order, look after my chickens and rabbits, and no longer think about revolutions and empires. But as soon as I am in town, the misery of the people, and the insolence of the rich reawaken my hatred of injustice and oppression. All my heart and soul is for the triumph of the great truths and the success of our regeneration.[22]

Roland returned to Lyon in early May, in the unlikely role of a public speaker, pleading in favour of open council meetings, i.e. building a public gallery:

Where does sovereignty reside? In the people. What is the law? The general will. Who can make the law? The people. In a nation too large to meet and pronounce, it does so through its representatives, freely elected.…Gentlemen [messieurs] we are the mandated delegates of the people, to watch over its interets, and run its affairs. Ought we, can we even, refuse that [the people] should be present when we are handling the most important of those affairs?[23]

From Le Clos, Mme Roland followed Lyon affairs with increasing exasperation. (When Bosc suggested they come to Paris, she replied 'how the devil do you get a *notable de Lyon* to move?') Nonetheless, she thoroughly identified herself with Roland's campaigns, writing a fiercely worded letter to Lanthenas on 30 April about the opposition to her husband's proposal for open sessions: 'our mayor is a *tartufe*, our councillors broomsticks'; the Lyon deputies in Paris (who had been applied to) were 'imbeciles'; all feared the people, and letting 'daylight' in on their doings. They were not budging on the serious question of accounts, while the people suffered. She also found time to wish the Assembly would get a move on with reforming the clergy:

I'm impatient with the whole boiling (*fatras*) of that old hierarchy of archbishops, primates, bishops, etc. Soon we will also be hanging on to canons. What a lot of useless insects (= *frelons*, lit. hornets) and theological muddlers, ambitious, sectarian, intolerant, bloodthirsty, spreading stupidity and corruption![24]

At a referendum on 17 May, a majority of active citizens supported Roland's proposal for open sessions, though the issue hung fire for material reasons.[25] However, it matched the optimistic mood, reflected in the popular Fête de la Fédération (of the National Guard) on 30 May.

Mme Roland returned to Lyon on 28 May to witness the festivities and wrote them up for Champagneux's paper, anonymously of course, having risen at five in the morning to see the fun. Her jubilant enthusiasm caught the cheerful spirit of spring 1790: 60,000 national guards and as many as 200,000 spectators from the town trooped out to the Brotteaux fields, where a huge artificial mound was topped by a statue of Liberty. With drums, trumpets, and much ceremony, preceded by the *Te Deum*, the guards pronounced the civic oath. Champagneux claimed that

---

[22] 17 May 1790 to Bosc, *Corr.*, II, pp. 88–90; ibid., Appendix O, pp. 724, ff.
[23] 1 May 1790, Edmonds (1990), pp. 54–6.
[24] 7 June 1790, *Corr.*, II, p. 93.
[25] Wahl (1894), pp. 160–1; proposal supported by Bret, Pressavin, Vitet, etc.

her article sold 60,000 copies of the *Courier*. It was syndicated to *Le Patriote*, and to Camille Desmoulins's paper, *Révolutions de France et de Brabant*.[26] The Lyon festivities are credited with inspiring the national festivities later in the summer. Mme Roland's writings were reaching well beyond Lyon, but few people knew her identity.

In June, her husband raised the looming question of the city's 'immense debt'. Between 30 and 36 million *livres*, it resulted largely from royal exactions during the ancien régime, and payments to farmers of the *octrois*. The Consulat had simply borrowed to meet it, using the *octrois* to pay the interest. In an annual budget of 2,407,000 *livres*, these duties represented 2,218,000.[27] Unless the system was re-formed, the choice, as Roland put it, was between paying up or going bankrupt. After a chaotic session in which he stood his ground, the council resolved to send a representative to Paris to request a bail-out by the national authorities. Roland's ex-friend Blot (now estranged over politics) went to the capital on 22 June.[28]

INCITEMENT TO RIOT?

Roland's insistence on home truths about finance was unpopular with the Lyon elite. However, what really damaged him in the eyes of the conservative establish-ment were the renewed violent attacks on the *octroi* barriers by exasperated workers in July. Roland recognized that the tolls could not be abolished until a replacement was found, but the drift of his writings was that it was high time to tax the rich, rather than the poor. He was not alone: the *octrois* were denounced in the *cahier* of the Third Estate, on the grounds that they increased the cost of labour and de-creased the city's competitiveness. A flood of pamphlets and articles against them appeared in 1790, by such as Blot, Champagneux, and Pressavin.[29] The National Assembly itself had abolished all *octrois* except municipal ones in March, encourag-ing the belief that they would soon abolish these, too. Any reform of the plight of artisans and silk-workers was likely to be blocked until there was a majority for change. Impatience among the people was not surprising. However, the immediate 'mainspring' (Edmonds) of the July unrest was probably general hardship and high prices. The council had tried to conserve grain by issuing only one kind of bread, most unpopular, at a fixed three *sous* a pound.[30] The *octrois* became the symbol of *la vie chère*.

---

[26] Champagneux, 1800, pp. xxiii–xxv: 'we rose at 5 a.m. and I entrusted [the description] to the brush of Citizeness Roland'; *Courier*, 1 June 1790, Desmoulins in *Révolutions de France et de Brabant*, no. 30; *Corr.*, II, p. 90 and note.

[27] 'Our friend' stated some 'harsh truths', *Corr.*, II, p. 94, to Lanthenas, 22 June 1790: probably from brochure, *Avis d'un des membres du conseil général de la commune de Lyon, 19 juin 1790*.

[28] Blot thought the Rolands 'extremists', 23 June to Lanthenas; Mme Blot's husband 'was being shouted at [*tympanisé*] for his connection to mine', *Corr.*, II, p. 100; cf. Edmonds (1990), p. 58; Wahl (1894), p. 17, and Perl-Rosenthal (2011) for reasons behind the estrangement.

[29] E.g. Pressavin's *Avis aux citoyens de la ville de Lyon sur les octrois*.

[30] Edmonds (1990), pp. 56–8.

The violence started with an invasion of the council meeting of 8 July. A customs barge was seized, and the tax collectors chased away. Roland could hardly be held directly responsible, since he was at Le Clos. There were threats to life, and the municipal officers did not care to test them. On 10 July, they capitulated and suspended collection of the *octrois*, not daring to obey the National Assembly's edicts of the 13th and 16th, calling for their reimposition. On 25–26 July, more violence broke out. The commander of the national guard, Dervieu de Villars, did not fire on the crowd, and was treated at first as a hero, before later being criticized for inaction. The *octrois* were reimposed on 21 August, by which time, at the council's request, there were 4600 regular troops in the city to enforce order. Popular opinion started to turn against the national guard, for siding with the authorities, notably searching houses in working-class districts for arms.

The patriots, cornered by these developments, took refuge in suggesting that the origin of the violence was counter-revolutionary provocation, engineered in order to call the troops in (the line taken by Mme Roland). A barrage of letters taking the side of the people flowed from Le Clos to Brissot, who had been given an alarmist version by Blot. Mme Roland undertook to set him right, blaming the administration for clumsy handling and leading the people to feel betrayed.[31] Roland protested in the *Courier* on 25 July, that he had never advocated disorder. To Lanthenas, privately, he exploded with irritation: 'What the devil am I supposed to do or say? The Lyonnais are mad; the council is made up of rogues and imbeciles. I am willing to appear in court in front of all the superiors and judges on earth with complete confidence. All my crimes are printed…and anyway I don't think they are crimes.'[32] Touched to the quick by 'odious rumours' about both him and his wife,[33] he shot off a defensive brochure entitled *Aux amis de la vérité*, protesting that he had never sought wealth, advancement, or even office, but had been pressed into it:

> I love the Revolution, I saw it come with enthusiasm because it consecrates principles dear to my heart…it has cost me some privileges, and may well deprive me of my post. So people have said that by supporting it in spite of that, I must have some secret hopes of compensation. This sordid calculation is so ridiculous that it just makes me smile. I live with such austerity that I will be able to manage whatever happens [and so on].[34]

Mme Roland agreed that the least said about women in public the better: it could never do them any good. However, since 'nobody in Lyon knew what she looked like', she could go there with impunity.[35] On 3 August, not trusting Roland to

---

[31] 23 July 1790, *Corr.*, II, pp. 114–20.

[32] To Champagneux, *Corr.*, II, p. 123–4; to Lanthenas, BNF MSS, naf 9532.

[33] Tittle-tattle represented Dervieu de Villars 'on his knees to Mme Roland'. 'Time was I would have died of chagrin to learn that people were speaking ill of me, but these flights of fancy do not trouble or even tickle me now,' 4 August 1790, *Corr.*, II, p. 133.

[34] *Aux Amis*; a malicious reply (BML, Fonds Coste 352351) accuses him (not inaccurately) of self-centredness. 'Who cares about Le Clos Laplatière, etc.'; cf. Mme Roland to Bancal, 13 October 1790, *Corr.*, II, p. 174 on receiving this 'impudent and scurrilous set of lies'.

[35] 'Even my name is unknown, because people take my husband for an *abbé* on account of his clothes. […] To justify a woman is almost always to compromise her,' 28 July 1790, to Lanthenas and Bosc, *Corr.*, II, pp. 124–5. Cf. Feuga (1985), p. 57; *Courier*, 18 March, 18 June, 7 August.

show his face there, in case he should be set upon, she went there on horseback to gauge reactions to his pamphlet. Her conversations confirmed her view that the *affaire des octrois* was a mixture of provocation and bungling by the authorities. She now described Lyon as no longer 'this fine city', but 'a sewer [*cloaque* = cesspit] of everything that was most disgusting in the ancien régime'. In early August, she thought her husband should stay out of town until the Martinmas elections (11 November) and hinted that he would do well to withdraw from the council and indeed give up on Lyon altogether.[36] 'My friend, the counter-revolution has begun here. This region is incurably lost [to the Revolution].'[37]

THE CLUBS

Marie-Jeanne was not alone in feeling discouraged. The June elections to the departmental council (Rhône-et-Loire) had resulted in more 'aristocratic' candidates being elected, mostly from outside Lyon; the district *directoire* was similar, so in all three tiers of the new local government, the patriots had little influence. Champagneux gave up trying to run the *Courier* in late September.[38] Although the unrest had settled by September 1790, the financial crisis deepened, as no taxes had been collected for forty days. Blot was having little luck in Paris.[39] By now the *menu peuple* were keen to take reform into their own hands. The journeymen successfully extracted from the council in April what they had not managed in 1786, imposition of the new tariff.[40] They had new-fangled ideas about citizenship and rights. But the Lyon bourgeoisie remained both indifferent to their claims and fearful of an uprising.

It was into this atmosphere, with troops still quartered in the town, that there began the initiative of the popular clubs, which the Rolands and their friends encouraged. The local Société des amis de la constitution (the equivalent of the Jacobin Club in Paris) had moderate politics, and very few members.[41] The Société *populaire* des amis de la constitution, with a far less well-to-do membership, started up in rivalry in late August. 'A few zealous patriots met and swore to [...] propagate the spirit with which they were fired and to overthrow the debris of the aristocratic domination.'[42] The new clubs met 'on Sunday after playing

---

[36] To Bancal, 4 August from Lyon. *Corr.*, II, pp. 132–8.

[37] Necker resigned on 4 Sept, followed by a Fayettist ministry—Duportail, Duport-Dutertre, De Lessart; see her letter to Brissot, 31 October, AN, 446 AP: 'The French are not sensible enough to put up with a seven-year parliament in the English manner.'

[38] Fatigue, ill health and opposition, Feuga (1991), p. 63; *Corr.*, II, pp. 138 ff.: 'Champagneux is inclined to retire from the fray; if Blot takes the paper, we won't have anything to do with it,' 8 August, p. 140; Brissot to Lanthenas: 'I see we shall have to go on fighting all our lives; our triumph will have been been short-lived', BNF MSS, naf 9534.

[39] Feuga (1985), p. 72: Blot asked the *octroi*-farmers in June for an advance, incurring Roland's wrath.

[40] Edmonds (1990), p. 29.

[41] Mme Roland, 30 December, *Corr.*, II, p. 211. Only 40, according to Wahl (1894), p. 226: 'a rich man's club with high entry dues'.

[42] Feuga (1985), p. 67 note; Edmonds (1990), pp. 70–1.

boules', and recruited among working men. By January 1791, they claimed about 3000 members. Officially the Jacobin Club in Paris did not allow the existence of two branches in the same town, so the initiative was bound to be divisive.

Roland himself was not directly involved at first: he planned to stay out of Lyon until after the elections. In any case, his 92-year-old mother died that November, which kept him home dealing with family business.[43] He and his allies among the *notables* no doubt saw the new clubs as a way of bringing the popular classes into an alliance with middle-class reformers, thus heading off uncontrolled violence. However, some of his close friends were certainly involved, as Perl-Rosenthal's thesis makes clear.

Both Lanthenas and Bancal, who were visiting the Rolands that autumn, actively encouraged the new clubs. They tried at first, unsuccessfully, to persuade them to merge with the 'official' Jacobin version. The older Lyon club took to calling itself the Société du Concert, while the popular clubs based in the sections sent representatives to a new Comité central des 31 Clubs. When Roland reached Lyon, in late December, he joined Lanthenas, working for the new club.[44] Mme Roland commented:

> Lanthenas is beginning to be out of favour with the [official club]…composed mostly of merchants. He finds it easier to spread the right kind of ideas among the societies in the sections: there *tout est peuple*, and the feeling of equality is developing a singular aptitude to grasp the correct principles, but a terrible amount of work will be needed to get them all really known, and teach people to apply them. Days are passed drafting or imagining motions, addresses, petitions, pamphlets, letters, and instructions; commenting on news, collecting opinions, watching, acting, thinking. While this activity, directed to the public good and devoted to the *patrie*, lifts and fills the soul, one must admit it doesn't offer all the pleasures of the peaceful rural life.[45]

An 'uneasy coexistence' lasted, until the Société du Concert dwindled to a rump. In the short term, the new clubs benefited the *patriotes* electorally. Edmonds considers them responsible for the increased numbers of both *patriotes* and artisans holding municipal office between 1790 and 1792. The city council was partly renewed in November–December 1790. Turnout was low, and when the mayor and two former *échevins* resigned, replacements moved up from the *notables* to full

---

[43] Roland's PS to Bancal, 28 October 1790: 'at my name, the aristocrats react like the possessed being sprinkled with holy water. We laugh at this foolishness, but I shall not budge from here till the elections are finished,' *Corr.*, II, p. 190; and ibid., pp. 200–1, to Bancal, 30 November 1790.

[44] See Kennedy (1988), p. 72 for 'exceptional success' of Lyon clubs; his claims, p. 46, that Roland and Lanthenas 'founded' them are doubtful: *Corr.*, II, p. 163 note, Roland to Bosc from Lyon on 15 September: 'we got here today and our friends will join us'; cf. Lanthenas to Bosc, 25 September, ibid., II, pp 165–6 note (Coll. Morrison); Lanthenas on Lyon clubs *Le Patriote*, 28 February 1791; Wahl (1894), p. 115; Edmonds (1990), pp. 86 ff.

[45] To Bancal, 30 December 1790, *Corr.*, II, p. 211; joint letter from Lanthenas and Mme Roland to Bancal, 10 January 1791, *Corr.*, II, pp. 216–17: efforts to reconcile the 'clubs populaires' and the official Jacobin branch. See Wahl (1894), p. 365, and letter from Lanthenas, 22 January, *Corr.*, II, pp. 223–4.

membership, under the rules: one of them was Jean-Marie Roland. On 23 December, Louis Vitet (1736–1809) became mayor, and François Bret *procureur*, while Roland became chair of the municipal finance committee.[46]

Roland addressed the clubs' central committee quite soberly on 2 January 1791. He gave advice on how to run their affairs, and urged the need to recognize the new laws and the thinking behind them. Ignorance was 'the greatest evil' for the people. The ancien régime, he said:

> held you under oppression and a sort of abasement, by keeping you far removed from all public affairs; the new Constitution gives you back all your rights by declaring equality between men…so the first thing to do is to seek enlightenment, since it is only possible to enjoy the benefits of the law once you know it, what it allows and what it forbids and how to apply it. [...] We are [he rather movingly said] so to speak, like beings who find themselves in a new creation: we find the environment strange not because of nature, the source of our rights, but because we are not used to using them, since until now they were forbidden us.

He recommended rotating office-holders to avoid dictatorships; the need to shun factional strife; a commitment to education, by reading improving texts at meetings (he came, after all, from an ecclesiastical family). And he reiterated that the rule of law was 'the mark of all free peoples'. The clubs must have approved of his speech, since they asked for the text, to print it.[47]

So by 1791, the *patriotes* found themselves running the town, the result of an exceptional alliance with *le menu peuple*, as reflected in the popular clubs. They shared hostility to the royal garrison—on which the departmental council was still insisting—and faced renewed fears of counter-revolution. However, they were awkwardly placed, between the still economically-dominant merchant class and the mass of citizens. Louis Vitet as mayor managed to keep a 'moderately *patriote*' administration running for the next eighteen months without a major crisis. This was the so-called 'Rolandin' council, although Roland himself was practically never present after January 1791. It is true that the Vitet-Champagneux administration, when in office, had his sympathies, and he kept constantly in touch by letter, intervening from Paris, when the tensions in the *patriote–peuple* alliance eventually erupted (see Chapter 21). His local input had been crucial, but his influence would from now on be exerted mainly from a distance.

The reason for his absence in 1791 was the perennial problem of the city's debts. Having received unsatisfactory information from his predecessors, Roland made some economies in January. However, these scarcely dented the massive municipal

---

[46] Edmonds (1990); Feuga (1991), p. 65. Results 26 November: 13,400 enrolled, 3652 voters. 'Uneasy coexistence', Perl-Rosenthal (2011), chapter 7, on the 'Roland circle's involvement', based on Brissot's papers. See Lefebvre (1957) on the royalist plot and Lyon's counter-revolutionary reputation.

[47] Fonds Coste 352352: 'Discours prononcé à la société centrale formée des commissaires des sociétés populaires des amis de la constitution de Lyon', le 6 janvier 1791, par J.-M. Roland. Was Mme Roland behind the 'new creation' sentence?

deficit.[48] Blot had returned empty-handed from Paris, so the council voted to send two official 'extraordinary deputies' to the Assembly, to join their four regular representatives. Roland himself and Bret were elected to go, with travel costs and a per diem of 12 *livres*. Champagneux replaced Roland as chair of the finance committee.

*

The Rolands had never intended to go to Paris. Mme Roland wrote on 30 November 1790 to Bancal, 'We shall live in Lyon for two years, and only abandon it when it has been entirely regenerated.'[49] This chapter has shown how deeply involved they were with Lyon politics, yet at the same time unhopeful of rapid progress, in a city so firmly under conservative management until the November 1790 elections.

The mission to sort out the city debt was meant to be brief. No doubt Mme Roland jumped at the chance to revisit her native city, and a journey that would have been out of the question privately was made possible by their expense account. However, their future was still tied to Lyon and to their bases in Villefranche and Le Clos.

Above all, they were still entertaining an idea they had talked and written about throughout 1790, without taking any final decision. This was for an ideal community, quite separate from municipalities and assemblies: an association of friends with an educational aspect. Mme Roland had written to Bancal in June 1790 that she thought 'the people' were the only section of society that cherished the Revolution, but that it was still uneducated, and bearing 'the mark of the chains it had borne so long'. It would take a generation to remove all traces of these and engender 'that noble pride which will maintain men at the level required by their liberty'.[50] Perhaps their best hope of 'regeneration' was to try to create a small-scale revolution locally. This plan is usually a footnote in biographies of Mme Roland, but it warrants more attention, and is the subject of the next chapter.

---

[48] Feuga (1991), pp. 70–1, note, confirms from AML series L that (a) the debt was 33.8 million *livres*; (b) the service on it was 1,800,000, i.e. three quarters of their income; (c) that the *octrois* formed 94 per cent of the city income, in 1788, the last year for full figures, 2,373,000. It would take time to work out a new equitable tax base. Asking for a *contribution patriotique* was unlikely to get far, though Champagneux donated 1250 *livres*.

[49] *Corr.*, II, p. 201.

[50] 22 June, *Corr.*, II, p. 99.

13

1790: A Community of Friends?

> Perhaps we are building castles in Spain with all this, but it offers such a pleasant prospect of enjoyment: we will preach patriotism, the doctor [Lanthenas] will ply his trade, my wife is the apothecary of the canton; you and I will sort out the business side, and we will all work for peace and concord.
>
> J.-M. Roland to Henri Bancal, October 1790.[1]

Alongside the turmoil of local politics in 1790, the Rolands seriously considered an ambitious scheme to create a rural community of like-minded people, by buying land formerly owned by the church. The Constituent Assembly's decree of 2 November 1789 had designated church property as *biens nationaux* to be offered for sale, although in practice it was several months before it became legally possible.[2]

Buying up these estates could be seen as a legitimate activity for supporters of the Revolution. The point was to raise funds to meet the expenses of the church and to relieve the national debt. In the end, most small rural properties were bought by fair-to-middling-size farmers (*paysans*) with the straightforward aim of enlarging their holdings, and larger ones by well-off bourgeois or nobles; really extensive estates, like abbeys with farms attached, could hardly be bought by anything less than a consortium. The Assembly did not aim to redistribute land to tenant farmers or others working it, but to sell to private bidders for cash. The *assignat* was created on 19 December 1789 as a state bond guaranteed by the *biens nationaux*—to which Crown possessions as well as those of émigrés were later added. (Only later did it mutate into paper currency.)[3]

The plan was to support several families by farming, but also to create a school and printing-press, with the aim of winning local people over to the new thinking. It was the sort of thing that could probably only have been imagined in the early phase of the Revolution, for several paradoxical reasons: because of the atmosphere of freedom to experiment, inspired by visions of the New World; because of the sudden availability of large and fertile tracts of land with buildings attached, once

---

[1] BNF MSS, naf 9532.

[2] *DCRF*, 'Biens nationaux'; cf. Bodinier *et al.* (2000), pp. 309–10, 388–9, on the 'budgetary imperatives'. Sales peaked in August 1791; by December, 'the vast majority' had been sold.

[3] Ibid., and Kennedy (1982) Chapter VII: many Jacobins, in Michelet's words, 'became acquirers; the acquirers became Jacobins', p. 142. See *DCRF*, 'Assignats'.

owned by abbeys and priories; but also because enthusiasts already feared that the Revolution was being stopped in its tracks by reaction, especially in the provinces, and would remain so, without grassroots evangelical work. Even in the cities, people found it difficult to adapt their mindset to the bewildering speed of change—holding elections for example. Most French people lived in small towns, villages, and hamlets, where the structures of everyday life had been deeply shaped by the feudal hierarchy and the institutions of the church. Throughout the 1790s, the urban–rural divide remained. Revolutionaries of every tendency were obsessed with the question of public opinion.

Biographies of Mme Roland pass quickly over the plan for communal living, because it is awkward to fit in chronologically; it moved in and out of focus over two years. But although it never took the shape originally dreamed of, the project was constantly in mind between the Rolands, Brissot, Lanthenas, and others, and is an essential background to understanding their friendship and later developments—especially the so-called, disputed *bureau d'esprit public* of 1792. It illustrates the closeness of the contacts between members of their circle, that they could have seriously considered living together. It also, incidentally, led to the first known crack in the Roland marriage, although that was papered over for the time being.

To Jean-Marie Roland, it looked like a genuinely idealistic alternative to official politics. Retrospectively, in February 1792, regretting that it had never happened, he wrote to Champagneux, one of the original partners:

> I was as sure of this as of my existence—to create a monument to patriotism and the useful arts [i.e. making things], such as does not exist even in Paris, where there are a hundred times more resources than we would have been able to bring to it; but they are widely scattered there, and we would have made a community [*réunion*] such as never existed before in the provinces, which could have become famous and would have rewarded our pains with either reputation or profit.[4]

The idea probably originated with Brissot: he had long dreamed of taking his family into a community—if not in America, which his wife favoured, then on American lines—combining philosophy and agriculture. He was one of many visionaries in old Europe who thought of regenerating human nature through ideal communities: Southey and Coleridge later (1794) dreamed of a community they called Pantisocracy, again in America. The novelty of the Roland project was that it would be tried in France, in the new atmosphere of liberty, rather than overseas. I have encountered no records of another scheme quite like this on French soil.[5]

Brissot's ambitious outline survives in the Roland archives. His plan for 'an agricultural society, or one between friends', outlined an estate big enough to

---

[4] BNF MSS, naf 9534, fos 356–8. First analysed in Perroud (1902b).
[5] Cf. Desan (2008) on 'Sciotomanie', when French people were tempted to buy up land in Ohio. Holmes (1989), pp. 59 ff.

support twenty families, each in a simple house without luxury, and centred on the need for educating country people (a secular alternative to the church). 'This society would have as its effects to regenerate [its members] by returning to the cultivation of the soil, and to regenerate [their fellow-men] through rural education.' It would teach morality, 'the simplest religious opinions', and manual labour. There would be a library and printing-press. It would mean pooling resources. Even so, payment would have to be by instalments. Brissot, far from rich himself, proposed three levels of participation: benefactors, who would put in the bulk of funds—perhaps with public help; associates, putting in more modest investments (between 12,000 and 20,000 *livres*); and ordinary members who would contribute their talents and services. Membership would be by probation and the community would be self-governing.[6]

In spring 1790, Brissot approached Lanthenas and Bosc, and through them Bancal. Bosc was chronically short of funds, but Lanthenas had money to invest. (Despite his strictures on primogeniture, he inherited a house worth *c.* 20,000 *livres* from his parents.) They naturally thought of the Rolands, with their small country estate, who would—they assumed—have exactly the right attitude. The couple had money due from Panckoucke, plus what remained from their marriage settlement, tied up in *rentes*. They were already predicting that the inspectorate would be abolished, taking with it their regular income.[7]

Overtures were also made to an eccentric rich Englishman, Robert Pigott (1736?–1793), in Geneva. His name surfaced at intervals over the next year, but as a wayward and unreliable investor—the French partners mistakenly thought he was a Quaker. Mme Roland called him an 'inconstant Pythagorean' (vegetarian) subject only to whim.[8] Blot, and Champagneux were approached. The support of some *pères de famille* was important, since several of the early enthusiastic members were youngish and unmarried (Bosc, Lanthenas, Bancal). Blot, having quarrelled with Roland about politics, withdrew and Champagneux followed suit.[9] Of the original group, Henri Bancal had most money, from his family and the sale of his solicitor's office, so he was a key player, but the plan was never likely to match Brissot's original ambitions.[10]

Lanthenas wrote to Bancal early in 1790: 'I have proposed to several philosophers that we set up an association like the Moravian Brothers, bringing together a few families who know each other'.[11] In May he wrote again:

---

[6] BNF MSS, naf 9534, fos 349–61.

[7] On Lanthenas, see *Corr.*, II, Appendix L; the Rolands later (1791) offered 40–60,000.

[8] On Pigott: 'un franc original', *Corr.*, II, pp. 150, note and 193; *ODNB* (2004); Alger (1889), pp. 39 ff.

[9] *Corr.*, II, pp. 81, 93, June 1790, and later references in summer.

[10] On Bancal's resources: *Corr.*, II, Appendix Q.

[11] See *Corr.* II, p.741; Perroud (1902b), p. 263; Lanthenas even tried to interest Julien Raimond, the free black planter from Saint-Domingue. Thanks to Nathan Perl-Rosenthal for this reference (BNF MSS, naf 9534).

There's a plan afoot to buy in common enough church property to support several families, and where we might install a paper mill, a printworks and an agricultural school. Monsieur Pigot [*sic*] would put up some money, I would put in my little contribution, [and so would] our friends in Lyon [the Rolands]. We need someone to suggest a property that might suit us.[12]

There was serious talk of emigrating to America to set it up, Mme Brissot's preferred option.[13] It is unlikely the Rolands would have agreed. Lanthenas reported that they would prefer to buy a religious house in town, over a twelve-year agreement. (By the decree of 14 May 1790, property was to be auctioned, with payments spread over twelve years.) They considered the original scheme over-ambitious, 'a fiction impossible to realise in the present state of attitudes [*moeurs*]'. However, they would back a more modest plan—an educational farm in the countryside, plus a printing-house in town, which could also include 'a garden and a lower floor which could be a coffee-house and patriotic club'.[14] Brissot hoped to change their minds, explaining to Bancal that he was increasingly drawn to the countryside, since the patriot cause seemed to be so hard to implant:

> Our Lyon friends will come back to it when they see the advantages. The essential point is to discover the income of the [religious establishment] you have seen, the quality of the property, to calculate what one might sell off and what one should keep…Monsieur Pigott favours Burgundy, but that's a flat region and we want some hills, and it is a vine-growing area, which means there is much drunkenness and poverty.[15]

On 22 June, Mme Roland wrote her first 'very studied' and courteous letter to Henri Bancal (M. Desissart, as she called him), inviting him to visit Le Clos and join them in planning the community.[16] Bancal was a delegate from the Auvergne for the Fête de la Fédération on 14 July in Paris, so he travelled via Lyon, where he met both Rolands. He accompanied them briefly to Le Clos on 7 July, before going to the Bastille Day festivities. Their meeting made an immediate impression on Mme Roland, such that her letters to him at once adopted a friendly and intimate tone. It is to this very full correspondence—reaching almost continuously into 1792—that we owe much of our later information. As Mme Roland put it on 18 July, 'revolutionary times [...] are favourable to immediate and durable friendships [*liaisons*] born of the energies on both sides'.[17] Her husband too was very taken with Bancal, who was warmly invited to return later in the summer with Lanthenas.

---

[12] BNF, MSS, naf 9534: Lanthenas to Bancal, 14 May 1790.

[13] Perroud, (1902b), p. 264, quoting Lanthenas to Bancal, 17 May 1790. Cf. Lanthenas to Bancal, early January 1791, *Corr.*, II, pp. 217–18.

[14] BNF MSS, fo 235, quoted Perroud (1902b) p. 264. See also ibid., fo 238, 16 June.

[15] To Bancal, 5 June 1790. BNF MSS, naf 9534.

[16] *Corr.*, II, pp. 97–9, signed 'Phlipon-Delaplatière'. Blot 'has abandoned us', ibid., pp. 94, ff.

[17] 18 July 1790, *Corr.*, II, p. 107. Cf. letter to Bosc on 20 July, *Corr.*, NS, II, supplement, p. 525, envisaging the abolition of the inspectorate: 'I will even feel happiness in concentrating on the countryside; [the tranquillity of being farmers] is well worth the reduction in situation.'

During July and August, the Rolands were preoccupied by the events in Lyon described in the last chapter. But when the *octrois* crisis seemed temporarily over, Bancal arrived back at Le Clos with Lanthenas. It was a longer visit—five weeks in each other's company—30 August–7 October, mostly in the countryside, with intermittent visits to Lyon to encourage the clubs. The project took more serious shape. Brissot wrote to Lanthenas: 'I read with pleasure the details you sent about the abbeys you have seen. Carry on. The plan is in your hands and Bancal's.'[18] The atmosphere in the Beaujolais hills was convivial, after the anxieties of midsummer. The friends walked round the village of Theizé, visited the poor, tried to convert the local curate and schoolmaster to the Revolution, played shuttlecock at Le Clos—and, it seems very likely, two of them developed feelings going beyond friendly affection. Mme Roland walked through the autumn woods with Bancal as he left for Clermont and was, perhaps for the first time, shaken in her resolve to keep her male friends at an amicable distance.[19]

Most of her letters to Bancal were written while Roland was present and presumably reading them, and some were jointly written with Lanthenas, but one from Le Clos on 8 October, while her husband was in Lyon, expresses strong emotion, in *Nouvelle Héloïse* mode:

> Why are my eyes full of tears which spill all the time but fill them up again? My will is firm, my heart is pure, and I am not at peace. '*It will be the greatest charm of our lives and we shall not be without use to our fellow-men*', was what you said about the affection that unites us, and this consoling sentence has not yet brought me peace [...] I believe I have observed you attaching your happiness to a hope which I must forbid [...] Why is it that this sheet on which I'm writing can't be sent without mystery? Why can't it be visible to all eyes [so pure is my heart]. When shall we see each other again? I often ask myself this question, but dare not resolve it. Why seek to penetrate the future when nature has hidden it from us? Let us leave it under the imposing veil in which she covers it [and so on].[20]

The language of the next few letters makes it clear that something had been said, but that Marie-Jeanne Roland had 'forbidden' Bancal to go any further. Absence made her heart grow fonder. She *appears* to have sent him a fable about 'the finch and the nightingale', which is little short of a declaration of love. The finch lives in 'a pleasant aviary' with a 'good master', but when a nightingale with a charming voice and tender accents turns up, they fall in love. Alas, the nightingale has to fly, while the finch must 'repay, with her caressing wing and gentle cooing', the 'care of the good master who cherishes her'.[21]

Several historians, though mentioning it only in passing, have described this quasi-affair to illustrate the vulnerability of the Roland marriage. Perhaps the most

---

[18] BNF MSS, naf 9534, 18 September 1790; *Corr.*, II, p. 742.
[19] *Corr.*, II, p. 187. See ibid., p. 742, for dates: Bancal was at Le Clos *c.*20 September to 2 October. Warm affection, letters of 8 and 28 October 1790, and 24, 26 January and 11 February 1791.
[20] 8 October 1790, *Corr.*, II, pp. 165–8.
[21] *Corr.*, II, pp. 202–3. Perroud notes this fable, *apparently* inserted in the letter, in very small handwriting—possibly, but not indisputably, Mme Roland's: original in BNF MSS, naf 9534, fol 77.

neutral construction to put on it is that Marie-Jeanne was seduced into a private *amitié amoureuse*, indulging in a Rousseau-esque fantasy, which cost her a few tears. She had no serious intention of being unfaithful to her husband, and Roland assumed that her affection for Bancal was like his, the warmth inspired by thinking alike on philosophical and political matters. A darker view might be that with a husband so much older and in fragile health, she might—without betraying him—envisage a future without him. Her letters to Bancal over several months, although mostly reporting on public affairs, are far more intimate in tone than those to her other friends. A close reading of this correspondence (we do not have Bancal's, but he annotated some of hers) suggests he cooled first. At any rate, she did not see him again until summer 1791. Had the attachment continued, it would have complicated the communal project.[22]

Meantime, Jean-Marie Roland, writing from Lyon and seemingly unaware of this sub-plot, enthused to Bancal in warm and affectionate terms:

You share our frank and straightforward way of being; one doesn't change at my age if one has always been this way. We [i.e. my wife and I] talk every day of our friendship with you, and certainly a clerical property in Villefranche would offer a good proposition: they are fetching between 2 and 300,000 *livres*, and as for lodging, one needn't despair of finding some. Perhaps we are building castles in Spain with all this, but it offers such a pleasant prospect of enjoyment: we will preach patriotism, the doctor [Lanthenas] will ply his trade, my wife is the apothecary of the canton; you and I will sort out the business side, and we will all work for peace and concord, but although it will be in common, it will also mean all the individual independence imaginable.[23]

Bancal reported on two abbeys, Beauregard and Monpeyroux; Mme Roland teasingly offered to initiate him into his agricultural future, and hoped he would find something 'within visiting distance'.[24] Lanthenas tried to tempt Pigott to take an interest. Then, in mid-October, Bancal—for reasons one can half-guess—suddenly bolted. Roland and Lanthenas expressed astonishment on hearing that, instead of 'looking for convents and monasteries for us', he was in Paris. What was more, he planned to go to England, on an ill-defined mission of spreading the word about the Revolution among English radicals, with introductions to some of Brissot's contacts. He would stay in London for several months. Mme Roland, who evidently learned his plans earlier than the others, warned him of the risks (war might be declared) and the weather ('nothing but mist and fog in London at this time of year').[25]

With the Auvergne ruled out, the Beaujolais was the more serious prospect. Lanthenas inspected Savigny Abbey, four leagues from Le Clos and the priory of

---

[22] See 26 January 1791, *Corr.*, II, pp. 228–9: a hint at secret letters, only to be opened 'when destiny has claimed me'—a letter ending with a *tutoiement*; cf. ibid, p. 237, irritable annotation by Bancal on a letter, where she preaches about duty; he had devoted himself to duty since 1789, except for 'one month which was not after all entirely wasted for her'!

[23] BNF, MSS naf 9534, J.-M. Roland to Bancal, 7 October 1790.

[24] *Corr.*, II, p. 183, 26 October.

[25] Roland's reaction, *Corr.*, II, p. 188; cf. Mme Roland's 12 and 28 October: on 'English ladies', whom 'Lanthenas has met in Paris', possibly Helen Maria Williams (*Corr.*, II, p. 194).

Monroman, between Lyon and Villefranche, which he described in lyrical terms.[26] Jean-Marie Roland suggested land adjoining Le Clos, belonging to local landowners who were moving to Paris, perhaps the best solution, making the Rolands central to the project. 'We have built singular plans on this arrangement, and I think for you, him, them and us, we could hardly do better.'[27] Typically and rather belatedly, Lanthenas got cold feet: 'Having to look after property which would tie me down, otherwise it might deteriorate, and finding myself without an income, I might one day be reduced to slavery [...] and will regret too much my former liberty.'[28]

For the Rolands meanwhile, life kept intervening—as mentioned above, first Mme Roland de la Platière senior died in November 1790, then the elections precipitated Roland into full membership of the Lyon council. To complicate matters further, he fell ill with erysipelas in December, and postponed going to Lyon for some weeks. Once there, he soon found himself chairing the council's finance committee, and plunged into sorting out the massive burden of debt. When he and his wife left for Paris in February 1791, the communal project perforce went into abeyance. Bancal was still in England;[29] Lanthenas was due to accompany the couple to Paris; Pigott had become invisible; Champagneux and Blot had long since dropped out. The Rolands had not yet even clapped eyes on the prime mover, Brissot, although they had been corresponding with him for years.

What is one to make of this scheme? At least one biographer has seen it as an only slightly more worthy version of the rush by small proprietors to profit from the sale of church lands,[30] but that is probably unfair. There was a good dose of idealism in it, inspired by pioneer communities in America and by various strands of eighteenth-century educational and philosophical thought. Roland himself had always taken the plans seriously and was later strangely reproachful to Champagneux for pulling out:

> You can never have appreciated the grandeur of my ideas, and the beauty of my project in the establishment I proposed to you [...] You showed no enthusiasm and really it was because of you that we gave up on it. We had the right circumstances, time, expressions [of interest]. You alone destroyed the illusion and forced me to abandon a project we [i.e. he and his wife] have talked about every day since, and always with regret.[31]

As will become clear, the idea had not gone away, and resurfaced in other forms. Its key attraction for the Rolands and Lanthenas was not so much agriculture, as the idea of a publishing house. Brissot already had his newspaper, but their dealings with him had shown that their views might diverge. During 1791, the perceived need for a reliable means of 'educating popular opinion' was something that had occurred to other groups of intellectuals whom the Rolands were about to meet in Paris.

---

[26] To Bancal, 15 October 1790, *Corr.*, II, pp. 179–80.
[27] To Bosc, *Corr.*, NS, II, supplement, p. 527, 10 November: 'it would be delightful if [...] our hermitage could become the focal point.' *Corr.*, II, pp. 188–9 and note; Roland's PS, 28 October.
[28] Lanthenas from Le Clos, 9 November 1790:, BNF MSS, naf 9534; *Corr.*, II, p. 698.
[29] *Corr.*, II, p. 222, 24 January 1791, to Bancal.
[30] Kermina (1976) p. 223.
[31] BNF MSS, naf 6241.

14

1791

When is a Salon Not a Salon? Parisian Circles

> My dear, you won't have a brilliant wife, whose charms, witty sallies, and finesse will make her the ornament of a circle or the subject of praise, such as to make you an object of envy.
>
> Marie-Jeanne Phlipon to Jean-Marie Roland, 17 May 1779.[1]

The Rolands arrived in Paris on 20 February 1791. Eudora was left behind, but their party included Lanthenas and Bret, a manservant, and a maidservant (Fleury). Bosc had found them furnished rooms in the Hôtel Britannique, in the narrow rue Guénégaud, two minutes from Mme Roland's childhood home on the Pont-Neuf: 'I have revisited, to my unimaginable delight, all the places where my earliest years were spent.'[2] It was conveniently central for callers, and for outings to clubs and the Assembly.[3]

Revolutionary Paris was a small world. The left bank, especially the area round the Théâtre Français (the Odeon today) was a publishing district. A few minutes from the hotel, the Cordeliers Club was holding sessions in the rue Dauphine by spring 1791, though the Rolands, who attended the Jacobins, never went there. Across the Seine, via the Pont-Neuf, was the much frequented Palais-Royal, a favourite meeting place. The Constituent Assembly sat in the former *manège* or riding school, on the north side of the Tuileries Palace, home to the royal family since autumn 1789. The Assembly's committees and offices were nearby. The Jacobin Club met in a monastery building round the corner. Deputies and journalists often lived within walking distance: of those the Rolands now met, Pétion lived on the rue du Faubourg Saint-Honoré, Buzot on the quai Malaquet [Malaquais]; Robespierre further off, 'in the depths of the Marais'. Brissot lodged in the rue Grétry, near the Palais-Royal.[4]

---

[1] *Lettres d'amour*, p. 125.   [2] *Corr.*, II, p. 241, 7 March 1791.
[3] Ibid., p. 213, cf. request to Bosc, p. 234, asking for a clean, but not luxurious location, with room for two servants and parking for two carriages. They hoped to be near Delandine, and his wife, *ibid.*, p. 235; cf. Perroud (1899); on the Hôtel Britannique, Lemay (1987), p. 119.
[4] Lemay (1987), pp. 120 ff. Robespierre was in 'a third-floor lodging in the rue de Saintonge', ibid., p. 122.

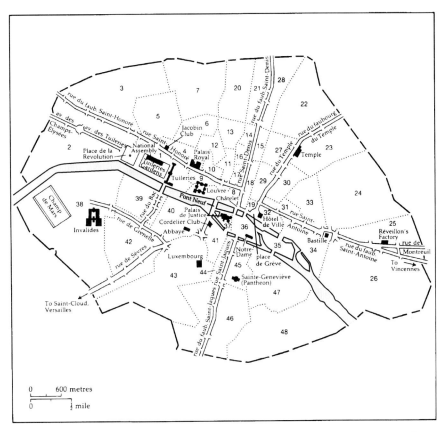

Figure 4. Revolutionary Paris. Source: G. Rudé (1959), *The Crowd in the French Revolution* (Oxford: Oxford University Press, 1959).

The Rolands' stay is well-documented. Jean-Marie sent regular reports to Champagneux, while his wife sent a string of informative letters to Henri Bancal in London.[5] The Paris of 1791 was very different from the one they had known before 1789. Everyday life in the capital had been radicalized: men and women even wore different clothes from the old days, in brighter colours, including tricolour cockades; Paris was 'saturated' with revolutionary newspapers and pamphlets, political discussions took place in the streets, meetings of all kinds were being held in venues large and small. News—and rumours—spread fast. There were constant whispers of aristocratic or counter-revolutionary plots. Parisian political clubs were much better organized and attended than in the provinces: numerous *sociétés fraternelles* had been set up. The 48 Paris *sections*, originally electoral units limited to active citizens, acted as a channel to wider local communities. The National Guard, commanded by General Lafayette, was intervening 'almost daily' in minor but unsettling

[5] On Bancal in London, see *Corr.* II, Appendix Q, pp. 743 ff.

disturbances, some connected to difficult living conditions and unemployment. In January 1791, 'Parisian politics were already seething with doubt and fear'.[6]

The Rolands had an immediate entry to this cauldron. Roland and Bret began lobbying deputies, ministers, and committee chairs at the Constituent Assembly, to get someone to take notice of Lyon's debt-burdened plight.[7] Three weeks in, Roland wrote in despair that he had made no progress: 'I think they are fobbing me off.'[8] He had 'little cooperation' from the Lyon deputies.[9] The new envoys pleaded that Lyon was a special case with its *octrois* undermining industry and causing a vicious circle. Their request fell on unsympathetic ears and Bret went home in April, leaving Roland to fight on alone. In May, he wrote, 'we may not be moving like crayfishes, backwards, but certainly like tortoises, very slowly [...] I am bound now to Sisyphus's rock, now to Ixion's wheel, and my task is like that of the Danaides'.[10]

Marie-Jeanne also lost patience ('my blood boils'). She was helping Jean-Marie, copying and possibly composing two of his letters. Tactfully worded, they appealed for an interim advance, including urgent aid for the charitable Hôtel-Dieu, which was partially granted. But by mid-June, he was no nearer achieving his principal object. His wife often 'wished she were a man', so as to spare him his perpetual errands to the Assembly.[11] As a woman, she was only allowed into the public gallery, unless she had a petition. She did, however, take full advantage of being in Paris to become acquainted with the Assembly and the Jacobin Club, and before long the Rolands had met several rising young politicians.

Marie-Jeanne had been ill, with 'terrible colic' on their arrival, but it did not hold her up for long. Roland wrote with aristocratic crudity to his men-friends: 'My wife used to make up pretty little verses [*des vers*], but she has just been passing some very big fat ones from her backside [*des vers* also meant worms].'[12] But as soon as she felt better, she was so keen to see the debates that she would rise 'at five in the morning to queue up for her place' in the public gallery. Sessions began at nine and the public tribunes filled up at once—with a predominance of women.[13] Mme Roland reached the gallery (worms notwithstanding) in time to hear one of Mirabeau's last speeches: he died a few weeks later.[14] She was now seeing the faces of men who had been just names in the newspapers, but after a few visits was unimpressed by the deputies, most of whom she judged 'mediocre and corrupt'.

---

[6] Andress (2000), p. 39; Tackett (2003), pp. 88–96.

[7] Le Guin (1966), pp. 71–3 for quotations from their *Adresse préliminaire* (1791).

[8] BNF MSS, naf 6241, to Champagneux, fo 22.

[9] The Lyon deputies: J.J.F. Millanois (1749–1793), J. A. Périsse-Duluc (1738–1800), and G. B. Couderc (1741–1809) sent letters to Lyon (BML, Mss 1471–3) analysed by Tackett (1996); see also Lemay (1991).

[10] Roland to Champagneux, BNF MSS, naf 6241, 10 March, 17 and 24 May. Le Guin (1966), p. 72, quotes Coste, BML MS 1132, piece 50, Roland to finance committee. Mme Roland to Bancal, 5 April 1791, *Corr.*, II, pp. 254–5.

[11] *Corr.*, II, pp. 86–93, 7–11 June 1791: they granted an advance of 300,000 *livres*, plus 50,000 for *enfants trouvés*. Roland to Champagneux, 27 May 1791, BNF MSS, naf 6241.

[12] Ibid., 25 and 28 February 1791.

[13] On the Manège, see Brette (1902), p. 206; Lemay (1987), pp. 204 ff. The Assembly met from 9 a.m. to 3 or 4 p.m., then the deputies dined. There were sometimes evening sessions.

[14] *Mém.*, pp. 75, 127–8; Mirabeau spoke on 28 February, 23 and 27 March 1791, and died on 2 April.

The crowds of people and the chaotic accoustics in the *manège* didn't help. The long chamber was unsuited to clear debate, and a loud voice was essential.[15] A ferocious page of the memoirs deals out brickbats and the occasional compliment to Assembly orators. In particular, she regretted that speakers on the right, with all the wrong principles, were more impressive public speakers than their opponents.[16] By early March, she had concluded that liberty and the constitution were not really valued by 'the men who were in the forefront at the [first] moment of the Revolution'.[17] She stormed out of an April session, 'in a rage, convinced they would never produce anything, but nonsense, and promising myself never to set foot there again'.[18] The Assembly, debating the army and the National Guard, had voted (against the left-wing minority) to allow only active citizens into the latter. As a radical sympathizer, she sent Brissot a letter, which he printed in *Le Patriote*:

> [How was it] that nobody pointed out that in all cities with large industrial plants, there are vast numbers of workers who, because of industrial crises and competition between manufacturers, find themselves temporarily unemployed, unable to pay their taxes, even forced to resort to public relief? In Lyon alone, over 25,000 souls were reduced to poverty during the terrible winter of 1789. These workers were nevertheless useful citizens, honest family men, very devoted to the constitution.[19]

The debates at the Jacobins were more interesting; both the Rolands attended meetings four evenings a week.[20] As the Société des amis de la constitution, the Paris Jacobin Club was the 'mother institution' of the clubs with which Jean-Marie had been concerned in Lyon. Members had to subscribe; non-members, including women, could listen from the gallery. By 1791, it was moving from its early association with the constitutional monarchist 'triumvirate' of 1790 (Barnave, Duport, and the Lameths) towards a more radical mood. Michelet described this 'middle period' of its history as that of 'le jacobinisme mixte', associating journalists like Brissot and Choderlos de Laclos with Robespierre, by now starting to be a dominant presence.[21]

A more congenial alternative to seeing politicians from afar and hearing speeches through a confused hubbub, was to see them at home. At last, the Rolands met Brissot face to face. Mme Roland's memory of the meeting was that 'we were soon as affectionate as old friends, because we already felt sure of our moral characters'. Brissot's appearance pleased her: this slightly-built man of thirty-eight was simplicity itself, 'trusting to the point of imprudence, merry, naïve, and as unaffected as a fifteen-year-old'. Her words of praise are warm, but with hindsight her portrait of him is pierced with regrets. Brissot was, in her view, too disinterested, too unwilling to recognize vice and deception, and had too much *légèreté d'esprit et de caractère*. He was, in short, too 'lightweight' for his responsibilities—until it was too

[15] *Corr.*, II, p. 243; Brette (1902), chapter 3, esp. pp. 167–8. [16] *Mém.*, p. 128.
[17] *Corr.*, II, p. 240, Lanthenas to Bancal, 7 March 1791. [18] *Mém.*, p. 129.
[19] Ibid.; cf. May (1970), p. 187; *Corr.*, II, pp. 270–1, 28 April 1791; in the *Patriote* version, 'le vigoureux Robespierre* and *le sage Buzot* were shouted down'.
[20] Roland to Champagneux, 25 February, BNF MSS, naf 6241; Lemay (1987), pp. 216 ff.
[21] 'Jacobinisme' in *DCRF*, p. 751.

late, a judgement echoed by most historians.[22] She also met his wife, Félicite née Dupont, whose common sense she appreciated.[23]

Not yet a deputy, but an ex-member of the Paris municipal council, and an influential journalist, Brissot knew just about everybody. He introduced the Rolands to the most radical politicians and journalists in Paris. That spring, most of the debates were over the new Constitution, with the left-wing minority trying to inflect it in a more democratic direction. Meetings outside the Assembly were devoted to discussing what should be proposed there next day. In April, one of these informal groups started to meet in the rue Guénégaud.

It is not clear whose idea it was. Mme Roland informed Bancal on 5–6 April that 'some of our best friends, deputies or not, have tried to arrange to meet to increase their potential for pressure ['*leurs forces*']. A postscript adds 'I believe that the gathering [*société*] I mentioned will be formed, and maybe it will even hold its sessions in our present lodgings'.[24] Her memoirs explain that because of the convenient location of the rue Guénégaud, 'it was agreed that those deputies who were accustomed to meeting to confer, would come *chez moi* four times a week, after the Assembly session [and after dining] and before the Jacobins'.[25] Thus began a period when the Rolands were in one of the inmost circles of revolutionary Paris.

WAS THIS A 'SALON'?

Mme Roland is often described as having her 'first salon' during these few months in 1791 (the so-called 'second salon' being in 1792, when Roland was a minister).[26] Indeed the word *salonnière* seems to have been attached so firmly to her that some writers imagine she was entertaining lavishly in Lyon before arriving in Paris, though anyone who has read this far may find it hard to see why. One writer compares her to the courtesan Ninon de Lenclos.[27] Another claims her marriage to 'the eminent state functionary, M. Roland de la Platiere', had brought her a salon.[28]

The word 'salon' has a slippery history. Its most recent historian, Antoine Lilti, refers to the 'sediment' of fragmentary sources, endlessly recycled, coating the history of the pre-revolutionary salon. The word itself, in the eighteenth century, usually meant simply a room for receiving guests. People referred rather to 'circles' or *soirées*. In the nineteenth century, the term was reinvented to refer to elite social gatherings. Applied retrospectively to previous centuries, it usually indicates a private function, held on fixed days, weekly or twice weekly, for invited guests and occasional visitors. Its origin lay in aristocratic traditions of hospitality. To provide

---

[22] Cf. Gueniffey (1991).   [23] *Mém.*, pp. 63, 129.   [24] *Corr.*, II, pp. 257–8.
[25] *Mém.*, pp. 63 and 131; cf. *Corr.*, II, p. 213, 'twice a week'.
[26] Cf. Pope-Hennessy (1917), Chapter 6: 'The First Salon'; May (1970), Chapter 12: 'A Revolutionary Salon'; Le Guin (1966), p. 71, her 'first political salon'. Sydenham (1961), pp. 86–91; Perroud (1899); Chaussinand-Nogaret (1985), pp. 93 and 105: 'salonnière d'instinct', 'enchanteresse', 'magicienne.'
[27] Bayard (1997), p. 305.
[28] Walter: 'Telle fut Mme Roland', editorial matter, in *Actes*, p.351; 5000 *livres* a year wasn't enough to run a salon.

food and drink, agreeable furnishings, lighting, heating, and service implied considerable outlay. Only wealthy hosts could regularly offer such a welcome. Some salons were literary and philosophical, although Lilti argues that not all salons were intellectual power-houses: they were often an opportunity for *mondanité*, polite social interaction, and networking in one's self-interest. Music, cards, and other amusements besides serious conversation, might be offered. There was usually a *maîtresse de maison*, whose role was to put guests at their ease and see that the evening passed smoothly. She need not be the only woman present, because salons could be mixed. One can conclude that there was probably no such thing as a 'typical' salon: the sociability of the ancien régime could embrace many forms: nevertheless, the word itself is almost always associated with the presence of a woman or women. It is a highly gendered term.[29]

Considering the Rolands' circumstances from March to August 1791, it is hard to see much in common with a 'salon' of this kind. Their material situation was modest. They were in rented accommodation—like many provincial deputies—and had just two rooms at their disposal: a public room in which their new friends (often living in 'bachelor' lodgings) could be received, and a private bedroom. They did not offer hospitality beyond the most basic kind: the visitors had already dined by late afternoon, and 'a jug of water and a sugar shaker', certainly nothing alcoholic, was what Mme Roland judged suitable refreshment.[30]

Secondly, there is Mme Roland's own conduct. She was virtually always the only woman present at these particular meetings, but if we are to believe her memoirs, during this *first* stay in Paris—an important distinction—she deliberately did not play the role of *maîtresse de maison*, beyond minimal politeness. She claims that she took care to station herself separately from the circle of men, sewing or writing letters at a little table, although not missing what was said. Her remark rings fairly true that, apart from the 'usual greetings as these gentlemen arrived or left, I never allowed myself to say a word, although I often had to press my lips together to stop myself'.[31] She develops this theme (the capacity of men for talking round in circles) at some length. Of course, her husband was there all the time, talking with the male visitors. Any previous entertaining, *pace* those who think she had a 'salon' in Lyon, had consisted of informal and basic, not to say earthy hospitality at Le Clos, with a few friends. A far cry from Ninon de Lenclos at any rate.

Thirdly, those who called on the Rolands were not there for social chitchat. They came to confer in private about their anxieties concerning the Revolution, the king's council of ministers, the Assembly majority, and the way it was—according to them—being influenced by the court. These men were already connected by many threads linking them to political, intellectual, or journalistic circles in Paris from both before and after the Revolution of 1789. As Leigh Whaley remarks, the radical press 'served as both an informal political club and a mutual support

---

[29] On salons see Lilti (2005), Kale (2004), Goodman (1994); Blanc (2006); Lemay (1987), pp. 93–105, on invitations and receptions, especially the Necker household.

[30] *Mem.*, p. 131.

[31] Ibid., the second, fuller version, under the heading 'Brissot'. Her account of her behaviour is backed up by Dumont (1832), II, p. 394, despite his mixing two periods.

network for radical politicians, whether or not they were deputies'.[32] Club meetings were another source of contacts. Apart from the Jacobin Club, several of the Rolands' new acquaintances belonged to the Société des amis des noirs, started by Brissot in 1788, and now presided over by Condorcet (not intimate with the Rolands, but they must have known him). Brissot was also connected to the Cercle social, set up by the Abbé Claude Fauchet (1744–1793) and the journalist Nicolas de Bonneville (1760–1828).[33]

With these multi-polar networks, they did not need the Rolands to bring them together. They can perhaps be described as fully participating in what modern commentators sometimes describe as the Habermasian 'public sphere', from which women were not necessarily excluded, but less often present. It was these men, and not Mme Roland, who had taken the initiative to meet. We know from her letters that the same people often met at other people's private houses, especially those who had families: Pétion's and Garran de Coulon's for example.[34] The meetings at the rue Guénégaud were only one among many gatherings. They were more like a modern think tank, than a salon in the usual sense, and they were private, not open to all comers.

That is not to say that there were not in Paris at the time gatherings more like a conventional salon. The meetings at the house of Louise de Kéralio (Mme Robert, of whom more later) might more accurately be so described, although historians hardly ever call her a *salonnière*. Mme Roland recalled being invited (in 1792) to Mme Robert's house, 'where she held an assembly two evenings a week', attended by many 'men of merit from the legislature, as well as women from the Société fraternelle [des patriotes des deux sexes]'. It would not be unreasonable to apply the word to the grander gatherings that Germaine de Staël held in the rue du Bac, or which Sophie de Grouchy, Condorcet's wife, held first in the Hotel de la Monnaie and then in the rue de Bourbon, and which better conformed to the pattern of the ancien régime.[35]

Mme Roland's own description of the people who met in her lodgings was *le petit comité*, and their gatherings were squeezed in on weekdays for an hour or two between Assembly, dinner, and Jacobin Club. Who was in the 'little committee'? It's 'basic core consisted of Pétion, Buzot, and Robespierre', alongside non-deputies Brissot and Clavière.[36] The only other men mentioned by name in the memoirs are 'Louis Noailles, Volfius, and *le petit* Antoine', of whom we hear little, although 'a few others' came. Individuals mentioned in letters between April and June were the Englishman Thomas Paine, the Abbé Grégoire, Garran de Coulon, and Etienne Dumont, but it is not clear whether they actually visited the rue Guénégaud.[37]

---

[32] Whaley (2000), p. 35.   [33] On the Cercle social see Kates (1985).

[34] Garran de Coulon (1748–1816), university friend of Bancal's *Corr.*, II, pp. 736 and 245.

[35] Lilti (2005); Blanc (2006); *Mém.*, p. 117.

[36] *Mém.*, p. 131.

[37] Noailles (1756–1804), Wolfius (1743–1805), and Antoine (1758–1793) do not figure in the inner circle. On Paine, *Corr.*, II, p. 262 and *Mém.*, p. 194. By June, Grégoire (1750–1831) was 'among our friends: and I could say the same of Pétion, Buzot and Robespierre', *Corr.*, II, pp. 308 ff., to Bancal.

These men already knew each other, with Brissot often the linkman. Jérôme Pétion (1756–1794), now a deputy, was his boyhood friend from Chartres.[38] Brissot's business associate Etienne Clavière (1735–1793) a banker, in exile, but a banker all the same, was regarded as a financial expert to rival Necker. Mme Roland was never very warm towards him—'irascible and opinionated' are two of her terms. No doubt his lifelong deafness did not help. According to his compatriot, Etienne Dumont, he entertained often at his house in Suresnes: 'we dined there the other day', Mme Roland wrote in April.[39]

References to Mme Roland's 'salon' do not usually dwell on Robespierre's presence at the Hôtel Britannique. However, Maximilien [de] Robespierre (1758–1794), whom the Rolands now met for the first time, was someone with whom they were in complete political sympathy. Mme Roland had heard him speak in the Assembly, and remarked on his 'courage', although she was probably thinking of him when she said the right had better orators than the left.[40] After being elected to the Estates-General, Robespierre became well-known for his consistently democratic views in the Constituent Assembly. He had spoken in favour of opening the National Guard to 'all citizens of an age to bear arms', instead of to active citizens only, exactly reflecting Mme Roland's own views.[41] It is not clear how regularly Robespierre visited, but Marie-Jeanne knew him well: 'even when he was not attending the *petit comité* so often, he came from time to time, to ask if he could dine'.[42] It was almost certainly from the Rolands that Robespierre was returning home when he left behind in a cab some manuscripts by Lanthenas on popular societies and press freedom. An advertisement in *Le Patriote* said that Citizen Robespierre had left the quai des Grands Augustins (near the rue Guénégaud) at 9.30 p.m. on 12 May: he would be grateful for the return of papers he had forgotten on the seat.[43]

For obvious reasons, Mme Roland's memoirs are not kind to Robespierre. She paints a retrospectively unflattering picture of him chewing his fingernails (she may not have made this up) and sitting silently listening to points he later put forward as his own in the Assembly, where his 'trivial' voice, poor use of language and boring delivery made him an orator 'below mediocrity'. But even from the memoirs, and certainly from the letters, it is clear that she and her husband were, in early 1791, thoroughly sympathetic to his views, on friendly terms with him, and among his fiercest defenders. Later the same year, although they were to differ somewhat in their reactions to the king's flight, they went on respecting him as a man of principle.

[38] On Pétion, *Mém.*, p. 101, a nuanced portrait. While his 'serenity', 'gentleness' and probity were praised, he was too trusting and complacent.

[39] *Corr.*, II, p. 260. On the under-estimated Clavière, Le Guin (1966), p. 80. Brissot, Malesherbes, La Fayette, La Rochefoucauld-Liancourt, Lubersac, Sieyes and Mirabeau dined at Suresnes in 1789, Dumont (1832), pp. 43 and 64; cf. Lemay (1987), p. 96.

[40] *Corr.*, II, p. 244, 15 March to Bancal.

[41] Scurr (2007), pp. 140–1, for his defence of 'le peuple' in similar terms to Mme Roland; May (1970), p. 186, and *Corr.*, II, pp. 343, 356 for similarity of views.

[42] *Mém.*, p.133 and cf. May (1970), pp. 192–3.

[43] *Corr.*, II, p. 280 and note, Lanthenas on the incident, 27 April 92, BNF MSS, naf 9534: 'Robespierre lost a mansucript of mine last *March* [sic]'. Advertisement in *Patriote*, 17 May 1791.

François-Nicolas-Léonard Buzot (1760–1794) was a lawyer from Evreux, who had come to Paris only in 1789. He was accompanied by his wife, Marie-Anne-Victoire Baudry, whom Mme Roland visited and liked. Less prominent than Robespierre, he was his most regular supporter in the Assembly, for example over the so-called 'self-denying ordinance', whereby on Robespierre's proposal, deputies sitting in the Constituent Assembly ruled themselves out as candidates for the forthcoming new Legislative Assembly; the aim was not so much self-denying as to reduce the numbers of conservatives, hangovers from the Constituante—though with hindsight this tactic brought its own problems.[44]

All these men were to be closely associated with the Rolands one way or another. Camille Desmoulins (1760–1794) never visited the rue Guénégaud, and it is not clear when, if ever, he and the Rolands really met. He was, with Danton (whom they also did not meet yet) a member of the Cordeliers Club, sometimes described as 'the more plebeian' equivalent of the Jacobins. However, Desmoulins was a link between the Cordeliers and the visitors to the rue Guénégaud. His newspaper, *Révolutions de France et de Brabant*, provided updates on the closeness of members of the 'little committee'. A schoolfriend of Robespierre's, he was already a 'street-figure and pamphleteer of verve', well-known for his role in July 1789.[45] In February and March 1791, as the Rolands arrived, he was reporting that 'one cannot speak of Robespierre without Pétion'; and that Brissot, Pétion, Robespierre, and Desmoulins himself were 'the Jacobins of the Jacobins'. The witnesses at his wedding to Lucile Duplessis a few months earlier, in September 1790, had been Pétion, Robespierre, Brissot, and Louis-Sébastien Mercier.[46]

This was a 'Brissotin', not a 'Girondin' circle. Mme Roland's remarks, specifically of this group, about the ability of men to talk in circles, are often wrongly quoted in relation to the politicians later known as the 'Girondins', but the famous deputies from the Gironde had not yet even arrived in Paris. Perhaps there was some retrospective confusion in her mind between the two, but in 1791, she was intimate only with the small Brissot circle.[47]

It wasn't the only group the Rolands frequented. They were also drawn into the orbit of the Cercle social: to the large meetings which it organized as the Confédération des amis de la vérité, and possibly to its smaller sessions. The first mention in the correspondence is on 22 March, when Mme Roland declared: 'I heard the greatest principles of liberty deduced with firmness, warmth, and clarity.' Claude Fauchet, its founder, was 'an excellent and vigorous apostle of the best doctrine'.

[44] On Buzot, Lemay (1991); Vatel (1872), II, pp. 279 ff.; *Corr.*, II, Appendix R.

[45] Jones (1990), p. 339, etc.: 'Qui faut-il élire?' by Mme Roland, *le Patriote*, 12 June 91, reproduced by Desmoulins *Corr.*, II, p. 293 and note: 'we need men of character, enlightened, honest, and able to run finances without putting their hand in the till'.

[46] Whaley (2000), p. 35; Lemay (1987), p. 128: the masonic Loge des Neuf-Soeurs numbered Condorcet, Bailly, Brissot, Desmoulins, Danton, Pétion, and Rabaut de Saint-Etienne. On Pétion, cf. Vatel (1872), II, pp. 261–2, quoting Mercier: 'inseparable from Robespierre', they were called 'two fingers on the same hand'.

[47] Inexplicably, Charles Le Guin confuses the two periods, pp. 82–3, despite the discrepancy of presuming Robespierre to have been present in 1792.

The Cercle was a forum for ideas for a range of individuals and fraternal societies, standing aloof as yet from more committed politics. Gary Kates suggests that Jean-Marie Roland was a 'core member' of the Cercle's inner councils: certainly several men he knew well were key figures, but it is not clear that he was much involved at this stage.[48]

Life wasn't all politics. Marie-Jeanne renewed old connections, visiting the aged Besnards, and her cousin by marriage, Mme Trude, at Meulan. Henriette Cannet, recently widowed, was in Paris, and one of the *demoiselles* Malortie from Rouen, was in town on family business. There are references to dining with their old and new friends, Bosc, the Brissots, etc. Tomorrow, she wrote in March, we will be spending the whole day with 'Caton-Garran and his amiable family: a real party'. Bancal too was briefly in Paris in May: a jaunty note to him in English refers to meeting at six that evening.[49]

By the time of the dramatic events of midsummer 1791 then, the Rolands, if not 'salon-holders', were familiar with a radical, if rather confined, sector of Parisian opinion. Their views and acquaintances predisposed them to react strongly to the news to which Parisians woke up on 21 June: that the royal family was missing from the Tuileries Palace.

---

[48] Kates (1985), p. 5. First mention by Mme Roland in letter to Bancal, 22 March 1791, *Corr.*, II, pp. 247–8, and cf. ibid., pp. 262, 268.

[49] See *Corr.*, II, pp. 241, 245, 247, 249, 284, 296–8.

15

1791: After Varennes

There was no [executive] under our Constitution other than the one abandoned to the heredity of a family, and the absurd inviolable status of a chief.

Marie-Jeanne Roland to Brissot, 1 July 1791.

The core members of the *petit comité* (including the Rolands, Buzot, Robespierre, and Brissot) met at Pétion's lodgings to discuss the bombshell of the king's disappearance. The 'flight to Varennes', was a turning-point in the Revolution. The king and queen, their two children, the king's sister, Madame Elisabeth, and their attendants, had been driven from the Tuileries Palace at night. Their escape, organized by Count Fersen, was intended to link up with General Bouillé's forces at the Montmédy camp near the frontier. It almost succeeded, despite many mishaps, but the royal party was recognized by vigilant citizens and held under arrest in Varennes in north-eastern France on 22 June, before being brought back to Paris under escort, on Lafayette's orders.[1]

On that first day, when it seemed that Louis had gone for good, several of those who dined with Pétion regarded the king as having committed the irreparable. They enthusiastically imagined the possibility of a 'virtuous republic'. Until then, although radical deputies favoured a more democratic constitution, there had been little open mention of a republic—that is the formal abolition of the monarchy. Robespierre himself was not particularly in favour. He had said, 'I hate this form of government where factious men reign', and was not disposed to suggest it, even at the height of the June crisis.[2] According to Mme Roland's memoirs, Robespierre remained anxious and depressed, rather than elated by the king's flight, saying 'that the royal family would not have taken this step without having a coalition in Paris ready to launch a St Bartholomew's massacre of patriots'. He assumed he would be on the list, and would 'not last twenty-four hours'. There is some retrospective malice in her wording, but as she reported to Bancal at the time, she shared his fear. 'Yesterday [i.e. before the king's recapture], with Robespierre and several others, we thought we were under the knife.'[3] Nevertheless, at the Jacobin Club, Robespierre made an impassioned speech, which she warmly praised for its courage, attacking both the king and the majority in the Assembly as being counter-revolutionary.[4]

---

[1] Tackett (2003), pp. 42–4.
[2] 'République' in *DCRF*, p. 834; cf. Scurr (2007), pp. 148–54, 209–10.
[3] *Mém.*, p. 133; *Corr.*, II, p. 306, 23 June 1791.   [4] Ibid., 22 June, p. 304.

The club was quickly plunged into division and schism by the crisis, with most of the deputies, led by Barnave, hoping to preserve the monarchy, others (Laclos, and possibly Danton) manoeuvring on behalf of the duc d'Orléans, while the radicals, although stopping short of a republic, favoured an elected executive council, at least temporarily.

Other people were galvanized by Varennes into open republicanism. 'Within hours of learning about the king's flight', the Cercle social endorsed the idea of a republic. Its paper, *La Bouche de Fer* went daily, with an article by Nicolas Bonneville entitled: 'No more kings'. A Cordeliers petition claimed: 'France is no longer a monarchy; it is a republic, at least until all the *départements* and primary assemblies have spoken.'[5] Mme Roland reported that the buzzword 'republic' was being spoken aloud. She and her husband sympathized, seeing no future for the monarchy. No words were strong enough to express their contempt for the king ('crowned rascal'; 'monstrous phantom', etc.).[6] To Brissot, Mme Roland wrote of the 'perverse ministers' and 'more than suspect committees' in the Assembly, which should be 'purged'. Louis XVI might be in Brussels, but 'his agents are still here'. Why were the sections not demanding 'a change of ministry, a renewal of the committees, and the solemn convocation of all the primary assemblies of the kingdom, to examine whether we still need a crowned puppet?' In short, immediately Varennes was known about, she was fully endorsing the Cercle-social/Cordeliers reaction.[7]

Fresh turmoil followed the news of the king's recapture on 22 June. When he fled, he had left behind a document revealing how much he disliked both the Revolution's policy on the church and its limitation of his powers, alongside a list of petty complaints. It became public, and popular agitation and club meetings were at their height. Mme Roland was feverishly excited. 'We are living ten years in twenty-four hours,' as she put it on 11 July. She threw down on paper her thoughts about the way forward, which she saw as without the king: 'the fall of thrones is written into the destiny of empires'. 'We get home at eleven or midnight every night, thinking how different are the interests for which the people assemble today, when only a few years ago they would sleepily have said Amen.' She had watched with enthusiasm citizens marching from the working-class suburb of Saint-Antoine to the Assembly on 23 June. Bancal, in Clermont, was exhorted to press for a national meeting to approve 'an elective temporary council'. In the same important letter of 1 July, she reiterated her own uncompromising republicanism:

> It is obvious that if a republican government is one in which all powers are exercised by the people's elected representatives, [...] then we are under a republic if we entrust executive power to an elected council, since there was no [executive] under our Constitution other than the one abandoned to the heredity of a family, and the absurd inviolable status of a chief. We need the council to balance the Legislative Body, in the same way as in the United States Congress the Senate balances the legislative arm.

---

[5] Kates (1985), pp. 158–9.

[6] Roland to Champagneux, 25 June, 29 June, BNF MSS, naf 6241; Mme Roland to Bancal, *Corr.*, II, pp. 303–6.

[7] Undated, AN, 446 AP, 31/99; *Corr.*, II, p. 304, 22 June; on Cordeliers, cf. Hammersley (2005).

Brissot had not initially come out strongly in print on this score, to her disapproval ('he describes merely').[8]

She warmly approved the Cercle social and Cordeliers: 'today [1 July] the Cercle social is openly discussing whether or not we should maintain our kings; it is the only club, after the Cordeliers, that dares act so openly in the capital'. Meanwhile, 'the Jacobins, like the Assembly, go into convulsions at the name of republic, although they accept the *thing*, because they more or less decided on the elective council'.[9]

Fewer documents by her husband survive, but the signs are that they were in total agreement. Mme Roland was, perhaps for the first time, reconsidering her views about women and politics. She literally found it hard to sit still: 'I can't stay home, and I go round to see the valiant people I know, to excite them to some grand action.' She actually joined a women's club in her own name, the only time she was tempted to do anything like this:

> While things were peaceful, I maintained the tranquil role and the kind of influence [informal] that seemed proper for my sex. But when the king's departure declared war, it seemed to me that every person should devote him or herself without reserve. I have been to sign up to the Fraternal societies, thinking that zeal and the right kind of thoughts [*la bonne pensée*] might sometimes be very useful in times of crisis.[10]

This suggests that she considered speaking in public, though alas, she gives no clear identification either of the Société fraternelle des deux sexes, or of the Société fraternelle des amies de la vérité (Etta Palm d'Aelders's group within the Cercle social).[11]

Among other calls for a republic, Condorcet gave a surprisingly bold address to the Cercle social on 8 July: '*De la République, or is a king necessary for the preservation of liberty?*'[12] With Bonneville, Lanthenas, and Tom Paine, he started a newspaper: *Le Républicain*. It ran for four issues, starting on 3 July, and the Rolands read and even distributed it. Mme Roland reported that 'Thomas Payne' was 'at its head'. Jean-Marie sent Champagneux 'my last copy' of the paper. Despite her habitual coolness whenever the name of Condorcet comes up, Mme Roland dispatched one to Bancal.[13]

The republicans were, however, in a minority in the country. Despite the collapse of the king's popularity, the provinces apparently wanted peace to return, with the constitution restored. Most people, when the word 'republic' was pronounced, thought either of ancient models, or of a city-republic like Geneva, considered

---

[8] A conciliatory note inviting Brissot to supper, 29 June, cf. AN, 446 AP, 22/88 and 22bis/89, on the Champ de Mars. *Corr.*, II, p. 321: two letters to Bancal dated 1 July brim with republicanism. One contains the words, often reproached Mme Roland, where she appears to justify bloodshed: 'the impulse to liberty is so strong and widespread that we must reach that liberty, even if it is through a sea of blood.' *Corr.*, II, p. 317.

[9] 24 June and 1 and 6 July, *Corr.*, II, pp. 309, 317, 319–22, 325.

[10] Ibid., p. 307, 23 June 1791.

[11] On Etta Palm d'Aelders, see Kates (1985), pp. 122–6.

[12] Baker (1975), pp. 304–5: causing 'a sensation' among former friends like Lafayette.

[13] Subtitle: *le Défenseur du gouvernement représentatif; Corr.*, II, p. 301, no love lost between Mme Roland and Condorcet, *Corr.*, II, pp. 319, 323; Kates (1985) pp. 162–4; *Mém.*, p. 170.

unworkable in its pure Rousseauist form in a large country. They were less likely to think of the United States of America (as Brissot and the Rolands evidently were).[14]

During these tumultuous weeks, the Assembly tried to rein in the crisis, by broadcasting the fiction that the king had been 'morally kidnapped' by Bouillé (who 'confessed' to it, from over the border). A temporary ministerial committee was handling current business, but the deputies still hoped to maintain the precarious balance of the new Constitution, getting the chastened king to cooperate. The Bastille Day celebrations took place surprisingly peacefully, with no royal presence, and only a few deputies. Lafayette was there on his white horse, but the brewing unrest was about to come to a head.

Since the stream of anti-monarchist petitions launched by the Cordeliers and their allies had been ignored by the Assembly, the club decided to bypass it, and launched an 'Address to the Nation'. It called on *départements* to send delegates to a new 'executive authority'—that is to replace the king and, by implication, the Assembly.[15] On 15 July, under pressure from these quarters, a committee of Jacobins (including Brissot, Lanthenas and Laclos) drafted another petition calling on the Assembly to accept Louis's abdication. Its final words were: 'and to provide for his replacement by constitutional means'. This was controversial (and its authorship disputed), since it could be read as replacing the king with a regent or successor from the royal family—code for an Orleanist succession. The plan was to place it on the 'people's altar' of 14 July, still standing on the Champ de Mars, where it would be signed by 'the people'. Danton read out the Jacobin version on the morning of 16 July, but sensing discontent, he agreed to present a more satisfactory text next day.[16]

However, the same day, the Assembly took a contrary decision: the king's person was inviolable, and he could *not* be brought to book for the events surrounding Varennes (an 'indecent farce', according to Mme Roland). Temporarily suspended, he would be reinstated when he formally ratified the Constitution. The Jacobins at once withdrew their petition, regarding it as irrelevant, if not illegal. Radicals like Robespierre were in any case reluctant to call openly for a republic, although they thought the king might be put on trial. However, the change of heart came too late to stop the majority of 'moderate' deputies among the Jacobins walking out—over 250 of them, led by Barnave. Committed to trying to rescue the monarchical constitution, they became known from now on as the 'Feuillants', since they reconvened in the Feuillants building, across the street. Behind them, they left 'a handful of the faithful [= radical] clustered round Pétion and Robespierre'. The Rolands both appear to have attended these Jacobin meetings.[17]

[14] Hammersley (2005), pp. 54–5, distinguishes between the Brissot representative model and the Cordeliers' 'delegate or semi-direct democracy;' cf. Tackett (2003), Chapter 7.

[15] *DCRE* 'Varennes'.

[16] Mme Roland on Orleans, 17 July to Bancal, *Corr.*, II, p. 333; ibid., p. 760.

[17] Mme Roland to Bancal, 15–22 July: running commentary, but not clear when she was an eye-witness, *Corr.*, II, pp. 327–46.

THE MASSACRE OF THE CHAMP DE MARS

The Cordeliers didn't give up. They decided to launch their revised petition during a huge rally by the 'fraternal societies' held on the Champ de Mars on 17 July. A violent incident occurred early on: two men hiding under the altar (they turned out to be peeping toms) were suspected of planning to blow it up and brutally lynched. This event alerted the city authorities. Meanwhile François Robert, a prominent Cordelier, and husband of Louise Kéralio, drew up the final wording and circulated copies of the petition on the field. None now survive. Although it avoided the word republic, it called on the deputies to reconsider and to replace the king by a different form of executive. It is generally agreed that it attracted some six thousand signatures before the demonstration was disrupted.[18]

Despite the earlier violence, the crowd was largely peaceful, with women and children present. It was only a petition after all. Under pressure to react against the challenge to authority, Mayor Bailly and General Lafayette, as commander of the national guard, ordered the red flag signifying martial law to be hoisted on the city hall. What happened next is disputed, but no official summons to disperse, as the law required, was issued. Stones were thrown at the national guards, shots were fired, and troopers on foot and horseback moved in. Firing continued for several minutes, there was panic and confusion, and when the smoke cleared, at least fifty people were dead and many more, possibly hundreds, wounded. The flight to Varennes had ended in a bloodbath.

Both Rolands were present on the Champ de Mars, though not apparently during the actual shooting. Mme Roland expressed sorrow and furious indignation to Bancal. 'Having attended out of curiosity, at midday', she reported next day on the events of the evening, probably at second hand: 'Mourning and death are among us, tyranny sits on a bloodstained throne... there is no liberty in Paris now except for those national guards who wish to cut the throats of their brothers.' Jean-Marie was also present the day of the massacre, as appears from a letter he later received from the painter Jacques-Louis David, saying: 'I wouldn't be so frank if you were not so good-hearted, and if our acquaintance did not date from 17 July, on the Champ de Mars, by the Altar of the Fatherland.'[19]

The subsequent wave of repression sent many radicals into exile (Danton to England) or hiding (Marat); newspapers closed. Roland wrote in alarmist terms to Champagneux:

> We are, my friend, in days of horror here, and they are throwing anyone who supports the revolution into jail. About three hundred are in the Abbaye. [...] There were hundreds of deaths on the Champ de Mars: husbands killed wives, relatives killed each other, friends killed friends. St Bartholomew and the *dragonnades* were not more horrible. They chased people everywhere, and finished off the wounded with sabres or blows from the butts of their guns.[20]

[18] Petition burned during 1871 Commune; Andress (2000); Tackett (2003).
[19] *Corr.*, II, p. 335; BNF MSS, naf 9532, fo 291. In the Convention, it was customary to say 'Were you at the Champ de Mars?'
[20] BNF MSS, naf 6241, 22 July 1791.

Right away, on the evening of 17 July, the Rolands found themselves harbouring a key figure of the day. François and Louise Robert appeared at the Hôtel Britannique at eleven that night, asking for shelter. Robert, part-author of the petition circulated on the field, was indeed at risk. The episode is recounted in Mme Roland's memoirs. Although fearing the hotel was unsafe, she asked the landlady for two camp beds. François Robert and Jean-Marie Roland slept in the outer room, while Louise slept 'in my husband's bed' in Marie-Jeanne's bedroom. By 1793, Mme Roland had reason to detest the Roberts, and relates censoriously that next day, instead of keeping a low profile, the couple drew attention to themselves by calling to people from her balcony. They reappeared for a meal [*la soupe*] with Mme Robert wearing 'feathers and a lot of rouge' while her husband was wearing a sky-blue silk coat. ('Are they mad? I wondered.')[21]

The Roberts survived unscathed, and at the time, Mme Roland referred to 'le brave Robert' as 'a good patriot'.[22] They were not the only people she took trouble over. Following a stormy meeting at the Jacobins, Mme Roland hauled her husband off on a quixotic quest to rescue Robespierre from potential violence. They took a cab to Robespierre's lodgings in the Marais, 'to offer him shelter', arriving at midnight to find him absent. He had already been offered accommodation, from similar motives probably, by the carpenter Maurice Duplay, with whose family he lodged, when in Paris, for the rest of his life.[23]

There were obvious reasons (coals of fire) why Mme Roland describes both incidents in her memoirs, by which time Robert and Robespierre were among her fiercest enemies, but there is no reason to doubt that they happened. In a letter to Bancal of 18 July, she wrote of her surprise at seeing the Roberts, whom she scarcely knew. There is no dated reference to the Robespierre expedition, but Buzot's memoirs support it independently.[24] In several letters in late July, Mme Roland refers warmly to Robespierre ('ce digne homme'), to Danton, and even—despite his 'excesses'—to Marat, whom she saw as equally unjustly under threat, 'for speaking the truth'. She reported to Bancal that 'fallacious tracts, agents provocateurs, every kind of prejudice and fabricated testimony' were being employed against 'good patriots'.[25]

Through that summer of repression, a mood of pessimism took hold. Mme Roland pined for 'my trees again' and the Beaujolais hills. Perhaps after all, 'private virtues' would be the only consolation, as we 'bury ourselves in a retreat somewhere', hoping to pass on 'the sacred flame of liberty in its purity to a happier generation'.[26] But she also encouraged Bancal to help confront the damaging split in the Jacobins. Nathan Perl-Rosenthal stresses the role of the 'Roland circle'

[21] *Mém.*, p. 116.
[22] BNF MSS, naf 6241: 14 August, PS on Roland's letter. Robert, turned down for an embassy post, spoke 'at length' against Roland, *Jacobins*, IV, p. 595, December 1792.
[23] *Mém.*, p. 136; Scurr (2007), pp. 154–5; before or after sheltering the Roberts? *Corr.*, II, p. 334. Robespierre was at the Jacobins every evening 15–18 July, *Jacobins*, III, pp. 14 ff.
[24] Buzot (1823), pp. 163–4, remembered because the Rolands asked for his help.
[25] *Corr.*, II, p. 344, 21 July 1791; ibid., p. 351, 27 July; Tackett (2003), pp. 203–5.
[26] Ibid., p. 336, letter begun on 17 July, finished on 18.

that summer, as their private networks worked to attach provincial branches to the radical Paris club, rather than secede with the Feuillants.[27]

One cheering element was the final success of Roland's mission. The Constituent Assembly, in its dying days—so it would not have to suffer the consequences—agreed a bail-out for Lyon. A decree of 5–10 August ('debts contracted by [...] municipalities') wrote off 33 million *livres*, leaving the city only 6 million to find.[28] It was an extraordinary achievement, and Mme Roland understandably complained of ingratitude: 'In the week before the decree, we would get many letters of lamentation, but since things have been settled, we have not yet had the pleasure of receiving a single expression of happiness or the slightest feeling of relief.'[29]

Even more annoyingly, the Rolands had not been reimbursed correctly by Lyon and had to borrow money for living expenses. Roland wrote a string of letters to Champagneux asking for funds: 'You have to *live* in Paris, and for someone who has no base there, at a time when paper money is losing 20 per cent of its value against cash, which you need even to shop in the market,' not receiving what was due meant they were 'only just managing'.[30] He also wondered whether his name would go forward for the forthcoming elections to the Legislative Assembly. He warned his wife not to go to Lyon on her return, so as not to provoke his enemies, but to go straight to Le Clos. The countryside would be their fallback position:

> If I'm elected, [...] I will forget nothing, attending to general matters and working away for particular matters [i.e. Lyon's interests]. If the opposite happens, I shall [...] go to the mountains and woods of my hermitage, and [...] try to revive the people and matters there.

He remained philosophical ('vienne que pourra' = what will be will be), but reminded Champagneux that 'everything—friends, acquaintances, my own affairs, anything of taste and pleasure—all have been sacrificed to my mission'.[31] His final report on the success of his Paris mission was dated 9 September. He might legitimately expect the Lyonnais to elect him to the Legislative Assembly out of gratitude.[32]

---

[27] Perl-Rosenthal (2011), chapter 7.
[28] Another grant of 450,000 *livres* obtained in October. As minister he managed another 2 million, *Patriote*, 29 April 1792, *Corr.*, II, note p. 288; Wahl (1894), p. 404.
[29] *Corr.*, II, p. 359.
[30] BNF MSS, naf 6241, 18 August: 1200 *livres* needed to pay off debts; cf. 11, 14, 21, 23, 27 August, ibid.
[31] Cf. letters of 30 August, 9 September, and *Corr.*, II, p. 214; BNF MSS, naf 6241, fol 105.
[32] Cf. Le Guin (1966) pp. 72–3; Mme Roland to Champagneux, 31 July, *Corr.*, II, pp. 354–5.

16

1791

Provincial Life Has Lost Its Charms

> I find myself, now that my job [as inspector] has been abolished, reminded
> [...] that the only alternatives for a man who has seen the world enough to
> know it are: Paris or the countryside.
>
> Jean-Marie Roland, autumn 1791.

Marie-Jeanne Roland prepared to return home ahead of her husband in late August.
Their daughter was pining for her parents. Mme Champagneux reported that
Eudora had read a letter from her papa, 'with astonishing avidity, and soon knew
it by heart'. The house in Villefranche was half-empty, and the wine-harvest was
approaching.[1] Jean-Marie could not yet follow, but Mme Roland's travelling companion was her new friend: Sophie Grandchamp.

This somewhat mysterious woman wrote her recollections in the 1800s, by
which time she had become a royalist; she also took the view, which colours her
account, that Roland should never have accepted the ministry in 1792. Much of
what Mme Grandchamp has to say rings true, other aspects of it are harder to
credit, but her testimony is valuable, as one of the Mme Roland's few close female
friends at this time.[2] The two women were introduced by Louis Bosc in August
1791, and took to each other. Sophie left a striking account of their first meeting:

> I can still see this famous woman sitting at a little table, *en habit d'amazone*, her dark
> hair in a 'jockey cut' [tied back, leaving short locks round the face, the coachmen's
> style]. She had an animated expression and gentle penetrating eyes, and spoke with a
> purity and choice of expressions which the silvery tone of her voice rendered more
> remarkable.[3]

Of Jean-Marie Roland, Sophie remarked less warmly that he was thin, above average height, with 'fine and intelligent features, on which were imprinted rigidity,
sarcasm, and disdain'.[4]

---

[1] BNF, MSS, naf 6241 (13 April 1791); cf. Mme Roland to Robespierre, 27 September 1791,
Corr., II, p. 386; to Bancal, ibid., p. 384.

[2] Sophie Grandchamp's memoirs (hereafter: Grandchamp) reproduced in *Mém.*/Perroud (1905),
pp. 461–97; manuscript in BNF MSS, naf 9533.

[3] Grandchamp, p. 462. A portrait—not Mme Roland—by Adelaïde Labille-Guiard (1787) illustrates the 'riding-habit' dress, Goodman (2009a), cover.

[4] Grandchamp, p. 463.

Bosc was surprised, put out even, when a friendship developed between the two women whom he described as 'an Athenian and a Spartan'. This remark also suggests that Mme Grandchamp (the Athenian) moved in worldlier, or perhaps the right word is *demi-mondaine* circles. Unlike most acquaintances of the strait-laced Rolands, she was not in a regular situation. Bosc later said that he 'had had a fling [*une passade*] with her, which engaged nothing, but the senses on either side'.[5] In 1792, she was possibly already living with Grandpré, later inspector of prisons, and *may* have been the mother of his young son. An educated woman, she gave unpaid lessons in 'astronomy, geography, and literature' and later translated Helen Maria Williams's *Sketches*.

A few days after their meeting, Mme Grandchamp received a pressing invitation to accompany Marie-Jeanne to the country. Mme Roland went to some lengths (leaving Fleury behind) to find Sophie a place in the crowded stagecoach. The two women spent the next few weeks together companionably in the Beaujolais, where Roland joined them in late September. Both the euphoria and the anxiety of the summer had subsided. However, it was far from clear what the couple's next move would be.

How was it that scarcely six months later, they were back in Paris and moving into the grand residence of the ministry of the Interior? This development was apparently as unforeseen by themselves as by anyone else. References to Mme Roland's 'ambition', which punctuate historical accounts of this time, hardly seem relevant. The obvious focus for ambition was election to the Legislative Assembly. But Roland was not elected. He could understandably feel disappointed, after his efforts on the debt bail-out, but his absence in the critical election period probably did him no good. According to his wife and Lanthenas, 'the cabal' of his enemies had been active during his enforced absence: the new deputies from the *département* were a few 'wrong-headed people from the city, peasants from the countryside, and several absolutely unknown men, although they are reputed to be honest'.[6]

Mme Roland told Bancal—who had also failed to be elected—that she was sorry her husband would not be a deputy, because 'he's become accustomed to public life; it is more necessary to him than he thinks himself; his energy and activity become very bad for his health when they are not being used as he would wish'.[7] There may be some wishful thinking here, but Roland himself showed signs of restlessness. Frustratingly, the Lyon municipality had written in September asking him to stay on in Paris, as a supernumerary *deputy*, but the letter had reached the capital too late, and the offer was not repeated. He raised the question again in October—showing that he would not have minded returning—'but it didn't catch on'.[8] Any political ambitions would have to be local ones. Roland was, in fact,

    [5] See *Corr.*, II, p. 676, 'passade' from *Notes et archives* online, based on Perroud (1899); Grandpré = possibly Pierre-Claude Lemoyne de Grandpré, see *Mém.*/Perroud (1905), p. 30.
    [6] To Bancal, *Corr.*, II, p. 381, 11 September; cf. Lanthenas to Bancal, 8 September 1791, on the 'cabal', PS by Roland: 'It will be back to slavery by a primrose path', BNF MSS, naf 9533.
    [7] To Bancal, 11 September 1791, *Corr.*, II, p. 382.
    [8] BNF MSS, naf 6241.

elected to the district council in September, then re-elected to the city council in December—both of which, after some thought, he refused.[9]

A decision was urgent though, because one of the last acts of the outgoing Constituent Assembly, on 27 September, was to abolish the inspectorate of manufactures. Although not unexpected, it was a blow.[10] As Mme Roland put it: 'it is not very agreeable to lose an income of 5000 *livres* after forty years service, without the slightest compensation'. Roland might qualify for a pension related to length of service, but 'you have to ask for it, and these days, those who don't ask don't get [...] I wish we were not so far from the capital'.[11]

Roland was evidently torn between returning to Paris or making his home more permanently in the Beaujolais—or elsewhere in the country. As he wrote to Champagneux in mid-October:

If Paris can be a stormy sea, at least you can always find an anchorage there [...] so I find myself, now that my job has been abolished, reminded of my former opinion that the only alternatives for a man who has seen the world enough to know it are: Paris or the countryside. However, before I make a final decision, or to give it a firmer basis, I shall go to Paris this winter, perhaps alone, perhaps with my family.[12]

Mention of *la campagne* refers not only to Le Clos, but to the revived possibility of the communal scheme. Of the original partners, Brissot, newly elected to the Assembly, was out of it: 'he has his future mapped out for two years and is making his arrangements up here [in Paris]'.[13] But some of the others were still interested, and as everyone well knew, the *assignat* was depreciating.[14] In July, Bancal had unilaterally bought an ex-church property, Bonneval, in the Limousin.[15] In June, Marie-Jeanne, with a little inherited money, had bought a field and a wood adjoining Le Clos. They had hesitated too long to buy the whole neighbouring property. Nothing acquired so far was of a size to meet the ambitious original plans. On the other hand, Lanthenas was still keen to find a safe place for his funds.[16]

Back in August, just before Mme Roland had left Paris, she and Lanthenas had written jointly to Bancal:

We think it prudent and necessary to put our money somewhere and our circumstances make this very urgent, because Lanthenas' money is sleeping in a portfolio, and for us the time has come to renew some bills which we have either to cash in or

---

[9] Wahl (1894), pp. 426 and 450.

[10] *Corr.*, II, p. 201, 30 November 1790, to Bancal: they already envisaged having to go to Paris on that account. Cf. Le Guin (1966), p. 73.

[11] To Champagneux, 12 October 1791, *Corr.*, II, pp. 389–90 and 396. Cf. letter to Brissot with 'reflections' for *Le Patriote*: AN, 446 AP, 25/92: undated, but this autumn.

[12] BNF, MSS, naf 6241, 18 October 1791.

[13] BNF, MSS, naf 9534, 22 September 1791, Lanthenas to Bancal.

[14] See *Corr.*, II, July 1791; 29, 30 August 1791, pp. 361–4.

[15] Corr., II, Appendix Q.

[16] *Corr.*, II, p. 396, and note (re letter in Morrison Collection); Lanthenas to Bancal, 16 June 1790, BNF MSS, naf 9534, fo 238: a property in Le Puy worth 15,000 *livres,* and capital of 24,000 *livres* invested locally.

they will hold us up afterwards. The ties that unite all three parties make us think it possible and agreeable to place them in common. [...] The *nec plus ultra* for us is 60,000 *livres*.[17]

The property they now had in mind was the ruined priory and dependencies of Sainte-Radegonde, in the forest of Montmorency, a district well known to Bosc and Bancal from their botanizing trips. It would have been a convenient base, if Roland had been elected to the Legislative Assembly. However, in the end, it was the well-off Bancal, not the Rolands, who bought Sainte-Radegonde in January 1792, asking Bosc to look after it for him. (It plays a significant part in the end of this story.)[18]

In October, Mme Roland asked Champagneux whether he knew of any property in the Dauphiné, or near Lyon, *without* a vineyard—her husband had specified 'not for anything in the world would I want vines'. Was Savigny still for sale? In a final throw of the dice, in mid-October, Lanthenas visited the ex-Cistercian abbey of Mortemer, in Normandy. A great estate, now in disrepair, it contained several farms, listed in a detailed schedule. If they created an *école nationale* there, the plan would possibly be viable. As the Roland family eventually prepared to leave for Paris, Marie-Jeanne wrote on 30 November: 'Here is the latest from the faithful Lanthenas, who is waiting for us; as soon as we get to Paris, one of us will probably have to make the trip to Mortemer with him, to decide once and for all if we should settle somewhere, or else give up thinking about this scheme.'[19]

All these hesitations show that the Rolands were trying to reconcile their interests as a family with the changed landscape of revolutionary France. For the time being, they could hardly have any political ambition, and were rather gloomy about the Revolution. 'If public life does not improve, the only thing left to good citizens will be to love each other'—in other words to set up their grass-roots community.[20] If they couldn't do that, Mme Roland's own vote went for a return to Paris. She certainly felt restless in the Beaujolais. According to Sophie, who shared in family discussions of what to do next, her friend was dreading more work on the encyclopedia, which she now considered very boring:

> How I am to be pitied, my friend would say to me. The work I have to do disgusts and exhausts me. I shall be shut up in the countryside with no distractions to break the sad monotony of my life or to comfort my secret sorrows. Why can I not spend my life with you?[21]

It is true that Sophie's view is coloured by later events, and she hints at the 'secret sorrows' without being explicit. At the time, Mme Roland certainly used the much-quoted expression 'the desperate nullity of the provinces' more than once,

---

[17] *Corr.*, II, pp. 365–6, 31 August 1791, cf. previous letter of 29 August, pp. 361–4.
[18] Ibid., p. 364n., Roland also bought land at Villeron, district de Gonesse, restored to Eudora in 1795.
[19] *Corr.*, II, p. 391, 30 November, to Roland in Lyon, my italics. Lanthenas did later buy property near Mortemer.
[20] Mme Roland to Bancal, 30 August 1791, *Corr.*, II, p. 364.
[21] Grandchamp, p. 467.

including in an effusive fan letter to Robespierre. However, it should also be noted that the phrase originally referred to election results, and that she was simultaneously writing apparently cheerful letters claiming to enjoy country life.[22]

There were practical reasons for returning to Paris, at least for the winter, agreed by husband and wife: it was easier to lobby for a pension in person than if one was 'far from the capital'. There was Eudora's education to think about. When Marie-Jeanne had visited the ten-year-old at the convent on arriving from Paris, they had both broken down in tears, and instead of leaving Eudora behind while she dealt with the 'layers of dust' in the Villefranche house, Mme Roland took her straight home. However, she was disappointed (all over again) at her child's lack of intellectual progress. Eudora had learnt nothing in the convent—perhaps a stay in Paris would provide some stimulus. By late November, Eudora was more promisingly reading Homer and Ovid in translation in the evenings with her mother, but Mme Roland revealingly wrote to Jean-Marie that she could not see any way of devoting herself entirely to the education of one child.[23] The hope was for Eudora to have a broader education, as well as to start thinking of her future marriage prospects. As for Le Clos, once the grape harvest and the winemaking was complete, it virtually shut down until the spring, while there was little to tempt the family in Villefranche society.

The clearest summary of their thinking (though not without a little spin) occurs retrospectively in Mme Roland's letter to their Swiss friends the Gosses, after they had arrived in Paris:

> Retiring [to the country] is wise and agreeable for philosophizing; but our rustic manor is a real hermitage [*une thébaïde*], difficult of access, wild and without neighbours; a solitude where the only society is the farmyard. For a man used to political life and communicating with cultivated minds, such a life should not be embraced unthinkingly; besides we only have one daughter, but she exists, and nobody will come looking for her in a desert. Having been obliged to come to Paris for business [the pension], we have decided to stay seven or eight months [which would take them up to the grape harvest] during which we will try to occupy ourselves usefully and if it succeeds, that will be a way of keeping us here, where activity, taste, and friendships can always be satisfied, despite the rumblings of politics. We are thinking of a periodical, totally devoted to agriculture, the [practical] arts and trade, which will interest even foreigners by its subject.[24]

The reference to the periodical (plans for which only jelled once they were in Paris) hints at the most convincing reason why the Rolands chose to leave the Beaujolais in early December 1791. With his post abolished, Roland's chief source of a cash income was his writing. Indeed, the first thing he wanted to do in Paris was supervise for Panckoucke the long-delayed printing of Volume III of the *Dictionnaire des manufactures*. However, he hoped to have other irons in the fire. In late November

---

[22] *Corr.*, II, p. 378, to Roland, 8 September; to Bancal, p. 382; to Robespierre 27 September, p. 384: did he ever reply?

[23] To Roland, 30 November 1791, *Corr.,* II, p. 392.

[24] *Corr.*, II, pp. 408–9, 24 January 1792; cf. *Corr.*, NS, II, supplement, p. 534.

1791, Lanthenas had finally abandoned the rural plan and taken a decision: he invested 26,000 *livres* in the Imprimerie du Cercle social in Paris, run by the printer Jean-Louis Reynier and their old contact, Bonneville. There is no record of the Rolands following suit, but it is not impossible. In retrospect, Lanthenas's choice tells us how central the idea of a printing house and publication had been to the communal idea in all its variants.[25]

The Cercle social's printing press was 'one of the nation's most important publishing houses'. While the Jacobins and Cordeliers published news sheets containing minutes and developing club ideas, no other group had 'collectively owned an entire publishing house or planned and executed a full publishing programme'. The Cercle's political activities had been abruptly curtailed by the Champ de Mars fallout, and publishing was now its main activity. Lanthenas was to involve himself substantially in future propaganda, and the Imprimerie du Cercle social was his printer of choice.[26] The Rolands' plans for a periodical were with the same publishing house. This helps make sense of a rather cryptic letter that Roland wrote to his friend Champagneux on 2 December:

> I leave tomorrow for Paris. At last, this is the execution of the grand project [...] I do not know how favourable circumstances will be. [...] The fact is that mistrust is growing, fears are spreading, and we are close to some violent crisis. Let us hope that it will be of a kind to decide our fate which has been so long uncertain. When I have understood or at least registered the state of affairs in Paris, I'll write to you. You can contact me via Bosc.[27]

So *pace* historians and biographers who have assumed otherwise, analysis of the family papers tends not to support any long-laid political ambition in the decision to travel to Paris, which turned out to be fateful. The Rolands cannot have dreamed of ministerial office at this stage, though the letter hints that Jean-Marie meant to pick up some threads. Their correspondence shows them still considering the plan for a provincial community until November. When it fell through, a visit to the capital became attractive for various reasons, but largely to help their financial situation through contact with publishing circles. They both preferred Paris to Villefranche, and a winter on the farm tempted neither of them. They left it to be cared for temporarily by their faithful servant, Marguerite Fleury, planning to return in time for the next grape harvest. (When their fortunes abruptly changed three months later, they summoned her so suddenly to Paris that she had to leave on a washday, leaving half her clothes behind.) Neither Jean-Marie nor Marie-Jeanne Roland would ever see Le Clos again.[28]

[25] Kates (1985), p. 183.
[26] Ibid., pp. 190, 178.
[27] BNF MSS, naf 6241; See *Corr.*, II, Appendix L p. 695, on Lanthenas's campaigns and possible effect on the laws of 15 March 1790, 8 April 1791, 4 January and 7 March 1793, and his articles in Brissot's *Patriote*.
[28] Fleury's clothes, BNF MSS, naf 22424.

PART IV

IN THE THICK OF IT

17

March 1792
What, No Buckles? The Brissotin Ministry

'We are not deserting the countryside,'
Mme Roland to Mme Gosse, 20 March 1792.[1]

The Rolands arrived back in Paris, with Eudora, on 15 December 1791. No longer on an expense account, they occupied cramped quarters on the top floor of the Hôtel Britannique. Sophie Grandchamp had booked their rooms, and her account of their arrival bears the plausible marks of a perceived slight. They had left word at the stagecoach terminal that they were too tired to receive visitors. On persevering, she found Roland sitting by the fire reading a book, from which he scarcely bothered to look up. She sent round a sharp note: M. Roland had used her as a proofreader and adviser in Le Clos, so why was he now incapable of common courtesy? Shortly afterwards, he came round to apologize, telling his wife: 'She is quite right. I shall take her my reply in person.' To Sophie he said: 'You have humiliated me; and I think all the better of you for it.'[2]

The upshot, which Mme Grandchamp may not have greatly appreciated, was that she was indeed asked to help with editorial work, since Mme Roland was unwell. Sophie claims that from then on, Jean-Marie came round to her apartment at eight in the morning and they worked until two, after which she spent the afternoon with his wife. Sophie was presumably editing or proof-reading—the kind of thing Marie-Jeanne now found excruciatingly boring, but which remained her husband's chief priority.[3] Production began of the long-delayed Volume III. Its preface states: 'Begun in October 1790, the printing has been delayed until now [January 1792] because there is no work which should not be subordinated to the duty of the citizen.'[4]

Roland was also re-drafting his *Mémoire des services* for pension purposes, stressing his record of near-forty years of service. One version is dated December 1791, another February 1792: some of the text is in Mme Roland's handwriting.[5] The fact that there are two suggests it was not easy to get a hearing, and by March, no progress had been made.

Reconnecting with political life was not automatic. *Le petit comité* in its original form did not exist. Mme Roland in her memoirs remarks that the old sociability

---

[1] *Corr.*, NS, II, suppl., p. 534.   [2] Grandchamp, pp. 470–1.
[3] *Corr.*, II., p. 396.   [4] *Dictionnaire*, vol. 3, p. 493.
[5] Ibid., p. 397; BNF MSS, naf 6243, December 1791; ibid., naf 9532, 20 February 1792.

was no longer there: not even their original friends still in the capital were regular visitors. Pétion, now mayor of Paris, lived in the official residence on the Ile de la Cité. Both the Rolands paid visits, but were rather miffed by the Pétions' cool reception. Brissot, now a leading deputy, was less available for informal dinners. In a letter to Mme Gosse in March, Marie-Jeanne frankly contrasted their situation in 1791 and 1792: the previous year her husband had had a mission and status; they were well-lodged and 'the most renowned patriotic deputies' came to visit them four or five times a week. 'Our position was really interesting.' Whereas now, modestly lodged and fighting for a pension, they were without their friends, who were either 'back home, or in high posts and have forgotten us'. Last year she was seeing plenty of people and occupied with politics, now she is just 'shut up in my room reading'—and this the very day before Roland was first approached about the ministry.[6]

Her husband had, however, been regularly attending the Jacobin Club, which had an increasingly radical identity. Bosc, Lanthenas, and Bancal were all members and by February they had recruited Roland to the correspondence committee.[7] But the Jacobins were increasingly dividing along new lines. Robespierre, back from Arras and a dominant speaker, was at ever more bitter odds with Brissot (who attended less often because of his Assembly role). The split was over the question of war (see below under 'Taking sides'). In these early months of 1792, while this disagreement was evident, but fairly muted, the Rolands might hope to remain on good terms with both men, but apparently saw little of either of them.[8]

Marie-Jeanne, although under the weather, did have one outlet: helping her husband deal with the club's correspondence. Committee members were responsible for a number of provincial centres, replying to letters sent to the Paris mother-club. It was a crucial process, as the Jacobins evolved into a sort of shadow Assembly. Mme Roland reports that she took pleasure in composing letters ('the epistolary genre has always seemed singularly easy and agreeable to me') and that between them they got through a lot of work. In this respect, the Rolands were being drawn into the political debate.[9]

Jacobin circulars were printed by the Imprimerie du Cercle social, into which, as we saw, Lanthenas had sunk his funds, in the interests of propagating the ideals of the new state to clubs all over France. Since the previous July, Bonneville and Reynier's publishing house had been putting out the monthly *Chronique du mois*, and in January 1792 began the academic *Journal d'histoire naturelle*. This may have been the context for the Rolands' own project, a journal on 'agriculture, the [industrial] arts and trade', to be published and printed by the Cercle social.[10] The

[6] *Corr.*, NS, II, supplement, pp. 534–5, 20 March. Cf. *Mém.*, p. 64.
[7] *Corr.*, II, p. 397; joint secretary on 20, 27 February, and 2 March.
[8] Whaley (2000) pp. 46–7, suggests that Brissot and Robespierre originally differed mainly on tactical grounds.
[9] *Mém.*, p. 147; M. Kennedy (1988); *Jacobins*, III, pp. 323 ff; on *noyautage* of the Jacobins, Perl-Rosenthal (2011).
[10] Sophie Grandchamp (p. 472) claimed she helped arrange it; cf. Kates (1985) pp. 183 ff.; *Corr.*, II, p. 396. Panckoucke advertised it, but was not the proposed publisher.

Moniteur of 28 February and 1 March 1792 carried an advertisement for a *Journal des Arts utiles*, edited by Jean-Marie Roland. The archives contain the original agreement whereby Roland undertook '*jointly with my wife*, the composition of a periodical' with this title, for a duration of six years—he would provide six pages of copy per month. It can be seen as part of the larger Cercle social project: 'the moral regeneration of the people would come from books'.[11]

The idea was to spend half the year in Paris. On 10 March 1792, Jean-Marie Roland signed a six-year lease (corresponding to the *Journal* contract) at 450 *livres*, for a small second-floor flat looking on to the courtyard at 51 rue de La Harpe, in the Latin quarter, opposite the church of Saint Côme. The house is long since demolished: its site was roughly where the boulevard Saint-Michel meets the rue de l'Ecole de Médecine. The landlord, Jean-Alexandre Cauchois, was a Jacobin, The Roland family planned to move at Easter to this Paris *pied-a-terre*, and then go to Le Clos in the summer: 'We are not deserting the countryside'.

In connection with his new plans, Roland delivered a lecture on a quasi-agricultural topic: 'Usury and hoarding', to 'a circle of friends' (presumably the Cercle social) and printed it as a brochure, in February. A key text for understanding his later position, it rehearsed arguments about the distribution of grain and other foodstuffs. A central point was that given the geography of France, the price of transport had to be factored into grain prices. Farmers who clung on to their grain when there was plenty and prices were low, waiting for better returns that would also pay for transport, were not necessarily to be condemned. The real villains were speculators who bought up massive sections of the harvest (a form of the futures market), hoarded them, and speculated in the high prices they had themselves created. These men of 'insatiable cupidity' were speculating on public poverty. However, he concluded, with no law against usury or hoarding, the only legitimate sanction was to 'expose such men to public opprobrium'. We do not know how this rather theoretical, not to say idealist, appeal to public opinion was received. At the time, while there was no bread crisis, there were shortages in Paris of items like coffee and sugar, now becoming staples of the general diet, but these colonial products were subject to different obstacles.[12]

For Roland himself then, unlike his wife, these early weeks were full of activity and contacts. In March, he wrote to Champagneux, he 'scarcely had time to breathe'. 'I belong to three societies, not counting the Jacobins, for whom I have just stopped being secretary, and where I am still on the correspondence committee, which gives me five or six *départements* to deal with.' He was also still advising the Lyon city council on how to lobby the Assembly. Champagneux as municipal officer, was now allied with the radical Joseph Chalier against the more conservative district and departmental councils, and needing help from Paris.[13] In his usual forthright style, Roland told him there was no point writing to the president of the

[11] Dorigny (1989a), p. 205; agreement in BNF MSS, naf 22423, fo 54; cf. ibid., naf 9532, fos 194–7; *Corr.*, II, p. 397, Roland to Gosse, 24 January; *Mém.*, p. 64; AN, W294, doss. 227, cote 28.
[12] *Des usuriers et accapareurs*, Paris: Cercle social, 1792 (BNF).
[13] *Corr.*, II, p. 410 note; Wahl (1894), pp. 429–89; BNF MSS, naf 6241; cf. *Corr.*, II, p. 717.

Assembly ('you might as well save the paper to wipe your backside') and that persistent lobbying and networking was the only way. The same letter tells us that he had revived links with Pétion, 'at whose house, we [whoever this means] had a meeting with twelve or fifteen of our best deputies, to confer and decide the measures to take'.[14]

This clearly indicates that Roland was the one who had willingly reconnected with Parisian political circles, while his wife remained unwell. He was having to run domestic errands, since 'I've had my wife ill for three weeks now, giving me much anxiety'. Sophie Grandchamp suggests in her memoir that Mme Roland was depressed 'with secret cares', and even—although this sounds unlikely—suicidal. How true this is, or whether it might be fallout from the Bancal attachment, is unknowable. One wonders, too, how keen Marie-Jeanne was on the proposed periodical.[15]

TAKING SIDES

The vision of a manageable combination of 'Paris and the countryside' was about to be changed for ever. As the foregoing suggests, there is no sign (and plenty of counter-evidence) of hopes for any political office. The Rolands must have had some contact with Brissot and other old friends, and been aware of the dissension between Brissot's sphere of influence—the Legislative Assembly—and Robespierre's—the Jacobin Club. But there is every indication that Roland's appointment as minister of the Interior before the end of March came as a complete surprise.[16] To understand it, a brief outline of the situation in March 1791, in which Brissot played a key role, is called for.

Brissot was a much occupied man, at the centre of Assembly affairs. He sat on the diplomatic committee, and in the new political configuration was—along with Condorcet—one of the emergent leaders of the left and a frequent speaker. Since autumn 1791 he had acquired new allies, chief among them three newly-elected deputies from the Gironde *département*, all lawyers from Bordeaux: Pierre-Victurnien Vergniaud (1753–1793); Armand Gensonné (1758–1793); and Marguerite-Elie Guadet (1755–1793), president of the Bordeaux criminal court. It was of this trio, augmented by others, that the name 'Gironde' and 'Girondin' started to be used, although in these early days 'Brissotin' was the more usual term.

How did these people get together? At his trial in 1793, when replying to Chabot's testimony about his meetings with the Gironde deputies, Brissot said that they had contacted him when the Legislative Assembly convened in October 1791, 'because of my opinions on the colonies', i.e. about the slave trade, for which

---

[14] BNF MSS, naf 6241, fo 147, March 1792.

[15] Grandchamp, pp. 472–5. Mme Roland described the journal as 'a distraction' from politics, *Mém.*, p. 64.

[16] I can find no documentary basis for G. Walter's reference to 'lobbying for the ministry', *Actes*, p. 352, although Grandchamp (p. 475) claimed later that Mme Roland 'nourished a secret ambition, envying those who were not as worthy as her husband', etc.

Bordeaux was a major port. They, too, had liberal and emancipationist views on slavery—*against* the economic interests of Bordeaux merchants. Brissot said that they agreed to meet to lunch (*déjeuner*) three times a week before going to the Assembly. It was a new version of the *petit comité* (as Mme Roland called it), although Brissot said the meetings were open to anyone who wished to come. It certainly became a place of power-broking.[17]

The meetings in question—more exclusive than Brissot claimed, by dint of being between friends—were held during the winter of 1791–1792 'chez Madame Dodun'. The word '*salon*' has been used of this venue too, but it hardly applies. Mme Dodun, née Louise-Marie-Julie Bourgeois, was the wife, later divorced to save their property, of a director of the French East India Company. They owned a large house at 5, now 12, Place Vendôme, (ex-Place Louis-le-Grand, later Place des Piques). The elusive Mme Dodun, whom nobody ever mentions meeting in person, seems simply to have been Vergniaud's landlady. He and another deputy from the south-west, Pierre-Roger Ducos (1765–1793), lodged in her house. She made available a larger meeting room (literally a *salon),* even when she was not in residence. Mme Roland in her memoirs refers to these meetings as happening 'sometimes', and that Roland was invited, but 'usually thought it too far to go' (although in fact it was near the Jacobins). Lanthenas was, however, a regular attender.[18]

The men who met at the Place Vendôme shared Brissot's view on war, the critical issue of that spring. Vergniaud had made a rousing speech in favour of war in December. Their 'hawkish' stance triggered the ministerial crisis of March 1792—and thus Roland's appointment. But it was also the major cause of the Brissot–Robespierre split. Robespierre, although initially sympathetic to the idea of a preventive war with Austria, set his face firmly against it in December 1791, on the grounds that the French potential armies were under-prepared (he was right about that); and that the more important problem was 'the enemy within'—which increasingly meant not only the remaining aristocrats, the Feuillants, and the court, but also—eventually—some of his former associates among radical politicians. In particular, he feared, not implausibly, that army generals, above all Lafayette, would take advantage of war to stage a coup. Responding to pro-war Assembly speeches by Brissot, Robespierre on 18 January declared at the Jacobins that he did not attack M. Brissot: 'our principles are the same, but I have refuted his opinion [...] The National Assembly should show great mettle, restore order to the kingdom and exhaust all the good legislators can do, and [only] then declare war.' Brissot replied with another long speech in the Assembly favouring war, yet he and Robespierre embraced at the Jacobins on the evening of 20 January.[19]

[17] *Actes,* p. 302; *Mém.,* p. 147.
[18] *Mém.,* pp. 146–9; neither Senevas (1938) nor Lintilhac (1918) offers evidence of Mme Dodun being at any meeting. Rivalry between 'her salon' and 'Mme Roland's', cf. Sydenham (1961), pp. 75 ff., is wholly fictional. *Corr.,* II, p. 398n., one reference to Roland dining 'at Mme Dodun's', September 1792.
[19] *Jacobins,* III, pp. 333 ff.; Brissot, 15 December: 'War, war, that is the cry of all patriots'; Vergniaud, 30 December: 'Aux armes, donc aux armes.'

Although the French *émigrés* in Coblenz were agitating for allied intervention, most historians now discount the seriousness of the war threat posed by the emperor Leopold II and Frederick-William of Prussia. Despite the belligerence of the Declaration of Pillnitz back in August 1791, it appears that they were not really eager to use force to maintain monarchic rule in France.[20] Brissot, however, brandished the threat as an argument. He was the key speaker in favour of war and there is no doubt he influenced the Assembly in this direction, arguing for a conflict that would unite progressive nations against the 'dark forces' of the courts of Europe. He argued both from principle—an ideological war would rouse other peoples to freedom—and pragmatism; pre-empting a possible war would deprive France's enemies of advantage. He and his Girondin colleagues also had a political agenda. War would unite patriots, expose traitors, and force the king to make a choice, probably showing him in his true colours.

The consensus of history is that Brissot 'grossly underestimated the dangers of war', and seems to have been carried away by his own rhetoric. Apparently believing that the subject peoples of western Europe would rise up and greet the French as liberators, he irresponsibly started something he would never be able to control. Given the sabre-rattling tone of Austrian and Prussian diplomatic moves, the 'preventive' thesis could be viewed as plausible, and Brissot's views were not confined to a minority, but one undeniable effect of his stance was to split radical opinion, with disastrous future consequences.[21]

The Feuillant leaders (Barnave and the Lameths, out of the Assembly, but still active) favoured peace, in order to uphold the 1791 Constitution, but were frustrated by the foreign allies' refusal to recognize it and by Louis XVI's indecision. They eventually withdrew from the political battle. The Lafayette faction favoured war, as likely to boost their fortunes, while certain elements at court were hopeful of a defeat for France. The king himself, while aware of these calculations, was said to be personally reluctant.

His minister of War, the count of Narbonne-Lara (b. 1755), a Fayettist and career soldier, favoured a limited war against the elector of Trèves and the emperor. That pleased neither the court, which hoped to provoke massive armed intervention by all the powers, nor the Assembly, influenced by Brissot, which was prepared to let loose a 'true and passionate national war [...] to consolidate [France's] liberty and purge it of the evils of despotism'.[22] Brissot and his allies were waiting for Narbonne to complete his useful military preparations before turning against him. Louis, who was not short of advice, often contradictory, sacked Narbonne on 9 March, replacing him with another soldier, De Grave. The Brissotins riposted, accusing the foreign minister, Valdec De Lessart, Narbonne's chief opponent, of treachery by concealing information. A domino crisis followed: Cahier de Gerville,

---

[20] On war, Blanning (1986); Sutherland (1985), p. 135; Doyle (2002), pp. 178 ff.; Whaley (2000), pp. 46 ff.

[21] Blanning's verdict (1986), pp. 103 ff.—uncomfortable reading for Brissotins!—is large-scale 'mutual miscalculation' by both France and its enemies. Cf. Hampson (1978/1988), p. 68.

[22] Le Guin (1966), pp. 77–8, Brissot speech, 16 December.

minister of the Interior, resigned on 10 March; Molleville, minister of the Navy, followed suit on 11 March.[23]

Constitutionally, it was the king's prerogative alone to hire and fire ministers. He could not choose any member of the Legislative Assembly, and had to take advice in finding men who would be both competent and politically acceptable. The increasing turnover of ministers in the winter of 1791–1792 illustrated the difficulty of filling posts. On 15 March, Louis decided, against his personal wishes, but in the interests of short-term accord, to appoint ministers agreeable to the Assembly. He invited General Dumouriez to take over at Foreign Affairs. Dumouriez, while apparently just about acceptable at court,[24] was also favoured by Brissot for his pro-war stance, and known to the 'patriot' left in the Assembly. In particular, he was friendly with Gensonné, a *habitué* of the Place Vendôme. The two men had become close when posted to the Vendée, and Gensonné regularly consulted Dumouriez about foreign affairs during the first months of the Legislative.[25]

Charles-François du Périer, aka Dumouriez (1739–1823), was nearer Roland's age than Brissot's. A long career in (secret) diplomacy and the army lay behind him, and he had the not undeserved reputation of being a *roué* in private life. Mme Roland described him as having 'the confident air of a military man, the manners of a cunning courtier and the way of speaking of a wit, but nowhere showing the character of truth'.[26] The key figure in what became known as the 'Brissotin' ministry, he neither shared all Brissot's views nor even felt any loyalty towards him. Still, it was natural for Dumouriez to ask the Place Vendôme 'committee' to suggest ministers: initially for the Interior and for Public Contributions, as Brissot later stated during his trial. Although these consultations took place with the emerging progressive majority of the Assembly, they were not opened to the further shores of radical opinion in the Jacobin Club, for what may seem obvious reasons.[27] Nonetheless, Dumouriez did take the unusual step—for a minister—of going to the Jacobins on the evening of 19 March and sporting a liberty cap, before warmly embracing Robespierre.[28]

Brissot's friend, Clavière, looked a reasonable choice for *Contributions publiques* (taxation), as a financial expert.[29] When it came to the Interior, the need was for a good administrator who was politically reliable. Who first suggested Roland's name is not clear. Sophie Grandchamp later claimed, plausibly, that it was Lanthenas, and that she herself advised against, on the grounds that the Rolands were

[23] On Narbonne, Whaley (2000), p. 52: De Lessart (1742–1792), was charged with 'concealing the intentions of the foreign powers from the Assembly, and carrying on secret negotiations with them'. Cf. Bernardin (1964), pp. 61–2.

[24] 'Less extreme than he is thought,' Jaurès (1983 edn), II, note by Soboul, p. 259 (Piece 10, *Troisième recueil de l'armoire de fer*).

[25] Howe (2008), pp. 45–51. She argues *passim* that Dumouriez's agenda was the liberation of Belgium and the Low Countries.

[26] *Mém.*, p. 149.

[27] Ibid., p. 148: 'if Jacobin hotheads were appointed that would have discredited the patriots'—nor would they have accepted.

[28] *Jacobins*, III, pp. 439–40, for his speech, and Robespierre's cautious reply.

[29] On Clavière, Whatmore (1996); Shovlin (2006), esp. pp. 157–9, 185.

provincials, who would be victims of court manoeuvres. Brissot's approval, readily given, was essential, but he unwisely concealed his choice under cover of two other names, Dietrich, mayor of Strasbourg, and Jean-Marie Collot d'Herbois. Dietrich later defected, but Collot, whether seriously expecting the post or not, became a ferocious opponent of the minister.[30]

Roland's appointment astonished everyone. The night before he was approached, according to Sophie Grandchamp, he had even remarked to her: 'at least my obscurity saves me from having any fear, and I bless it'.[31] He was so unknown among deputies that Brissot had to deny the old rumour that he was his brother-in-law.[32] But it was not necessarily such an eccentric choice. Dumouriez, who had never met Roland, later wrote that he was 'known for some very good books on trade and manufacture'. After all, he had experience of administration and foreign travel, of municipal politics, and of Parisian political circles. He was totally committed to the Revolution and, approaching sixty, he gave every sign of being a safe pair of hands. Indeed, to the rakish Dumouriez, he seemed a quaint sobersides: 'He looked like Plutarch or a Quaker in his Sunday best: his straight white hair with very little powder and his black coat [...] meant that he seemed at court to be as exotic as a rhinoceros.' Mme Roland herself repeated the anecdote of her husband's first appearance there. Since his shoes had ribbons instead of silver buckles, a footman whispered in alarm to Dumouriez: 'What! no buckles, Monsieur!' to which Dumouriez replied with mock-panic, 'Ah, all is lost!' After this incident, courtiers apparently muttered about the 'sans-culotte ministry'.[33]

The first the Rolands heard of the proposal was a hint from Lanthenas, which they did not take seriously. An evening visit by Brissot followed on 21 March, to see whether Roland would accept. Mme Roland later said she still thought he was joking. According to her memoirs, the couple talked it over, and Mme Roland recalled that her husband had laughed, saying that he had often wondered how things got done, since most ministers were so inefficient.[34] He eventually accepted it, one must conclude, in a spirit of public duty, pressed hard by Brissot, who represented to him that the Interior ministry was both delicate and wide-ranging, so that it would be a relief to know it was in politically reliable hands. Finally, late at night on 23 March, Dumouriez himself arrived at the Hôtel Britannique and advised them that Roland had been proposed, and was invited to kiss hands at the Tuileries next day. To what extent his wife 'pushed' him to accept, a frequent assertion, is not an easy question to answer, in the absence of clear evidence. She appears to have seen it as a call from destiny that should not be refused

Sophie Grandchamp provides a vivid (though is it quite reliable?) account of their reaction. She called early in the morning of 24 March—according to her because they had sent her a note seeking her advice. They were still in bed—no

---

[30] Bernardin (1964), p. 41; cf. Brissot in *Chronique du mois*, November 1792, cited Whaley (2000), p. 53. Collot d'Herbois (1749–*c.*1796) former actor and playwright, Jacobin, later Montagnard deputy to Convention.

[31] Grandchamp, p. 474.   [32] Ellery (1970), p. 78; *Corr.*, II, p. 401.

[33] Bois (2005), p. 185; *Mém.*, p. 150.   [34] *Mém.*, pp. 148–9.

doubt after a sleepless night—and in a state of high anxiety, but at a reception later that day, she found them surrounded by well-wishers (and job-hunters), the fragile Mme Roland of the morning transformed into a beaming *châtelaine*, welcoming all the attention. It's perfectly possible.[35] Mme Roland certainly hastened to write to her friends announcing the turn of events. To Gosse she wrote that she could not 'consider except with a kind of panic [*effroi*] everything there is to do, and the obstacles to overcome to do good. [...] Now we have to hoist ourselves to the level of our destiny.' To Champagneux, she wrote that she was still preparing the little flat in the rue de La Harpe. And to Bancal she said, rather prophetically, that she and her husband proposed to keep the apartment in reserve, 'as certain philosophers keep their coffins'.[36]

---

[35] Grandchamp, pp. 475–6; oddly, Mme Roland was simultaneously mediating in a private quarrel between Bosc and Sophie, *Corr.*, II, pp. 414–18.

[36] *Corr.*, II, pp. 413, 410, 412, 23 March.

18

Summer 1792:
Minister of the King

Among the ministers, there is one whom I will not name, who has the most upright intentions, and I hope he is not thwarted by any obstacle.

Maximilien Robespierre, spring 1792.

Marie-Jeanne Roland was surely right to have feelings of panic and also to predict that their tenure at the ministry would be short. This was when the provincial couple really entered history. Until now, apart from Roland's local reputation in Lyon (where he actually spent little time) they had moved in restricted circles, and were unknown to the public. Roland was not even in the first rank of Jacobins, for he never spoke at the rostrum. Becoming a minister thrust him into an exposed position: he appeared first at court, then before the Assembly, on 26 March, to make a brief statement of acceptance, reported in the papers. No one mentioned his wife. However, by carrying on as she had always done, with increasing assurance—sharing his correspondence, drafting papers, discussing everything, writing to political friends—his wife would (so far as we know) be different from any other ministerial wives. Of this aspect of their partnership, not common knowledge at first, more later.

The job of minister of the Interior was overwhelming (cf. Chapter 24). Clearly, revolutionary leaders took some time to appreciate the difficulty of the administrative changeover from the ancien régime: it had depended on a huge bureaucracy to run the country, even before the immense reform programme of 1789–1791. The potential power of which the Convention later became suspicious was less evident during Roland's first ministry, but the size of his remit was already there. 'A huge, sprawling affair', it resulted from a merger of the Maison du roi and the Contrôle général, in 1790. It was renamed 'ministry of the Interior', a name it keeps to this day, by the law of 25 May 1791, which defined its scope: its brief covered elections, subsistence, education, agriculture, industry and trade, religious institutions, highways and public buildings; security and public order, poor relief and most importantly, communicating decisions to the *départements* and *communes* ('recalling them to their duties and enlightening them on the way to execute the laws'). In short, it covered virtually everything except justice, foreign affairs, war, the navy, and finance (i.e. taxation), which had their own ministries.[1]

---

[1] Parker (1979), p. ix; Terson (1913); Church (1981); Bernardin (1964), *passim*.

Reporting, much later, to the Convention, in February 1793, Bertrand de Barère concluded that in the minister of the Interior, the Constituent Assembly had created 'a kind of monarch, extending his empire over the entire surface of France—a despot governing all the constituted authorities and directing the citizens' opinions'. Anyone taking it on was doomed either to nullity (by depending on his administrators) or to calumny (for having too much power). Barère proposed dividing it in two, but eventually the Convention by-passed or abolished ministries, replacing them with committees, above all the Committee of Public Safety. The American ambassador, Gouverneur Morris had remarked in autumn 1792 that 'the ministers [possess] far more patronage than any monarch since Louis the Fourteenth'.[2]

The ministry was housed in a grand building, formerly the Contrôle Géneral—ironically the very one Roland had visited as an inspector, in the rue Neuve-des-Petits-Champs. His former bosses Blondel and Tolozan were now his subordinates: it must have seemed the world upside-down to them. The Hôtel de Lionne Pontchartrain is on the 1734 Plan Turgot, and was not unlike the Hôtel Tubeuf still standing on the same street. Since De Lessart had combined the posts of Interior and Finances briefly in 1791, the building became that of the Interior, for a while (it reverted to the Finance ministry after 1795, and was demolished in 1829). Alongside its offices and reception rooms was an apartment for the minister, grandly furnished by Calonne. Mme Roland frostily commented that it looked 'like an inn'.[3] De Lessart had organized its five divisions in autumn 1791. During

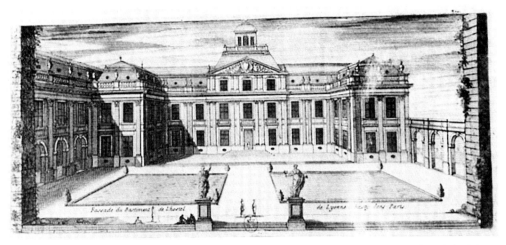

Figure 5. L'Hôtel de Lionne Pontchartrain, rue Neuve-des-Petits-Champs, Paris, now demolished, location of the ministry of the Interior in 1792–1793. © Ministères de l'économie et du budget—SAEF "Un ministère dans la ville", reproduced with permission.

---

[2] Morris (1889), II, p. 547; Barère, *AP,* LIX: 6 February 1793.
[3] Dumont (1832), II, p. 414.

his first ministry, Roland did not substantially change the structures he had inherited, nor the staff, many of whom dated from the ancien régime and were unsympathetic to the Revolution. It would have been too risky, Mme Roland recalled, to upset the workings of 'the great machine' at such a delicate moment.[4]

The basic unit was the bureau. As described by Harold Parker, this was a 'rather intimate group': the *garçon de bureau* trimmed the pens and fed the fire and lamps; two or three *expéditionnaires* copied outgoing correspondence and reports; the *rédacteurs* drafted letters, under the eyes of a *sous-chef*, supervised by the *chef de bureau*, a permanent civil servant. They shared an office, with an archive room attached. A *chef de division* might group three bureaux, in five (later six) divisions. Day-to-day business consisted largely of receiving and sending messages, letters, and reports. The archives contain a receipt from the stationer Delavoye, almost literally for red tape—it lists reams of paper, 'a pound of red sealing wax, inkwells, red string, one ebony ruler, packet of pens, pint of ink, sponges, black sealing wax, total price 247 *livres*'. (This was incidentally for 'Monsieur Lanthenas' who immediately became a sort of private secretary to Roland.)[5]

Heads of division singled out correspondence needing the minister's personal attention. He signed letters prepared for him, or in Roland's case, increasingly, drafted his own messages to the Assembly and elsewhere. The archives bulge with thousands of these documents. To deal with the 'chaos of the first days', Roland called on a contact of his wife's: Jean-Nicolas Pache (1749–1823), a former functionary in the naval ministry. Pache, an efficient administrator, insisted on working without pay as a sort of political supervisor of the potentially unreliable officials—not the least of his peculiarities, as will appear. Roland regarded him as 'a precious friend', but after a few weeks he moved to the war ministry, where the newly-appointed Joseph Servan was begging for his help.[6]

Some idea of the paperwork emerges from the partial summary by Alexandre Tuetey (1917), concentrating on subsistence and public order. This refers 'only' to 926 letters between mid-April and mid-October 1792, but Edith Bernardin found the register of dispatches recording 2720 in April; 2937 in May; 5528 in July–August; 4826 in Sept; 6926 in October; 6640 in November; 5681 in December 1792, and 5160 in January 1793. Champagneux, who joined Roland's second ministry, said about 200 letters arrived every day.[7] They covered every subject, from food supplies to building works. Many were applications from individuals for pensions, jobs, lodgings, etc., absorbing a disproportionate amount of time, but explaining why ministers were thought to exercise patronage. The earliest documents concern purchases of foreign grain: in April–May, Roland was personally and minutely concerned with buying cereals, to ward off the regular

---

[4] *Mém.*, p. 104.
[5] BNF MSS, naf 22422; see Parker (1979); Bernardin (1964).
[6] *Mém.*, pp. 104–7, on Pache; she knew him from before the Revolution via Gibert. See Gillispie (2004) for the 'Pache-Monge connection'.
[7] Bernardin (1964), p. 223. Tuetey (1917).

spring shortages. (Most policy questions will be discussed more fully in relation to the second ministry.)

One controversial aspect of the ministry's role began operating at once: the subsidizing of pro-government propaganda. The first clear example was that of Jean-Baptiste Louvet de Couvray (1760–1797), introduced to the Rolands—as so many others were—by Lanthenas. Known previously as the author of a rather salacious novel, *Les aventures de Faublias*, Louvet started the poster paper, the *Sentinelle*, in April 1792, with government money. Wherever the idea came from, it fully supported the Brissotin ministry 'to balance the influence of the court',[8] and once hostilities started, the war effort. Its subsidies came not directly from the ministry of the Interior, but from 'secret funds' at Dumouriez's disposal, which passed via the budget of the mayor of Paris (Pétion) so as not to alert the court. However, the Interior minister 'supervised' Louvet's paper: Roland received 6000 *livres* from Pétion on 13 May, intended as a first monthly instalment.[9] At the time, the *Sentinelle* directed its criticism whole-heartedly at the enemies within, especially the supposed 'Austrian committee'. The question of subsidizing selected newspapers became a more burning issue in the next government.[10]

How competent was Roland when he took over this huge department? One has to dig through a certain number of *parti pris* to discover the answer. Gita May is unquestionably wrong on several counts in her snap judgement that 'everyone knew [...] that without his wife's imagination, conviction, boldness, and literary know-how, he could be rated barely higher than a superior clerk'.[11] Mme Roland's role is discussed below, but from Bernardin's thesis (which can't be accused of partiality) a picture emerges of a man hardworking to the point of exhaustion, a thorough, but also imaginative administrator, professing firmly-held principles, and with an acute sense of his responsibilities. He was idealistically devoted to the public good (by his own lights), rigid and opinionated (according to others). Tuetey's nuanced judgement is that Roland, while

> highly competent, especially in matters of trade and industry, had extremely forceful ideas, which he maintained energetically, with the obstinacy [*raideur*] of an absolute character, who did not tolerate being contradicted and with the conscientiousness he brought to defending the country's interests [...] He did not overly restrain his criticism whether of the administration and of individuals.[12]

Jaurès, a harsh critic of both Rolands, commented that 'he brought to the Revolution the qualities and faults of an inspector of manufactures', the rather disdainful judgement of a graduate of the Ecole Normale Supérieure. But he had a point if he meant that Roland paid too much attention to detail. Plenty of documents show

[8] *Mém.*, pp. 72–3.
[9] Ibid., and Perroud (1912), pp. 207–12; printed by the Reynier brothers; only 9000 *livres* ever came through.
[10] *Corr.*, II, p. 426, 18 May and note, p. 427.
[11] May (1970), p. 206.   [12] Tuetey (1917), pp. xxv–xxvi.

him often drafting letters himself over fairly minor issues. On the other hand, as Bernardin remarks, many ministry memos show his marginal comments to be decisive and to the point. Understandably, he proceeded cautiously at first. With time, he acquired formidable experience and an overview of the administration, but he was in no sense an orator or charismatic leader. Had he later taken his seat in the Convention, little might have been heard of him. Roland was above all a great believer in the written word, which turned out to be both a strength and a weakness.[13]

MINISTERIAL SOLIDARITY

Ministers did not just have to run their departments. They were appointed by the king, and attended council meetings three times a week. Mme Roland reports, with some head-shaking, that both Roland and Clavière were at first 'enchanted with the king's attitude', and 'dreamed that the revolution was over', since he was willing to cooperate.[14] She, by contrast, could not forget Varennes, and claimed to see through the king's *bon enfant* tactics. Louis went out of his way to be affable—to Roland he made small-talk about industry, to Dumouriez about court tittle-tattle. Once non-controversial papers had been rubber-stamped, she comments tartly, 'the council of ministers was no more than a coffee-house, where they chatted about unimportant things. No minutes were taken'. The king refused Roland's request for a written record. Louis never openly said he would veto anything, but refused to sanction significant decrees, perpetually postponing discussion. In this way, she argued, by procrastination, he was lulling his ministers into false confidence.

Dumouriez had his own agenda. But at first, a degree of collegiality united the six ministers, who had been appointed more or less as a group. In his memoirs, long afterwards, Dumouriez said they had agreed to dine with each other by turns, three days a week. They came to the Hotel de Lionne Pontchartrain on Fridays. Each would produce his most important dispatches, and they discussed business to be put to the king, in order to avoid disputes in front of him and form a common opinion. It was the closest the Revolution came to having a cabinet government.

While the collegiality sounded reasonable, it also enabled Dumouriez to dominate the group, notably over the declaration of war and foreign policy, since none of the other ministers had competence in these areas. They did not agree with him on all matters. Mme Roland recounts an apparently trivial episode, which rankled. Dumouriez's subordinate, Bonnecarrère, a *beau garçon* of doubtful reputation. had obtained a place for someone, resulting in a large payment to Dumouriez's mistress,

[13] Jaurès (1983), vol. II, p. 536; Bernardin, (1964); Tuetey cites AN, F1c III Seine 27 1, example of memo on 20 May.
[14] *Mém.*, p. 152; Cf. 24 March 1792—cf. Roland's first memo to *départements*, in *Lettres et pièces intéressantes*.

Mme de Beauvert. The other ministers cornered Dumouriez after dinner, when 'some deputies' (read: Brissot) were present, and Roland lectured him about these goings-on. After that, she says, the minister of Foreign Affairs objected to meeting deputies at the ministry, and came round less often.[15]

Dumouriez had his own version of this (minus the Bonnecarrère reference). He claimed that Roland started insisting that his wife and later his friends, such as Brissot, join the diners at his apartment. Other ministers stopped bringing their portfolios, and by implication it became a social occasion.[16] Neither Mme Roland nor Dumouriez are entirely neutral witnesses of course. Mme Roland had, typically, commented on his lack of decorum in having Mme de Beauvert preside at his own house. His portrait of Mme Roland in return runs as follows:

> She was virtuously coquettish; always elegantly dressed, speaking very well, perhaps with too much application of wit, she had become the muse for a society of metaphysicians, literary men, and ministers. None of the wives of the other ministers was admitted to these political mysteries. Although intelligent [*ayant beaucoup d'esprit*] Mme Roland was presumptuous and arrogant. She was quite happy for it to be known that she dominated her husband; and this did him more harm than her advice did good.[17]

THE MINISTER'S WIFE

This posthumous description shares features with other judgements on Mme Roland as a hostess at the dinner table. Their reliability or otherwise is discussed in Chapter 25. Some are more complimentary, others far more hostile. What they have in common is the view that it was rare for a woman to hear 'political mysteries' and perhaps exert unofficial influence. At one level, this could be seen as an unavoidable and perhaps insoluble aspect of being the spouse (usually the wife) of a political figure. In recent times, the wives of not a few presidents and prime ministers have all been seen as having an unusual degree of access to and perhaps influence on their husbands' politics.

In Mme Roland's case, there is a historiographical problem, because of a tendency to confuse different periods of her short life in the spotlight. As argued above, her 1791 stay in Paris is often mistakenly described as holding a 'salon'. Notions about her so-called 'second salon' of spring 1792 also need some deconstructing, to find out quite what lies behind them.

Obviously, the Rolands now had the space and resources to entertain on a larger scale. Previous ministers, men of aristocratic origins and wealth, had regularly entertained and held (sometimes mixed) dinner parties. By her own account, however, Mme Roland did not wish to imitate these ancien régime ways. Explicitly

[15] *Mém.*, pp. 68–70; Bois (2005), p. 185; *Actes*, pp. 302–3: Brissot, at his trial, claimed that the Bonnecarrère affair caused enmity and calumny.

[16] Mme Roland, incidentally, reports convincingly a good-natured conversation between Brissot and Dumouriez about the unsuitability of François Robert, *Mém.*, pp. 118–19.

[17] Quoted Bois (2005), p. 186.

referring to spring 1792, she wrote: 'when my husband was in the [first] ministry, I made it a rule not to make or receive visits [i.e. in 'society'] and never to invite any women to a meal'. Again, this is revealing. To the Rolands, ancien régime-type mixed gatherings, such as those *chez* Dumouriez, were too frivolous to be continued by conscientious politicians. One should distinguish between this time, and the later period in the autumn. Roland's presence in the Dumouriez ministry lasted a mere twelve weeks, from 23 March to 13 June, and his wife did not move into the Hôtel Pontchartrain until the second week in April. Over the next two months, the couple certainly received visitors one or two days a week. The rest of the time, things were quiet. On 15 April, she told Bosc: 'I have people invited here only on Mondays and Fridays. You will find me *en famille* the other days and almost alone on Sundays and Wednesdays.'[18]

But if ministers came on Fridays, there was a more open house on Mondays. On 13 May, Lanthenas—acting as private secretary to Roland—wrote to Dulaure, editor of the *Thermomètre du Jour*: 'Mme Roland is having a few patriots to dinner with her husband tomorrow, Monday. She invites M. Dulaure to come and give both of them the pleasure of getting to know a good citizen of whom M. Lanthenas has often spoken.'[19] A few days later, Mme Roland wrote to Dulaure, thanking him for a copy of his paper and adding, 'remember that M. Roland always dines at home on Mondays, whenever it is convenient for you to add to the number of good citizens with whom he likes to surround himself'.[20] Apart from these fragments, there is little hard evidence about who, during the first ministry, actually came to dine (i.e. eat the late-afternoon meal at five) at the apartment. There is no record for instance of the 'trio of Girondins' being visitors, though clearly Brissot had a permanent entrée, and in her memoirs, Mme Roland writes of the first ministry that 'various members of the [Legislative] Assembly were sometimes *chez moi* with the ministers'. It may be fair to conclude, though, that these eight weeks were an apprenticeship in political entertaining for both the minister and his wife.[21]

But there was more to Mme Roland's role from the start than presiding at the dinner table. She undoubtedly had a hand in some appointments—for example, suggesting Pache as an assistant. When in May Clavière reorganized the post office, the preferment of her friends Gibert and Bosc, both already in the service, cannot have been without her knowledge and perhaps sponsorship.[22] Bosc told Bancal on 14 May that the point was to 'de-aristocratize the postal service and give it back all the trust it should enjoy'. 'Honest Gibert' was a Phlipon family friend from the 1770s who lived in the village of Monceaux, where the Rolands sometimes escaped for country air. Furthermore, while the post of minister of Justice was vacant, with Roland handling it in the interim, the couple thought seri-

[18] *Corr.*, II, pp. 418; cf. 3 May, *Corr.*, II, p. 422. Sundays and Wednesdays, Roland was at the other ministries.
[19] BNF MSS, naf, 9533, 13 May 1792, also quoted, *Corr.*, II, p. 401.
[20] *Corr.*, II, p. 426, 18 May 1792.
[21] *Mém.*, p. 68.
[22] *Corr.*, II, pp. 425, 678; note to him, 10 May; *Mém.*, pp. 102–4.

ously of proposing their lawyer friend, Bancal. (It went in the end, with or without Vergniaud's approval, to Duranthon, *procureur-général* of Bordeaux.)[23]

In the case of the minister for War, there is a smoking gun. When after the first reverses of French armies on 8 May, De Grave resigned, Mme Roland appears to have pushed forward the name of Joseph Servan de Gerbey (1741–1808), a serving officer who had contributed articles on military subjects to the *Encyclopédie*, and was known to Brissot. The Rolands had met him in Lyon. Mme Roland sent Servan two unequivocal letters, dated 9 and 10 May 1792. 'Yes, Monsieur, I wished and desired it; I hold to this opinion and you will justify it [i.e. your appointment].' She hoped he would bring determination to running the war: the previous 'inadequate' minister, a '*ci-devant*', had made 'culpable concessions to the revolution's enemies'. 'Now that you are all plebeians, more or less, and true revolutionaries,' she urged stronger measures, not hesitating to suggest specific policy: distrust of General Rochambeau (an ally of Lafayette's), and 'the need for a big force, not a few small armies, on the frontier with Brabant'.[24]

Servan remained a political ally of Roland and Clavière, and an obstacle to Dumouriez's schemes. He was relatively unknown before his appointment, but given the problem of finding loyal army leaders, this did not damage him with the left. At the Jacobins, Carra vouched for him as a patriot, and even Robespierre remarked that although 'apparently he had never had command of more than 200 men', Servan's speech to the Assembly had been impressive: 'he is the first minister whom we can praise in this way, but it is so dangerous to praise a minister that I will immediately withdraw that remark'.[25] However, Robespierre also reiterated, as usual, that war was too important to be left to the generals, and that the ministry had to demonstrate its independence from them.

THE BREACH WITH ROBESPIERRE

The 'Brissotin' ministry transformed revolutionary politics.[26] It was suspect to many people from the start: to the king, for one; to the court, or what was left of it; to the remaining Feuillants; and no doubt to the Fayettists. Even Brissot was rather taken aback, feeling the need to express his visceral distrust of ministers by saying of Roland: 'I have the deep certainty that he will stop being a minister the minute it is not possible for him to be a patriot of the strictest kind. *That is the only way I would be a friend of a minister.*'[27] Above all, despite a wary acceptance at first, the trickiest relationship for the new ministry would be with the radical left in the

---

[23] *Corr.*, I., p. 543; II, pp. 399–401, cf. 678; Bosc to Bancal on 12 April, 'Lanthenas sounded me out whether you would accept the post of secretary of this ministry'.

[24] *Corr.*, II, p. 425.

[25] *Jacobins*, III, p. 633, 30 May 1792.

[26] The new ministers 'could not play the passive role of their predecessors in relation to the royal prerogative', Jaurès (1983), III, pp. 263–4.

[27] *Le Patriote*, 28 March 1792, my italics.

Paris Jacobin Club, of whom Robespierre was chief spokesman. Here lay the seeds of dissensions to come.

The distrust of personal power that had marked the constitutional debates made ministers vulnerable to the charge of ambition, although they were the uneasy servants of two masters: answerable officially to the king and indirectly to the Assembly. Mirabeau had remarked: 'By a pious fiction of the law, the king cannot be mistaken; [...] but people sometimes need victims and the ministers are those victims.'[28] They could be categorized as bad advisers, or power-hungry individuals, and there was a constant fear of corruption. Their salaries were fixed by the Assembly high enough to make them independent, but this did not protect them from accusations of greed: during Roland's first ministry, their pay was halved from 100,000 *livres* to 50,000, but that was still a lot, even with the necessary outgoings on staff, etc.[29]

Although he had been one of the first to warn against ministerial power during the Constituent Assembly, Robespierre did not immediately attack the ministry.[30] He had, after all, embraced Dumouriez, saying, 'I am not among those who think it is absolutely impossible for a minister to be a patriot.' However, he had also warned that ministers should not consider they were in any way 'above a single Jacobin'.[31] Mme Roland, whose political antennae were acute, realized the importance of winning him over, and was almost immediately on the case. Again, her involvement in the political dimensions of the ministry is significant. One of the first letters she wrote after Roland's appointment was, it seems, to Robespierre, in reply to a glimpsed nod of approval. On 26 March, at the Jacobins, as the ministers went before the Legislative Assembly to take the oath, Robespierre, while reserving his judgement on the executive, let fall a semi-complimentary remark:

> Among the ministers, there is one whom I will not name, who has the most upright intentions and I hope he is not thwarted by any obstacle. [...] I don't want to speak well or badly of them; I said the ministers are members of the Jacobin Club, and that that did not impress us one way or another; I have said that the ministry was announced in favourable circumstances, that's what I said, I could do no more, my conscience wouldn't allow me.[32]

As a welcome, it is very cool, but it allowed Mme Roland to assume the 'upright' reference was to her husband. She opened her letter of the following day, 27 March, by saying 'Vous me justifiez' (i.e. you justify our decision):

> You justify me, Monsieur, and my reaction is a joy which I leave you to judge, since you are the right person to appreciate it. [...] I am staying at the Hôtel Britannique at least for a while; you will regularly find me there at dinner time, and I maintain there, as I shall wherever I go, the simplicity which makes me worthy not to be disdained,

[28] 5 October 1789, Bernardin (1964), p. 23; Church (1981), p. 47.
[29] 27 May 1792: Robespierre: 'paid patriotism is always suspect to me' (*Jacobins*, III, p. 615).
[30] In 1791, he had said 'nothing would be more dangerous than to create a new ministerial power', Bernardin (1964), p. 27.
[31] *Jacobins*, III, pp. 440–1.
[32] Robespierre, *Oeuvres complètes*, 8, p. 236. Not included by Aulard.

despite the misfortune of finding myself the wife of a minister. I hope only to contribute to the [general] good with the enlightenment and the help of wise patriots. For me, you are *at the head of that category*. Do come soon. I am anxious to see you and to assure you once more of my regard, which nothing will alter. Signed, Roland, née Phlipon.[33]

This is an extraordinary letter, in its use of the first person, although it may have had more context in terms of meetings than has survived. Mme Roland was appointing herself her husband's political spokeswoman. Evidently, Robespierre *did* go to see her: she wrote a note to Bosc, undated, but probably from April, saying 'I'm at home and R.b.p. is with me, having requested a meeting'. We know nothing about this meeting or whether it led anywhere.[34] What is clear is that after the declaration of war, relations between Robespierre and Brissot's friends would deteriorate badly, and Robespierre would increasingly make accusations of ambition and greed against those who took 'places'. He did not attack Roland directly at first, and as noted, even offered a qualified welcome to Servan, but his opposition to the war had put them on opposite sides.

BRISSOT AND DUMOURIEZ GO TO WAR

The slide to war, encouraged by Dumouriez, had begun with an ultimatum to the new emperor Francis II on 25 March. On 20 April, the king announced to the Assembly that since it had not been answered, France was at war with the 'king of Bohemia and Hungary' (i.e. not his subjects), and Francis II. Only seven deputies opposed the declaration of war. Robespierre was increasingly isolated in his opposition, though with some backing at the Jacobin Club.[35]

Brissot, once the scourge of ministers himself, naïvely could not understand why others did not think the situation had changed for the better—after all, the Jacobins had complained previously of court influence. He came to explain on 23 April:

> What are my crimes? [...] even if it is true that I had a hand in creating the current ministers, since when is it a crime to entrust the people's interests to friends of the people? [...] I just wish *all* the positions [of power] were occupied by Jacobins—from the public servant [*fonctionnaire*] on the throne to the most junior clerk.

In particular, he denied having any contact with General Lafayette—he had not seen him since the previous summer.[36] The rejection of Lafayette in Brissot's self-justification is crucial: one of Robespierre's repeated objections to the war was his fear that Lafayette would turn into 'a Cromwell'. When Robespierre spoke of

---

[33] *Corr.,* II, pp. 413–14, my italics. Perroud's analysis of this letter's identity is convincing.

[34] Ibid., p. 417: undated, but probably April 1792. Cf. Robespierre, *Oeuvres complètes,* 8, pp. 227–8 and Bernardin (1964), p. 42.

[35] See e.g. Whaley (2000) p. 47: Desmoulins, Marat and Billaud-Varenne supported his anti-war stance. See Scurr (2007), chapter 7.

[36] *Jacobins,* III, pp. 526–8, Lafayette 'no Cromwell', 25 April.

internal enemies of the Revolution, that was what he meant. It was not an unreasonable assumption, though in the event, the general proved a less than effective
counter-revolutionary. Jaurès remarks that Robespierre linked the ministers with
Lafayette in the public mind. But with armies taking the field, it was unlikely the
government would dispense with the best-known general in France, or that he
would be openly attacked in the Assembly.[37]

Once war was declared, Robespierre, in a speech not often quoted, claimed his
chief enemies were not Brissot or Guadet, and conceded that unity behind the
army would be a good thing: 'Since war has been declared, I too am in favour of
conquering Brabant, the Netherlands, Liège, Flanders, etc. The only thing that
should now occupy us is the right means to carry out this useful enterprise.' That
meant, as he had so often said, not just 'following the generals', but 'arming the
whole people', so that it would rise up against its internal enemies, once more
identified as the court, 'intriguers', and Lafayette.[38] But an irreparable breach was
on the way. In a stormy session at the Jacobins on 25 April, harsh words were exchanged between Robespierre, Brissot, and Guadet. It was in reaction to this that
Pétion, a man acceptable to all parties and still a friend of Robespierre's, wrote to
him in anguished terms, imploring him to heal the split inside the club ('I tremble
when I consider how we are behaving'). Robespierre, who soon afterwards created
his own newspaper, *Le Défenseur de la Constitution,* did not reply.[39]

Nor, it seems, did he reply to a disapproving, priggish, but not entirely hostile
letter from Mme Roland, written late that night, 25 April. It is worth quoting at
length for the insight it gives into their relations. She had obviously—and
revealingly—been listening to Robespierre from the public gallery:

> It was with pain that I saw you convinced that anyone with knowledge *who thought
> differently from you about the war was not a good citizen.* I have not committed the same
> injustice towards you; I know some excellent citizens who have the opposite opinion
> from you, and I do not find you any less estimable because you disagree with them.
> I have wept [*gémi,* literally 'groaned'] at your strictures, and wishing to avoid having
> any of my own to form, I wanted to know your reasons. You promised to let me know
> them, and you were going to come and see me. But you have avoided me, you haven't
> told me anything, and in the meantime you have been stirring up public opinion
> against those who don't see eye to eye with you. I'm too straightforward [*franche*] not
> to tell you that your action did not seem so to me. I don't know who you regard as
> your mortal enemies; I don't know of any; and certainly I don't receive them at home
> [...], because I only see here citizens whose integrity has been demonstrated, and who
> have no other enemies than those opposed to the salvation of France. Be so good as to
> recall, Monsieur, that the last time I had the honour of meeting you, I said that sup-
> porting the Constitution, making it work with popular support, seemed to me to be

---

[37] Guenniffey (1991), p. 442: Brissot had long been a friend of Lafayette, as was Condorcet, Whaley
(2000), p. 68. Mme Roland considered Lafayette ready to betray the revolution at any moment.
[38] 20 April, *Jacobins,* III, pp. 518 and 531; Cf. Jaurès (1983), III, p. 540.
[39] Scurr (2007) pp. 179–81; 29 April to the Jacobins, noted without text, *Jacobins,* III, p. 541;
Whaley (2000), p. 56. Lanthenas, 27 April 1792 (to Roland?) expressing despair at being unable to
get Robespierre ('whom I sincerely love') to cooperate, BNF MSS, naf 9534. Cf. *Jacobins,* III, p. 531,
Guadet's attack on Robespierre.

the compass by which the citizen should steer [...] That is the intention of the respectable men whom I know, the aim of all their actions; and I look about me in vain to apply the term 'intriguers' that you have used.[40]

The rather schoolmarmish letter was hardly likely to mend the breach, and indeed signalled the end of their friendship. However, she wasn't wrong to see that Robespierre had turned his face resolutely from anyone who did not agree with him.

Although the question was central to their breach with Robespierre, there is little contemporary evidence about either of the Rolands' personal views on the war. This is odd, considering that Roland countersigned the king's declaration of war, so he was certainly associated with it by default. He and his wife were, in private, enemies of Lafayette, whom Mme Roland called in a warning letter to Brissot later that summer *le polisson des deux mondes*, 'a rascal in both the old and the new world'.[41] One might expect her to be wholehearted one way or the other, but in her memoirs she is reticent about the 1792 debates on the war. Her two accounts of this period concentrate on internal politics, and her mentions of the war are all pragmatic, based on strategic advantage rather than principle (it is true that she had had time to change her mind). She says first: 'The enemies were getting ready; it was necessary to declare war, about which there were animated discussions.'[42] She expands a little on this in her *Observations* on Amar's act of accusation of the Girondins: 'it seemed to me that on the whole the mass of enlightened people were for it, agreeing with Brissot [...] that our enemies were preparing for it at their leisure, and our inaction would have delivered us up to them without defence'.[43]

As for Roland, we have to assume that by his closeness to Brissot, he was drawn into support for the war, or at least felt unable to oppose it. Etienne Dumont's memoirs refer—at second hand, of course—to a ministerial meeting of 11 April, where Dumouriez left his plans for attacking Belgium on the table, and the other ministers were intimidated into silence: Roland 'would have preferred negotiations', Clavière was worried about funds, and De Grave about military preparations, but none of them dared oppose Dumouriez. 'Neither Roland nor Clavière were warriors.'[44] Whatever their views, in the event, it was not, or not directly, the war which precipitated the end of the experiment in the 'parliamentary ministry', which fell apart in a matter of weeks.

---

[40] *Corr.*, II, pp. 418–19, my italics. Found among Robespierre's papers.
[41] AN, 446 AP (8), letter dated 31 July [1792]; he is 'un faquin', a puppet.
[42] *Mém.*, pp. 153 and 351.   [43] *Mém.*, p. 351.
[44] Dumont (1832), p. 412.

19

June–August 1792
Out of the Frying Pan Into the Fire

> I wasn't proud of his entry to the ministry, but I was proud of the way he left it.
>
> Mme Roland, *Mémoires*.[1]

For the first six weeks of the ministry, there was no open dissent between its members and it met guarded tolerance from the Jacobins. But the disastrous start to the war after 20 April had its impact on politics. The first serious encounter on the frontier had seen French troops turn tail and lynch a commander, General Théobald Dillon, accusing him of treason. No short sharp victory was on the horizon.[2] The Brissotins in the Assembly, realizing that success or failure in war would determine their own position, were quick to accuse others of treason—counter-revolutionaries and the so-called 'Austrian committee' of fifth columnists were their principal target.[3]

One of Servan's first actions in mid-May was to propose that the army be strengthened by mobilizing the National Guard in the frontier *départements*, and at the same time that the king's 1800-strong personal guard—suspected of counter-revolution—be disbanded. Louis, perhaps surprisingly, agreed to the relevant decrees that were passed by the Assembly,[4] but two other decrees, passed after pressure from the left of the Assembly, sat on the table. The king refused to sanction them, while stopping short of applying his constitutional veto. The first concerned the non-juring or 'refractory' priests, who had refused to take the civic oath of allegiance introduced in 1790. Although they covered many shades of opinion, some were accused of encouraging counter-revolution. Roland, as minister responsible for church–state relations, at first tried to maintain some balance between the 'prêtres perturbateurs' and freedom of worship, invoking the king's support. His 5 April circular warned local authorities of 'factional and hypocritical' priests stirring up fanaticism in the countryside and persecuting constitutional priests, who had accepted the oath. He claimed that the king was 'profoundly distressed' by such disorders, and asked that they should stop.[5] But the 27 May decree went fur-

---

[1] *Mém.*, p. 157.   [2] Blanning (1996).
[3] *Corr.*, II, p. 402. The king was thought to have a 'secret council': Montmorin, Molleville, and Justice minister Duranthon. Cf. Roland to Bancal 28–9 May, quoted, *Corr.*, II, p. 403.
[4] Le Guin (1966), p. 85; Campbell (2010), p. 520; Howe (2008), pp. 81–2.
[5] Quoted in *Lettres et pièces intéressantes*; cf. Scurr (2007) p. 184.

ther. Apparently argued for by Roland, this provided for the expulsion of non-jurors, if twenty citizens in good standing petitioned—not too hard to organize. At this point, the king's religious scruples were tried too far and he refused to agree.[6]

The second decree, approved by the Assembly on 8 June, was Servan's proposal for a body of 20,000 troops from all over France to encamp near Paris, to replace the regular troops sent to the front. (Robespierre had apparently once favoured a similar idea.)[7] The arrival of the provincials was timed to celebrate the feast of the Federation on 14 July. The king, possibly emboldened by a counter-petition from the National Guard (the 'petition of the 8000'), told his ministers that he proposed to veto the decree.

The ministerial council was divided. Distrust between Dumouriez, Lacoste, and Duranthon, on one hand, and the three Brissotins on the other, had already been fuelled by disagreements. Roland had proposed in mid-May that they all sign a letter to the king, warning him that failing to sanction the Assembly's decrees would cause a crisis and threatening resignation. According to his wife, although the ministers agreed in principle, in practice they were less keen. Clavière, in a letter later made public, wrote prophetically: 'My dear colleague, why irritate the King against us, since we only accepted these positions in order to make public policy run smoothly?' The moderates would be alienated, and the king was 'most unlikely to take any notice and isolate himself from the palace'. A letter would be either 'pointless or dangerous', and would almost certainly become public, exposing the king to 'popular risings which we wish to prevent'. However, Clavière agreed to bow to the majority, for the important thing 'is that we should march in step'.[8] Roland took heed at first, but after the renewed threat of veto, decided to send a letter to the king on his own.

A LETTER TO LOUIS

Much ink has been spilled over the famous letter of 10 June, which provoked a ministerial crisis. It is possible that the king and Dumouriez had already decided to dismiss the three increasingly uncooperative 'Jacobin' ministers. Gouverneur Morris, the American envoy privy to court gossip, certainly thought so.[9] But the letter was the immediate trigger for the sacking of Servan on 12, then of Roland and Clavière on 13 June.

---

[6] *Défenseur de la Constitution*, no. 3, p. 92, quoted Bernardin (1964) p. 80; *Lettres et pièces*, 5 April, esp. p. 16. Cf. *Mém.*, p. 153, Mme Roland defends both decrees as necessary, because of court intrigues. Cf. ibid., pp. 69–71.

[7] Scurr (2007), pp. 184–5—Servan's proposal was 'disconcertingly familiar'. The idea was to prevent a court-led coup.

[8] *Mém.*, p. 154; BNF MSS, naf 9534, 26 May 1792; also in *Lettres et pièces*, pp. 41–2, plus version of Roland's letter.

[9] Morris (1889), I, pp. 435–6, 4 June: 'already there exists a serious breach between the members of the present Administration and a Part of them must go out', Cf. *Mém.*, p. 154, Bernardin (1964), p. 63.

What did it say? It was a 2000-word long civic sermon, couched—to royal eyes—in language thoroughly lacking in deference. Mme Roland undoubtedly had a large hand in writing it. She gave two accounts in her memoirs. Her first version says: 'We felt that the council did not have the nerve or unity to pronounce as a group, so it was appropriate to Roland's integrity and courage to take the step himself. *Between the two of us*, we drew up [*nous arrêtâmes*] his famous letter to the king.' When her husband took it to council, intending to read it out, Louis asked the ministers for written views on the decrees, so it could be seen as a response to that request.[10]

Her second version is more peremptory—in May, she had 'sketched out a letter after agreeing its main lines with Roland'. Then in June 'Je fis la fameuse lettre'— 'I wrote the famous letter'. She adds for good measure: 'it was written at a sitting, like almost everything of that kind I did'.[11] Champagneux maintained that Mme Roland was always called in when there was some particularly important text to be written, because she was so gifted at finding the right words. On the other hand, Sophie Grandchamp was adamant that the letter was dictated by Jean-Marie Roland, and that his wife acted merely as his scribe, perhaps polishing it a bit. Whichever version is true, she was surely at least partly responsible for this text.[12]

'Sire', the letter began dramatically, 'the present state of France cannot subsist much longer; there is a state of crisis, the violence of which is reaching the highest degree.' It moved on to make judgements about the king's education for his role:

> Your Majesty has constantly been faced with the alternative of either giving way to his earliest habits and affections [acquired by being brought up a monarch], or to make the sacrifices dictated by philosophy and called for by necessity: either to embolden the rebels [i.e. court intriguers, émigrés] and distress the nation, or to calm the nation by taking its side. [...] It is now time to end the uncertainty. Will Your Majesty openly side with those who wish to change the Constitution [foreign powers]? Or generously devote himself without reservation to making it triumph?

The kernel of the letter—but one had to read a long way through, before finding it—ran as follows:

> The moment when your Majesty, wishing thoroughly for the triumph of the Constitution, supports the legislative body with the full power of execution, will remove any excuse for the people's anxiety and all hope from the malcontents. For example, two important decrees have been passed, both essentially concerning public tranquillity and the safety of the state. Delaying their sanction is inspiring distrust; if the delay is prolonged it will cause discontent, and I have to say that with the current heated opinions, discontent could lead anywhere. This is no time to hang back, or even to try to buy time. The revolution has already happened in hearts and minds, and it will end in bloodshed and be sealed in it, if wise counsel does not prevent the misfortunes it is still possible to avoid.

[10] *Mém.*, p. 69; Cf. Chaussinand-Nogaret (1985), p. 168. Text in *Moniteur*, XII, pp. 658 ff.
[11] *Mém.*, pp. 154–7; BNF MSS, naf 9534, fol 178, 10 June. Several drafts actually.
[12] Grandchamp, pp. 481–2.

The letter also contained various moral admonitions, including a sentence that was probably the last straw for Louis: 'I know that the austere language of truth is rarely welcomed close to the throne; I also know that it is because it is practically never heard there that revolutions become necessary.'

The letter has been variously described as impertinent, inspiring, cynical, and naïve. Some historians completely ignore it (Furet), yet it was almost certainly a precipitating factor in the fall of the monarchy. Jaurès called it 'Mme Roland's insolent letter'.[13] There is no doubt that it lacks deference, and the Rolands were aware that it would lead to dismissal. However, it does propose a solution to the stalemate. Whether or not the decrees were wise or justified—they are both debatable—it suggested that the king was placing the Constitution under severe strain, and urged him to reconsider.

Writing her second version of events a year later, Mme Roland depicted her own state of mind in June 1792 as a kind of 'moral fever', prompted by distress at obstacles put in the way of the Constitution, which, 'with all its vices' had to be supported (as she had written to Robespierre). The ministers would be seen by deputies and radicals outside the Assembly as ineffective puppets, if their view had no purchase on the king. 'The king's prevarication showed his bad faith,' so all 'an honest minister' could do was resign, although the door was perhaps just open for a royal change of heart.[14]

Louis was having none of it. He sacked all three 'Jacobin' ministers. His curt handwritten note to Roland survives: 'You will, Monsieur, pass the portfolio of the department of the Interior which I had entrusted to you, to M. Mourgues, whom I have just appointed to it.'[15] Given the dramatic dismissal not only of Roland and Clavière, but also of War minister Servan, in the middle of hostilities, the gist of the letter would unavoidably have become public soon, but Mme Roland claimed it was her idea to send a copy to the Assembly, forestalling the king. The Assembly immediately sent its regrets to the three sacked ministers.[16] Not everyone was best pleased. We may guess that Brissot felt it as a body-blow. Gouverneur Morris even thought Brissot contacted Dumouriez to plan the next move: to persuade the king, after all, to sanction the decrees—and reinstate the ministers. If there was such a plan, it backfired, because a few days later, the king also let Dumouriez go; he took up an army command, but his entire strategy had been thwarted.[17]

The dismissal of the ministers led to a temporary truce between elements in the Jacobin Club. Its circular, signed by Chabot, Audouin, Fabre, and Collot (what a line-up!) urged provincial societies to 'circulate and spread profusely the letter written to the king by the patriot Roland', thus opening a period when Roland's popularity rose sharply in provincial France. Robespierre stood somewhat apart. His

---

[13] Jaurès (1983), II, p. 60, and note p. 565, quoted Whaley (2000) p. 56 and note: 'a point-blank shot in the king's face.' Neither Furet and Richet (1973 edn) nor Hardman (1981) mention it.

[14] *Mém.*, p. 154.

[15] Original in BNF MSS, naf 6241.

[16] *Mém.*, pp. 1 and 157. The Jacobin Albitte had 'never seen anything as patriotic as the minister's letter', *Jacobins,* III, p. 690, 13 June.

[17] Morris (1939), II, pp. 447–9.

reaction (no doubt eagerly awaited in the rue de la Harpe) was studied indifference: the fate of a few ministers was not the end of the world, he pointed out.
Camille Desmoulins expressed warm approval, interestingly, but inaccurately giving credit for the letter to Lanthenas, as Roland's 'secretary.'[18]

For the first, but not the last time, Jean-Marie Roland had been at the centre of
an initiative that would eventually contribute to the downfall of Louis XVI. His
wife was an active partner in his action, but there were good political reasons why
Roland might have wanted to pull out of government, and he was not the man to
do something simply because his wife suggested it; they were agreed that this was
the right step to take. He was certainly not taking instructions from Brissot, who
was seriously put out by this development. It is unlikely that the Rolands foresaw
quite where it would lead—dismissal, and re-appointment perhaps (Sophie Grandchamp's view). For the moment, Roland and his fellow-ministers were receiving
intoxicating congratulations from almost every quarter. Mme Roland later wrote:
'I was not proud of his entry to the ministry, but I was proud of the way he left it.'
In the terminology later used of ministerial resignations in France, they had 'fallen
to the left', i.e. over a progressive issue.

JUNE TO AUGUST: THE END OF THE MONARCHY

The Rolands immediately moved into the small flat in the rue de la Harpe, organized for their everyday needs by Sophie Grandchamp. As private citizens again,
they went on seeing political friends, meeting new ones, and following public
events. Surviving documents show that, at the very least, they were taking a keen
interest in what was happening—as how could they fail to? It could hardly be
called retiring from public view to publish the letter to the king, with other papers,
in a brochure sold in bookshops (*Lettres et pièces intéressantes*).

Louis's defiance of the Assembly by sacking his ministers lit the fuse for a
Parisian movement against the monarchy that gathered pace very quickly that
summer. The key choice was between trying to persuade the king to back down
and withdraw his veto, perhaps with new ministers, or joining a protest movement of confrontation with the crown, already discussed in the Paris sections.
Leading politicians did not openly declare either way, but private conversations
bubbled.

What might have been a minor cabinet reshuffle quickly turned into a crisis.
Competent and willing ministers were hard to find, as the king called on one Feuillant after another. To lose one minister of War in the middle of hostilities was bad
enough, but the revolving door at the War ministry meant that war was indeed left
(disastrously) to the generals. There were no fewer than three ministers of Finance
and three of the Interior between June and August, plus two ministers each at War

---

[18] Whaley (2000), pp. 57 ff. for reactions; *Jacobins*, IV, p. 8, proposal to circulate Roland's letter.
Chabot,18 June, said Roland's stern letter to 'Motier', (i.e. Lafayette), was also worth circulating,
Jacobins, IV, p. 15.

and Foreign Affairs.[19] In the heated Paris atmosphere, one persistent rumour was that the king was about to be 'kidnapped' again and spirited away. According to Gouverneur Morris, this was not for want of offers. Louis did not take them up and Morris noted on 19 June: 'there is to be a sort of Riot tomorrow'.[20] Within a week of the ministerial purge, and therefore in some sense associated with it, the revolutionary *journée* of 20 June took place.

That day, following an application to plant a tree of Liberty in memory of the Tennis Court Oath of 20 June 1789, and to petition the Assembly and the king over the disputed decrees, thousands of demonstrators, some armed, converged on the Tuileries Palace. There were calls for the king to give up the veto, and to reinstate the ministers (temporary heroes). Louis showed unsuspected sang-froid. Surrounded by *sans-culottes*, the name now being claimed by Parisian insurgents, he donned a red liberty cap and drank to the revolution, but refused to abandon his veto. Bloodshed was avoided when Pétion as mayor, after initially hesitating, persuaded the crowd to withdraw. It could be seen as an anti-climax.[21]

One result was a temporary—and fragile—reconciliation between Brissot and Robespierre, encouraged by Lafayette's last attempt to rally moderate opinion. The general left his army post to address the Assembly on 28 June, calling the Jacobin Club 'a sect that has tyrannized citizens'. Brissot apologized for his previous 'support' for him, but Brissot's agenda was probably still to get 'his' ministers reinstated, seeing the crisis as resolvable by an English-type reshuffle. He attacked the king's current ministers on 9 July: 'The present ministry […] does not have the confidence of the nation; there is no need for the ministers to be guilty, it is sufficient that they have lost that confidence.'[22]

Brissot was still vexed with the Rolands for precipitating the crisis. Mme Roland, hearing this, wrote to him twice in late July, from Champigny-sur-Marne, outside Paris. Indicating that she knew of the threats to the throne, she warned Brissot of rumours that he had accepted 'six million *livres* from the court, either to ensure the king's safety', or to prevent his *déchéance* (dethronement). She suggested he issue a denial, and went on to advise him on what she (and presumably Roland) considered the best course of action:

> I have been re-reading the Constitution; I have always felt that our dangers lie not in our external enemies…but in the weakness or corruption of the legislative power and the inertia and treason of the executive power [i.e. the king].

The *déchéance* of the king was not the most urgent task, she suggested, rather his *temporary suspension* (as in 1791), which could be 'hooked, so to speak, on to an article of the Constitution'. The Assembly, taking into account the 'wishes' of the sections, should appoint a 'patriotic ministry', then hold primary assemblies to convoke a Convention, which would embark on reforming the Constitution. 'I see

---

[19] Jones (1990), p. 79 for full list.   [20] Morris (1889), vol. II, p. 547.
[21] On the term, cf. *DCRF*, 'Sans-culottes'.
[22] Bernardin (1964), p. 67; Brissot had still not finally broken with Lafayette according to Gueniffey (1991).

no other way to avoid anarchy and civil war, during which the legislative body would be dissolved, and there would be no centre round which to rally.'[23]

This project is both bold and disingenuous. Given the current popularity of the Brissotin ministers, their names would surely be the first to be proposed. Mme Roland is frequently described as ambitious, and pushing her husband into power. Her letter at this point certainly bears this interpretation, but is also a considered attempt, with its reference to sections and primary assemblies, to think through how the more radical forces could remain united.

It also shows that she had moved beyond a position of negotiating with the king. In the same letter, she warned Brissot against all three 'Girondin' allies: Gensonné lacked resolution, Guadet was too impetuous, and 'as for Vergniaud, whose sudden change of heart has turned opinion against him, I won't allow myself to pass judgement on him, but I would be wary of a man who is lazy, vain about his appearance, and insincere in his expression'. This passage is often quoted alongside another harsh judgement on Vergniaud in her memoirs: 'the most eloquent orator in the Assembly', was 'disdainful of his fellow men' and therefore lazy, 'which is a crime' in public life.[24]

But the chief reason for her distrust was—presumably—Vergniaud's retreat from a radical stance. On 3 July, he made a passionate speech criticizing the king, but leaving the door open to maintaining the status quo. 'The harmony between the two powers [legislative and executive] will be sufficient to extinguish hatred, bring together divided citizens, and stop the monarchy from sliding into the abyss…so I want the message [to the king] to have as its aim to maintain or produce [such harmony] not to render it impossible […] a signal for reunion, not a manifesto of war.' Vergniaud's speech seems to have been welcomed at the Jacobins, where most members were still reluctant to move into illegality.[25]

On 7 July 1792, Mme Roland wrote to Bancal: 'Will Vergniaud be at Mme Dodun's? If so, don't be afraid to say to him that he has a lot of headway to make up to restore his reputation in public opinion, if he still wants this as an honest man, which I doubt.'[26] Her words *might* suggest she already had wind of the famous last-ditch move by the Gironde three to get the king to cooperate with the Assembly and appoint new ministers. This incident, later in July, which became public knowledge only six months later (see Chapter 29), was initiated by the king's portrait painter, Joseph Boze, and his valet, Thierry. Gensonné was approached by Boze for advice: he answered with a note suggesting, among other things, that the king choose new ministers, if he wanted to defuse the brewing crisis. His two colleagues signed it. 'A truly patriotic ministry would be one of the greatest means that the king could use to regain confidence.'[27] They did not *necessarily* advocate

---

[23] Mme Roland letters to Brissot of 23 and 31 July 1792, AN, 446 AP (8); not in Perroud's edition.

[24] *Mém.*, p. 109.

[25] *AP*, XLVI, p. 82; Whaley (2000), p. 65.

[26] *Corr.*, II, p. 428 (Perroud's dating).

[27] Whaley (2000), p. 65, quoting Gensonné's interrogation, AN W 292, letter sent on 17 July; text in *AHRF* (1931) pp. 198–201, and Hardman (1981), pp. 142–5.

the reinstatement of Roland and the others, since another document suggests taking four members of the Constituent Assembly into the ministry. The proposals, which were arguably no more than a final attempt to save the Constitution, were in any case never considered seriously by the king, but they later did terrible retrospective damage to the Gironde.[28]

Robespierre, for his part, unequivocally saw any reinstatement of the ministers as retrograde, and repeatedly accused Brissot and his allies of thinking simply in terms of restoring their friends to power. Back on the offensive by late July, he told the Jacobins: 'The members of the present legislature [have been] scandalously soliciting the ministry for their creatures, sacrificing to this vile interest any principles and the energetic measures which alone can save the state.' He called for a new 'pure' Assembly, from which members of the present one would disqualify themselves. Robespierre's proposal, complete with its new 'self-denying ordinance'—to stop Assembly members such as Brissot and his friends standing for re-election—was, of course, as disingenuous as Mme Roland's, and was seen as such by Brissot, who viciously attacked him next day.[29] But Robespierre was also on a knife-edge, moving from support for the status quo towards direct action. He 'wanted his "constitutional uprising against the constitution", but he both feared it and was afraid for it'.[30]

Both proposals were made in the shadow of foreign invasion. On 1 August, news reached Paris of the declaration by the duke of Brunswick on 25 July: this bombastic pronouncement threatened exemplary and forever memorable vengeance on the city of Paris, if it took any action against the king. Louis's re-establishment in full authority was now the allies' war aim; foreign armies were massing for an attack.

THE FALL OF THE TUILERIES: 10 AUGUST

The degree to which the Rolands were aware of preparations either for the *journée* of 20 June, or for the critical events of 10 August, is difficult to estimate. In her memoirs, Mme Roland rather loftily says: 'Of the revolution of 10 August, I know no more than the general public; having been *au courant* with state affairs when Roland was a public figure, I was never party to what might be termed petty manoeuvres, any more than he was an agent of any such.'[31] Despite this glib disclaimer, one would have had to be blind and deaf not to suspect that trouble was brewing.

The Rolands had recently met Charles-Jean Barbaroux (1767–1794). A radical young politician from Marseille, he had helped raise the famous battalion of the Marseillais to come to Paris in response to the *patrie en danger* call. Barbaroux

---

[28] Whaley (2000), p. 66, AP, LIII, 3 January 1793. Mme Roland was more inclined to pardon it by 1793: 'only the most blatant malice could describe this as treason', *Mem.*, p. 352.

[29] Hampson (1974/1988), p. 114.

[30] Scurr (2007), p. 194.   [31] *Mém.*, p. 75.

remembered meeting Roland and Lanthenas walking in the Tuileries Gardens during June. Both he and Mme Roland refer in their memoirs to their discussions in following weeks in the flat in the rue de la Harpe.[32] This was the period—later to be anachronistically linked to 'federalism' charges—when they discussed 'a conditional project' for 'a republic in the south', if the north of France were to be invaded. But they talked about more immediate matters too. Mme Roland later wrote that Barbaroux stopped calling, and told them that 'this was so as not to compromise us'. They had already judged from some words he let fall 'that an insurrection was being prepared', but since he said no more, 'we didn't ask further'.[33]

Paris was full of ferment, which could hardly be ignored, such as petitions to the Jacobin Club from the newly-arrived *fédérés*. By late July, there were upwards of 5000 such troops, including the Marseillais, who marched in on 30 July, singing Rouget de Lisle's *chant de guerre*, later named after them. In the Cordeliers Club, (no distance from the rue de la Harpe) and in the sections there was constant agitation. Either the Rolands stopped their ears to details, or they took steps to avoid drawing attention to themselves. As noted above, they went out of Paris for a few days in late July—perhaps to avert suspicion of being involved. They were very far from alone in this.[34]

Moves were well under way for a rising against the crown, spurred on by the Brunswick Declaration. Barbaroux was involved, as he states in his memoirs, giving circumstantial details of the groups coordinating their efforts to dethrone the king, and being in close touch with the Marseillais. But most prominent figures—Robespierre, certainly Marat, and others—kept their heads down, like the Rolands, until it was all over. Leigh Whaley's conclusion is that there was wide involvement in the 10 August insurrection by elements of the Jacobins, Cordeliers, certain Paris sections, and federal troops. Post-mortems are not exactly reliable, since people later had their own motives for claiming to have been involved—or not. Few openly backed the insurrection before it happened. On the other hand, the Assembly, by failing to impeach Lafayette on 8 August, by 406 to 224 votes, sent a signal that moderate (Feuillant) politics had prevailed there, while the general on the white horse was perceived as the enemy by the left. Brissot had personally (if insincerely) voted for impeachment, as did Guadet and Vergniaud, but the vote disappointed many at the Jacobins.[35]

Late at night on 9 August, the tocsin was rung, as new men from the sections replaced the Paris municipal council, now seen as too moderate: they formed what became the revolutionary Commune (to remain in power in the city for many months thereafter). The commander of the national guard was killed at the Hôtel de Ville, and his place taken by Antoine-Joseph Santerre (1752–1809), a brewer

---

[32] *Mém.*, p. 110; Barbaroux, *Mémoires* 1936 edn, pp. 123 and 331 ff.

[33] *Mém.*, p. 111; on Barbaroux, p. 73: fear of the court and its allies triumphing in the north.

[34] Louvet's *Sentinelle*, 8 August, opposed attack on the palace, as being only 'in the interests of the enemies of the people', Whaley (2000), p. 70. The Rolands had permission to leave Paris, perhaps for Beaujolais, BNF MSS, naf 6243, fo 136.

[35] Cf. Hampson (1974/1988a) p. 115; Hampson (1978/1988b), pp. 71–2; Whaley (2000) pp. 68 and 71–4 for a careful attempt to work out who was involved.

from the Faubourg St Antoine. In the early morning of 10 August, federal troops and armed citizens from some sections marched on the Tuileries Palace. It was defended by over 3000 men, 2000 of them national guards—who immediately changed sides. The rest were mostly Swiss guards and courtiers. The king and royal family fled, taking refuge in the Assembly (presided over by a hastily-summoned Vergniaud). At the Tuileries, the beginnings of fraternization between insurgents and defenders (who now had nobody to defend) ended in confusion, as firing started, from the Swiss side. Lethal fighting followed, including the massacre of some of the fleeing defenders. The total death toll—figures vary according to source—was between about 700 and 1000: perhaps 600 Swiss and about 300 *fédérés* and Parisians were killed. This was the bloodiest episode so far in the Revolution.[36]

Confronted with the *fait accompli*, and the obvious impossibility of reinstating the king, the Legislative Assembly—by now missing many deputies who had discreetly or fearfully vanished—had to react quickly. It had somehow to share its authority with the enlarged Paris Commune, which had emerged from the events of 10 August cloaked in its newly-claimed legitimacy for having 'saved the nation'. The Commune was quickly augmented by some big hitters chosen by the sections: they included Robespierre, Collot, Billaud, Fabre, and Robert, as well as Pétion. Through speeches at the Jacobins and articles in the press—including some from Marat, who had been in total eclipse during the events of 10 August—radical milieux in Paris were already creating a sort of parallel power to the lame-duck Assembly.

For the first few days after 10 August, although not everyone agreed with the Assembly's emergency decisions, they were broadly accepted. An extraordinary commission of twenty-five was formed: perhaps inevitably, Brissot became a strong voice on it. It was decided not to dethrone Louis XVI and declare a republic, but to suspend the king, and effectively the monarchy, pending the election of a National Convention, whose role would be to decide on the future form of government, the recipe Mme Roland had advocated. The royal family was interned in the fortress of the Temple in north-east Paris, under the formal supervision of the Commune.

The Assembly, in the voice of Vergniaud, proposed (against the wishes of some) that a version of the 1791 Constitution would have to remain temporarily in force, minus the king, so as to avoid a power vacuum. In practice, without the monarchy, there was no formal agreement over exactly what relations should be between Assembly and executive. As after Varennes, the executive would be the council of ministers, minus the royal veto, and its role would be to enact Assembly decrees. However, the law-making body was now a rump, waiting for the Convention to take over. (Not that this prevented it passing some last-minute laws later seen as significant, on divorce for example.)[37] Meanwhile there was a

---

[36] See Doyle (2002) p. 189; Sutherland (1985), p. 151, etc., for accounts.
[37] On divorce and inheritance laws, see Desan (2004).

war on. Almost any combination of politicians would have encountered problems in the circumstances.[38]

The council of ministers was therefore hastily reconstituted and given the new name Provisional Executive Council [PEC]. It included the three Brissotins in their old posts: Servan at War, Clavière at Public Contributions, and Roland at the Interior. Their reappointment went through the Assembly without a formal vote— in fact, remarkably, Clavière had to handle the War ministry for ten days until Servan could be fetched back from the south. Danton was overwhelmingly elected minister of Justice, with the approval both of Brissot and Condorcet, but especially that of the *sans-culottes*. The Foreign ministry went to Pierre-Henri Lebrun (or Lebrun-Tondu, 1763–1793), an associate of Dumouriez, and the Navy to Pache's associate, mathematician Gaspard Monge (1746–1818).[39] With Danton in post, there was no doubt who was the dominant personality, but the whole ministry was initially generally accepted.

The immediate consequence for the Rolands—whatever they had expected during the previous weeks—was their move back to the rue Neuve-des-Petits-Champs. Following the insurrection, they were plunged straight into a far more exposed and explosive situation, as the Prussian army invaded French territory, fear of fifth columnists took hold, and there was a real risk that Paris would be taken. 10 August had been a turning-point even greater than Varennes. In the few weeks since Roland left the ministry, things had changed in unpredictable and volatile ways. The Brissotin ministers had unquestionably 'benefited' from the uprising, but the chalice was a particularly poisoned one. Historians have argued for many years over the responsibilities for the ferocious splits that soon opened up in the political arena. The Rolands have often been at the centre of their analyses.

---

[38] See Gueniffey, 'Les assemblées et la représentation' in Lucas (1988), II, pp. 233–59.
[39] Mme Roland's character assassination of Monge, *Mém.*, p. 75–6; on the Pache-Monge connection, Gillispie (1980); Monge was also proposed by Condorcet.

20

August–September 1792
Invasion and Massacre

> …We owe the whole of France a declaration that the executive power was unable to predict or to prevent these excesses. I know that it is the duty of the constituted authorities to put an end to it, or see themselves reduced to nothing.
>
> J.-M. Roland to the Assembly, 3 September.

In theory, after 10 August, despite undercurrents of dislike and distrust, ministers and assemblies might have cooperated in the face of the foreign threat. The new executive had been appointed unanimously. Danton—who devoted much of his energy to the war effort—was acceptable to the Paris Commune; and in troubled times, the 'Brissotin' ministers' familiarity with their portfolios might be seen as providing initial stability. But any consensus did not last long. There was already potential for divisions in appointments to ministry teams, or proposing names for political tasks. When the unexpected events of September put pressure on these apparently minor fault lines, large cracks began to open up in political allegiances, driving divisions deep inside the Provisional Executive Council, notably between Roland and Danton.[1]

In the early days, all ministers needed dependable colleagues. Roland immediately purged his offices of suspected royalists—of *c.* 150 employees in the ministry, 22 (14 per cent) were let go on 11 August.[2] He again called on Lanthenas—a doubtful administrator, but assumed to be loyal. (The person on whom he relied most was of course his wife, of whom more in Chapter 24). Roland also summoned from Lyon his friends Champagneux and Le Camus, who proved efficient and reliable.[3] He was later attacked for making further partisan appointments: an undated note from Brissot to Mme Roland, recommending names, was found among his papers: 'I am sending [you] for your husband and Lanthenas, a list of patriots to place: for he should always have a list like this to hand'. Roland argued that this simply applied to purging the ministry of counter-revolutionaries, although of course it was open to charges of cronyism.[4]

---

[1] Cf. rather uninformative council minutes, AN, AF II/2.

[2] Kawa (1996), p. 182, and article in Vovelle (1995) *passim*; Bernardin (1964), pp. 206–8; Le Guin (1966), p. 91; *Mém.*, p. 76: 'the renewal for which he felt the need'; AN, H 1 1439 for several appeals against dismissal.

[3] Gabriel-E. Le Camus, botanist and *receveur de gabelle* in Lyon; Kermina (1976), pp. 106–7; Le Guin (1966), p. 90.

[4] Brissot later said this was sent during the *first* ministry, *Actes,* p. 315: cf. Rapport Brival and Roland's reply (Chapter 24 below); Bernardin (1964), p. 229.

Other ministers did much the same—political reliability was an urgent priority. Danton immediately appointed associates, such as Fabre d'Eglantine, Desmoulins, and Robert, as secretaries in the ministry of Justice.[5] Patricia Howe notes that the new foreign minister, Lebrun, was glad to inherit offices staffed by Dumouriez appointments. Within a week, Dumouriez himself was appointed Commander-in-Chief of the army of the Centre, following the dismissal and defection of Lafayette (17 August). Roland wrote to him on 16 August burying the hatchet.[6] Howard Brown mentions a list of applicants for jobs under Servan as war minister, prepared in late August 1792, with personal and political backing from such as 'Danton, Brissot, Claviere and Pétion, as well as leaders of the 10 August insurrection'.[7]

Another urgent matter was the dispatch of *commissaires* to the *départements*, to explain and justify events in Paris, rally support for the revolution, and recruit for the army. This was not simply a matter for ministers. At least three sets of *commissaires* went out from Paris in August–September, and many of their doings have been studied in detail. The Assembly started sending emissaries to ensure the reliability of the four armies on 15 August. The Commune quickly followed suit. When Longwy fell on 23 August, leaving the road to Paris vulnerable, the Assembly instructed the Provisional Executive Council (PEC) to send out further commissioners, to recruit volunteers and promote patriotic sentiments in the provinces. Roland asked for time to propose names. But next morning, Danton arrived at council with a list of up to thirty commissioners, including members of the Commune and/or leading Cordeliers (Chaumette, Momoro, Billaud).

These appointments were certainly political, but Mme Roland's description of them as 'little-known men, intriguers from the sections or loudmouths from the clubs' was unduly negative. She candidly wrote that she considered the list 'one of Danton's greatest coups and the most humiliating for the council'.[8] Most historians regard the appointments less luridly. In the fullest study, Caron argues that while benefiting from Danton's Paris network, they were not his protégés nor necessarily known to him personally. They were sent on 29 and 31 August, on orders signed by all the ministers, so Roland either did not, or dared not, object. Mme Roland was writing after certain *commissaires* had been accused of stirring up trouble (giving partisan versions of 10 August, campaigning against moderate candidates in the elections, exacerbating political differences in Paris, or simply throwing their weight about). Roland himself particularly objected to the Commune's *commissaires*, as a usurpation of power. Caron argues that these, too, were slandered in the contentious atmosphere after the September massacres, and that most of them did what they were asked to do, as far as possible. Whether they were an important

---

  [5] Hampson (1978/1988), pp. 75–6: also Paré and Billaud-Varenne.

  [6] Howe (2008); Roland's letter, see *Mém.*, p. 159. Could this *possibly* have been the letter later (mis?)dated to 1793? See Chapter 24. Dumouriez thanked Clavière, but Danton must have approved. Roland called on the Sedanais not to support Lafayette, Le Guin (1966), p. 92.

  [7] Brown (1995), p. 276. Mme Roland recalled Servan's impatience at having to recruit politically correct engineers for Paris's defence, instead of technical experts, *Mém.*, p. 121.

  [8] *Mém.*, p. 80.

reason for the rift between the two ministers is not clear, but they must have contributed to it.[9]

The immediate preoccupation of both Roland and Danton was the fear of invasion. Emergency measures were urged by both ministers. Danton was perpetually at the War office, while Roland was concerned with rousing the provinces. His biographer, Le Guin, suggests that 'by energetic use of his power to suspend and purge' (including sacking the 'moderate' departmental council as a favour to his 'radical' friends on the Lyon city council), Roland had 'helped guarantee acceptance of the "second revolution" in France'—and deserved the praise he got from some provincial quarters. He urged public officials to embrace and publicize the principles of liberty and equality. According to Le Guin, the *Proclamation du conseil exécutif provisoire de la nation française du 25 Août*, enjoining the provinces to resist invasion, was probably written by Roland.[10] He also issued bracing circulars:

> See to it that all metals are melted into weapons, that everywhere cannon, rifles, sabres, pikes, are made, that you are provided with bullets, cartridges, powder, and that these provisions and those of food and fodder are kept from locations threatened by the enemy and placed in safe keeping. Let every city, every village close its gates…and be prepared for fierce resistance. […] Enemy armies are on our soil: arm all hands already raised to exterminate them.[11]

But closer to home, Roland's relations with the Paris Commune got off on the wrong foot. He incurred its opposition almost at once, by writing to the mayor urging that regular elections be held as soon as possible, under the law of 11 August. Pétion agreed, but members of the Commune did not see this as a priority, to put it mildly.[12] Thus began Roland's long-running battle with the Paris municipal authorities, an important element in the factional struggles of the autumn. The tensions brewing between the remains of the Assembly, the PEC, and the Paris Commune were fatefully thrown into high relief by the advance of enemy forces, and the events that came to be known as the September massacres.

Up to this point, there had been no open conflict between ministerial colleagues. Mme Roland's retrospective dislike of Danton was far from being as pronounced at first. It is true that the puritanical Rolands viewed his appointment with some apprehension, in view of his boisterous (*débraillé*) reputation.[13] Yet Mme Roland's memoirs and correspondence clearly tell us that during August, she saw Danton and Fabre d'Eglantine regularly:

[9] Caron (1950), pp. 71–2; Whaley (2000), pp. 78–9, and the recall of all on 22 September after Valmy; Le Guin (1966), p. 99; *Mém.*, p. 80; Hampson (1974/1988), p. 76; Walton (2009), pp. 210–13. On Roland's emissaries see below, Chapter 23.

[10] *Moniteur*, 13, pp. 605 ff.; Le Guin (1966), pp. 92–4; Roland still backed Chalier in Lyon at this stage, *AP*, XLVIII, p. 158.

[11] Circulars quoted Le Guin (1966), p. 94, from *Moniteur*, 13, pp. 441–2, 546; AN, AF II/2, council minutes, orders sent 1 Sept for defence of cities, and search for arms, to be distributed for defence of Paris, signed by all ministers.

[12] Le Guin (1966), p. 93.   [13] *Mém.*, p. 75.

> Danton hardly let a day go past without coming to see me; sometimes it was for a council meeting: he would arrive a little early and come into my apartment, or stop off there afterwards, usually with Fabre d'Eglantine; other times he came to ask if he could eat with us [*il venait me demander la soupe*] in order to have a private conversation with Roland.[14]

She frankly reports that she thought his overwhelming physical appearance reflected his moral character. However, she tried to overcome her first impressions of 'that repulsive and terrifying face'. While admitting that he expressed 'an air of great jovial bonhomie', she also mentions his 'amazing audacity'—which in context could be a coded reference to Danton making a pass at her. It wouldn't be entirely out of character. Still their first relations must have been reasonably amicable. No one, she admits, on the same page, 'could have *shown*[15] greater signs of zeal [than Danton] or have had a greater love of liberty and the strongest desire to agree with his colleagues so as to serve it [liberty] effectively'. However, their reactions to the prison massacres were a key element in their later regrettable estrangement.

THE SEPTEMBER MASSACRES

The invasion scare inspired rumours about fifth-columnists inside Paris. Nonjuring priests in particular were suspected of being spies. At Danton's request, house-to-house searches were ordered, ostensibly for weapons. Many arrests resulted, and the city's prisons were soon packed with 'suspects'. Roland himself shared the anxiety about counter-revolutionaries: he signed the PEC declaration of 25 August saying 'You have traitors in your midst, but your active vigilance is sure to thwart them. Remain calm and united.'[16] He wrote to the Paris *département* (not the Commune) expressing anxiety about prison security, but in terms of escapes. Guards were scarce at the prison of La Force, but the many prisoners required 'the most firm and close supervision. There could be many escapes if the concierge does not get reinforcements, [...]. Please send four extra men, from whatever source.'[17]

If four extra guards materialized, they would hardly have been much use. On Sunday 2 September, news reached Paris that Verdun was threatened, and the fort fell that day. This fuelled rumours about a 'prison plot' to arm counter-revolutionaries in a mass breakout. That afternoon, a convoy of prisoners being transferred from the *mairie* to the Abbaye prison was attacked by *sans-culottes*, subjected to a sort of instant trial, and a number of them hacked to death.[18] Between 4 and 6 p.m. that day, a hundred or more priests were killed in the Carmes convent, again after some form of trial. Further assaults followed overnight, and by next

---

[14] *Mém.*, pp. 76 ff., *Corr.*, II, p. 436, 'mon ami Danton' [ironic.] Philippe-François Fabre d'Eglantine (1750–1794), described by Mme Roland as 'a perfect *tartufe*, i.e., hypocrite', ibid., p. 77.
[15] She uses the slightly ambiguous term 'faire montre' for 'shown', *Mém.*, p. 76.
[16] Quoted Bluche (1986), p. 33.
[17] AN, F^{12} 178.
[18] Bluche (1986), pp. 47–9. Numbers vary: 16, 18, 25.

day, most of the Parisian prisons had been broken into and makeshift tribunals set up in courtyards: impromptu trials, later described as the people's justice, were held. The slaughter was not entirely indiscriminate: some prisoners were 'acquitted'.

Nevertheless, according to the most authoritative accounts, about half the prison population, between 1000 and 1400 people, were killed between 2 September and the last incidents on 6–7 September. The majority were 'droit commun', i.e. common law, rather than political prisoners. Some were forgers of *assignats* (detested by the public, though not treasonable). Caron estimated about 72 per cent of the total in this category, with priests making up about 17 per cent (223 individuals: three-quarters of the priests in jail). The dead also included Swiss survivors from the Tuileries, and aristocrats, notoriously Marie-Antoinette's friend, the princesse de Lamballe. It was both the expeditious nature of the 'trials' and the atrociously cruel manner of execution that came to be seen as the most appalling aspects of the massacres: the condemned prisoners (who included women at the Salpêtrière and teenagers in Bicêtre) were hacked or bludgeoned to death, minutes after being pronounced guilty.[19]

Throughout this time, several elected bodies were meeting continuously, but without apparently being able, or willing, to stop the slaughter. Accusations of counter-revolutionary treachery at the top were being made. Robespierre, at the Commune General Council on the night of 30–31 August, accused Brissot, Condorcet, and Roland of 'misinforming' against him, and repeated his accusation on following days. On 2 September, the surveillance committee of the Paris Commune issued arrest warrants for several people, including Brissot and Roland. It is not clear who was responsible, but Marat had joined the committee that afternoon, and had already denounced dozens of Assembly members. Pétion later stated that on 4 September, he and Danton confronted Robespierre, who confirmed that he was in favour of the arrest warrants. Apparently sincerely, but surely quite wrongly, he claimed Brissot was a traitor, in league with Brunswick. Brissot later testified that the Commune had accused him of being an agent of Brunswick at this time. Three magistrates inspected his papers on 3 September, finding nothing suspicious.[20]

If these arrests had been carried out, Brissot and Roland, and several of their colleagues (perhaps even Mme Roland, according to Louvet) would almost certainly have been sent to their deaths, since the prison killings had started. Braesch describes Robespierre's approval—there is no evidence that he *proposed* the arrests—as 'no more or less than a hypocritical incitement to assassination', presumably to remove political opponents.[21] When later, in November, Pétion defended Robespierre, his one-time bosom friend, from charges of would-be dictatorship, he did describe him as 'a misanthrope [*atrabilaire*] who saw conspiracy everywhere; once he had an idea in his head, he would not admit to being wrong'.[22] Whatever

---

[19] Figures from Caron (1935) reproduced and amended by Bluche, ibid., p. 99. Cf. Scurr (2007), p. 199 for a summary.

[20] Whaley (2000), p. 80; cf. Louvet (1889); Hampson (1978/1988), p. 83, quoting Mortimer-Ternaux, III, 189; *Actes*, p. 261; Braesch (1911), p. 517; I have not found any document by Roland mentioning Robespierre at this time.

[21] Braesch (1911), p. 519.

[22] Whaley (2000), p. 81; *Moniteur*, XIII, p. 617, November 1792.

Robespierre thought or didn't think, Danton and Pétion poohpoohed the charges, and Danton tore up the warrants, arguably saving Roland's life.[23]

Both Danton and Roland were still preoccupied with the invasion, but taking different views. Mme Roland herself was retrospectively sceptical over the panic, saying a moment's thought should have been enough to realize an army from Verdun would take more than a few days to reach Paris.[24] Still, it was at this stage that her husband apparently suggested to the council of ministers that in the event of the enemy's arrival, perhaps the capital (i.e. the Assembly and the executive) should move to Blois on the Loire.[25] As noted earlier, the Rolands and Barbaroux had already discussed in June a possible strategic response if the capital were to be invested (rallying from the south). Roland's proposal had support from other ministers, including Clavière and Servan. The idea was not in itself treacherous: any government would be expected to have a contingency plan, and during invasions in later centuries, French governments did indeed leave Paris to try to continue governing. Roland later said as much in a message of 30 September: 'It is not true that any of us *advised* leaving Paris. It is true that [ministers] discussed whether if the enemy actually got near, [...] the nation's Assembly, Treasury, executive, and indeed Louis XVI, which all belong to the whole of France, should be moved', since they would be 'the enemy's chief targets. [...] We would have been unworthy or inept had we not judged it necessary to foresee all eventualities.'[26]

However, Danton stoutly opposed it, and went off to give the most famous speech of his career to the Assembly, calling citizens to arms:

> We demand that each citizen who refuses to serve against the enemy or take up arms will be punished with death. [...] To defeat [the enemy] Messieurs, we need audacity, more audacity, always audacity, and France will be saved: *il nous faut de l'audace, encore de l'audace, toujours de l'audace et la France est sauvée!*[27]

It was a terrific rallying call, which has echoed down the ages, and Danton was no doubt right (as well as inspirational) in the sense that moving the government might send the wrong signal to the enemy and the Parisians. In the end, of course, his bluff was never called. The invasion threat was removed, at least for a while, after the unexpected victory at the battle of Valmy (20 September), when under Dumouriez, the French army provoked a Prussian retreat. It never came to defending Paris with pikes, as Danton implied—and indeed as Roland had already called for. However, it was easy, when the two men later crossed swords, to accuse Roland of being 'an old driveller who sees ghosts everywhere'.[28] In personal terms, neither

---

[23] *Mém.*, pp. 83–4, for Mme Roland's version, presumably from Pétion; she refused to believe Danton's motives were good. cf. Le Guin (1966), p. 98.

[24] *Mém.*, p. 81.

[25] Caron (1950) pp. 233–4; Whaley (2000), p. 81.

[26] *Moniteur*, XIV, p. 89; Le Guin (1966), p. 98. Roland, letter of 30 September, Crawford Collection, p. 6. Cf *Mém.*, pp. 354–5, Mme Roland says, correctly, that the discussion was 'hypothetical', and (probably correctly) that Danton later used it as a stick to beat Roland.

[27] *AP,* XLIX, 2 September 1792.

[28] Whaley (2000), p. 94, 26 September.

of the Rolands can seriously be accused of cowardice, but the proposal for a strategic retreat, however prudent, could be seen as not showing enough determination to resist.[29]

POST-MORTEM ON A MASSACRE

Given the invasion fever, could the September killings have been prevented or brought under control? And who was responsible? When the slaughter finally ended, it would cast a long shadow, as politicians pondered their reactions. The tribunal of history has been out a long time, and given various answers.

No serious evidence of coordination has been found. No speaker at the Jacobins called for the killings. The massacres were carried out by people whose names are mostly obscure and who were never charged. Almost certainly, as Robespierre later implied, they included some of the 'men of 10 August', but they did not necessarily have any record of indiscriminate violence. Fear of a prison breakout, far-fetched though the scenario looks in retrospect, might have been credited in the frantic atmosphere of those days, encouraging some spontaneous attacks. Men called to the army were said to have feared leaving their families behind, at the mercy of counter-revolutionaries.[30]

Mme Roland later came to believe, like some of her political friends, that the killings were prompted by the Commune, and implicated Robespierre, Danton, and Marat. It is less clear in her writings at the time. Although she mentioned all three, and 'our insane Commune', in letters to Bancal on 2 and 5 September, as responsible for disorder, and for encouraging hostility to the Assembly and the PEC, she did not specifically accuse them of the killings. On 2 September, she wrote of the invasion: 'we'll be saved only by a miracle', and said she had heard of the massacre of 'fifteen' prisoners at the Abbaye. On 5 September, she wrote that Robespierre had 'a little army at his command', 'my friend Danton is the ringleader', and 'we are under the knife of Robespierre and Marat', but this wording is perhaps ambiguous, and might even apply to the arrest warrants, not the massacres.[31]

There is no evidence that either Robespierre or Danton was behind the massacres, although later both tended to excuse or belittle them, and Danton did not trouble to deny the accusations.[32] Robespierre made no statement at the time. As for Marat, the charge has plenty to make it stick. He had repeatedly called for attacks on politicians he considered traitors and enemies, and was famous for

[29] *Corr.*, II, pp. 433–4: Mme Roland shows resolution in her letter of 2 September: cf. note 25 above.

[30] *Mém.*, p. 80; Whaley (2000), pp. 81–2; Bluche (1986).

[31] *Corr.*, II, pp. 434–6, 5 and 9 September: 'My friend Dton is driving everything; Robp. is his puppet. Mat holds his torch and dagger; this wild tribune rules us and we are oppressed while waiting to be his victims.' Cf. *Mém.*, p. 87, suspicion of Danton.

[32] Hampson (1974/1988) on Danton; Hampson (1978/1988), pp. 123–215 says Robespierre was less than frank about his knowledge and whereabouts, but does not conclude; Bluche (1986), pp. 34–8; Scurr (2007), pp. 200–1.

sanguinary remarks.[33] At any rate, the General Council of the Paris Commune, while powerless to stop the killings, did not dissociate itself from them. On the contrary, on 3 September, it sent out a circular to the provinces, signed by Marat, explicitly justifying them, and calling for similar measures against traitors in the provinces.[34]

Danton's ministry was contacted by the Commune for a signature to that circular, and in his absence one was provided by Fabre, who backed the massacres. Mme Roland reports in her memoirs that Grandpré, the inspector of prisons, told her he had approached Danton early on 2 September, fearing violence, and that Danton had said something like, 'The prisoners will just damn well have to fend for themselves.'[35] His mind was no doubt elsewhere, on his 'audace' speech to the Assembly. If the anecdote is true, he could be reproached for callousness, and failure to recognize what was happening. However, in any case, he was completely powerless to stop it—and perhaps seeing it as beyond recall, did not even try. His biographer remarks that once the massacres had happened, Danton not only did not repudiate them, but even claimed they were his work: so 'the Girondins could scarcely be blamed if they took him at his word'.[36]

So, finally, what was Roland's own responsibility, as minister of the Interior? Undoubtedly, the massacres mark a turning-point in both the Rolands' attitude to the Revolution, or at least its insurrectionary aspects. On 9 September, Marie-Jeanne wrote to Bancal, 'You know my enthusiasm for the Revolution, well now I am ashamed of it! It has been besmirched by criminals, and become hideous'.[37] Jean-Marie Roland literally fell ill, developing jaundice, and being unable to eat or sleep, according to his wife, although he continued to work. She herself was enraged, following the first day which, she agreed, had taken everyone by surprise, by the fact that the killings continued for days which, while bystanders stood and watched. She claimed that the attackers were relatively few, and divided into small bands who could easily have been overpowered. Could nobody have intervened to stop them?[38]

The situation glaringly highlighted the confusion over executive responsibilities. Between them, the Assembly, the Commune, the mayor, and the ministers were all seemingly paralysed. Some historians have concluded that Danton and Roland, as the ministers responsible for justice, prisons, and public order, 'did nothing', or

[33] Placard of 30 August accusing Brissot and others of warmongering and betrayal, Marat, *OC*, 8, pp. 4704–5: he accuses not Roland directly, but Lanthenas, 'puppet of la femme Roland'. He had called on people to go to the Abbaye and kill the Swiss and their accomplices, quoted Bluche (1986), pp. 34–5: 'let traitors' blood start to flow'.
[34] On the circular, see Doyle (2002), p. 191, signed by Marat, Panis, Sergent etc.: 'a terrible plot to cut the throats of patriots: [...] some of these ferocious conspirators held in prisons have been put to death by the people, acts of justice which appeared indispensable, to contain by terror the legions of traitors hidden in their walls', Marat, *OC*, 8, pp. 4710 ff.; Bluche (1986), p. 60.
[35] Whaley (2000), p. 82, quotes Bluche, but the only source for this is actually Mme Roland: *Mém.*, p. 47.
[36] See Hampson (1974/1988), pp. 80, 82, etc. for comments on Danton's tendency to contradict himself, say what his listeners wanted to hear, etc.
[37] *Corr.*, II, p. 436.   [38] *Mém.*, pp. 86–7.

were even 'complicit' in the massacres.[39] Leaving Danton's case to his biographers, what did Roland do?

As minister in charge of prisons and public order, Roland was theoretically empowered to call on the police or National Guard, in practice the only possible force that could intervene. Mme Roland claims that he contacted both Pétion as mayor and Santerre as commander of the guard at an early stage, even before the violence, calling on them to strengthen the guards on the prisons. It is possible that messages exchanged between Roland, Pétion, and Santerre on 2 and 3 September led Santerre as commander to make an effort, to call on the guard and that, as he later claimed, he was confronted with refusal to move.[40] Rightly or wrongly, at the time, and afterwards, it has been claimed that the guard's intervention could have caused an even greater bloodbath. But in any case, it was apparently determined not to intervene.

Mme Roland's later version of events can't be regarded as an entirely reliable chronological record. But there is no reason to disbelieve her account of the arrival at the Interior ministry of a crowd of men demanding arms on the afternoon of 2 September. She recounts that she immediately took a cab to the ministry of the Navy, where the council was meeting, to warn them about this. Whether, as she claims, neither she nor Roland realized the full scope of the killings until next morning, is more open to question. Where we are on firmer ground is that a letter from Roland was certainly read out by the president of the Assembly at the evening session of 3 September.

One sentence of this letter has been endlessly quoted (and slightly misquoted) to indicate Roland's complicity in the massacres.[41] It goes like this: 'Yesterday! [*sic*] was a day over whose events it is perhaps necessary to leave a veil' [*Hier! fut un jour sur les événements duquel il faut peut-être laisser un voile*]. The last words are sometimes mis-translated as '*draw* a veil', which is not quite the same thing as 'leave'. In any event, Roland and everyone else were undoubtedly operating in a climate of fear, and there are plenty of precautions in the letter, plus a partial excuse for the earliest actions. This sentence, however, is embedded several pages into a careful, but arguably quite courageous text, condemning the massacres, and calling for their immediate end. For all we know, Mme Roland may have helped compose it, even the 'veil' sentence.[42]

Roland's letter conceded that revolutions do not operate by the usual rules: the people's anger was like a torrent that, if not soon brought within its banks, would sweep everything away. He agreed that 'without the tenth of August, we were lost':

[39] Whaley (2000), pp. 83 (wrongly I think) states that Roland's objection was 'not to the massacres themselves', but to the warrants. Cf. Bluche (1986).

[40] *Mém.*, p. 82; Le Guin (1966), p. 97 and BNF MSS, naf 9532, fol 245 ff., Roland to Santerre and Pétion on 4 September, referring to earlier messages, which if written, did not survive. Whaley and Hampson argue that calling out the National Guard might have resulted in a 'second Champ de Mars massacre'. Cf. AN, F[12] 178: Roland to Pétion, 4 September.

[41] Bluche calls this letter 'full of cowardice and hypocrisy'; Whaley (2000), pp. 82–3 says: 'he did not denounce the massacres', and was, like Robespierre, 'complicit' (also gives 'draw' for 'leave'.).

[42] 'Paris, ce 3 septembre, 1792, l'an 4e de la liberté'; quoted from the printed copy in NLS, Crawford Collection, FR 1014, no. 11.

the royal court was 'biding its time to deploy the standard of death over Paris and reign through terror'. But if disorganization and denunciations continued, it would become impossible to govern. The 'provisional' Commune had rendered great services, but was now abusing its power. He referred back to June, perhaps to establish his credentials: 'One owes it to the people as much as to kings, to tell them the truth.' With the enemy soon at the gates, mayor and ministers were faced with orders coming from all directions, and with total lack of control, knowledge, and unity. Ministers had even been denounced in the Commune chamber, and a climate of suspicion was 'fomenting trouble and hindering operations'.[43] At this point comes the famous sentence about the veil. What follows deserves quoting in full:

> I know that the people, terrible in its vengeance, is operating a form of justice: it has not been making a victim of everybody in its fury, which is directed at those it sees as having been too long spared by the sword of the law, and whom the perilous circumstances suggested should be sacrificed at once. But I [also] know it is easy for *scélérats* [criminals] and traitors to abuse this outburst of feeling, and that it must be stopped. I know that we owe the whole of France a declaration that the executive power was unable to predict or to prevent these excesses. I know that it is the duty of the constituted authorities to put an end to it, or see themselves reduced to nothing. And I know that this declaration exposes me to the fury of certain agitators. Well, they can take my life! I would only want to preserve it in the cause of liberty and equality, and if these are violated and destroyed, whether by foreign despots or the misled and abused people, I wouldn't want to go on living.

There was no time to lose: 'the legislators must speak, the people must listen, and the reign of law must be established'. Roland insisted he would stay in his post until death, if he could be useful and was judged to be so, but asked permission to resign if anyone else was recognized as better to occupy it, or if the silence of the laws stopped him having the means of action.[44]

There is no documentary evidence that he yet knew about the proposal to arrest him. Danton apparently tore it up *next* day, and Mme Roland insists that Roland did not hear about it (though she did) until days later. This seems doubtful: she mentions it in a letter dated 5 September, and Roland's final words indicate that he felt threatened. His wife wanted to answer the charge that if he protested at the massacres, it was *only* because he was himself endangered. If he did know, it would add a personal motive to his protest. However, her argument that the threat would simply have made him more vociferous in condemning the massacres is probably fair comment.

Whatever the truth about the arrest warrant, I agree with his biographer Le Guin, who defends Roland from charges of complicity. 'Almost alone', on the evidence of this text, he made a conscientious effort to stop the massacres on the second day. Although he wrapped up his message in his habitual 'pious verbiage',

---

[43] He had been to a meeting of the sections convened by Pétion on 2 September, as his wife reported that day, *Corr.*, II, p. 433.
[44] See note 41.

and prudent praise of the 'people's justice', and semi-excused the first day as explained by panic, there is no mistaking his call for the killing to stop.[45] It is well-nigh impossible to find any other contemporary documents which go as far, or were issued so soon, as his 3 September letter. Several other future Girondins or sympathizers went much further in excusing the massacres.[46] Gorsas on 3 September (early on, it is true) wrote, 'The people being furious, knowing the prisons to be full of conspirators, have carried out justice which is terrible, but necessary [...] we are in open war with the enemies of our freedom. We shall die at their hands if they do not die by ours.' Carra wrote that the victims had given 'outstanding proof of their lack of civic spirit'. Louvet, silent until 8 September, wrote cautiously: 'the people's prompt justice spared many innocent prisoners, and apparently only struck down the guilty'. Brissot reported the deaths saying, 'Here are the chief details, without comment. What comment could say more than the facts?' Bluche, while hostile to the Gironde, exempts Brissot from the 'chorus of approval of the press', and reproduces several articles from the *Patriote* in an appendix.'[47]

The Assembly voted the posting up of Roland's letter of 3 September. However, the killings did not stop, going on sporadically until 6 or 7 September. In his message to the Parisians, dated 13 September, Roland again took a stand against the Commune, stoking its lasting enmity. 'I admired 10 August. I shuddered at the consequences of 2 September [...]; *I did not condemn a first and terrible movement,* [of the people's 'long-deluded justice', but] I believed that its continuance should be avoided, and that those working to perpetuate it were deceived by their imagination, or by cruel and ill-intentioned men.'[48]

The trauma of these days did not go away. Robespierre, when later refusing to condemn the massacres outright, argued, correctly, that there had been illegitimate violence at earlier stages in the Revolution: 14 July 1789 and 10 August had both been 'illegal' and violent, he pointed out, but had it not been for those events, there would be no Revolution. This is sometimes regarded as a good knock-down argument. However, it stretches moral relativism to extremes.[49] Massacre of unarmed prisoners, most of whom were not guilty of anything remotely like treason, was hardly the same as an armed crowd of citizens tackling armed troops and facing the power of the official state. It is true that some politicians later condemned the events more loudly than they had at the time. However, the horror inspired by the killings, nationally, and internationally, had devastating consequences. It became critical to the factional divide, and lay behind the call for a provincial force to protect the Assembly, which became another bitter bone of contention under the Convention.

[45] Le Guin (1966), pp. 96–7 ff.: 'he got no support.' See BNF MSS, naf 9532 for letters between Roland, Pétion and Santerre.

[46] See Hampson (1978/1988), p. 82.

[47] Quoted by Dorigny in Soboul (1980), though Gorsas and Louvet are hardly all 'the Girondins'. Bluche and Whaley (2000), p. 83, give the same quotations.

[48] *Moniteur*, XIII, pp. 673 ff., quoted Le Guin (1966), p. 99. On the 4th, Bluche agrees, Roland tried to alert Santerre about the risk to signatories of July petitions.

[49] *AP*, LIII, pp. 49 ff., 52 ff., 170 ff., November 1792, see Chapter 23 below. Scurr (2007), p. 216, agrees that this speech is 'morally disturbing'.

ELECTIONS TO THE CONVENTION

In the short term, the massacres coincided with the start of elections to the Convention, casting a serious shadow across them.

The September events prompted Roland to envisage resigning from the ministry, and standing for election to the Convention. Both he and his wife viewed this (perhaps understandably) as a protective measure. On 11 September, Mme Roland wrote to Bancal, saying Brissot had upbraided her for seeking nomination, because 'he claims that for our friend to leave the ministry would be a public calamity. However, his health makes me fear any continuation of this terrible workload, even if he escapes the tempest still thundering over our heads.'[50] A year later, the deputy Duroy told the Convention that Buzot had read him a similar letter, in which Mme Roland complained that the Commune had issued a warrant against 'the virtuous Roland': 'She explained the dangers awaiting her husband, and said the only way to save him was to get him a nomination to the Convention'.[51]

The elections began in the first week of September, with lists circulated earlier.[52] In Paris, the Commune and Jacobins successfully garnered most of the votes for their favoured radical candidates. There were protests from other quarters that the sections were being manipulated or marginalized, and the upshot was that Brissot and his Parisian friends had to turn to the provinces to get elected. Whaley argues, no doubt correctly, that manipulation and marginalization went on in the provinces too.[53]

There must have been some fancy footwork in the Somme *département* to get Roland elected.[54] He had friends in patriot circles in Amiens, and the Somme electors unexpectedly revoked two deputies already selected, replacing their names by those of Roland and Héraut de Séchelles. (Héraut opted for another *département*.) On 25 September, Roland informed the Convention that he would resign his ministry in order to take his seat, staying only for current business until a successor was found. However, he later changed his mind: partly because of pressure from Brissot and others—'la foule des députés', according to his wife. One pressing letter came from Camille (later Gracchus) Babeuf, telling him that 'the welfare of the country' demanded that he stay. In fact, Roland already knew that the Somme seat could be challenged, as his wife admits.[55] In a stormy session on 29 September, the Convention made heavy weather about the rules on ministers staying on temporarily. It was in that session that Danton, in a moment of impatience, uttered his famous sound-bite, which probably deeply envenomed his relations with the Rolands: 'If you decide to offer his ministry back to Roland, you had better offer it to Mme Roland as well. Everyone knows he was not alone in his ministry as I was in mine.' It was both insulting and inaccurate of course, given

---

[50] *Corr.*, II, p. 437.   [51] Bernardin (1964), p. 43.
[52] The distinction between active and passive citizens was abolished: male citizens over 21, resident for one year and not servants, could vote. Jones (1988), p. 68; see Crook (1996) and Gueniffey (1992); not that it expanded the number of voters *au contraire*, elections analysed in Patrick (1972).
[53] Whaley (2000), p. 87.
[54] Patrick (1972), p. 178.   [55] Babeuf, AN, H 1 1439; Somme, *Mém.*, p. 92.

Danton's reliance on Fabre and other assistants, though not his wife.[56] Next day, Roland claimed (possibly with some truth, see Chapter 22) that he was staying *mainly* because he had been accused of cowardice by Danton. The Convention agreed, and validated the original deputies from the Somme.[57]

Roland was also accused by Camille Desmoulins of wanting to hang on to power: he had to choose, Camille wrote, between 'a palace or a second-floor flat, a carriage or his sexagenarian legs, 75,000 or 6,000 *livres* income'.[58] Roland's habitual self-righteousness made him an obvious target for mockery, but the evidence does not stand up that he was motivated either by greed for money, or overweening ambition. He undoubtedly had a high idea of his own efficiency, but he well knew he was accepting a dangerous job. It appears that it was, indeed, pressure from the 'Brissotin', or non-Parisian faction, combined with an elevated sense of duty and wounded pride, that drove him to carry on.[59]

---

[56] *AP*, LII, p. 229.

[57] *Corr.*, II, p. 437, note; Le Guin (1966), p. 101; original in AN, in H1 1439. The irregularities in the Somme meant he would have ended up 'nowhere', an outcome Mme Roland claims the 'Parisian gang' wanted, *Mém.*, p. 105; Gosse says she wrote his acceptance speech (see Chapter 22).

[58] *Révolutions de France et de Brabant*, 10, p. 75, Quoted Bernardin (1964), p. 69; ministerial salaries were *c.* 50,000 *livres* at this time.

[59] *Moniteur*, XIV, p. 78, Danton opted for the Assembly on 8 October, and Garat took over Justice.

21
1792–1793
Minister of the Republic
Grain and Museums

The extent of my department, the immensity of the work attached to it, have been considered as a kind of monstrosity. People started to think I had a great deal of power because I had a great deal to do.

Jean-Marie Roland, January 1793.[1]

How did the minister of the Interior spend his time during his second term of office? The point is not to ask whether Jean-Marie Roland was a 'good' or 'bad' minister: the answer is probably 'both', but the question is irrelevant. The suggestion here is that, for good or ill, in the absence of any other clearly-defined executive power, he now became more active and interventionist in everyday administration than any of his immediate predecessors—or indeed successors—in ways that have been largely overlooked.[2]

The period from September 1792 to 21 January 1793 (when Louis XVI was executed) was the seedbed of the split within the Convention: Brissotin–Montagnard or Girondin–Jacobin. (I shall usually use the term *Brissotin* as a shorthand for associates of Brissot, up till Roland's resignation in January 1793; the term *Girondin* after that.) Narrative histories have often devoted more time to the political battles than to policy and ministerial action at this stage in the Revolution. It is admittedly difficult to keep the two distinct, so a word about the divided context is needed.

The September massacres made a pre-existing gulf wider, but during the autumn the dividing lines were not set in stone. When the Convention met on 20 September, returning deputies from previous assemblies brought their political baggage with them, Robespierre and Brissot in particular. But many others were

---

[1] Bernardin (1964), p. 192; *AP*, 57, p. 599 and statement.
[2] Predecessors: Saint Priest, De Lessart, Cahier de Gréville; successors 13 June–10 August 1792, three Feuillants, in office briefly. All were royal appointments. Successors: Garat ('too insignificant to attack under the Terror') January–August 1793; J-F. Paré, August 1793–April 1794, 'manifestly not up to the job'. Dates and comments from Jones (1988), pp. 77–80, 349 and 378. In this company, Roland stands out.

newly elected.[3] The scrupulous, if slightly conflicting, studies by M. J. Sydenham and Alison Patrick have formed the basis for most discussions of the Jacobin–Girondin question, using the head-counts in a series of six critical votes starting with the king's trial at the turn of the year, by which time Roland's term of office was on the point of ending. During the autumn of 1792, it is harder to be precise, but there was a quite small nucleus on each wing of the Convention, the so-called 'left' and 'right'.

The slate of deputies for Paris, including Robespierre and Marat, perhaps formed the core of the 'Montagne'—occupying a perch in the highest seats on the left of the chamber. They defended the Paris Commune, and took an increasingly radical stance, reaching a peak over Louis's trial. 'The Montagne forged its identity by its implacable desire to obtain the judgement, sentencing and execution of the king.'[4] Brissot and his associates, including the original Gironde three, but extending to a number of others, were, and are, a more difficult group to define. Some 'Brissotin' speakers and journalists identified themselves by their greater readiness to condemn the September massacres, and call for prosecution of those responsible; some of them backed the idea of a 'departmental', i.e. provincial, force in Paris to protect the Assembly. During the king's trial in January, all the 'Girondins' voted him guilty, and a few voted for immediate death; more of them proposed amendments to the death sentence, in particular an 'appeal to the people' or national referendum on Louis's fate. Before the trial, Danton had a somewhat unaligned position for a while; and many deputies caught in the centre ('the Plain') did not give their allegiance clearly to either side at first. After the king's trial, most choices became somewhat clearer. Retrospectively, the vote on the *appel au peuple* in particular was used as a key criterion of division.[5]

As a minister long identified with the Brissot 'faction'—however much he denied this[6]—Roland was an obvious focus for its opponents' attacks, largely because he kept complaining about the non-cooperation of the Paris Commune. Many of the more damaging Girondin–Montagne confrontations in fact occurred later, in 1793, after he had resigned; and his views, and his wife's, did not always coincide with those of their friends.[7] One issue that became prominent towards the end of his ministry, however, was the charge that he was 'manipulating public opinion', through propaganda in favour of the Brissotins. This inspired the most violent Montagnard attacks on Roland in December (and is often singled out by historians). It is certainly important, and its significance will be considered closely in Chapter 26, but it should not obscure what else was going on, day after day, that eventful autumn. For surprisingly, much business went on during these months without arousing too much

---

[3] 78 of the 750 deputies were from the Constituent Assembly, 191 from the Legislative Assembly, Patrick (1972), Appendix 1.

[4] Lewis-Beck et al. (1991), p. 178.

[5] Discussed in Sydenham (1961), Patrick (1972), Lewis-Beck et al (1991), and by many articles since. See Jones (1988) pp. 170–92 for useful summaries.

[6] *Compte moral*, p. 12, NLS, Crawford Collection, Fr 1014, no 17.

[7] Whaley (2000) does not count the Rolands as 'radicals'; there is no article on ministers in *DCRF*; see Doyle (2002), pp. 235–7, for an analysis of the Girondins as revolutionary intransigents.

confrontation. 'In truth very little divided the factions of the Year II [and by implication, Year I]: the leading revolutionaries shared much in the way of ideology.'[8] There
were many policy issues (the church, education, conduct of the war, even subsistence), which did not necessarily divide the Convention along factional lines.

DAILY LIFE IN THE RUE NEUVE-DES-PETITS-CHAMPS

The two existing studies of Jean-Marie Roland as minister, now out of print, are
detailed and informative. Both faced the complexity of analysing a huge body of
archival evidence—selection is inevitable, neutrality difficult to maintain. Edith
Bernardin's thesis takes a thematic and institutional, not a chronological approach.
Policy is not ignored, but is marginalized. The author's default position (anti-
Gironde) is modified by scrupulous inclusion of evidence that does not always fit,
leading to tensions if not contradictions. Le Guin's chronological biography is
more sympathetic, while not shrinking from criticism, especially of Roland's character, but gives little detail about how the ministry operated. Both these writers,
incidentally, say comparatively little, and that fairly dismissive, about Mme
Roland's political contribution.

Robespierre was not wrong to assume that Roland was in a position of potentially great power after 10 August, though not perhaps quite in the way he meant
it. One could almost argue that with the king under lock and key, the offices of the
ministry of the Interior, replacing the royal bureaucracy, provided the only machinery for running everyday life in France. There was no formal constitution for the
Republic yet; improvisation reigned. All ministers were subordinate to the Assembly and its decrees, and Roland was—ostentatiously—scrupulous about asking for
permission or guidance. Because he did not have the right to speak at the Convention unless invited, historians have overlooked the fact that his almost daily reports,
usually letters read out by the president or secretary, were therefore *heard*—and
reported in the *Moniteur*—as much as leading deputies' speeches. His name was
constantly in public view. It is quite difficult otherwise to understand why he was
sometimes accused of being the head of a faction, planning to be regent, etc.[9]

As often as not, he requested clarification. To implement decrees, the minister
had to take literally hundreds of executive actions, for which individual permission
was not always possible. The revolutionary assemblies, as historians have noted,
seem to have assumed that it was enough to vote the laws and communicate them
to citizens for them to start operating. The 1791 Constitution ('an anachronism
before it went into effect') was badly suited to the new situation. There was no
prime minister, so the door was open for rifts inside the Provisional Executive
Council; nor were there guidelines for dealings between local and central authorities;
and there was virtually no machinery for enforcing Assembly decisions (a situation
that led to the later creation of Napoleonic prefects). The rain of decrees in 1792

---

[8] Linton (2008), p. 59.
[9] This seems an oversight in Whaley's otherwise full narrative (2000).

gave the Interior minister plenty to handle, and the only method open to him was constant communication in writing.[10]

Crucially, as the archives show, messages and queries flowed into the minister from all over France, on every subject, and from every political standpoint. Nobody else was in this position, since deputies were responsible to their electors, and other ministers' remit was far less wide. This link to the provinces was arguably the deep-seated root of Roland's quarrel with the Paris Commune (and its defenders, the Paris deputies). He took the admittedly provocative view that 10 August notwith-standing, the Paris municipal council had no more right than any other city coun-cil to speak for the whole of France on every matter. In his *Compte moral* in October, he wrote that it should 'be restricted to its eighty-third part of influence'—there were 83 *départements*—and in one heated exchange over the appropriation of national property, he said Paris had 'no greater right to claiming it than the com-munes of Perpignan or Gravelines'.[11]

His stance might be disingenuous, but there was a reality behind it, which cannot be described as 'federalism', the charge later levelled at the Gironde. Roland repeat-edly insisted on the unity of the republic, which he saw as threatened not from the provinces, but on the contrary, by Paris claiming special privileges. The Montagnard view, also repeatedly stated, was that 'Paris' was responsible for the heroic establish-ment of the Republic since 10 August, and *should* therefore be specially respected. Perhaps there was some pragmatism, or anxiety, in the unwillingness of other depu-ties to criticize 'Paris', where they had to sit, for fear of further violence. The minis-ter of the Interior was awkwardly positioned, if not on a collision course, vis-à-vis Paris. His ministry was a vast centralizing office for *provincial* affairs, reflected in many policy issues, from (crucially) law and order to subsistence.

A daily diary would refer to half a dozen different questions before breakfast, when the minister was briefed by his officials. Sometimes, Roland claimed, he had four hours' sleep. As well as purging the ministry of royalists, he reorganized its offices. The five new divisions were run by trusted 'patriots': their odd head-ings were devised to separate the routine from the contentious. According to the *Almanach national* (1793), Division 1, headed by Champagneux' handled cor-respondence with the departments on execution of laws, deportations of non-juror priests, postal services, prisons, hospitals, charitable works, grain—and gunpowder; the second, under Guillaume-Charles Faipoult, gendarmes, foreign-ers, pensions; the third, with Lanthenas sporadically in charge, education, cul-ture, and the arts; the fourth, under Le Camus, public works and buildings, mines, forests, shipping and ports. The fifth, under Jean Guillaume, trade and subsistence. There was a special bureau for opening, registering, and expediting dispatches—A.F. Le Tellier was 'particularly charged with correspondence relat-ing to the formation and propagation of *l'esprit public*', on which more later.[12]

---

[10] Church (1981), p. 47; Le Guin (1966), pp.118–19, Bernardin (1964), *passim*.

[11] Report of 30 September, NLS Crawford Collection 16. *Comte moral*, ibid., p. 17; *Moniteur*, XXX, p. 701; Le Guin (1966) pp. 99–100.

[12] *Almanach national* 1793, pp. 130–1; Bernardin (1964), p. 205, based on Perroud: Pache had started the reorganization in April.

It would strain the reader's patience to list the policy issues, great and small, arising over five months. The indexes of the *Archives parlementaires* give an idea of the range. To take relatively non-contentious issues during two weeks picked at random in December—when a lot else was going on, e.g. the king's trial—Roland's reports or queries covered: government bonds; the projected Directory of army and navy purchases; the need to send copies of laws to the Moselle, because the enemy had burnt them; purchases of foreign grain; requests for more funds for same; back payment to construction workers for the festival of the Federation (of 1790!); memos on external maritime trade; the Sèvres china manufacture; the *gendarmerie nationale*; the need for indemnities to Thionville—and so on.[13]

The minister also had to liaise with Assembly committees, one for every major policy heading. Ministerial letters were usually referred to the relevant committee, which might bury the issue. Take weights and measures. Roland suggested back in spring 1792 that the chaos of local weights and measures in France was a major obstacle to the free circulation of grain, at the time supported by all sides. On 14 May, he proposed to the committee of public instruction that until the Académie des Sciences finished measuring the meridian (later the basis of the metric system), a common measure should temporarily be adopted, preferably the Paris units. The deputy chosen to handle it never reported, and no statement of standarization was introduced until August 1793.[14] Dilatory committees were frustrating to an executive, but Bernardin argues, no doubt rightly, that Roland never really worked out a policy for dealing with committees, so his relations with them became politicized and antagonistic.[15]

The ministry's daily post contained a mass of requests from local statutory bodies: municipal, district, and departmental councils, virtually all run by 'new men' of all shades, coping with new problems. After several purges ('suspensions') of oppositional, i.e. 'moderate' councils during August, Bernardin states that 'despite a few tiffs, the usual harmony between the minister and the local administrations cannot be denied'—leading to complaints at the Jacobin Club that Roland was 'venerated in the provinces'.[16]

The minister predictably took a special interest in Lyon, from where his friends besieged him with letters. After a relative calm since 1791, the city was now in turmoil. In September 1792, it witnessed its own prison massacres, on a smaller scale, during which the 'Rolandin' mayor and councillors bravely, but vainly tried to intervene physically. The real problem remained *la vie chère*. Violent popular movements with pillaging and radical price-fixing broke out, which the authorities could not handle. By late October, 'our patriot municipal men, hitherto loved by

---

[13] *AP*, LV, 11–27 December 1792. He was constantly receiving death threats at this time and some nights sleeping away from home.

[14] *AP*, LXX, 1793, pp. 73–4, pending full introduction of the metric system. See Guillaume (1889), pp. 294, 296, and Alder (2002); Gillispie (2004), p. 279; Bernardin (1964), p. 156. Guillaume's index references often end with note 'no report'.

[15] Bernardin (1964), pp. 157–9 and 163.   [16] Ibid., p. 387.

the people, are the objects of scorn and threats'.[17] Roland, opposed to local price-fixing, was in constant touch with his allies on the council during autumn. However, the old alliance between the city's elected representatives and the popular clubs he had once supported was blowing up in his face. In the November council elections, the radicals around Chalier won most seats, although Chalier himself lost the mayoral election to a moderate, Nivière-Chol. Roland wrote on 10 November approving this last choice 'with all my heart'. He was aware that the city was 'riven by many different interests', but maintained that if the law was not firmly protected, 'everything will fall into anarchy and we are lost'.[18] Billemaz, a founder of the popular clubs, felt he had been outflanked by men whose 'ignorance and incompetence' he deplored.[19] The clubs had 'opened the way to power for the unpropertied and for men of violence whose respect for property and for the rule of law was at best doubtful'.[20] Vitet wrote in November that 'public opinion has been perverted since the arrival of Challier' [*sic*]. He feared 'the lethal effects of agitators', whom he called 'Maratistes', unless Roland could help alleviate distress and provide work for the silk industry—something probably well beyond the minister's powers, although he had done his best to send financial aid to the city.[21] In any case, Roland was out of office by late January. A few months later, Lyon would be the scene of the most dramatic political conflict outside Paris, and Roland would be suspected (quite wrongly) of leading its revolt against Paris.

Collective replies to the provinces took the form of ministry circulars. Bernardin regards these as wrongly neglected by historians, dismissed as routine correspondence. During Roland's tenure, they were more often like sermons or mission statements. Champagneux's remarks about Mme Roland suggest she may have helped compose them. However, Roland was well able to take on a lecturing tone himself. 'Without suggesting that he had a special taste for domination, [or] a clear plan, one can agree that almost imperceptibly he modified his brief, as he sent out circulars to citizens and elected bodies.'[22] His approach sounds eerily like paternalist presidential TV chats today: 'On entering the ministry of the Interior, I've come now to talk with you about the matters which will be the backbone of our dealings.'[23] One particularly stirring message, after the declaration of the Republic on 21 September, reads:

France will no longer be the property of an individual, the prey of courtiers; the numerous class of industrious inhabitants will no longer have to bend a humiliated

[17] Villieux to Roland, 28 October 1792, quoted Edmonds (1990), p. 128.
[18] AN, F⁷ 3686/6, ministry correspondence with Lyon 1790–1792, 29 November 1792.
[19] Billemaz to Roland, ibid., 29 November 1792.
[20] Edmonds (1990), pp. 126–37; Hanson (2003).
[21] AN, F⁷ 3683/6, 20 November 1792; also Billemaz, 9 October; cf. letter from silk-manufacturers, 6 November, suggesting the ministry order silk fabric and pretend the demand was from overseas. Vitet's letter, in Brival report, see Chapter 24. Cf. Hanson (2003), pp. 148–50.
[22] Bernardin (1964), pp. 257–9.
[23] 8 April, in *Lettres et pièces*: several circulars of a headmasterly nature.

brow before the idol [...] France has declared that she no longer wants a King, so every man recognizes no master or power other than the LAW. The spirit of tolerance, humanity and universal benevolence should not just be in the books of philosophers. It must be the National Spirit.[24]

Possibly because of this paternalist image, but also because old habits die hard (and certainly did not vanish during the Revolution) the minister continued to receive a flood of letters from individuals asking for favours—exemptions, jobs, lodgings, appeals against sacking. In January 1793, Roland declared that the volume of such requests was so great and the scope for satisfying them so small, that they would not be acknowledged in future.[25]

FEEDING THE NATION

A couple of case-studies may illustrate Roland's handling of policy. Subsistence was one of the time's most critical issues. Supplying grain and flour to cities—in particular to Paris—had been a major worry under the ancien régime. Shortages or high prices invariably led to urban unrest or even riots. So the royal government had always stepped in resolutely to subsidize bread, keeping its price steady, especially in the capital. Most economic thinkers argued that free trade and circulation of grain would be a more efficient method of supply, even if prices might rise before they settled. But this was hard to enforce, given the archaic economic structures of the time, and naturally not appreciated by ordinary townspeople, who spent a large share of their income on food. If prices rose, they felt it at once, and called for price-fixing on the old model (*taxation,* or as it became known, the *maximum*). Although by 1792, Parisians were protesting about other shortages (sugar, coffee, etc.), bread was still central to their diet, certainly for low-income families. Obstacles to the equitable distribution of grain included: hoarders and speculators, especially once the *assignat* dwindled in value, transport conditions on an inadequate road system, incompatible measurements, and one-off interventions by municipal authorities to fix prices, which satisfied townspeople, but might make matters worse in surrounding areas.[26]

In 1792–1793, it was unlikely that any nationwide policy, whether the *maximum* or so-called free trade, could square the circle of providing regular, equitably-priced supplies both to the towns and countryside, and to the armies, which expected priority.[27] In September 1792, given the military crisis, and the reluctance of farmers to accept *assignats,* the rump of the Legislative Assembly had adopted coercive measures (emergency aid, and a compulsory census of stores, which

[24] Address to Corps administratifs, 21 September, BNF MSS, naf 9532.
[25] AN, H 1439, carton full of such requests.
[26] Kaplan (1976): Roland sent out a questionnaire about grain prices in the spring: they varied from 21 *livres* in Calvados to 52 in Hautes-Alpes; meat shortages were explained by destruction of game, people eating meat on fast days, feeding the armies, etc. See BNF MSS, naf 22422.
[27] Kaplan (1976), I, pp. 682 ff. sums up: the police system ignored economics, the free trade system ignored politics. For Roland's approach in September see Le Guin (1966), pp. 102 ff. and 119–20.

Roland considered on the whole counter-productive).[28] Although fierce debates pitted some partisans of controls against those of free trade, most deputies had absorbed the economists' thinking. The argument was more political than economic. Left-wingers may not have believed in price controls any more than their opponents, but 'acceded to them as a tactical exigency', because of their electoral clientele in Paris—and because the fear of rioting was as real as ever. Some Brissotins—Creuzé-Latouche, for example—preached free trade long and loud, incurring popular disapproval, but there is no need to jump to the conclusion that one side was devoted to 'the people' and the other to 'the bourgeoisie', if one envisages the quarrel from the point of view of practical consequences. John Shovlin argues that both Montagne and Gironde, especially in 1793, tried to balance 'wealth and virtue [...] The Girondins had more confidence in the power of market forces to create abundance, but ultimately, like the Montagnards, they were instrumental liberals—economic freedom for them was a means to achieve republican goals.'[29]

Roland, as his whole career illustrated, was a fully-paid-up member of the free-trade school, but this belief coexisted with what appears to be a genuinely egalitarian, if gradualist, approach to levelling-up. He was emphatically not in favour of an all-out 'agrarian law' (nor was the Convention: on 18 March 1793, the death penalty was imposed for proponents of the *loi agraire*, i.e. compulsory expropriation of landowners). However, this 'arch-liberal' as he is sometimes called, did for instance advocate the free distribution of émigré lands to soldiers, 'a measure strikingly similar to the one proposed by the Gracchi' in ancient Rome. He wrote in January 1793:

> It is important for the republican government to multiply the number of proprietors, since nothing will attach them more strongly to the country, to respect for law, than property; and because nothing is more favourable to the system of equality which forms our political religion than the disappearance of inequality in fortunes.[30]

Roland's usual remedy for grain shortages remained the well-tried one of importing cereals from abroad, but it was the distribution of grain inside France that caused problems. One is struck by the pragmatic nature of his many interventions on this point. Because of their detailed listing of conditions on the ground, his reports to the Convention carried weight: they often concerned links in the supply chain—farmers, convoys, transport, measures, mills, and bakers.[31] On 19 November, he wrote to the Paris municipality:

---

[28] Cf. O'Connor (2008) p. 225 quoting Furet, 'Revolutionary politics were not concerned with means.'

[29] Shovlin (2006) pp. 202 ff.: those described as Girondins had a range of views, including equal inheritance, redistribution, and progressive taxation; Clavière advocated an estate tax.

[30] *Compte rendu*, p. 195. Cf. Le Guin (1966), pp. 120, 123. Shovlin (2006), p. 203, quoting from Dorigny (1980); BNF MSS, naf 22423.

[31] Cf. AN, F¹² 178, Roland to Cousin, 9 September 1792, requisitioning emergency supply for Paris because of invasion threat: grain, vegetables, forage, poultry, wood, coal etc. 'Get all bread ovens repaired to bake enough bread for 150,000 extra men, plus the daily usual, and see all the flourmills near Paris are working full stretch.' He asked the Commune to make sure all this was paid for.

I don't know why you have bought flour at 62 *livres* per sack and sold it to the bakers at 54. They quickly started selling it outside Paris at a profit. [...] I must advise you that this is as ruinous to the city of Paris as to the freedom of trade and the true interests of the people...merchants are unable now to sell these goods to the bakers.[32]

What was more, the linked subsidy of 12,000 *livres* a day couldn't go on forever. On 28 November, he reported that it was becoming hard for anyone to load a cart without being treated as a hoarder and suffering armed raids. 'Aristocrats and enemies of the republic' and 'rich individuals' were making capital out of distributing free grain, while people were flooding into Paris to buy it up, because it was cheaper there—thus emptying the market. Knowing that shortages often resulted from panic buying, he repeatedly assured Parisians that the city's suburban mills were all grinding away and well-provided with grain, so shortages were imaginary. Supplies should be normal in the autumn—real penury did not usually happen until the spring. As so often, Roland couldn't resist a tirade against 'trouble-makers', who were fomenting disturbances, and—as usual—this raised hackles. However, it bears repeating that this question was not yet really divisive in the Convention. Saint-Just gave his famous speech on the economy next day, 29 November, advocating the principles of free trade, while suggesting some possible interim measures. Several speakers, including Danton, Buzot, Pétion, and Robespierre, also defended free circulation, Robespierre on this occasion saying that the Convention was 'the supreme power' and that anyone who attacked it should be severely punished.[33]

In a retrospective summary on 6 January 1793, Roland gave his own version of the subsistence situation. The census in September had resulted, as he expected, in false returns—regions with supplies for two years claimed they had only enough for six months, etc. When the 8 December decree restored free circulation and told local authorities they must protect it, things improved—or so, at any rate, he claimed. 'A week before the decree, I was besieged with complaints of hunger and shortage. A week after, the complaints had dried up, the granaries had opened because they felt protected by the law, and *départements* without grain started to receive some.' His opponents had talked up a panic, he reckoned.[34] On the other hand, he warned strongly in his farewell report in January, the Convention would be faced with worse problems in the spring. Not only had autumn rain spoiled the maize and buckwheat, the principal grains of the poor in the countryside (Paris always insisted on wheat flour), but the demands of the army had bought up much

[32] *AP*, LIII, p. 477.

[33] *AP*, LIII, pp. 198 ff., 476 ff. 641 ff; Saint-Just's speech reproduced in English in Hardman (1973), pp. 37–46. He supported free circulation of grain inside France. *Moniteur*, 1 December; cf. Whaley (2000) p.117. See also BNF MSS, naf 22423.

[34] BNF MSS, naf 6243. (Well, he would say that, wouldn't he! But there are no counter-indications.)

of the autumn grain. Long-standing obstacles to free circulation meant that the price of the *sétier* varied from 96 to 27 *livres* nationwide. 'I cannot conceal from the Convention that there will be great need in the spring [...] it is urgent to take preventive measures now, which may not be practicable if deferred.' More grain would have to be brought in from abroad, and the money for it made available. The war with Britain would, of course. soon gravely affect imports.[35]

Civilian subsistence had to compete with the needs of the army and navy. Roland fought constantly to protect supplies from being unjustifiably diverted to the armies, while recognizing that the military often had to take priority. However, divisions between him and the War minister, ironically his own nominee, J.N. Pache since October, led to a stalemate here, too. Pache changed allegiance during the autumn and was now close to the Montagnard deputies. Mme Roland wrote that he was an excellent administrator, but the most 'Jeanfesse' (= useless) minister you could find'. He purged the ministry so ruthlessly, according to Howard Brown, that 'common sense was discarded, experienced personnel were sacrificed, and administrative action was retarded'.[36] Early in November, a Directory of Purchases was appointed, for the armies. Roland maintained that the War ministry was handling supplies and accounts inefficiently, and the Brissotins in the Assembly (although not only they) attacked Pache. Pache and Dumouriez, as commander in Belgium, were, moreover, unhelpfully involved with two rival groups of outside financiers, angling for government contracts to feed the troops, and driving up prices. Both men were also jockeying for power and appealed to the Convention. Roland was not a good team player; if he suspected his colleagues were inefficient or corrupt, he stopped cooperating. Some blame probably lay on both sides, but 'the real victim was the Directory of Purchases.'[37]

Overall, however, during Roland's tenure at the ministry, although there were constant scares over subsistence, there was no major crisis of the kind the authorities would have to face in 1793, so his free-circulation approach was not seriously challenged. The war was going relatively well, too, before the *levée en masse* created the need for huge army requisitions. Roland never succeeded in sorting out subsistence, but perhaps he did not entirely fail either: he accurately identified the bottlenecks. The rights and wrongs of the 'maximum' have long been debated, but really apply to the time after he had left office. It was opposed even by Montagnards at first, and eventually introduced as an emergency measure only in May 1793, under pressure. Its importance then and later was symbolic and political, as well as strategic. It is worth remarking though, that the difficulties of applying it encountered exactly the kind of problems Roland had foreseen: the means of enforcing maximum prices had, in the end, to be draconian (under the Terror) if they were to be effective in the face of evasion, hoarding, black marketeering, etc.

[35] Quoted from BNF MSS, naf 22423. On Paris, see Garrioch (2002), especially Chapter on 'Bread, police and protest'.
[36] 'Jeanfesse', *Corr.*, II, p. 446, to Servan (!), 25 December 1792, Brown (1995), p. 47. On Pache see Mme Roland's diatribe, *Mém.*, pp. 102–8.
[37] Le Guin (1966), p. 107; on the Directorate of Purchases, see esp. Brown (1995), pp. 52 ff. and Bernardin (1964), pp. 441–4.

One can only conclude that although he (as usual) believed he was right and everyone else was wrong, Roland's approach to this policy issue was grounded in more practical knowledge than that of the average deputy.[38]

FEEDING THE MIND? MUSEUMS, LIBRARIES, COLLECTIONS

Universal education, however important, does not make a good case study, since nothing concrete came of any plans put forward while Roland was minister. Condorcet's detailed educational proposals came to the Legislative Assembly on 20 April 1792, the day war was declared, and were sidelined, although they influenced later decisions. The Assembly committees on public instruction worked hard and continuously, but without clear results at first. In December 1792, both Lanthenas and Romme spoke on the committee's proposals, again not discussed fully because of other priorities. (Marat said discussing education was like planting trees while soldiers were dying.) Roland mostly had to deal with nuts-and-bolts matters, like the consequences of outlawing the religious teaching orders.[39] He had his own ideas, in particular on agricultural and veterinary education, as essential to any 'agricultural revolution' in France, and which he outlined, along with proposals for primary and secondary education, in his January *Compte rendu*.[40] However, the cultural matter on which he arguably made most impact was in setting the ground rules for cultural institutions, in particular the Louvre and the Bibliothèque nationale. It is no accident perhaps, that a question where the minister was allowed a fairly free hand, precisely because deputies thought it was a nuts-and-bolts matter, was the one where Roland made most progress towards what he believed in.

It is not surprising that the Assembly committees and the ministry devoted time to the arts and 'heritage' matters: in the symbolic economy of the Revolution, national identity and cultural ideals were seen as critical, reflected in numerous festivals and celebrations. The acquisition by the state of church property in 1789 had brought many monuments, books and works of art into 'national' ownership: 'overnight, an immense artistic and historic heritage ceased to function meaningfully in a religious context'.[41]

In 1792, the national heritage expanded even further. The Louvre, although a royal palace, was also an art gallery during the ancien régime. The annual Salons were held there, it housed the royal academies, and made lodgings available for privileged artists and craftsmen. The Bibliothèque royale, in the rue de Richelieu,

---

[38] *DCRF* article 'Maximum'.

[39] On education, see Guillaume (1891–1907) for Lanthenas and Romme proposals; Barnard (1969); Palmer (1985 and 1989); O'Connor in Armenteros (2008); Brockliss (1987) p. 238, etc. Romme to Roland, 14 November 92, about persistence of 'the same spirit of pride and aristocracy', AN, F[17] 1001, no 92.

[40] *Compte rendu*, quoted Le Guin (1966) pp. 120–1: he claims 'only Condorcet came up with more ideas', and Roland deserves more credit. BNF MSS, naf 6243.

[41] McLellan (1994), p. 92.

was also theoretically owned by the king. After 10 August, both were destined to become national repositories and 'glories of France'.

The first issues Roland faced had to do with destruction, not conservation. By an Assembly decree in May 1792, he was instructed to organize a 'bonfire of the vanities': 2500 boxes of 'titles and genealogies' from the royal libraries. He gave it his full support: it was 'useless and even dangerous' to conserve this collection. Interestingly, it contained requests and decisions about the granting of noble status (so presumably the record of his own 1784 application was in there—something he wouldn't be unhappy to see destroyed). He was out of office though, when the bonfires took place on the Place Vendôme on 19 June, 7 July, and 7 August.[42]

But the major attack on relics of the past came after 10 August when all royal property, including the Louvre and library, reverted to the nation. There was a simultaneous wave of popular, often passionate attacks on symbols of royalty— what the Abbé Grégoire later called 'vandalism', a term that caught on. Some monuments were requisitioned for the war effort—Roland himself authorized the statue of Louis XV in Nancy to be melted down for cannon on 2 September, despite local protests. The statue of Henri IV on the Pont-Neuf, which Mme Roland saw every day of her childhood, was pulled down too, although the *sans-culottes* who did so admitted they had hesitated, 'because his virtues gave us pause': still, he was 'king without the consent of the people', so down he came. Some citizens wanted to burn down the royal library, simply because it had belonged to the kings.[43]

But the deputies quickly agreed that works of art should be protected. Pierre-Joseph Cambon, in the last days of the Legislative Assembly, made an ingenious speech, distinguishing the symbolic and cultural value of royal possessions:

> We must certainly preserve artistic monuments, and keep them as models for the monuments we will put up to liberty. We should even preserve the images which remind us of the Bourbons, who will eternally merit our gratitude, since they made us detest kings. [...] Let us bring them all together in a single place to form a museum [...] which, while destroying the idea of royalty will preserve the masterpieces now kept in the detestable palaces of our ci-devant kings.[44]

There was already an Assembly committee for monuments, but perhaps emboldened by previous experience of committees and fearing a free-for-all, Roland asked for and got some autonomy in this area. 'It is indispensable', he argued, 'that I should not be thwarted by *commissaires* or by administrative bodies concerning artworks etc. from Versailles, Compiègne, Fontainebleau and Saint-Cloud,' if he was to be held responsible for them, as the decree stated.[45] He also favoured departmental museums, although the structures were not yet in place: 'We should do for the Nation what the industrious citizen would do for himself,' he wrote to the

---

[42] Bléchet (1992).
[43] Vandalism: *AP*, XLIII, p. 115; Bléchet (1992); Poulot (1997), p. 153; Pommier (1992), p. 101, etc.
[44] Pommier (1992), p. 104.
[45] *AP*, LIII, 27 October 1792.

corps administratifs in November.[46] For the Louvre, he obtained permission for an extra-parliamentary Commission du Museum, with the task of deciding what should go into the gallery and organizing its collection and display. He personally appointed its six members, all academicians. One of them was an old friend, Pierre Pasquier (1731–1806) from Villefranche, and another, Nicolas Jollain, had been known to Marie-Jeanne's father, so there is some evidence of hand-picking.

In the light of his later attacks on the work of this group, it is worth noting that Jacques-Louis David, the painter of the Revolution (1748–1825), was still on friendly terms with Roland at the time, and asking him favours. David, as noted earlier, wrote to him on 17 October ('at last a virtuous minister') reminding him that they had met on the Champ de Mars on 17 July 1791, a coded touchstone for revolutionary correctness. David requested and got lodgings in the Louvre for more than one of his nominees.[47] Roland's reply to David, published in *Le Moniteur*, was a statement of his vision of the Louvre:

> This Museum must develop the great wealth of drawings, paintings, sculptures, etc., that the nation possesses. *As I see it*, it should attract foreigners and draw their attention; encourage the taste for the Fine Arts; give pleasure to art-lovers; and be a school for artists. *It should be open to everyone*, and anyone should be able to set up his easel in front of a picture or statue to sketch or model. This is to be a national monument and *no individual will be deprived of the right to enjoy it.* [Like Ancient Greece] France must extend its glory to all times and all peoples [my italics]

—'and since you are one of the glories of France,' he added, 'I will displace a goldsmith to grant your friend's request.'[48]

This mutual admiration did not last. Before long, David lined up with the Montagne in the Convention. The fact that the Museum commissioners were academicians was one problem, since David was on his way to getting the old Academy abolished. More importantly, he sided with professional colleagues about the identity of the collection and how it was to be displayed.[49]

The dispute between Roland's commission and these colleagues engendered much acrimony, and is discussed at length by Edouard Pommier.[50] Jean-Baptiste Pierre Le Brun, art-dealer and divorced husband of court painter and émigrée Elisabeth Vigée-Le Brun, and J-M. Picault, who had been passed over for the job of restoring paintings from the ex-royal collection, had personal axes to grind—

---

[46] Quoted Poulot (1997), p. 389, who argues this fitted with a view of the community as owner of its patrimoine, 'both elitist and democratic'.

[47] BNF MSS, naf 9532, fo 291.

[48] Ibid., draft, and *Moniteur*, 22 October 1792; see circular to the administration, 3 November, AN, F⁷ 1035: 'it would empoverish the Republic to remove all the precious artworks [...] previously reserved for the fortunate owners of royal and religious houses, who have deserted their fatherland'.

[49] Before long, David was referring to the Museum Commission as the 'vile creatures of Roland', quoted Tuetey and Guiffrey (1910/1971), p. 11.

[50] Pommier (1992) and (1992): his edition of Le Brun's pamphlet against Roland, January 1793. AN, F¹⁷ 1035 and F¹⁷ 1059 for Roland's circulars.

Roland suspected their motives as commercial. But the difference was important. It could be described as 'access' versus 'pedagogy'. Le Brun was a knowledgeable scholar, in touch with thinking elsewhere in Europe and favouring a taxonomic approach; that is, to show paintings by school, chronologically, rather than mixing them up as did private collectors in their *cabinets* and the royal collections.[51] Roland, however, directed the commission on 25 December *not* to make the display didactic, but to 'mix together schools and centuries, so as to entertain curious visitors, by showing them a flowerbed [*parterre*] which must be decorated with the most brilliant colours'.[52] He also directed that it contain no works by living artists (a shrewd move, to avoid disputes, and one that has governed the Louvre ever since). He took a personal interest in how the Louvre should develop. On his resignation in January, he wrote a detailed memo about organizing the overhead lighting he thought essential for the Grande Galerie, which would mean piercing the roof.[53]

The Louvre was supposed to open on 10 August 1793. Roland was not there to see it, but his successor, Garat, pressured the commission to be finished. In their statement of 17 June, they directly quoted Roland's view: 'The arrangement we have adopted is that of a bed [*parterre*] of flowers, of infinite variety [...] We could have shown Art in its infancy, growth and last period, or separated schools, and then would have satisfied a few scholars.'[54] They took the line instead that the public didn't want a lesson in art history, but direct contact with the works of great artists. This view prevailed for the official hasty opening on 10 August, with 537 paintings, 124 marble and bronze sculptures, and a variety of 'other objects'.[55] David was busy orchestrating his set piece of Hercules (the French people) trampling the hydra of Federalism for the anniversary, but he eventually moved things in a different direction, with the creation of the Conservatoire instead of the Academy, and his approach to display. The Louvre is, however, an example of Roland deliberately outflanking the Convention's committee for monuments (which admittedly was not very helpful), and professional intervention, to try to push through his own detailed vision. He was helped both by a general consensus that the Museum would be a good thing, and the distraction of deputies by more controversial matters. What is not in doubt is Roland's passionate and lyrical defence of French cultural heritage (it would probably not be disavowed by ministers of culture today). He thought the arts contributed as much to a nation's glory as its armies:

> I seem to see the glory of our sciences and arts combining their illustriousness with those of our arms and consolidating the liberty which they should render beautiful. The sciences and the arts were in a degraded condition under despotism, but are

[51] Cf. Pommier (1992) *passim*, and (1991) pp. 110 ff. Modern scholars are divided about whether this could have been achieved successfully.

[52] Roland to the Commission, 25 December 1792, AN, F17 1059.

[53] AN, F13 502, 23 January 1793.

[54] Museum commission to Garat, 17 June 1793, AN, F17 1059.

[55] McLellan (1994), p. 95: it was closed down again.

the most fertile element and the most fitting foundation to all truly republican ideas. It is [only among] free peoples that they receive the purest and most universal homage.[56]

The Bibliothèque nationale was another example where he had a free hand, although not everyone agreed with his penny-pinching. One of his first acts on 11 August was to appoint as joint directors the journalist Jean-Louis Carra (1742–1793), already employed there, but also a deputy, and the intellectual Nicolas-Sebastien Roch, aka Chamfort (1741–1794). They were supposed to share the official residence in the rue de Richelieu and the 8000 *livres* salary (already reduced). Roland's letter to Chamfort, whom he had apparently not yet met, is strikingly informal:

> Accept this, my friend, and take up a situation which will reflect your tastes and which my wife and I envy you. Think about it, and come and dine with me [*venez un soir souper avec moi*], we'll talk about it some more. I'm the minister of money, you're the minister of intelligence.[57]

We know that Chamfort took up the offer to dine, since Mme Roland in her memoirs has an appreciative passage about him, reporting detailed conversations. In autumn 1793, Chamfort understandably tried to minimize these social contacts, when the whole staff of the library, bar one, was purged at Robespierre's request: Chamfort claimed that his links with Roland had been purely professional, and that he had hardly met any members of 'la Gironde'. (He did not long outlive them: fearing re-arrest, he died of infection from a failed suicide attempt in spring 1794.)[58]

Roland carried out his own purge at the library. His approach was reader-centred, but not so good for the staff. It was already an uncomfortable place to work; because of the fire risk, only natural light was allowed, and no heating. It had opened only certain days, from 10 a.m. to 2 p.m., for privileged readers. Roland sacked several employees (boasting to the Convention of his cost-cutting)—those who would not take the civic oath 'to be ready to die to defend liberty and equality', or who were under-occupied. It was to become a place of 'republican pride', operating on half the budget, opening more hours, but accessing twice the volume of books from religious and aristocratic libraries. Staff would work longer for less pay. Chamfort deployed 'almost maniacal integrity' in trying to get the system to work. Access to the public was to be increased, Roland specified, 'so that the public will benefit by its instruction, the nation in its economy'. Mme Roland comments on her husband's economies in her memoirs, in terms suggesting that even she thought them excessive. Here, Roland pushed through his austerity measures,

---

[56] Roland to Assembly, F 17 1002, quoted Pommier (1992), p.110. Roland's commission had bitter arguments with Alexandre Lenoir, who was saving sculptures in the Petits-Augustins, AN, F[17] 1059; cf. Oliver (2007); Courajod (1887/2009), Vol. I, while unsympathetic to Roland, calls him 'the most doctrinaire and perhaps the most honest of the Girondins', p. clxxi.

[57] Quoted Arnaud (1988), p. 260 from F. Albert-Buisson (1960).

[58] Mme Roland on Chamfort, *Mém.*, pp. 120–1: he evidently dined often, possibly after January 1793; AN, F[7] 4638; Arnaud (1988), p. 290, reference to interrogation 9 October 1793.

combined with an idealistic policy of universal education, in one area where the Convention did not interfere.[59]

Both the Louvre and the Bibliothèque later developed a complex history, but where Roland's early vision and personal intervention had some purchase. His tendency to act unilaterally, especially in this area, and to appropriate decision-making into the relevant division of the ministry, is on display in these striking examples, but in less-well-known areas, too. The Bureau des Arts et Métiers, a body in charge of grants for inventions, is discussed at length by Charles Gillispie, who has little time for Roland, (a 'know-it-all bureaucrat, not to say haughty scold') and who reckons he over-reached himself by hijacking the Bureau, before being reined in by the Convention on 4 January 1793.[60] Gillispie does allow, however, that Roland's intervention was useful in helping preserve the Paris botanical garden, the Jardin des Plantes—for which he and his wife had great affection. We know that they invited its director, Bernardin de Saint-Pierre, to dine at the ministry, and Roland also corresponded with head gardener André Thouin, the great friend of Bosc, about preserving specimens from royal palaces, to stock both national and provincial public gardens.[61]

*

In conclusion to this brief summary, although Roland's second ministry lasted only a few months, he was in a unique position, as the first Interior minister to be freed from the king's constitutional oversight. Under the *de facto* republic from August, and officially from September, he carried out his duties as he saw them, in ways the men who came before and after him, between 1789 and 1793, rarely did. He exploited his new position in a number of ways, driven largely by an administrator's exasperation at the difficulty of getting things done, and exerting an influence that is now hard to assess, in the wake of the tidal wave that swept away the Girondins in 1793. He apparently inspired devotion among his officials[62] and was extravagantly praised in some of the messages from around France. On many policy matters, too numerous to list here, he settled disputes, angled for funds, and dispatched instructions and encouragements (see Chapter 23 for the most controversial aspect of this).

In Paris, his rigid manner in public did not help him: even his friends no doubt regretted his tendency to self-righteousness and self-praise (not that he was alone in that). The term 'le vertueux Roland' became a bit of a joke among his contemporaries, but arguably they did not make the same mistake as historians in underestimating him. His enemies went to the other extreme indeed, in overestimating his role as a potential figurehead for an imagined conspiracy; the Jacobins were regularly calling him the most powerful man in France by January. Did they also overestimate his wife's role? This will be explored next.

[59] 'Mémoire sur la Bibliothèque nationale', *AP*, LIV, 2 December 1792, p. 43 ff.: 'It is consoling to me' he began 'to turn my attention to these noble and useful establishments which despotism set up without perhaps realizing that they were preparing its downfall [...] Liberty and light. Everything had to be done.' On staff cuts, see Arnaud (1988), pp. 263–4.

[60] Gillispie (2004), pp. 206–8. The relevant archive is full of applications for patents.

[61] Ibid., pp. 290 ff. The menagerie (still there) was proposed by Bernardin de Saint-Pierre. Cf. *Corr.*, II, p. 431, 23 August 1792.

[62] Gillispie's view that he treated 'underlings' with arrogance and disdain, p. 208, seems an over-harsh judgement. The jury must be out on it.

22

'This Astonishing Lady':
What Did the Minister's Wife Do All Day?

You tell me there are only a few patriotic women [...] it's the fault of the age and education, more than of [our] sex. The same sensibility that can waste itself on trivia [...] can become sublime for greater things.

Mme Roland to Bancal, 20 June 1791.[1]

If you offer his ministry back to Roland, be sure to offer it to his wife as well. Everyone knows he was not alone in his ministry as I was in mine. The nation needs ministers who can act without being led by their wife.

Danton to the Convention, 29 September 1792.[2]

Mme Roland was more fully involved in the affairs of the ministry and political life than she ever admits in her memoirs. But not until Roland's second term in office was her name spoken in public. Danton's outburst was the first time she was mentioned in the Convention. It is usually interpreted as a criticism, since he clearly intended to insult her husband. But he was aware of her grasp of public affairs. She wrote to Servan in December that she thought Danton and Fabre had guessed back in August 'that I sometimes wield the pen'.[3] How important, really, was 'Roland's wife' in revolutionary politics?

The very evening Danton made his jibe, 29 September, Jean-Marie Roland (stung to the quick) decided to remain in the ministry, rather than take his seat in the Convention. The Rolands' Genevan friend Gosse happened to be staying with them, and described how it happened:

It was nine at night before Monsieur Roland, who was unwell, had taken a decision about this. Suddenly the brave decision was taken, and after a private consultation between the spouses, Madame Roland, as if inspired, took the pen and set about composing a speech [*discours*] to the Convention of eight pages in close writing, in folio size. This speech [...] which had no mistakes in French or spelling, was brought to me by this astonishing lady at half-past three in the morning, to make a second copy, which I finished only at seven.[4]

---

[1] *Corr.*, II, pp. 301–2.   [2] *AP*, LII, p. 229.   [3] *Corr.*, II, p. 445, 25 December 1792.
[4] Perroud (1909), pp. 489–90. Gosse also commented that Roland 'is no longer an old man: few youngsters would have his degree of activity, fine judgement and vigour in maintaining his views when he is persuaded that it is in for the greater good', while his 'rare wife' combined the qualities of her sex with 'the energy and fine judgement of our own'. He had heard her 'combat her husband's views,

It is almost as if Mme Roland were sending a reply to Danton. (Certainly none of his assistants wrote *his* speeches for him! They were mostly improvised.) The defi-antly-worded document was technically a letter from the minister, read out in the Convention:

> Yesterday from the nation's rostrum, I was accused of lacking courage at a critical moment. [...] The citizen's duty is to remain at his post. I should remain at mine, since the great majority of the Convention has shown its wish in this regard: the desire of the representatives of the 83 *départements* is a new law, superior to that, as yet unclear, of one of them [i.e. Paris...] I am remaining at my post, *because* there are dangers. [...] I will sacrifice the calm due to my old age, and devote myself even until death.[5]

Champagneux's comment remains relevant, that on 'big occasions', Mme Roland held the pen. This was surely not the only time that she wrote some of her hus-band's messages to the deputies that autumn. But she was not necessarily putting words into his mouth: draft manuscripts in the archives contain examples of both their handwriting, one correcting the other and vice versa. Roland had far more calls on his time than a deputy to the Assembly. Whereas the deputy's job was to make or listen to speeches, ministers worked at their desks. Roland was his own man on policy issues, as I hope appeared in the previous chapter, but the couple thought alike on politics.

Mme Roland was well aware of her drafting talents. In modern French admin-istration, a *rédacteur*, document drafter, became an important civil service rank. Dumont said she had 'an energetic and fluent style, and urged her husband to write all the time. It was a ministry of writers.'[6] A page in her memoirs sets out her account of how they worked:

> I took *no part in administration*, but if there was *a circular, an instruction, an important public statement*, we would confer, with the mutual trust we were used to; and fully briefed on his ideas, augmented by my own [*pénétrée de ses idées, nourrie des miennes*], I picked up the pen, which I *had more time to wield* than he did. Since we had the same principles and were of one mind, we ended up agreeing a form of words, [I could not express anything he would not have agreed with] but I put it better. Without me, he would have been just as good an administrator, [...] but with me, he made *more of an impact* because I put into these writings the mixture of forcefulness and gentleness, authority and sentiments which perhaps are found only in a woman of feeling who also has a degree of common sense. [my italics][7]

When Mme Roland claimed not to take part in 'administration', she probably meant day-to-day matters, anything of a technical or economic nature. We know from her own account that she had a little office in the ministry: if not an ante-room to her husband's office, such as a modern secretary or receptionist might have, it was 'an austere cabinet'—not a 'boudoir' as Marat insisted on calling it.[8] Petitioners certainly believed her to have influence, and many requests came her way—'people

---

temper them and convince him' and 'hold her own against fifteen members of the Convention at din-ner and be widely applauded by them'; cf. Bernardin (1964), p. 69, and Chapter 20 above.

[5] *AP*, LII, 30 September 1792.   [6] Dumont (1832), p. 396.
[7] *Mém.* pp. 155, 304–5.   [8] Ibid.

tried to see me, because they thought it was like in the ancien régime, when you approached wives to ask their husbands for favours'. Applications for lodgings in the Louvre she 'simply passed on [to a clerk called Coqueau] and told people to apply to the minister or the relevant official, because I had nothing to do with this kind of request'.[9] Champagneux later contested the accusations that 'she was more of a minister than her husband'. This opinion, he wrote, was absolutely false:

> Not only did she take no part in administration of the ministry, but she would not have wanted to. A hundred times a day she was importuned by people asking for things [*sollicitations*] and when she did consent to take them forward, which was very rare, she annotated the memos in such a way as to alert the bureaux not to grant any undeserved favours [*contre toute espèce de complaisance*].[10]

While he may be right that it was not common, we know from fragments of evidence in the memoirs and elsewhere that she *did* sometimes put in a word. She unquestionably had a say in some appointments (Pache, Servan). Her finger-prints survive in other cases. She pleaded the cause of Sophie Grandchamp's friend, Grandpré, as prison inspector, hardly suspecting he would later help her.[11] Helen Maria Williams (c.1762–1837), the English enthusiast for the Revolution, intro-duced Francisco de Miranda to Mme Roland during Servan's ministry: he received his unexpected commission as a general as a result.[12] Mme Roland also—by her own admission and disastrously in the event—encouraged Roland to promote Pache further, when Servan resigned from the War office in autumn 1792. She and Roland cooperated on it: '*We* wrote to [Pache] about his appointment [...] he came to see *us*, *we* spoke to him with confidence that our views coincided.' Her friends thereafter 'accused *me* of insouciance', when Pache's volte-face caused prob-lems.[13] In retrospect, she commented on the difficulty of finding competent min-istry staff, indicating her own serious interest in doing so. By January, she said, Roland had appointed an efficient set of colleagues: 'another three months, and the mechanism would have been perfect'.[14] Garat admitted as much to Champagneux, on taking over.

These scattered mentions, when the dots are joined up, point to her role as a virtually irreplaceable personal assistant, who could anticipate or modify her hus-band's wishes, sift applicants, draft documents, handle some accounts (see below) or make useful personnel suggestions, sitting up late at night with him. But the point bears repetition that Roland was sufficiently strong-minded not to have been pushed by her into anything against his will, and that he put total trust in both her efficiency and her loyalty—Champagneux had his hands full, and Lanthenas was not only incompetent, but increasingly out of sympathy.

---

[9] To Jany-Mentelle, 27 October 1793, *Corr.*, II, pp. 536–7.
[10] Champagneux (1800), p. xxxvj.
[11] On Grandpré, *Corr.*, II, p. 485, to Buzot, 22 June 1793.
[12] Woodward (1930), p. 62. Miranda (1750–1816) served with Dumouriez at Valmy, survived the Revolutionary Tribunal, and ended his career in South America.
[13] *Mém.*, pp. 106–7.
[14] Roland's officials, *Corr.*, II, p. 537.

Few contemporary references describe this officially subordinate, but immeasurable 'helpmeet' role: Lasource gallantly but unhelpfully replied to Danton: 'What does it matter if Roland has an intelligent wife who gives him advice? What matters to the *patrie* is that the minister should have governed the Republic well: this snide comment [*ce petit moyen*] is unworthy of Danton.'[15] In the absence of detailed research, it is not obvious that any other political wives played such a role. (Mme Clavière, Mme Pétion? Certainly not Mme Brissot.) Was Mme Roland unique in this respect? She was far from the only intelligent and committed woman married to a revolutionary. However, there was surely no other woman so involved with the minutiae of government. She herself said: 'The only odd thing is its rarity: why shouldn't a wife act as secretary to her husband, without somehow detracting from his merit?'[16]

What came to dominate journalistic attacks on her, however, repeated by posterity, were two particular accusations: that she 'ran the *bureau d'esprit public*' (discussed in the next chapter); and that in the more familiar, 'womanly' role as hostess, she 'plotted' with guests who came to dinner at the ministry.

DINNER AT THE HÔTEL DE L'INTÉRIEUR

Marat was probably the first journalist to start referring to Mme Roland as presiding at the dinner table. He did not, of course, use the term 'salon' or even 'circle', but his target was the informal, after-hours kind of contact that went with dining:

> *La femme* Roland [a dismissive term] uses a very simple method of recruiting. Does a deputy need to see her husband about matters concerning his *département*? Roland says he is terribly busy, and invites him to come round after the Assembly, at dinner time. 'Come and eat soup with me, citizen deputy, [*mangez donc la soupe avec moi*] and we'll have a word about your affair.' *La femme* Roland, who spends her time cajoling her guests one after another, [...] will then pay special attention to the newcomer, who will soon become a supporter of her clique.[17]

It is quite a mild comment (by Marat's standards). Camille Desmoulins, in his often-quoted *Histoire des Brissotins* (May 1793), wrote later with particular vitriol of the Girondins sitting round Mme Roland's table, implying sexual favours:

> One should not believe that the only people at Roland's table were greedy deputies, and that the Circe of the house could do nothing but change Barbaroux's companions into pigs; she has recourse to other enchantments, which at her age, and with so little beauty, suggest she is an even greater magician.[18]

Historians too have been inclined to see entertaining guests as the key focus of Mme Roland's participation in politics, even if they admired her. Lamartine is

---

[15] *AP*, LII, p. 230. [16] *Mém.*, p. 305.
[17] Quoted Kermina (1976), without reference or date.
[18] Quoted here from *Mém.*, p. 404, and much reproduced.

admittedly an extreme case. He *appears* to have invented a romantic scene, set on 22 September 1792—a dinner 'at Mme Roland's', to celebrate the republic, with the entire Girondin general staff present. He portrays Vergniaud (actually a rare visitor) putting rose petals in the wine, at Mme Roland's request, while whispering to Barbaroux that since the republic's cradle is soaked in September's blood, they may be drinking to their own death. Guadet's nephew later commented that this *imagined* 'moment of ecstasy by a great poet' soon started to be taken seriously and indeed it was.[19]

Such myth-making, whether by admirers or enemies, ignores both the role of Jean-Marie Roland as host, and the wider context of dining and entertaining in revolutionary Paris. While Marie-Jeanne Roland did the conventional honours at the table, and often issued the invitations, the visitors were not coming to dine with her. She could hold her own in any company, but they were coming to dine with her husband, the minister. Applying the same rules as Mme Pétion, she claims, she was the only woman present, since to invite other women would mean 'having a social circle'. Most references write her husband entirely out of entertaining, whereas we know, and not only from Marat (cf. Roland's letter to Chamfort), that Roland himself regularly offered invitations to come to dinner, with Lanthenas free to propose names.

The Girondins weren't the only guests at his table of course. In her memoirs, Mme Roland confirmed that her husband received guests on Mondays and Fridays in the autumn: one evening for ministers and deputies; another for heads of bureaux or 'others occupied with public affairs', such as journalists (Dulaure), writers and scientists (Bernardin de Saint-Pierre, Chamfort). The couple also received English visitors: Tom Paine, who spoke little French, and David Williams, of whom Mme Roland had a good opinion. A conversation she reports with him, about the chaotic nature of Convention debates, probably took place over dinner. Helen Maria Williams (no relation) visited Mme Roland at the ministry, though perhaps not at dinner time (the no-women rule?) Most of these foreigners were admittedly closer to the Gironde than to the Montagne.[20]

To imagine that such dinners were unique would be to ignore Parisian social life in the fraught context of 1792. Olivier Blanc suggests that 'circles were never as present and active as at this time', although his evidence covers a longer period.[21] Who you dined with was a marker of your politics. Networking, or as contemporaries called it 'conciliabules' (conferences) by 'factions', went on, day in day out— in the Convention; in the Commune and its committees; in the clubs; in printed news sheets; and in informal gatherings, of which less record remains—such as 'dinners'. There were dinners all over town. Everyone had to eat. Many of the

---

[19] Lamartine referred to by Guadet (1861), vol 2, p. 5, quoted Hanson (2003), p. 232. Cf. Lamartine (1851), vol. XL, pp. 239–40.

[20] *Mém.*, pp. 168–9 on Paine and David Williams; D. Williams (1980). Both entertained guests themselves in the winter of 1792–1793. Mary Wollstonecraft moved in the same circles, but never met Mme Roland. Alger (1889) p. 70: Miss Williams's Sunday-evening receptions in the rue du Bac were attended by Vergniaud and Barère. Mme Roland agreed to promote Bancal's courtship of Miss Williams, *Corr.*, II, pp. 466–9, letters unfortunately undated.

[21] Blanc (2006).

deputies were far from home, without wives or relations, so they patronized coffee-houses, restaurants—or the homes of Paris-based colleagues. Gouverneur Morris regularly dined at the affluent houses of people notable for their lack of sympathy with the Revolution.[22] All ministers, as well as prominent officials or generals, routinely entertained guests. Dumont recalled the 'entertaining and witty atmosphere'—typically French, he said—at several ministers' dinners in the spring (Grave, Clavière, Roland). One 'grand dîner de la Gironde' hosted by his fellow Genevan, Clavière (rich, as well as a minister), was attended by most of the pre-10 August diplomatic committee. In retrospect, Dumont remarked that he had not paid as much attention to Mme Roland as he should have, while commenting slightingly of Mme Clavière that she 'would have liked to play the role of a Mme Roland, but she had only vanity, rather than talent and strength'—which at least tells us that Clavière's wife regularly presided at the table, as would be normal.[23] Edmond-Charles Genet, former *chargé d'affaires* in Russia, dined all over Paris during December 1792, including with the Rolands. At the Foreign Affairs ministry, when Lebrun was in office, Genet's fellow guests included Fauchet, Tom Paine, and 'most of the leaders of the Gironde'.[24] Genet also refers to an evening hosted by Dumouriez in December, where the guests included Brissot, Guadet, Vergniaud, Louvet, Danton, General Miranda, and 'several actresses'. 'As I was not used to such orgies,' he claimed, 'I made an excuse and left this unsavoury company' as soon as possible.[25]

Even ministers acceptable to the Montagne entertained (and sometimes even invited Girondins). In February 1793, a *citoyenne* from the Société fraternelle complained to the Jacobins that Roland's successor, Garat, had 'thirty people to dine last Wednesday'—including Brissot, Louvet, Barbaroux, and Beurnonville (War minister). 'Patriots don't have admission to the ministry, but Brissot can go in any time he likes.'[26] On Pache as minister, we have only Mme Roland's extremely hostile testimony, but interestingly it remarks on entertaining too: 'He did not accept the invitations of his colleague [Roland], claiming that he lived a very retired life, because of his workload, but I learnt that he *received at his table* Fabre, Chabot, and other Montagnards [...] and gave jobs to their friends.'[27]

It is true that contemporaries tended to view ministry dinners as particularly extravagant. After all, ministers had entertained grandly during the monarchy. 'A good dinner and as many as the table could hold', reported Morris after dining at the ministry of Marine in December 1791.[28] A particular rumour about entertainment in the Hôtel de l'Intérieur was its reputed 'luxurious' nature, as Desmoulins's reference to pigs indicates. The kind of meal served was important in the

---

[22] Morris's diary entries for autumn 1792 *passim*, usually giving marks for the quality of the dinner.

[23] Dumont (1832), pp. 448, 406.

[24] Genet in Conway (1900), Appendix, pp. 439–40.

[25] Ibid.

[26] *Jacobins*, V, pp. 23–4, 10 February 1793.

[27] *Mém.*, p. 106, my italics.

[28] Morris (1939), II, p. 325, the minister of the Marine at that date was no longer the well-named Claret de Fleurieu, but Molleville.

symbolic economy of 1792—the evocation of luxury was enough to tar an opponent with the brush of 'aristocratic' habits. As Rebecca Spang remarks, 'site of frugal repast or decadent feast, the table became a material and symbolic battleground'. Again, the presence of women, or the presiding role of a hostess, seemed to be code for aristocratic decadence.[29]

The most hostile journalism in this vein, specifically referring to the former kings' mistresses, came from the pen of Hébert:

> The tender other half of the virtuous Roland now has France on leading strings, like the Pompadours and Du Barrys of the past. Brissot is the grand *écuyer* of this new queen, Louvet her chamberlain, Buzot her chancellor, Fauchet her almoner, Barbaroux her captain of the guard, Vergniaud the master of ceremonies, Guadet the cup bearer, Lanthenas the herald; [this is] the new court which dictates rain or fair weather in the Convention and the *départements*. It is held every night, at the twilight hour. Like the ci-devant queen, Mme Coco, reclining on a sofa, surrounded by her favourite wits, discourses unendingly on war, politics, subsistence, etc.[30]

Hébert later claimed, at the Girondins' trial, to have seen when visiting the ministry with a petition, 'the entire deputation from the Gironde around a *delicately served table*, where these gentlemen were no doubt plotting some machinations' [my italics].[31]

Mme Roland had heard the charges of epicureanism, and was puritanically keen to deny them: her table was sober, guests sat down at five, there was a 'little chat over coffee' afterwards and people then went about their business; the room was empty by nine:

> Good taste and cleanliness reigned at my table, without any profusion, and there were no luxurious decorations; people were comfortable, without sitting long at table, because I provided only one course and would not let anyone else have the task of doing the honours. The normal number of guests was fifteen, rarely eighteen, and once twenty. Such were the meals that popular orators described at the Jacobins as 'sumptuous feasts' where I was a 'new Circe'.[32]

Unfortunately, no menu survives, but there is no reason to suppose that the Rolands' simple personal tastes changed much, even if they now could afford to sit down with fifteen instead of two or three guests. One piquant detail is that meat to the Roland household was provided by the butcher Legendre, Danton's associate at the Cordeliers, later the Rolands' fierce enemy. Good meat then, but not Lucullan fantasy.[33] Genet once contrasted his dinner chez Dumouriez with a visit to the Rolands, for 'what the French call "un petit souper",' which does not suggest luxury, though it was a political evening.[34]

---

[29] Spang (2000), p. 91; see also Jones and Spang (1999).

[30] Quoted Jaurès (1983), vol. 3, p. 597: no 202, *Père Duchêne*.

[31] If literal (unlikely) eight deputies: cf. *Actes*, p. 270. Hébert pressed harder than anyone for the Girondins to be brought to trial, because of his brief arrest in May.

[32] *Mém.*, p. 168.

[33] Legendre, Champagneux (1800), p. lxxxvij.

[34] Genet in Conway (1900), p. 439.

But was a political evening the same as a conspiracy? At Mme Roland's interrogation (11 brumaire 1793):

> The accused was asked whether [...] she had not habitually received at her home: Vergniaud, Guadet, Gensonné, Duprat, Duperret, Carra, Fauchet, Sillery, Brissot, Fonfrède, Ducos, Barbaroux, Birotteau, Buzot, Salle, Louvet, Lehardy, Mainville, Dufriche-Valazé, and others known under the denomination of Brissotins, Girondins etc. and whether in the different *conferences* which took place, the departmental force [was] not discussed.[35]

This list names thirteen of the twenty-two Girondins executed on 31 October, plus some in hiding. Replying, Mme Roland naturally sought to downplay any suggestion of conspiracy (while making it clear that the guests were her husband's). 'She had never had a circle or conferences' at her home; her husband received at his table once a week ministers, longstanding acquaintances, and persons who knew he would be 'at home that day'. She agreed that Brissot, Pétion, and Buzot (friends from 1791) were among these, as were Barbaroux, Louvet, Guadet, and Gensonné, from 1792. They did not hold 'conferences', but 'conversations in public' about public affairs.[36] She conceded what could not be denied, viz., that seven of the most prominent Brissotins/Girondins were regular visitors.[37]

The Rolands' dinners (twice a week, not once) undoubtedly afforded the occasion for the like-minded to meet—and the unlike-minded, such as Jean-Baptiste (Anacharsis) Cloots, to feel out of place. Still the latter had at least been asked and returned several times—invitations appear to have been quite widely and casually offered, at least at first.[38] Other coteries ate and drank elsewhere, sometimes with women present, sometimes not. The Girondins themselves had other meeting places where they could have 'concocted conspiracies', or to put it more neutrally, agreed on policy. Many of them rarely or never visited the Interior ministry. Sydenham refers in particular to gatherings at the lodgings of the Girondin deputy, Charles-Eléonore de Friche de Valazé.[39] Valazé testified openly at his trial that thirty or forty people regularly met at his lodgings between nine and twelve at night, 'because the sessions of the Convention ended late, so we could see each other only at night'.[40] He specifically told his constituents in January 1793, that they met to discuss the *appel au peuple*. Virtually all the leading Girondins were cited by name during his interrogation, but neither Roland nor Mme Roland was mentioned.

---

[35] *Actes*, p. 364, my italics; Cf. Sydenham (1961), pp. 86 ff., Mme Roland was accused of 'being its inspiration', in which there is some truth.

[36] Conspicuously absent is Vergniaud: at his trial he said he dined with Roland 'only five or six times.' *Actes*, pp. 273–4.

[37] Sydenham(1961) appendix, identifies 17 people as guests of 'Mme Roland' (note that he does not say 'of Jean-Marie Roland'); none of their names are a surprise. Valazé 'admitted' dining twice at the Rolands' during January 1793 (ibid. pp. 88–9).

[38] Duhem testified at the Girondins' trial: 'Mme Roland wrote to me and asked me to bring as many patriots as possible.' Anacharsis Cloots (J. B. du Val de Grâce, baron Cloots, 1755–1794), in his pamphlet *Ni Marat ni Roland*, stated he dined four times at the ministry in September and heard 'federalist' discussions. Cf. *Mem.*, pp. 85–6, and Roland *et al.*, counter-pamphlet, *Réponse au prussien Klootz*.

[39] Sydenham (1961), pp. 91–7.   [40] *Actes*, p. 310.

On the other side, so to speak, Danton's friend Fabre d'Eglantine was a regular diner-out at other people's expense. A key witness against the Girondins, he reported dining before 10 August with Danton at Pétion's, where 'a great number of the accused also were'. He also said 'after the Convention, one day' (so post-20 September) 'seven of *us patriots* met for dinner [...] when conversation turned to the characters of members of the [Girondin] faction and their goings-on'.[41] From Fabre's perhaps naïve, and certainly self-serving testimony, it is clear that politically motivated groups dined together—as why would they not? Fabre's dinner above was probably Cordelier based and in a restaurant. Even the *sans-culotte* groups who organized the uprisings of 31 May and 2 June 1793 were in the habit of meeting together to dine—in the case of Gusman, Desfieux, Proli, and others, at the Café Corrazza in the Palais-Royal.[42]

How then to judge the Rolands' dinners in this context of ubiquitous dining-out with political allies? Their significance was no doubt exaggerated, then and since. Mona Ozouf comments that Girondin 'salons' were 'not what they seemed in the Jacobin imagination, dark cabinets in which Gironde policy was concocted', but she does refer to 'luxurious places', with 'amiable women', with favourites and enemies, which looks like a covert reference to Mme Roland.[43] Less luridly, it could be argued that the reason the Rolands' entertaining is often singled out is firstly that, plain or fancy, it was paid for from public funds; and secondly that it combined an increasingly limited guest list with *power-dining*. The guests were not there just to enjoy Mme Roland's wit, or to conspire with people they met every day anyway. They were coming to eat with a minister, who had a very extensive portfolio. There was probably more useful networking to be done in the ministry of the Interior than anywhere else.

Their guest list can be seen as a set of concentric circles, varying over time, during the relatively short periods when the Rolands entertained (April–June and September–mid-January)—an inner circle of close friends, old or new; a mixture of deputies, at first from a fairly wide range of positions, but gradually narrowing down to consist chiefly of those whose politics agreed with Roland's; and an outer circle of occasional or one-off visitors, celebrities, foreigners, and intellectuals, attracted by their host's prominence, and invited for their conversation. To judge from references to favours asked or granted, insignificant individually, but adding up to quite a network of influence, dinners could be a useful time to put in a word for a friend.

Inevitably, this constellation attracted gossip and criticism, which the couple seems to have defiantly ignored. Perhaps the most telling testimony comes from their loyal friend Champagneux—it was not only the Rolands' enemies who commented unfavourably on their entertaining:

Roland [my italics] has been criticized for the meals that he hosted during his two ministries. I do think that *he* would have done better, in his own interests, not to do

[41] *Actes*, p. 311.   [42] Harder (2008), p. 295, and cf. Slavin (1986), p. 87.
[43] *DCRF*, 'Girondins' p. 376.

this. Since they [obviously] couldn't receive at their table all the people who thought they had a right to be there, Roland and his wife more willingly invited the people they considered their friends, or whose principles were closest to their own. From this arose dissatisfaction and jealousy, which only made more sensitive the demarcation line beginning to be established between the parties. If sometimes men of different views found themselves at the same meal, those who were already starting to be in opposition to those known as the Girondins noticed, or thought they had detected, a preference for the latter and withdrew in dudgeon (*mécontents*). If, during the meal, a political discussion started, tempers ran high and hotheads started calling others counter-revolutionaries.

When Champagneux remonstrated that 'I really wasn't in favour of their dinners', the Rolands disagreed, significantly arguing that it was necessary to have a meeting place for 'right-thinking people (*les bons esprits*) to be able to galvanize themselves (*s'electriser*) and gather strength against 'the ill-intentioned (*les méchants*)'. They were 'convinced that a Maratiste party was taking shape in the Convention[...] and that it would be better to wage war against it openly, if the alternative was to wait for it to bring about their death'. Champagneux, holding to his opinion, concluded that ministers should not have an entertainment allowance.[44]

THE MINISTER'S WIFE AS MEDIATOR?

The personal was political, all right. However, the boundaries were not necessarily clear and unchangeable. What about people who are sometimes regarded as in a midway position? The Rolands—Mme Roland in particular—are often taken to task for their antipathy to Danton. This is easy to document, because her hostility appears in such unvarnished form in her memoirs, and it was certainly unfortunate. Much contemporary evidence about Danton himself, his friends and foes, has vanished, so her views have always had a high profile. Danton dined often at the Rolands' in August, as we saw. But thereafter he had publicly insulted Roland, both by calling him a coward, and by claiming he was ruled by his wife. Such personal attacks rankled.

Perhaps equally relevant was the Rolands' (apparently sincere) conviction that Danton was behind the September massacres, as many of the Girondins came to think too. But the issue on which Danton was attacked in the Convention was his use of public money. On this count, he was admittedly vulnerable, and never provided a satisfactory answer. Later historians held a vociferous debate over his 'corruption'.[45] The issue was raised first not by Roland, but by the centrist deputy Cambon, who criticized all the ministers over expenses, prompting Roland to present a set of self-righteous and scrupulous figures: one of the grounds for his being described as 'virtuous'. Corruption and *laissez-aller* were two things Roland crusaded against, and Danton, whatever his other qualities, seemed to represent

[44] Champagneux (1800), pp. xxxiij–xxxiv.
[45] Hampson: 'early historians took [Danton's venality] for granted, the positivists thought they had refuted it, and Mathiez believed he had proved it beyond any doubt' (1978/1988), p. 78.

both. In her memoirs, Mme Roland reserves her sharpest barbs for him, conclud-
ing that in 1793, 'he went to Belgium to increase his wealth; he dares boast of a
fortune of 1,400,000 livres, and displays his luxury while preaching *sans-culottisme*
and sleeping on heaps of corpses, his victims'.[46]

Insofar as both the Rolands self-righteously contributed to or condoned attacks
on Danton's financial or ministerial record, they helped drive a wedge between him
and the Gironde. Their hostility, comprehensible perhaps, wasn't helpful. It cannot, however, be described as decisive, or the *sole* cause of that particular divide,
which developed far more drastically, thanks to intransigeance or evasiveness by all
those concerned, in the early months of 1793, when the Rolands were outside
public affairs. Danton did sometimes urge deputies on both sides to try to resolve
their differences, but his own complex manoeuvres meant that he did not do so
consistently, and he himself went on saying some fairly unforgivable things about
Roland.[47]

But it so happens that we have evidence from another quarter of an approach to
Madame Roland, possibly a bid for mediation, by Charles-Gilbert Romme (1750–
1795). Not firmly aligned at first, but usually voting with the Montagne, Romme
was a deputy from the Puy-de-Dôme and knew Bancal. He had been friendly with
Bosc since the early days of the Revolution, and sat on the education committee
with Lanthenas, so he was acceptable to the Roland's 'inner circle'. One of Mme
Roland's letters to Lanthenas (alas undated, but convincingly placed by Perroud in
October or November 1792) runs as follows:

> To wait for a fortnight with the wish to see a person when one thinks it might be
> interesting to talk to [her?] in order to save public affairs [*sauver la chose publique* = code
> for 'do the right thing'] is certainly to display a very great tranquillity! Monsieur
> Rome [*sic*] wants to see me, in the presence of my friends, [but] none of the gentlemen
> of the Gironde or Brissot must be there; perhaps he would like to indicate which of
> the other friends. It will be tomorrow at 10 or 11 in the morning; or tonight at 6 if he
> wishes. It would be right now, if I were not afraid that Monsieur Rome would not
> wish to meet the people I might be seeing this morning. Find out the moment he has
> chosen, and the witnesses he wants and tell him that he would have found me as will-
> ing [*empressée*] 15 days ago as today.
>
> *Mille bonjours.*[48]

This letter has an ironic tone, but shows willingness to talk to Romme, without
either Brissot or (presumably) the three key Girondins. The letter is tantalizing, but
telling—the most convincing reading of it is that Mme Roland was seen by a leading deputy of the left as a woman of influence and a valid go-between, perhaps to
effect some reconciliation—or to detach her husband from Brissot. Alas, no more is
known. If the meeting with Romme took place, it brought no healing of the rift.

---

[46] *Mém.*, p. 145.
[47] *Mém.*, pp. 139–45 on Danton: Mme Roland was (wrongly, probably) persuaded that he was
behind her imprisonment: 'I feel his hand riveting the irons which are chaining me here, just as I
recognized that he had inspired the first attacks on me by Marat.'
[48] *Corr.*, II, pp. 450–1, October 1792 (?). Charles-Gilbert Romme (1750–1796), remained a
Jacobin after Thermidor, which led to his death.

PRIDE BEFORE THE FALL

Balancing her behind-the-scenes presence, Mme Roland had her quarter-hour of publicity on 7 December 1792, at the Convention. The circumstances remain obscure. Was it a put-up job, engineered by Chabot, as some claimed, or simply the fortuitous initiative of an adventurer? Briefly, one Achille Viard claimed to have discovered in London a conspiracy to 'restore the king's authority', orchestrated by Narbonne and Talleyrand: they 'were counting on Fauchet and Roland', for whom he brought some 'packets'. He further stated that he had 'received from Mme Roland an *invitation* to meet her between ten and dinner-time'.

Roland, being summoned, said he had only ever had contact with Talleyrand before the bishop left for England in August—he and the rest of the PEC had refused to give him any commission (applause). He firmly denied any communication with London, said he had never seen Viard in his life, and requested that his wife be allowed to reply to her implication in the affair. Mme Roland came to the bar of the Convention—presumably the first time many deputies or the public had seen her. Her testimony, as recorded, was straightforward. She had not summoned Viard, that much was clear. *He* had written to her, saying he had something to communicate to her husband, and asked for her to fix an interview. 'I replied by an unsigned note that if it was a public matter, I kept to my role as a woman: he was doubtless under a widely-shared misapprehension' that she would have anything to do with it. However, if it was a personal request, she could see him at ten next day. When he arrived, he had started to tell her about some conspiracy in London. 'I said I was surprised he was telling me all this instead of my husband; he said the minister was too busy to see him at once. [...] I replied that citizen Roland was far too much in charge of his timetable for me to interfere.' She concluded, 'although I am not skilled in these matters, I thought Monsieur was there to sound out what we thought [*ce qu'on pensait*] rather than anything else'. After her extremely anodine, but confidently-given statement, she was accorded the honours of the session (a fairly regular happening). Even a Jacobin later reported that Mme Roland had spoken with 'grace and intelligence'.[49] She walked out 'to the applause of the majority of the Assembly', though not, apparently, of the public gallery. Marat was heard to comment, 'Listen to the silence of the public—they are wiser than us.'[50] Whether Viard was a confused troublemaker or a more sinister agent provocateur, the incident finally died the death. Conspiracy theories were ten a penny that month.

CONCLUSION

Mme Roland is a difficult woman to pigeonhole in the 'women in the French Revolution' debates. It is possible to find entirely contradictory statements, in her writings, about the proper role for women in times of political upheaval. During

---

[49] Dubois-Crancé, *Jacobins*, IV, pp. 552–3.
[50] *AP*, LIV, pp. 413–19.

her youth, she chafed at not being a man, and felt, in a quite modern way, that women were too circumscribed by convention to enjoy any real freedom. At the same time, she often indicated that it was women's role to refine and civilize men, and that they should observe society's conventions if they were not to become ridiculous. However, the Revolution pushed her some way towards different conclusions. She did not criticize women for taking part in demonstrations and celebrations. Her article on the Fête de la Fédération in Lyon had praised warmly the *citoyennes* who paraded. She also wrote approvingly of the street demonstrations from the faubourg St Antoine in 1791, which included women.[51] There could be room in women's lives for politics, and indeed she was equally impatient with women who thought about nothing but their appearance, or women who made household duties their entire existence.[52] Yet that same spring, she wrote:

> I don't believe that our social habits [*moeurs*] yet allow women to show themselves; they should inspire the good, and nourish and kindle all the sentiments useful to the *patrie*, but should not appear to contribute to political matters. They will not be able to act *openly* until all the French have deserved the name of free men; until then, our frivolity and poor morals would cast ridicule on anything they [women] might try to do, and thus destroy the advantage which might otherwise have resulted from it.[53]

Soon after that, as noted earlier, during the post-Varennes crisis she actually joined one of the women's clubs, though there is no record of her attending meetings or speaking. She met some 'ardently civic women' and 'respectable' members of the Société fraternelle on her single visit to Mme Robert's evening 'circle', probably in December 1791, although she did not find the company very congenial.[54]

She indicates so often that 'being a woman', she had to struggle not to intervene in political discussions at her house, that it must contain some truth (confirmed by Dumont). However, she obviously held many private conversations, and tête-à-têtes, as well as presiding at the dinner table, and shared strong opinions with her husband. She was a veteran of *epistolary* discussions with her friends and contemporaries about revolutionary politics. Of the *sans-culotte* women, who were particularly fond of Robespierre, or who celebrated Marat, she was dismissive, seeing them as easily manoeuvred. (It is true that once women of the people started to show signs of dissidence from mainstream Jacobinism, in late summer 1793, there was a crackdown.) We certainly do not find her making claims for women's public role, like Olympe de Gouges. During her imprisonment and trial, she repeatedly used the 'I'm only a wife' defence, visible in the Viard case.

But at bottom she—like her husband—saw herself as a fully committed revolutionary, serving the Revolution as best she could—by working as an unpaid functionary and speech-writer. Had she been Roland's brother, say, this might have caused less comment. But since it was so unprecedented for a woman, contemporaries viewed her in old-fashioned 'power-behind-the minister terms, as Danton's remark showed, and as hostile journalism repeated *ad nauseam*. To those

---

[51] Champagneux (1800), pp. xxiii–xxv; cf. *Corr.*, II, p. 90.   [52] *Mém.*, p. 303.
[53] To Bancal, 5 April 1791, *Corr.*, II, p. 258.   [54] *Mém.*, p. 117.

who wanted to attack her husband, she offered an easy target.[55] When her Girondin friends remarked on how 'charming' she was, that only encouraged the perception—not of course inaccurate, but not the whole story—that her role was that of hostess to a faction. And her no-woman rule, whatever its reason, made her, inevitably, a queen bee.

The Jacobin view of women's role, as clarified in the course of 1793, was that they should be *visible non-participants*: always there to back up their menfolk when required, but not to raise discordant voices, or have any say in decisions. Mme Roland was the exact opposite—an *invisible participant*. She was playing a role that she thought of as legitimate enough, as a woman patriot. By a paradox, she was both highly visible in theory and invisible in practice. Her political conversations were virtually all held in private, since there was no space in public life for her to appear. That brief speech to the Convention underlined how unusual it was for a woman's voice to be heard from the bar. 'In private, I was attacked for my determination to remain concentrating on my duty, in public I was slandered out of envy, as if I was running everything.'[56] In the light of Mme Roland's fate, it seems she was one of very few women to be challenged for her political role: admittedly there is little research on the families or mistresses of other ministers during the Revolution with which to compare her.

[55] Outram (1987) describes this as Catch-22. Cf. *Mém.*, p. 305.   [56] *Mém.* p. 124.

23

1792–1793: Fact or Fantasy?

The *Bureau d'Esprit Public* and the Minister for the Gironde

[*L'esprit public*] is a most profound and religious sentiment which places the interest of our common mother [the nation] above our particular interests and inspires in us a fraternal affection for our fellow citizens.

Jean-Marie Roland, January 1793.

The so-called *bureau d'esprit public* (= 'office for public opinion') was probably the single element that caused most hostility to the Rolands. At her trial, Marie-Jeanne Roland was accused of running this bureau at the ministry.[1] After Jean-Marie Roland's death, the epitaph proposed by the Montagnard commissioner who identified the corpse was that he had 'poisoned public spirit'.[2]

Much smoke surrounds the charge that the minister of the Interior manipulated opinion, by subsidizing and/or dispatching to the provinces ideologically-selected journals, pamphlets, and circulars. Inseparable from the Gironde–Montagne split, the accusation was that the ministry was using 'enormous sums' of public money— a much-repeated expression—to favour the Gironde. How big was the fire?[3] For all the contentious issues between Roland, on one hand, and the Paris Commune and Montagnard deputies, on the other, the first public mention of a *bureau d'esprit public* appears to date only from December 1792, during the tense early days of the king's trial. A Jacobin, Chales, claimed on 12 December that a bureau had 'been established in the ministry', run by 'a writer with anti-civic principles' (Lanthenas?). Mme Roland's name was not mentioned.[4]

The term *esprit public* is not easy to define. Charles Walton quotes significantly from Jean-Marie Roland's statement in January 1793:

Public spirit is not what people often confuse unthinkingly with public opinion, whose flux and partial applications can take on an indefinite variety of forms. What I call public spirit is a natural tendency, imperious towards all that can contribute to

[1] *Actes*, p. 367.   [2] Champagneux (1800), p. lxxxvii.
[3] 'Sommes immenses', Marat, 2 November 1792; Robespierre, 6 January 1793: 'immense pecuniary resources', *AP*, LIV, p. 248; cf. Amar, *Acte d'accusation*; Kermina (1976), pp. 209 ff.; Patrick (1972) pp. 172–3.
[4] *Jacobins*, IV, p. 576, except to claim that she would preside at a 'new women's club in the Tuileries' (!)

the happiness of the country; it is a most profound and religious sentiment which places the interest of our common mother [the nation] above our particular interests and inspires in us a fraternal affection for fellow citizens; it prescribes as the most important duty to love one's country, to respect and obey its laws, and to regard as scandalous and punishable all who violate them, undermine them or even censure them; to honour as fathers the magistrates responsible for communicating the laws and executing them; and to recognize as unworthy of belonging to the social body those who isolate themselves, seeking only advantage without contributing to its harmony.[5]

In other words, Roland saw *esprit public* as a particular set of beliefs, including love of the common good and obedience to the laws (provided those laws had been made in the 'right spirit', of course).

Ministers all potentially had access to networks of informers and were authorized to use public funds to disseminate information. Patricia Howe suggests that the foreign minister Lebrun had 'greater authority' than his colleagues, because of his network of ambassadors, officials, and secret agents, reporting on opinion from streets, coffee-houses, and clubs.[6] The controversy over the commissioners sent out in August–September 1792 was noted earlier. Roland, too, had informers reporting to him (see Chapter 24).[7] Since he was obliged to dispatch information about Assembly decisions, circulars, and replies to requests from the provinces, the ministry had an official section for handling communications.

The key question was whether he used public funds for purposes going beyond his mandate—subsidizing selected newspapers, paying for printing or postal charges of partisan brochures or speeches, or sending out prejudiced agents. What might be 'legitimate' if the revolutionaries in Paris thought with one mind, could become 'factional' once serious splits had developed. All publications had their own sphere of influence, of course, whatever their funding. The Jacobin Club had an energetic correspondence committee, handling communications to and from Paris. As Jeremy Popkin has noted, 'cut-throat competition was the rule' in the 'viciously competitive marketplace' of the revolutionary press. The ministry's official channels of distribution could be seen as offering an advantage in provincial outreach.[8]

First-hand research on the use of Roland's funds for propaganda was done by Claude Perroud a century ago. Additional archive files have since been explored, notably by Dorigny and Walton.[9] Dorigny's broadly positive interpretation sees Roland's attitude to propaganda as part of the publishing project of the Cercle social, with which he was already associated. (It might also be seen as related to the friends' community scheme for spreading the 'right ideas' in the countryside.) The Cercle believed that the Revolution would never be anchored in hearts and minds

---

[5] Walton (2009) p. 94, his translation; see ibid., p. 204; he picks out 'even censure [= criticize] them' as intolerance on Roland's part. Cf. Cowans (2001), chapter 4.

[6] Howe (2008), p. 94, based on Aulard, *Révolution française*, 12, 1887, pp. 1117–28.

[7] *Mém.*, p. 93; BNF MSS, naf 22423; Champagneux (1800), p. xxix; Kermina (1976) p. 213 ff. See Walton, p. 231 ff. for more details.

[8] Popkin (1990), pp. 70–3.

[9] See Perroud (1912); Dorigny (1989a); Walton (2009). Relevant files AN, H1 1448: thanks to Charles Walton for this archive reference: my interpretation of the material does not always coincide with his, but his sophisticated account takes Roland's ministry seriously as part of a longer process.

until its ideals were propagated throughout the provinces, through writings, but also using 'traditional cultural intermediaries'—literate provincials like priests and schoolteachers. Walton interprets the forming of public opinion as a continuous process, beginning much earlier in the Revolution (and pre-Revolution) than usually thought; he takes a much more critical view of Roland's role.

The question concerns both timing and content. To start chronologically, the minister had, as noted earlier, channelled 'secret' funds in spring to Louvet's *Sentinelle*. Its role was to encourage acceptance of both Constitution and war effort, and oppose court intrigues and counter-revolutionaries. Even when retrospective accusations were common later in 1792, the charges scarcely ever mention the period March–June. Apparently it caused little or no controversy.[10]

The second period started on a similar course. On 17 August, a week after the storming of the Tuileries, the Legislative Assembly voted a sum of 100,000 *livres* to the ministry of the Interior (proposer Lasource) for the 'printing and distribution to the *départements* and armies of all the writings designed to enlighten minds about the criminal plots of enemies of the state and on the true causes of the evils which have so long divided the country'.[11] Roland took this to mean encouraging acceptance of the events in Paris, the fall of the monarchy, and the move towards the republic, and inspiring soldiers to join up for the war effort.

One person whom he failed to subsidize during August—with drastic consequences—was Marat, who approached him for money to publish his collected works. In Marat's version, the Rolands were not initially hostile, and Mme Roland (NB) agreed to try and fast-track it. However, '*le bonhomme* didn't refuse my request directly, but put a thousand ministerial obstacles in its way [...] sending me to the Greek Kalends'. This earned Roland the eternal enmity of L'Ami du Peuple, who quite openly turned for funds to the duc d'Orléans. Still, apart from Marat's pique, the issue was not yet in the forefront of minds.[12]

What Roland did do in September, before the Convention convened, and while there was still an invasion threat, was send out several emissaries, distinct from the other sets, on a mission of moral regeneration or, to put it another way, propaganda for the Revolution. The timing predates 'Montagnard–Girondin' factionalism, although not the emergent divisions over the massacres. His *commissaires* had clear, rather headmasterly 'Instructions intended to guide their conduct', of which printed copies exist.[13] They were to be missionaries, but to avoid interfering with local authorities; they were to be conspicuously frugal, travelling on foot, and inspiring people with their 'wise advice and honest and virtuous actions'. These were the men his wife described as 'a small number of men as sensible as they

[10] *Mém.*, pp. 72–3, for Mme Roland's well-informed account: Louvet's mandate was to 'publish good writings to enlighten the people'. Cf. Perroud (1912), p. 208.
[11] Perroud (1912), p. 318; three detailed articles. Cf. *AP* 18, August 1792. BNF MSS, naf 22423. See also Dorigny (1989a).
[12] Marat (1995), vol. 8, pp. 4708–9. Whaley (2000) p. 77, suggests Roland blocked funds for a journal by Fabre and Danton; Perroud (1912), p. 317, states that Danton used other ministerial funds instead. Cf. *Mém.*, p. 90.
[13] Copy in AN, H1 1448, dated 13 September 1792; Dorigny (1989a), p. 212. Their mission was to be 'purely moral and simply of influence, except in an emergency'.

were zealous', and whom Desmoulins later called 'an army of stipended orators'. Champagneux confirmed that Roland had sent agents to identify intermediaries, such as local *curés*, but insisted that while 'they were obedient to his voice' they 'only used the position the ministry gave them to preach peace, good works, and submission to the government'.[14] They were apparently chiefly concerned to combat royalist sentiments. On 23 September (just after Valmy), one agent requested 'everything necessary to totally de-Lafayettize and de-royalize the minds of people in Sedan'. Another wrote that he was trying to reach women, 'knowing the hold women have over men's minds, and their liking for domestic happiness [...] I think they will raise their children to be like those of Sparta'.[15]

These men, whose names are known (Enenon, Regnier, etc.), filled out chits for travelling expenses, ranging from 300 to 900 *livres*, and sent back regular reports. They persisted throughout September and into October, despite their recall. Roland was still dealing with a backlog of claims in November, sternly advising one emissary that he had no right to distribute money. As late as 16 November, he asked the PEC for an extra indemnity to cover extraordinary expenses. Whatever budget these envoys originally came under, they were certainly financed by the Interior ministry and can be called 'Roland's men'.[16]

If one considers the formally allotted sum of 100,000 *livres*, Roland stated when he resigned that he had spent [just over] 32,913 *livres*. The figures studied a century later by Perroud broadly confirm this sum. Robespierre evidently had exaggerated ideas both about the money at Roland's disposal and his use of it: he had claimed that these untold 'millions' would have 'fed 100,000 poor families'. This kind of statement, flung out in the heat of the moment, let us say, encouraged continual accusations of 'massive resources'.[17] While both Jean-Marie Roland and his wife were somewhat economical with the truth, their accounts stand up reasonably well to examination, give or take some omissions. To persist in talking of 'huge sums' and 'millions' was *de bonne guerre* perhaps, but inaccurate.

Where did the money go? Mme Roland denied both at her trial, understandably, and in her memoirs 'more speciously' (Perroud) that any 'bureau' existed as such. She could truthfully say she had never seen such a notice on a door, but something of the sort must have existed. The official *Almanach national* stated that 'correspondence relating to the formation and propagation of *l'esprit public*' was officially handled by A.F. Le Tellier.[18] Lanthenas was the director, even after his election to the Convention in September. (All the stranger, then, that he escaped proscription in 1793.)[19] Because Lanthenas was so disorganized, Mme Roland had

---

[14] *Mém.*, pp. 171, 355; Desmoulins, *Histoire des Brissotins*; Champagneux (1800), p. xxix.

[15] AN, H1 1448, also quoted Dorigny (1989a), p. 213.

[16] AN, H1 1448, many papers, discussed in Walton (2009), pp. 210–15.

[17] Bernardin (1964), pp. 514–19, despite her lack of sympathy for Roland, makes short work of Robespierre's exaggerated claims; Perroud (1912), p. 318; *AP*, XLVIII, 18 August 1792, p. 358.

[18] Presumably the one abolished 21 January at Robespierre's request: Robespierre, *Oeuvres complètes*, V, p. 210; cf. *Mém*, pp. 171–3, Mme Roland claimed 'a great scaffolding' had been invented, see also ibid., pp. 355 ff., her reply to Amar.

[19] BNF MSS, naf 6243: Lanthenas 18 September to Dulaure; many letters to him in AN, H1 1448.

to correct his accounts. The source Perroud used is a ledger entirely in her writing, relating to printed matter.

Chronologically, his figures show that Louvet's *Sentinelle* went on being subsidized even during July–August 1792, but published only twelve issues between 26 August and 27 October. Louvet later moved to editing the *Journal des Débats et Decrets*, but by then he had identified himself as a sworn enemy of Robespierre by his 'philippic' against him (this is discussed more fully in context under the next section, Minister for the Gironde). The earlier *Sentinelle* pre-dated the worst of the factional fighting, but was retrospectively damned by association. Some funds also went to the pre-Hébert version of *Le Père Duchesne*, written by Antoine Lemaire: Mme Roland thought his martial style would suit the armies best.[20]

During September and October, the ministry paid Anne-Félicité Colomb— Marat's sometime printer—for 200 copies per day of the *Journal des débats et de la correspondance des Jacobins*—the Jacobin newsletter—which was certainly not sympathetic to the Brissotins. However, over the autumn, the newsletter's editor, Deflers, fell out with the more radical membership, and the subscription did not continue into November. (Brissot, Roland, and Lanthenas were all excluded from the club in October–November: the club dispatched its newsletters using other resources.)

Some subscriptions had longer runs—Dulaure's *Thermomètre*, sympathetic to the ministry, was backed from the spring on.[21] The largest and longest-lasting subscription was to Gorsas's *Courrier de Paris dans les provinces et des provinces à Paris*— 100 copies a day from August to January. Perroud commented that this purchase, while not enough to make much difference, was quite enough to arouse 'inexpiable hatred', because Gorsas moved to the right during the Convention, and his presses were among those attacked in March 1793.[22]

The ministry apparently also subsidized directly, for smaller sums, writers and their books—Thomas Rousseau for patriotic songs, writings on education, and a few other apparently non-contentious 'patriotic' works. Roland's agent, Gonchon, was sent into occupied departments with books and pamphlets to be distributed— in his pack, Lanthenas included several of his own works, having managed to get them printed at ministry expense.

Perroud lists further printing/dispatch bills under three headings: appeals for patriotism against the invasion, support for republican ideas, and anti-Jacobin writings. The first two were uncontentious; that was what the funds had been voted for. Under the third heading, Perroud rightly criticizes Roland's official accounts for not attaching Brissot's *name* to a set of his speeches, reprinted in September (841 *livres*). During December, he also subsidized *reprints* of Brissot's paper, *Le Patriote*, containing works by Tom Paine and Pétion—notably the latter's reply to Robespierre's reply to Louvet. This document, while absolving Robespierre of dictatorial intentions,

[20] To Bosc, 18 August 1792, *Corr.*, II, p. 327.
[21] Lanthenas invited Dulaure to dinner, BNF MSS, naf 9533: 'the Minister wants to bring together people capable of directing *l'esprit public*', 14 May 1792.
[22] Gorsas: 'the 2000 copies a day I'm supposed to have been providing to Roland!', note on receipt, Perroud (1912), p. 332.

was critical of him for seeing conspiracies everywhere (500 copies). The number containing Louvet's *follow-up* reply to Robespierre's reply as a supplement was also reprinted (500 copies), as were 1000 copies of the pamphlet replying to Cloots's accusations of federalism. What is more, Perroud significantly points out that Mme Roland had taken a few particularly compromising bills out of the ministry accounts—these were presumably paid for from other (private?) sources. More copies of Louvet, a poster by Barbaroux against Marat; one short-lived, but undoubtedly pro-Girondin journal, *Le Fanal parisien*, written by one Jacques Lablée (5 numbers only, but not paid for from ministry funds, for whatever reason).[23]

According to Perroud's calculations, of the public funds allowed him, and out of the queried items, Roland paid 4500 *livres* for 'straightforward republican' propaganda; 5600 for encouraging national defence; 4000 to proclamations in favour of order—'all of which were absolutely legitimate'. On the other hand, 4800 *livres* went on subscriptions to newspapers, mostly in the Girondin interest, 1400 to printed books including 'elucubrations', by Lanthenas, 900 on the last gasps of *La Sentinelle*, and almost 3000 *livres* on brochures or reprints by Brissot, and polemics against Robespierre—acknowledged, and dating from earlier in the autumn, but wide open to criticism for partisanship. As Perroud concludes, in monetary terms this is quite modest, certainly not 'immense sums'—but it represents a lot of paper.

As to the contents, Le Guin argues, in Roland's defence, that it is hard to imagine a 'more inoffensive or harmless campaign of words' than most of his missives: circulars to the clergy exhorting them to hold services in French, discourses on good citizenship, etc. But this is leaning rather far over backwards to overlook what was undoubtedly the chief head of accusation: circulating speeches or writings by Brissot, Pétion, and Louvet, in which Robespierre was personally attacked. Robespierre was not the man to forgive this. Mme Roland herself says in her *Observations* on the Girondins' trial that Roland was entitled to pick and choose a bit.[24] Perhaps he would have had to be heroically self-denying not to, but as Perroud remarks, and it is an understatement, this was 'huge imprudence for very slim benefit'.[25]

As Perroud also points out, government propaganda, during the Terror, later moved into a completely different dimension. 50 million *livres* were allocated in August 1793 to the Committee of Public Safety, which paid for, among other things, 600 daily copies of Montagnard newspapers, and 10,000 copies of a political bulletin for the army.[26] The fact that others followed suit massively does not let the Rolands

---

[23] Perroud (1912), p. 412; *Réponse au prussien Klootz* in which Brissot, Kersaint, Guadet, and Roland countered Cloots's scatter-gun attacks in *Ni Marat ni Roland*. Brissot spelled out in this pamphlet his rejection of federalism.

[24] *Mém.*, pp. 353–4: 'supposing that he made a selection, he was free to send out fewer of those that seemed less good'; ibid., pp. 355–6: 'I have seen even Marat's speeches dispatched'.

[25] Perroud (1912), p. 419, not exactly a 'state-subsidised publishing empire' for the Gironde, Cowans (2001), p. 104. However, for a heated exchange with Arras (significantly) in January 1793, over sending out only his own selection and not at all what they wanted, see BNF MSS, naf 22423.

[26] Perroud (1912), p. 419, note, Perroud's reference for this is P. Caron (1910) 'Les publications officieuses du ministère de l'Intérieur en 1793 et 1794, *Revue d'histoire moderne et contemporaine* 14. Cf. Whaley (2000), p. 159, on 'Roland's propaganda network'.

off the hook of course. One could even say that their enemies learnt from their mistakes—to play this game, you really did need 'enormous sums'. (Le Guin argues that Roland's resignation must have come as a surprise to the Mountain—they abolished the 'bureau', just when it could have become available to a 'more suitable' minister).[27] While the battle raged in the Montagnard press, whatever its own resources, ministry funds undoubtedly subsidized some pro-Gironde prints. The ledger shows that Mme Roland was doing the accounts—like any artisan's or printer's wife might have done. (She was also the addressee of several communications from Roland's agent Gadolle in October.) So her self-defence in the *Observations* is some way short of the truth, when she says 'I didn't have any hand in this, still less did I direct it.'[28]

Another accusation was that Roland 'stopped' certain documents. A deputation to the Convention on 18 May 1793 (though why then?) accused him of having with '*truly scandalous profusion*', circularized and poisoned the departments with libels, and of having *stopped the circulation* of the best revolutionary writings.[29] As far as I can see, on only one occasion did Roland actually intervene to hold up any prints, and did so publicly. On 30 October, he himself reported to the Convention that an address by the 48 sections was being sent out to the departments without the Convention's authorization—it happened to be a protest at the proposal for a provincial force for the assembly's protection, which the Convention had in theory approved—a highly controversial subject! He asked the postal services to hold it for approval. When asked how he knew about it, Roland replied that he had been 'informed'—presumably by the postal officials. The latter all testified that the packets had been identified (by some insider?), but that no seals had been broken. This may have been the origin of later charges (impossible to confirm or deny) that Roland sometimes blocked materials or interfered with the mails. That would, indeed, have been an example of actually denying freedom of expression—he insisted he had never done so. Although by not sending out Montagnard papers, he was also considered to be blocking free speech, the two things are not quite the same.[30]

What conclusion can be suggested? First, on the substance of the question, Roland had embarked on the path of 'enlightening opinion' as a 'necessary response' to counter-revolutionary propaganda in the provinces. He probably attached more importance to his own circulars during the autumn, into which both he and, we may imagine, his wife, put much effort. Her memoirs refer not to the Brissotin polemics, but to general exhortations written by Roland himself (or by her): 'he made it a rule to reply to everything, to correspond with societies, priests [...] sending circulars to remind them of the spirit of their institution, of the fraternal need to instruct and enlighten'. He employed Champagneux (not named, but obvious) to organize this 'patriotic correspondence', which included 'his own circulars [...] always expressing the morality and charm of affection [!] that won

---

[27] Le Guin (1966), p. 113, quoting AN, C11 255.
[28] *Mém.*, p. 355. Perhaps she could square doing the accounts with a simple clerical job?
[29] Le Guin (1966), p. 113, quoting AN, C11 255, my italics.
[30] Bosc, who worked there, claimed no mails were interfered with before 31 May 1793. Suppression of dissent during the Terror was on a different scale.

hearts'. The aim was to 'interest and bind to the public interest men hitherto totally occupied by their work, but abandoned to ignorance'. All this was in the interests of 'wisdom, civic spirit and reason'. It is not unreasonable to assume that it applied to material that went out in September and October, but it leaves untroubled the sensitive spot relating to the Louvet–Robespierre polemic—on which, of course, Mme Roland took sides.[31]

Roland himself must have been aware that as opinions polarized, the dispatches became more selective. He either failed in time to appreciate the complexion put on the selection, or took the view that he had to combat both reactionary publications and the 'anarchist' press. In his own workload, it is unclear how large it bulked. Much was left to Lanthenas and perhaps Le Tellier, while Mme Roland supervised the accounts. If he underestimated it, his enemies overestimated it. The root of the conflict (although hard to assess) was that Montagnard and Parisian papers, such as Marat's and Hébert's, had great currency in the capital, less so in the provinces. It became a Jacobin article of faith that the 'provinces' were being stirred up against Paris, and that Roland 'was venerated' in the rest of France. If so, the means employed by Roland were hardly adequate to the job. Perroud thought it would take a great deal more than a meagre 34,000 *livres* to counter the pro-Jacobin, pro-Montagnard, or pro-Commune press.[32]

The dates of both the expenditures and the attacks suggest that this issue became critical only during late autumn, with the Louvet–Robespierre spat of early November as a particular stimulus. Many of the publications subsidized pre-date this (most of Brissot's speeches) and few post-date it, so it seems to have tailed off. Marat's fiercest attack—accusing Roland of subsidizing extra copies of Gorsas's and Dulaure's papers—dates from 2 November.[33] Perroud points out that there are hardly any payments to printers for the month of January and those mostly for earlier bills. The whole affair covers about four months during the second ministry. So one way to explore why 'Roland's propaganda' became such an issue, is to consider the chronology of the destructive Montagnard–Gironde conflict, as it reached a particularly acute phase. What had started out as an idealistic project in Roland's mind undoubtedly ended up as part of what Walton rightly describes as 'the culture of calumny'. It was, of course, a culture in which both sides heartily participated.

MINISTER FOR THE GIRONDE?

Patrice Gueniffey has pertinently remarked that it was not so much politics that brought Brissot's associates together, as friendship that brought together people with often divergent political views. Sydenham similarly points out that the 'inner circle' of Girondins voted less consistently together than the larger grouping.

---

[31] *Mém.*, pp. 93, 171–2. What Perroud (and the Convention) regarded as 'legitimate' was already manipulating opinion and suppressing dissent (from royalists) as Charles Walton has pointed out.

[32] Perroud (1912), p. 212, and cf. Walton (2009), pp. 215–16.

[33] Perroud (1912), pp. 413–14, comments that Marat's figures for the *Sentinelle* overall are a good guess, but his other figures are either wrong or irrelevant.

Marisa Linton shows how friendship itself became suspect and could be reinterpreted as conspiracy.[34] As we saw, Brissot was the prime mover in the plan for an association of 'friends' in 1790. A series of friendships and loyalties was the cement binding Brissot and the Rolands. The very casualness of their relationship emerges from an informal note from Brissot to Mme Roland—undated, but probably during the first ministry. In a few lines, it shows that Brissot was a frequent private dinner guest, since neither on Thursday nor Saturday were there formal dinners:

> I wish good day to the respectable Madame Roland. [...] I cannot have the pleasure
> of dining with my friends Thursday, because we are having a regular dinner then, and
> I hope my friend Roland will come. M. Clavière and I will pick him up at four o'clock.
> I will be free on Saturday and at Mme Roland's orders.[35]

Roland and Brissot did not always agree by any means, but their friendship apparently survived. Both suffered by turns as a result of the association, first Roland as a 'Brissot nominee', then Brissot for being the 'minister's friend'. Both of them incurred the deep hatred of Robespierre, which was to persist through all the various reconciliation moves.[36] It was inevitable that as the Montagne–Gironde split developed, Roland would be firmly identified as the 'minister for the Brissot faction'.

However, he would also be perceived as the 'minister against Paris' for reasons already mentioned. Following the semi-truce after Valmy, when things appeared to settle down, it was the in-built conflict between his role as minister and the Paris municipal authority that fuelled their confrontations. In his reports to the Convention, Roland complained of the unwillingness of the Paris Commune to communicate with him, to provide proper accounts (while asking all the time for more money), to repress disturbances in the capital, and in general to conform to the rules that ought to govern their relations. Braesch's (1911) thorough study of the Paris Commune is not sympathetic to Roland, and deplores the split between the Commune and majority in the Convention, preventing the emergence of a 'republican party united against [both] anarchy and privilege', but he agrees that there was much disorder in Paris that autumn, and that the power struggles within the sections were complex and often waged by small minorities who dominated sectional meetings.[37]

It was in the wake of Roland's contentious report on the state of Paris (29 October)[38] that the Louvet–Robespierre fight erupted. Edith Bernardin argues that this was a put-up job. It is hard to confirm or deny this, but Roland certainly helped

---

[34] Gueniffey (1991), p. 442; Sydenham (1961); Linton (2008), pp. 57–9; Perl-Rosenthal (2011), chapters 6 and 7 on the cement that held together the 'Roland circles' at various times.

[35] Picked up in the Brival report, see Chapter 24.

[36] Whaley (2000), p. 132, on Robespierre letting Danton off the hook, because of attacks on Brissot and Roland as 'friends' of Dumouriez.

[37] Braesch (1911), pp. 1042, 1172–3. Cf. Daunou, cited Hardman (1973), p. 26: 'the most indefatigable enemy of anarchy was Roland who [...] had no means of combating it other than by his frequent and energetic denunciations', but was himself 'accused', when false reports of 'tranquillity' were produced.

[38] *AP*, LIII, p. 38 ff.

trigger it. He appended some documents to his report, including an anonymous letter denouncing death threats to himself and Brissotin deputies, and containing the provocative phrase 'they want to hear only Robespierre'. Robespierre immediately protested at his name being mentioned and challenged anyone to accuse him of 'anything'. Danton tried sensibly but unsuccessfully to head off a debate, suggesting in moderate terms that Roland was perhaps taking unduly seriously 'some petty and miserable intrigues'.[39]

But Robespierre's challenge was taken up by Louvet—'the most rash and least reflective' of the Girondins (Perroud). He had apparently been carrying round in his pocket a denunciation of Robespierre as potential dictator, and was ready to deliver it, which he did ('*Je t'accuse*'...of a great many things). Robespierre, taken aback, asked for time to reply, and did so at length the following Monday. Louvet and Pétion both counter-replied, but were not allowed to deliver their interventions. Despite partisan referees of this stand-off, the sensible verdict is probably Braesch's that it degenerated into name-calling, 'without any practical result'.[40] But it went very deep into Robespierre's heart, becoming a festering abscess, and certainly a point of reference in attacks on Roland.

Soon afterwards, the tensions of the autumn culminated in the head-counts over the king's fate. The mid-twentieth-century debates about whether the Gironde was a party are based largely on the critical January votes deciding whether Louis should be condemned to death, reprieved, or whether his fate should be submitted to the *appel au peuple*. Roland, not being a deputy, did not have to state his views.[41] It is usually assumed that he would have voted for the *appel au peuple* and/or the reprieve. Although he gave different reasons, his resignation on 22 January, the day after the king's execution, is sometimes taken as a sign that he was against the death sentence.[42] Mme Roland comes closest to saying so, when she writes that while her husband 'abhorred tyranny and regarded Louis as guilty, he [...] thought liberty had been lost when the wrong-headed [*les mauvaises têtes*] gained the ascendant' during the votes, so there was no point staying on. What Roland pointedly claimed himself, in answer to 'royalist' charges, was that he had done as much as anyone to bring down the king. Not only had his letter in June sparked the slow burn leading to 10 August, he had also discovered, in a secret cupboard in the Tuileries, significant documents that were used in the king's trial. A word on this controversial incident is therefore necessary.

Roland being Roland, and his enemies being who they were, the affair of the *armoire de fer*, the iron safe, turned into another face-off, to be added to the factional dossier. This stickler for the rules can be blamed for imprudence or blindness in failing to cover himself from foreseeable charges of tampering with the papers. What appears to have happened is this: shortly after the Convention session opened

---

[39] Ibid., p. 51.
[40] Ibid., p. 1019. For Roland's report on the state of Paris, the speeches by Louvet and Robespierre, and replies by Louvet and Pétion, see *AP*, LIII (November 1793), pp. 49 ff., 170 ff.
[41] On the trial, see Walzer (1974), and Jordan (1979).
[42] Genet claimed (Conway 1900, appendix) that the Roland circle favoured exiling the royal family to the United States, as did Tom Paine.

at 10 a.m. on 20 November, Roland arrived breathlessly in the chamber, with two folders full of papers, and asked to make a statement: 'I have brought to the Convention several files of papers which seem important. They cast light on 10 August and the whole revolution. Several members of the Constituent and Legislative Assemblies appear to be compromised.'

The king's locksmith, François Gamain, had installed the safe near the royal bedroom. Troubled by his dangerous knowledge, he told Heurtier, the architect responsible for altering the Tuileries. Both men then informed Roland, who was nominally in overall charge of the palace. 'This morning', the minister told the deputies, he had opened the cupboard in the two men's presence. He said that he had 'rapidly looked at the papers', long enough to realize what kind of documents they were, and had brought them straight to the Convention, in the *Manège* next door. The Convention decided that to avoid any tampering, Roland and the two secretaries of the day would stay in the chamber until they had numbered all 625 pieces (they can still be seen today with the signatures).[43]

These papers, dating back to 1791 and notably incriminating Mirabeau of secret talks with the king, contributed to charges against Louis that he had never sincerely cooperated with the Constitution. Far from getting credit for the prompt revelation, Roland was criticized for not calling members of the Convention to witness the find, laying himself open to suspicion that he might perhaps have abstracted documents incriminating friends of his. Roland replied that he had been with the two royal employees all the time, and they backed him up with sworn statements, but it happened that two deputies were in the palace at the time, checking various other discoveries. Roland's argument that the palace came under his sole authority, which trumped any commissioners from the Convention, did not cut any ice with deputies on the left.

Later on, some play was made of the fact that his find did not contain the letter from the Gironde deputies in July—made public for the first time by a speaker on 4 January 1793. Gensonné replied at once, explaining that it was a letter to Boze, not to the king, and that he was perfectly willing to reproduce it, which he did, but in an atmosphere so highly charged, and with retrospective accusations common practice, this was yet another bone of contention. It was later blown up into a massive propaganda advantage by those accusing the Girondins of royalism, despite the fact that the letter dated from the confusion in July 1792, when the choices between cooperating with the king and Constitution, or backing an insurrection, were still unresolved. It was convenient to forget, as Robespierre seemed to, that back in June–July 1792, even he had made speeches in favour of the existing Constitution.[44]

As for Roland and the iron safe, given the number of documents, the short time involved, Roland's generally stiff-necked uprightness, and his view that he was

---

[43] *AP*, LIII, pp. 452–5; Roland later recommended Heurtier as 'one of the most honest people he had worked with', BNF MSS, naf 6241, fo 308.

[44] Gensonné's letter, Hardman (1981) pp. 142–4. See *Moniteur*, 6 January 1793, p. 119 for the issue raised.

entitled to use his own authority, it is unlikely that he filleted the papers before delivering them, but the smoke from the affair hung around and he had to justify himself more than once. Even his wife in her memoirs agreed that, while being 'a man of probity and [too] trusting', and having 'committed no wrong in this affair', he had probably made a mistake 'in his conduct and the precautions he should have taken'.[45]

To conclude on this question, both the Rolands—as Champagneux remarked a propos of their dinner parties—were deeply persuaded that there were forces of evil (= *les méchants*) emanating at first principally from Marat, whom they thought capable of exciting any amount of disorder, anarchy and bloodshed. Their partisanship extended to distrust of Danton and, increasingly, Robespierre. They certainly engaged in counter-propaganda. This chapter has not sought to exonerate them from that, although the extent of their efforts was probably exaggerated (sincerely or otherwise) by the Montagnards and the Jacobins in late autumn, with support from Robespierre, who appears to have taken the Louvet affair much to heart. It took two to tango. The affair of dispatches from the '*bureau d'esprit public*' occupied a relatively short period—but a week is a long time in politics, and its echoes were to go on forever.

From being warmly welcomed back into the ministry as a hero after 10 August, Roland had become a figure of hate within sections of Parisian, Jacobin, and Convention opinion. He was regularly receiving death threats by December. Being the stubborn man he was, these did not deter him from speaking his mind, or ploughing on with what he saw as his daily responsibilities, but it was clear to others, if not to himself, that he would not last much longer in the job.

---

[45] Le Guin (1966), p. 106, in Roland's defence. cf. *Mém.* pp. 356–7. There were also attempts to blame him for the break-in at the royal treasury (the *garde-meuble*) in September, a truly *ténébreuse affaire*, see BNF MSS, naf 22423, fo 166 and *Mém.*, p. 199.

PART V

A CLOSING TRAP

24

January–May 1793

Nobody's Minister

In all cases [of death threats] the minister ought to remain at his post, because his death [*sa perte*] would cry out for vengeance [...] I know this kind of reasoning will seem ridiculous to anyone who puts his own life above everything else, but someone who values [his own life] in the middle of a revolution will never regard virtue, honour, and the *patrie* as worth anything.

Mme Roland, Memoirs.[1]

Given the hostility he faced, it's hardly surprising that Roland resigned in January 1793—more surprising that he didn't do so sooner. Mme Roland recorded that during the last two months in the ministry (December and January), she and her husband were often urged to move out of their lodgings for their own security, and did so three times in December. Finally, in January, she decided not to leave the ministry building—better to die at one's post than try to escape. She had Roland's bed moved into her room, and kept a pistol under her pillow, which she intended for herself to avoid 'indignities'. Both Rolands believed that they were in mortal danger.[2]

On 25 December 1792, they wrote to Dominique in Villefranche, intending to send Eudora south for safety. They drew up a legal document saying that while they would face any risks, it was not right to expose 'our cherished child' to them. She would be accompanied by 'an excellent woman', Marie-Madeleine Mignot, aged 55, a former organist at the Bernardins monastery. The Rolands had hired her earlier as keyboard teacher and governess, and trusted her 'affectionate care and enlightened goodness' to see to Eudora's education. They even promised her a future annuity of 1000 *livres*. For whatever reason—perhaps simply Roland's decision to resign—they did not carry out this plan: Eudora stayed in Paris with them.[3]

The fears were understandable. The verbal attacks on the minister at the Jacobin Club and in certain newspapers were violent, and they escalated. If one takes just ten days in December, on 5 December, a deputation from the Commune accused

---

[1] *Mém.*, p. 41.   [2] Ibid.
[3] *Corr.*, II, pp. 447–8; Champagneux, p. xlij; Mlle Mignot left on 20 May and did not repay their trust well, see Chapter 27.

Roland of being anti-Paris and spreading a 'profusion of incendiary writings' in the provinces. On 7 December, both Rolands were obliged to defend themselves in the Viard case, of doubtful provenance. On 9 December, just before the king's trial began, Chales, the Jacobin who first mentioned the *bureau d'esprit public*, claimed that Brissot planned to institute a 'regency with Roland, during the minority of the dauphin'.[4] He was backed up by one Garnier, who called Roland 'a wild beast [!], a regent, an uncrowned king, this modest man who goes around looking like a cleric (*un recollet*). They tell me Roland is venerated in the provinces: he is a revered idol, dangerous to the *patrie*.' If he was so virtuous, he should imitate Aristides (to whom his friends had compared him) and go into exile.[5] Three days later, at the Jacobin Club, Robespierre launched a broadside against Roland in stronger language than he habitually used in the Convention, where it would have raised protests:

> As long as there exists a monster who holds in his hands freedom and above all freedom of thought, a minister who can dispose of the worldly goods of the ci-devant clergy, as long as no honest man can ask him to account for the immense sums he has in his hands, as long as he has the power to calumniate not only the people, but the friends of the people; as long as this minister exists, as long as he gives dinners and places, you will only have the *despotism of a single man*, who is ruled by thirty-odd scoundrels. As long as Roland exists, all the aristocrats will rally to him. [my italics][6]

Although such attacks continued, the king's trial, starting on 10 December, absorbed the deputies' attention—and that of watchers everywhere. Roland played no part in the trial, apart from discovering the *armoire de fer* papers, and being formally responsible for Louis XVI's transport between the Temple and the Convention during the trial, about which he was characteristically scrupulous. Neither of the Rolands was remotely royalist, and Jean-Marie regularly referred to the king as 'the despot' or 'the tyrant'. But his closest friends mostly voted the moderate options: Brissot for conditional reprieve. Buzot, Vergniaud, and Guadet the Mailhe amendment—death, but with the possibility of reprieve. Bancal the straight moderate ticket—*appel*, prison, reprieve; Louvet imprisonment. Barbaroux voted death without reprieve. All voted the *appel au peuple*.[7] But whatever Roland thought, it is not so much dissent from the trial's conclusion, as the fact that the trial was over at last, which may help to explain the date of his resignation, on 22 January, the day after the king's execution.

Why did Roland resign and why just then? Perroud and others have speculated about his motives: disagreement with the king's execution? Pique at Robespierre's successful cutting of the so-called *bureau d'esprit* public funds on 21 January? Was

---

[4] *Jacobins*, IV, p. 564; Danton was also sometimes accused of wanting to be regent.
[5] Ibid., IV, p. 565.
[6] Ibid., pp. 574–5, 12 December 1792.
[7] Patrick (1972) Appendix III). Louis was declared guilty by unanimous vote 14 January; the *appel au peuple* was rejected (424–283); he was sentenced to death on 16–17 January (387–334); reprieve was ruled out on 20 January (380–310). He was executed next day, figures from Jones (1990), pp. 25–6. Deputies who voted for the amendments were later accused of royalism.

it even the distress in his private life [see Chapter 25]? These could all have contributed, plus weariness, given his age and the stress of working in a hostile atmosphere. One persuasive reason was that the dissension between himself and Pache
over procurement of supplies had led to calls in the Convention that one of them,
or both, should resign, but *not until the king's trial was over*, to minimize disrup-
tion. This fits Roland's own explanation, in a fragment of memoir written in
February 1793, which Perroud concluded was the most convincing.

The text is dated '30 days after my resignation', so in late February, and '40 days
after thinking these things'—that is before any of the votes on the king's fate. People imagined, Roland wrote, that the denunciations, 'the death threats, the tirades
coming from the Commune, the sections and the clubs, in public squares and even
from the tribune in the Convention' had intimidated him. But in the Convention
hardly more than ten men actually accused him of anything. What really moved
him was that no one stood up to defend him. They were all:

> too devastated by present circumstances and bore the pallor of fear [. . .]. Some feared
> a dagger in the back, such as I was threatened with all the time; others, who had some
> popular support, were afraid to compromise it; they gave the excuse that they needed
> to save their credit for more important circumstances. Some said: 'just let them have
> their say; don't irritate them any more; it'll blow over' [*ils s'usent*].

He indicated that if he had been defended—even by one speaker, which seems
unrealistic—he might have carried on, because it was not a matter of indifference
to 'the good side [*le bon parti*] to have a minister of the Interior who was doing the
right things [*dans la bonne voie*] and whose honour was intact'. However, 'I'm
ashamed to say this, and my heart breaks, I cannot name a single man.' Perhaps
even the Brissotins now feared he was too much of a hate-figure in Paris to be
worth defending in public, and he was probably about right in his judgement of
how they reacted.[8]

He referred to the pragmatic reason: the 'indispensable and necessary dismissal
of the minister for War [Pache] which would have been impossible if I had stayed'.
He claimed with some reason that the War ministry was disorganized. The armies
lacked provisions and clothes, but the 'backers of disorder' would not dismiss
Pache unless the minister of the Interior went too. As we saw earlier, Dumouriez
had long been at odds with Pache, complaining of the inadequacy of army supplies. Roland had withdrawn from the Directorate of Purchases in December,
refusing to endorse War ministry accounts in the weeks before he resigned. (The
Convention, with Danton pushing, quickly took the chance to sack Pache on
2 February—only to see him become mayor of Paris.)[9] Increasingly at odds both
with his opponents in the Convention and with a powerful element in the PEC,
Roland's determination nevertheless to 'try and see things through' is undeniable.
It may not have been quite what Robespierre characterized as hunger for power, so

---

[8] Reproduced Champagneux (1800), pp. xi–xvi, and Bernardin (1964), p. 71.
[9] Champagneux (1800), p. xviii, and *Mém.*, p. 107. Mme Roland accused Pache of malversation
and nepotism. Cf. Brown (1995), pp. 57 ff.

much as a frustrated desire to get things done. Of course, they are arguably two sides of the same coin.

At any rate, Mme Roland was still writing on 15 January: 'proscription floats over our heads, but we shall have to keep battling on [...] and deserve ostracism [in the antique sense = banishment perhaps to the Beaujolais] if that is the price of virtue'.[10] On 19 January, her husband put up a poster saying 'dismiss me or sacrifice me, but I demand a proper judgement'. However, after the king's execution on 21 January, Roland formally resigned next day.[11]

His resignation letter was preceded by a long report of 200+ pages, the *Compte rendu*, on how he saw things (the 'ministry of writing' with a vengeance). Charles Le Guin calls it 'a summary of the achievements and an expression of the hopes of Roland's public career'. Although it contains much self-praise and justification, always an irritating feature of Roland's memoranda, it is a practical document too, full of suggestions, not really controversial, about the different headings of the ministry (agriculture, industry, subsistence, education, transport and roads, national monuments, and even the melting down of the church bells). It forms the basis of Le Guin's conclusion on Roland's ministry.[12]

The couple moved back to the little flat in the rue de la Harpe and Jean-Marie Roland immediately presented his accounts, which had to be approved by the Convention. He also set about claiming his modest pension as inspector (not as minister).[13] Perhaps some words spoken at the Jacobins did not reach him, although they explain why the Convention kept fobbing him off, and never gave him permission to leave Paris. A Jacobin known only as 'C' (Collot, Chales?) reported on his resignation as 'happy news' and added: 'Now he has to produce his accounts—and that's where we'll be waiting for him.'[14] Champagneux reports, by contrast, presumably from documents before him, that the minister's officials 'came to see him in his retirement to express the homage of their regrets: the mourning was general and [...] so touching that one cannot read the correspondence relating to it without tears'.[15] One might imagine that having voluntarily resigned, and so conceded defeat, Roland could be permitted to lapse into quiet obscurity, and that it would have brought some relief to be out of the hot seat. But worse, much worse, was to come.

It was unlikely that the accumulated hostility would vanish overnight, but as far as one can see from the surviving documents the ex-minister wanted nothing so much as to get his accounts signed off (he made about six applications, all virtually identical, all sidelined by the Convention) and to return to the Beaujolais. The only suggestion I have found of Roland being involved in *any* political discussion

---

[10] *Corr.*, II, p. 465, to Lavater, quoting Garnier at the Jacobins.
[11] BNF MSS, naf 9532, also in *Moniteur*, 21 January 1793.
[12] *Compte rendu*, see Le Guin (1966), pp. 113, 116–24. Parts of it are quoted throughout these chapters.
[13] See Desmoulins (1874), II, p. 344; *Corr.*, II, p. 462.
[14] *Jacobins*, V, p. 1, 23 January 1793.
[15] Champagneux (1800), p. xxix, note, if so, the correspondence does not appear to have survived.

after his resignation is David Williams's account of Lebrun and Brissot expressing private regret, early in February, at having been 'pushed' into the declaration of war against England, and appealing to Williams to help re-negotiate. He lists Roland as present at this meeting: possible, but was it likely?[16] Roland exchanged letters with Garat and Lanthenas, and wrote to Paoli and an old friend, Gamelin, in Palermo, all reflecting great bitterness, but nothing in this correspondence suggests a desire to stay in politics, or anything other than a wish to let 'posterity' judge him.[17]

A different kind of tribunal was, however, more imminent. There is persuasive evidence that the Revolutionary Tribunal was set up with Roland specifically in mind. Throughout January he had been the subject of continuing diatribes in the Jacobin Club. A 12-page circular dated 7 January, directed almost entirely at him accusing him of tyranny and more besides, was approved for printing by eight Jacobins, including Desfieux and Chales.[18] On 3 March at the Jacobins, Collot set out a list of accusations against Roland (see below). Bentabole 'added further complaints', and specifically proposed that a revolutionary tribunal be instituted, 'to try this ex-minister and his accomplices'. He was supported by Desfieux.[19] Dan Edelstein, following James Godfrey, suggests it was then put *to* the Paris sections, rather than originating with them. On 10 March, with the support of radical deputies, the proposal reached the Convention, where it was the occasion of Danton's famous remark, 'Let us be terrible to dispense the people from being so.' Despite Girondin opposition, the Revolutionary Tribunal was approved.[20] None of this can have been reassuring, and one can be sure it was reported to the rue de la Harpe. That same evening, 10 March, there was a minor insurrection. Apparently inspired by the 'little-known men' (Hampson): Desfieux again, Varlet, Proli and Pereira, this consisted largely of an attack on 'Girondin' printing houses, notably that of Gorsas.[21]

In mid-March, a last-ditch attempt to get an understanding between Danton, the Montagne, and the Gironde appears to have been made, indicating that the gulf between the deputies was not irreversible even at this stage.[22] It came to nothing and as far as we know, the Rolands were neither involved nor did they interfere. However, the Dumouriez affair, which followed on its heels, was a disaster for Girondin sympathizers, and the Rolands in particular. The fortunes of war combined with politics to deal them a reeling blow. Danton had to extricate himself

[16] D. Williams (1980), p. 29 ff. Williams was certainly privy to a 'Girondist' attempt to try to recapture political control.

[17] BNF MSS, naf 6243.

[18] *Jacobins*, IV, pp. 55–6: Monestier, Bourdon, Desfieux, Chales, Drouet, La Faye, Mitie, Auvrest: mostly obscure men, but ball set rolling by others perhaps.

[19] *Jacobins*, V, pp. 64–5. The minutes clearly indicate that the idea of tribunal was linked to Collot's accusations.

[20] *AP*, LX, pp. 3–5, 50–1, 59–70 and 93–5; Jones (1988), p. 113; Hampson (1978/1988), p. 101, Edelstein (2009), pp. 135–6.

[21] Whaley (2000), pp. 125 ff. for details of the complicated factionalism between certain Paris sections and the Jacobins.

[22] Ibid., p. 128, and references.

from his well-publicized association with Dumouriez, and he very quickly moved in the opposite direction—in the course of his move, specifically attacking Roland as a form of self-defence.

General Dumouriez, whose republicanism was largely a matter of opportunism, had been having a good war on the whole (Valmy, Jemappes). But his crushing defeat by an Austrian army at Neerwinden on 18 March turned things round. On 24 March, a previous irritable letter from him, virtually declaring war on the Convention, was made public. The French War minister, Beurnonville, and four deputies were dispatched to arrest him (they included the Rolands' friend Bancal). Dumouriez promptly handed all five over to the Austrians. When his soldiers refused to follow him in marching on Paris, he fled to the enemy himself, taking along the duc de Chartres (the future king Louis-Philippe).

Now unmasked as a double-dyed traitor, Dumouriez was, of course, regarded as a 'Girondin' general. Any link to him was suspect. But Danton had been in close contact with him almost until the end, and had a lot of explaining to do in the fraught situation with which the Convention was now faced. France was at war with Britain and Holland (since 1 February) and Spain (since 7 March). Attempts to enforce the levy of soldiers in late February had triggered a serious uprising against the draft in western France (the Vendée revolt). In this siege atmosphere, the first calls started to be heard (from Marat) for the proscription of the Girondins, defined as those who had voted for the *appel au peuple,* but also referring to the Dumouriez affair. Danton chose to claim in the Convention on 27 March and 1 April during an attack on the Girondins—no reconciliations, now that he needed to defend himself—that Roland had written to Dumouriez asking him to help destroy the Montagnards. Roland indignantly denied any such thing, and both Norman Hampson, and Leigh Whaley dismiss this as a diversionary tactic in Danton's self-exculpatory speech. However, it was accepted by Robespierre, since it suited him to see Roland attacked—and, indeed, 'that was the last that was heard of [...] Danton's own relations with Dumouriez'.[23]

What Danton's aside meant for the Rolands, however, was that commissioners turned up at their flat to perquisition their papers, putting them under seals. Jean-Marie Roland had already been attacked by Collot d'Herbois at the Jacobins, with a copy of that speech sent to the Convention in April. It was frankly a rant, from which it is difficult to extract any serious charges. Collot attacked the famous 10 June letter as a 'ministerial intrigue' (despite what he had put his name to at the time, cf. Chapter 19) and accused Roland of sending 12 million *livres* to England,

---

[23] Hampson (1978/1988), pp. 107–9; Whaley (2000), pp. 132–3, on Danton's speech. See *Mém.,* pp. 159–62, for Mme Roland's account of their relations with Dumouriez in the winter of 1792–1793. It is possible Danton was referring to some earlier letter from Roland to Dumouriez, but without documentary evidence, any view is speculative.

preparing a federalist constitution, writing anonymous pro-English posters, grant-ing over-generous salaries to priests, wanting to restore the *corvée*, breaking seals, and helping emigrés escape.

Most of Collot's accusations were, as far as can be judged, false, imaginary, mis-interpretations, or unwarranted extrapolations from real events such as the sugges-tion of moving the capital in September (i.e. that the ministers would 'seize the public treasury'). Couched in language of rare violence, they kept Roland's name in view, while his papers were being examined.[24]

The Rolands' confiscated papers were the basis for the report to the Conven-tion in May by deputy Jacques Brival (and were made available to Camille Desmoulins for his *Histoire des Brissotins*). The Brival report was more serious than Collot's attack, because it was based on genuine documentation. Its chief purpose, to discover whether Roland had any links with Dumouriez, resulted however in a negative. It found only a few copies of anodyne letters written long beforehand, when Dumouriez was still untainted by suspicion. Danton had much more to fear on that score. Brival had to fall back on a mixture of odds and ends that Roland had (unwisely in some cases) kept in his desk. The report is fairly tendentious, muddling dates and misinterpreting documents, but the pub-lished letters which were authentic certainly did no good to Roland's reputation. (Brival selected those he thought most incriminating.) Roland had anticipated on 19 April that it would be easy for his enemies to pounce on certain words (such as 'a letter in English' to try to accuse him of intelligence with England): 'I want to say what these papers are, and I want them judged on the basis of the time they were written.'[25]

Probably the most damaging were a series of letters from a man named Gadol or Gadolle, obviously a paid agent for the ministry of the Interior. A former police-man, he had also worked for Danton.[26] All the dated letters—nine in all—are from October 1792, and most of them are addressed to Mme Roland, which suggests, interestingly enough, that she was running this agent. Gadol was reporting on public opinion, and using ministry money to buy rounds of drinks in order to influence his hearers. He was also trying to spread the idea of the necessity of the departmental force. A typical example:

> To Citizeness Roland, 18 October 1792: I am so well backed up by my five current colleagues in directing true public opinion that my opponents are starting to despair: the public cryers [of newspapers] are quieter and the cunning have realized how ridic-ulous their efforts are. As I amiably tell them.

---

[24] J. M. Collot, 'Rapport [...] sur les nombreuses accusations à porter contre l'ex-ministre Roland', 1793, *AP*, LXII, 18 April 1793, pp. 665–72.

[25] Quoted Le Guin (1966), p. 114. Retrospective accusations were becoming common coin. Cf: *Rapport fait par le citoyen Jacques Brival au nom du comité de sûreté générale relativement aux papiers trouvés chez le citoyen Roland*, Imp. Patriotique et républicaine, 1793, pp. 68, reproduced in Buchez and Roux (1833–1838) vol. 28, pp. 68 ff.

[26] *AP*, LXIII; see also Walton (2009), pp. 209 ff.

As Richard Cobb said about police spies, they tend to tell their masters what they want to hear, in this case:

> the agitators will soon lose hope of influencing the chamber; their supporters among the deputies will be more modest; the winter will see off gatherings in the open air; and it will all pass off peacefully. Marat and Robespierre are lost to right-thinking people (*les bons esprits*). Danton will be clever enough to abandon them: like the mole, he uses underground ways.[27]

Gadol was extremely long-winded, and all the more damaging, in suggesting that he had argued successfully against supporters of the Paris deputation, to whom he refers dismissively. Roland, by contrast, was referred to as 'le patriarche'. A well-known *sans-culotte* from Saint-Antoine, named Gonchon, whom Roland had also sent out to the provinces, was implicated in Gadol's manoeuvres, by being paid 50 *livres* to back up a petition in favour of the departmental force. (Gonchon managed to extricate himself on 24 April and was let go.)

Among other letters selected by Brival were: one from Barbaroux to Mme Roland, asking a favour for a fellow Marseillais (29 December); a couple from Brissot—one acknowledging a favour for the 'respectable scholar' Goussier, and the one attached to the list of names for appointments; one from Roland's Lyon friend, Vitet, deploring the pro-Chalier faction; and one from Lafayette's wife, thanking him for helping her to satisfy the administration and leave France.

The commissioners had also found a pile of letters—not reproduced by Brival for obvious reasons—sent to the king to protest at the sacking of the ministers in June. Roland said these had simply ended up in the offices of the ministry.

All these letters are useful to the historian, and clearly indicate that both Jean-Marie and Marie-Jeanne Roland were in touch with paid agents in early autumn 1792, listening to Parisian coffee-house gossip, and trying to influence it in their favour. The sums involved were pretty small beer, but there they were in black and white. They also shed light on the generally informal way friends like Brissot and Barbaroux dropped in notes about favours to be dispensed, and men to be placed—apparently going via Mme Roland, to whom Barbaroux joked, 'I won't tell you about this, because Danton doesn't wish you to be a minister'. In the same chatty letter, he apologized for not accepting a dinner invitation, but said he hoped to come with Rebecqui for a '*dîner* en famille'. Brival mentioned that he had not impounded Mme Roland's writing desk: 'but perhaps I should have'.

One can argue that Roland's agents were far from the only ones running round Paris, and that it was not surprising if the ministry tried to counter virulent attacks from the Montagnard press, on account of Roland's constant warnings about anarchy. It is also true that if these were the most damaging letters Brival could find, despite his evident wish to inculpate Roland, they do not amount to anything very much, certainly not royalism, federalism, or recent links with Dumouriez. But when all that is said, Gadol's letters in particular could be used as evidence of the 'perverting public opinion' charges, to which with unfailing regularity Robespierre and others kept returning.

Roland certainly thought it worth replying to Brival.[28] The letters had been cherry-picked and taken out of context, he wrote. On the important question of public opinion, he was prepared to justify his position rather robustly. It was the minister's job to have 'eyes and ears, and correspondents, where he cannot go in person', because he is ultimately responsible for the maintenance of order. After the September massacres, he had been receiving unsolicited anonymous information of all kinds, with no way of judging how accurate it was. He needed a few trusted agents, and Gadol's information had been found reliable: had M. Brival publicized *all* the agent's letters, which he took care not to do, they would have given a frightening picture of the 'doctrine and tactics of the men of blood who were frequenting all the public places to excite trouble'.

As for corrupting public opinion himself, back in August France was full of manoeuvring priests and aristocrats who were poisoning public opinion: he had sent out a 'luminous and fraternal correspondence', expressing true revolutionary principles, of which he was proud, and when he left the ministry there was no counter-revolutionary agitation in the provinces. In fact, 'the way I ran things, I would have been so well-apprised of troubles, that those presently [raging] in the Vendée would not, in my time, have reached the state of things we are seeing there now'. He also gave his reasons for resigning: his continued presence in the council of ministers would have caused division, because 'I fought in vain for courage and principle'. There was a lot more in the same vein, ending with a reference to the Viard case as a plot by Chabot, and to Collot, Gauthier, 'Dessieux', Robespierre, and Marat in particular for 'vomiting lies'. This defence was published on 21 May 1793, by a printer in the rue St Jacques. It has survived, but it is difficult to know who will have read it—probably not many people, as it was not officially reproduced anywhere.[29]

Although it was impossible to pin on the ex-minister of the Interior any charges relating to Dumouriez's treachery, the Brival report was another nail in his coffin, and it was widely available, being printed by order of the Convention, as was Collot's attack, not to mention Desmoulins's *History*. So instead of being in anonymous retirement, after having, he angrily thought, deserved well of the *patrie*, Roland's name was exposed to even more vilification if anything after his resignation than before. It was not surprising then that he went on being a target of threats and calls for his arrest. A note to Bosc says that, although the family had taken refuge outside central Paris for a few days, they were returning, since the 'fear of death is worse than death itself'. Mme Roland is described by Champagneux as

---

[28] *Observations de l'ex-ministre Roland sur le rapport fait contre lui par le député Brival*, 21 mai 1793, 12 pp, Paris: Delorme (BNF).

[29] As far as I can see, this was the only time Roland criticized Robespierre in print.

having been so exasperated by a plan to disguise herself as a peasant woman to escape, that she threw the costume across the room.[30]

But although she loyally supported her husband in his retirement—most of his letters to the Convention about the accounts are in her writing for instance—the most devastating emotional blow of all for Jean-Marie Roland, at this trying time, came from his wife. She had fallen in love with someone else and did not spare him the knowledge. Life in the little flat had become intensely miserable.

---

[30] Champagneux (1800), p. xxxvij. 'I'm ashamed of being made to play a part. If they are going to murder me, let them do it in my house: I owe it [to people] to give an example of firmness.'

25

January–November 1793
Marie-Jeanne in Love

I honour and cherish my husband in the same way that a daughter with feelings adores her virtuous father, to whom she would even sacrifice her love; but I have found the man who might be that love.

Mme Roland, *Mémoires*.[1]

The Rolands' marriage had lasted over twelve years since 1780. It had progressed through love, intimacy, affection, and companionship, ending with a rock-solid political partnership. It had survived the test of younger men (Lanthenas, Bosc, Bancal) falling under Marie-Jeanne's spell. In Bancal's case, she was seriously tempted to reciprocate, but the moment passed. In her memoirs, however, Mme Roland was quite explicit that she had fallen in love with someone. The memoirs don't say when this happened, or name the man. During her lifetime, as we saw, it was frequently, but wrongly reported by such writers as Hébert, that she had romantic intrigues with several young Girondins, in particular Barbaroux, who was strikingly handsome.[2] Her first editors, who did know the truth, discreetly edited out most references to her confession.

It was not until the chance discovery in 1864 of some letters to him, together with his portrait, that it became clear that the man was the Girondin deputy, François-Nicolas-Léonard Buzot, whom she had first met in 1791.[3] The five letters, the only ones to survive, were written by Mme Roland from prison between June and August 1793, and received by Buzot when he was on the run in Caen and Brittany, so they do not explain the origins of the liaison. Nothing remains of earlier correspondence during 1791–1792, when Buzot was in Evreux. At that stage, it seems their relations were simply friendly, and Mme Roland wrote affectionately of his wife.[4] They did not meet again until mid-September 1792, when Buzot was elected to the Convention. This lawyer from Normandy was in his early thirties, six years younger than Marie-Jeanne—dark-haired, tall, and always elegantly turned out.

---

[1] *Mém.*, p. 333.
[2] Le Guin (1966), p. 111: Dumouriez thought Servan was her lover.
[3] *Corr.*, II. p. 480, note: papers confiscated after Buzot's death, now in BNF MSS, naf 1730; portrait of Buzot found in 1863, now in the municipal library of Versailles; a medallion 7cm diameter, with a eulogy in Mme Roland's writing, reproduced Perroud (1905), II, Appendix, p. 437. Cf. *Corr.* II, Appendix R, p. 499; May (1970), p. 265 and note, Vatel, (1872), II, pp. 279 ff. etc.
[4] E.g. 9 September 1791: 'Tell them both [the Buzots] how dear they are to us,' *Corr.*, II, pp. 378, to Roland; ibid., p. 754; cf. *Mém.*, p. 101, on an informal dinner at the Buzots'.

Something happened, during the troubled months after September, to tip friendship over into passion. Mme Roland in her memoirs hints that it began in October: 'my only ambition at this time [October 1792] was to keep myself pure, and my husband's reputation intact'.[5] Another clue was that in December she sent a portrait of herself to Servan, saying 'after my husband, my daughter and one other person, you are the only one who has been made aware of [this picture]'.[6]

The relationship had both political and personal repercussions. With hind-sight—but there were murmurs at the time—Buzot has been seen as a mouth-piece for both the Rolands in the Convention. Almost at once, after his arrival, he tabled three resolutions calling for a report on the state of the Republic, and the capital; a bill against 'those inciting murder and assassination; and an 'armed public force' from the 83 *départements*, to protect the assembly. This was the 'guard' favoured by Mme Roland, and the 'large armed force' requested by Roland

Figure 6. Miniature on glass of Mme Roland, found with Buzot's effects. Reproduced with permission from the Archives Nationales, Paris AE VI A 54. Photo from the author's collection.

[5] *Mém.*, p. 23.
[6] *Corr.*, II, p. 446. Buzot certainly had a version of this miniature portrait on glass of Marie-Jeanne Roland: it was found among his effects referred to in note 3, and is now in the Archives Nationales, see Figure 6.

in his report of 23 September.[7] Although voted for, the force was never formed. Buzot also warmly supported Roland's reappointment ('he is my friend'), and became a committed Brissotin. He voted for the *appel au peuple* and a reprieve for the king. More provokingly to some on the left, on 4 December, he proposed (and carried) the motion that the death penalty be applied to anyone seeking to restore the monarchy 'under any form', something interpreted as a deliberate attack on Orléans (aka Philippe Egalité, then a Montagnard deputy). Buzot was a regular dinner guest at the Hotel de l'Intérieur that autumn. To what extent his interventions were inspired by Mme Roland is unknowable, although that has not prevented such assumptions.

Inside the marriage, the relationship came as a devastating blow to Jean-Marie Roland. We do not know when he was told. Mme Roland later wrote:

> while I remained faithful to my duties, my ingenuous nature was unable to conceal the feelings that I was suppressing for their sake. My husband, a man of extreme sensitivity, both in affection and self-love, was unable to tolerate the slightest alteration of his rule (*empire*); his imagination painted things in the darkest colours, his jealousy irritated me; happiness had fled far away from us; he adored me, I was sacrificing myself to him, and both of us were unhappy.[8]

In other words, she made a clean breast of her love for Buzot to Jean-Marie, while assuring him that she would remain technically faithful to her marriage vows. The affair did remain platonic, as the letters make clear, consistent with the character of both lovers.

In her memoirs, Mme Roland made both explicit and veiled references to Buzot. She openly described him as 'of elevated character, proud mind, effervescent courage, a man of feeling, ardent and melancholy'. 'He would forget the universe in the sweetness of private virtues [if he found] a heart worthy of his'—the world well lost, in other words. She also made a point of praising all his initiatives in the Convention.[9] As devoted readers of Rousseau, she and Buzot perhaps imagined themselves tragic figures in a novel. Partly for security reasons, but it is a Rousseau-esque name, Marie-Jeanne referred to herself as 'your Sophie'.[10] Behind Sophie is perhaps *Julie*. Roland, however, was unwilling to play the part of Julie's all-forgiving, all-understanding husband, Wolmar.[11] He had even, unwisely, confided in a friend, and the gossip appeared in Desmoulins's *History*: 'Jérôme Pétion told Danton in confidence that "what makes poor Roland saddest about [the perquisition in April] is that people will discover his domestic sorrows and how bitter being a cuckold is to the old man, troubling the serenity of that great soul".' Desmoulins reported—regretfully—that no such private papers were found.[12] Perhaps, from

---

[7] Buzot got the principle voted next day, and reported on 8 October cf. *Corr.*, II, p. 435, Mme Roland to Bancal, 5 September: 'If the *départements* don't send a guard for the Assembly and the Council, you will lose them both'.

[8] *Mém.*, p. 333.

[9] Ibid., pp. 99–101.

[10] *Corr.* II, p. 509: 'How many tears I have seen this poor Sophie shed, as she kisses your letters and your portait!'

[11] Roulston (2010), chapter 2, on the representation of marriage in *La Nouvelle Héloïse*.

[12] Desmoulins (1874), p. 759.

Pétion's remarks, Roland suspected his wife was lying about her faithfulness. She, in turn, said little in her memoirs about the twelve years of affectionate marriage. The days of 'Bonjour Loup!' were over.[13]

Roland was not the only one in the know. Lanthenas had guessed. The couple's protégé had been living under the same roof, in the ministry. This long-lasting friendship, to everyone's unhappiness, now collapsed. A series of increasingly distressed letters from Mme Roland, probably from November–December 1792, traces an irrevocable break. Her key letter, in a sequence moving from affectionate reproach to stinging rebuke, goes as follows:

> You are making me desperately unhappy, because I hate to be the cause of pain, because I am attached to you, and dread the thought of causing you distress. But even if you were a thousand times right, the hold over me [*empire*] which I have recognized is established and I can no longer resist it. [...] I ask that you have the generosity to be my friend. This effort will prevent many mishaps, but none of them will be able to change my destiny.[14]

Decoded, this means that Lanthenas knew about Buzot, as emerges from other letters: 'If you feel able to come and see me and behave properly, I will receive you with the affection you deserve. But I warn you, I will not tolerate a third scene.'[15]

Lanthenas was simultaneously distancing himself from the Gironde. Mme Roland, perhaps mistakenly, assumed that sentiment, rather than politics, was the real reason for his estrangement. She later wrote, rather cruelly:

> When Lanthenas, [...] happy with what he had [i.e. friendship] as long as others did not obtain anything more, realized that I was not immune from feeling, he became unhappy and jealous... and he became distant from us, imagining the worst.[16]

By 20 January, the break was complete: a dated note coolly addresses him as 'Monsieur'.[17]

Whatever Lanthenas's faults, he did not gossip to Roland—their own split had a political edge. When Lanthenas's brother contacted the ex-minister in February, asking for news, Roland wrote to his former friend in bewilderment 'Although we lived under the same roof for six months, I have hardly seen you, and have not been privy to your thoughts: people have told me that our opinions have been getting further and further apart. [...] I have to believe that what you [now] are towards me is what you have wanted to be.'[18] In March, Lanthenas sent Roland his educational plan, with a bitter note:

> I want him to see, when he reads it, whether he was right to abandon a friend whose constant friendship went back eighteen years for new friends whom his elevation alone

---

[13] May (1970), p. 249, suggests that Roland offered her a divorce, but cites no source. *Corr.*, II, p. 529: 'the jealousy of the unhappy R[oland] has given away my secret by confiding in several people'.

[14] *Corr.*, II, p. 453; Perroud dates these letters from November, cf. ibid., p. 703.

[15] *Corr.*, II, p. 456 etc.   [16] *Mém.*, p. 334.   [17] *Corr.*, II, p. 466.

[18] BNF MSS, naf 6241, February 1793.

procured him; [his] foolish vanity and demented course of action, surrounding himself with all their follies, are the only reason for the persecution he still suffers.

This seems to indicate Lanthenas's definitive break with the Gironde, though personal animosity against Buzot is not impossible. Roland retorted that Lanthenas
had abandoned *him*, by his silence in the Assembly: he had not made a single new
friend: 'Moved entirely by fear and cowardice, you abandoned an old friend to the
insolent attacks of a band of brigands whose influence you feared.' Lanthenas did
stand up to Marat in May, yet for some reason Marat contemptuously crossed him
off the list of proscribed Girondin deputies on 2 June: 'Lanthenas is feeble-minded,
and not worth bothering about.' The idealistic educator ended up disorientated,
and with friends in both camps: he made no attempt to defend the arrested Girondins (as 75 deputies did), but survived in a kind of limbo. Bosc later shook his head
over him, and Mme Roland commented that Lanthenas ended up 'less than nothing, despised by both sides'.[19]

The love affair with Buzot was even more impossible than the earlier flirt with
Bancal. Mme Roland might have been able to foresee a future without her older
and ailing husband, but Buzot was married, and what was worse, she liked his wife;
the Buzot marriage, although arranged, was marked by affection and duty. Marie-
Jeanne's feelings of guilt may explain the complete absence of mention of Buzot's
wife in her letters to him, although she speaks a great deal of her husband's
jealousy.

The atmosphere in the rue de la Harpe was miserable, as she tells us. At the
ministry the Rolands could have separate quarters, but in the cramped little flat,
accommodating Eudora and Fleury as well, they had to share a bedroom, night
after night. Since so few letters survive from this period, it is hard to know quite
what kind of social life they had, removed from the regular entertaining in the
rue Neuve-des-Petits-Champs, but we do not have to take literally Mme Roland's claim that they saw 'very few' people at this time. She still had relatives in
Paris. Some members of the inner circle remained close, and were probably frequent visitors—Bosc, Bancal, Barbaroux, Brissot, Louvet. Presumably, Buzot
was no longer welcome, but we do not know how this was handled (his absence
might arouse comment). The Panckoucke family were in touch. There were also
English visitors with whom we know the couple still had links: Tom Paine and
David Williams, and perhaps especially Helen Maria Williams, who lodged with
her mother in the rue de Lille, a mile away. Helen Williams later wrote that
throughout the spring before the 'fatal 31 May, the Girondin deputies and Barère
spent most of the evenings at our house'.[20] The two women knew each other
from at least the previous summer: Helen Maria Williams referred warmly to
Mme Roland's 'full dark eyes', which 'beamed with the brightest rays of intelligence'. She had heard her talking at the ministry with 'an eloquence peculiar to
herself', and Mme Roland offered to put in a word for Bancal when he fell for

[19] *Corr.*, II, Appendix L, pp. 688–708.
[20] See Kennedy (2002), and Williams (1796), pp. 195–6.

the young Englishwoman: Helen Maria claimed she had persuaded him to vote against the king's death.[21] Possibly the would-be lovers, Marie-Jeanne and Buzot, met on this neutral territory, which we know them both to have visited. However, the hopelessness of the affair must have prompted Mme Roland towards the end of May to give up waiting and prepare to take Eudora back to the Beaujolais. It should not have been too difficult, but it never happened.

---

[21] *Corr.*, II, pp. 466–9, undated letters, possibly January 1793.

26

31 May 1793

One Night in Summer

Everything had long been heralding the approach of some necessary crisis. [...] Energetic characters hate uncertainty. [...] The sound of the cannon of alarm, and the agitation of the day excited me with the interest that great events inspire, without any painful emotion.

Mme Roland, Memoirs.[1]

The Roland household was destroyed irrevocably on the evening of 31 May 1793. For months, the unhappy couple had been waiting for permission to leave Paris, as Roland sent request after fruitless request for his accounts to be cleared. Mme Roland obtained passports for herself and her daughter, although they had been held up (she says) by 'Maratists'. Unluckily, she fell ill during the last week of May, when she was due to get final clearance. The insurrection of 31 May put an abrupt end to her plans.[2]

The ever-increasing confrontations in the Convention between the Gironde and the Montagnards, with Paris as their battle ground, continued through April and May. On 14 April, the Girondins unwisely had Marat impeached for a Jacobin circular attacking those who voted for the *appel au peuple*. But this backfired badly when the Revolutionary Tribunal acquitted him, to popular rejoicing, on 24 April. The attempt had breached parliamentary immunity and that would now be turned on them. Particularly provocative was Isnard's foolhardy declaration on 25 April: 'if ever there is an attack on national representatives, I declare in the name of all of France, Paris will be annihilated: soon people will be searching on the banks of the Seine to see if it ever existed'.[3]

On 1 May, the Convention was surrounded by demonstrators calling for the *maximum* on bread; spring was, as Roland had predicted, always a difficult time for food prices. The Convention yielded under pressure, and thereafter the Gironde more openly spoke against threats from the Paris crowd against the elected deputies. Calls from some Paris sections grew for the Convention to be purged of deputies who were thought to have wanted to 'protect the tyrant', and/or who 'oppose cheap bread'. On 24 May, the Girondin-dominated Commission des Douze had Hébert

---

[1] *Mém.*, p. 36.
[2] Had they gone home, they would probably have been caught up in Lyon's fate, as Dominique was.
[3] Quoted Hardman (1973), p. 67.

arrested, something he never forgave, despite his release a few days later. On 26 May, Robespierre had 'invited the people' to rise up against 'the corrupt deputies'.

Even so the circumstances of the rising of 31 May remain rather obscure. Both the existing Commune and the Jacobins in the Convention were apparently out-flanked by an insurrectionary 'revolutionary committee', sitting in the archbishop's palace (the Evéché). The tocsin was rung early in the morning. The city gates were closed, and a new commander of the National Guard (Hanriot) named. There was confusion both about who was leading the insurrection and what its aims were. As far as the Convention was concerned, a petition calling for the proscription of named deputies associated with the Gironde was eventually referred to the Com-mittee of Public Safety and the agitated crowds that had gathered went home. The proscription of the Girondins would have to wait another couple of days.[4]

However, for the Rolands, 31 May was the beginning of the end. As Mme Roland narrates in detail in her memoirs, on hearing bells rung from Notre-Dame, just across the river from her, in the early hours, she at first felt a paradoxical sense of relief that there would be some resolution of what she saw as the Convention's pusillanimity. Friends arrived, suggesting that Roland contact their local section (Beaurepaire), where he had supporters. They agreed he might do well not to sleep at home that night. All the same, she felt no sense of personal danger herself. At five-thirty in the afternoon, six men appeared at the door, and read to Roland an order from the 'revolutionary committee' for his arrest. The decision to arrest him appears to relate to an overall plan to apprehend the 'three Girondin ministers' at the same time as proscribing the deputies, since orders went out to arrest Clavière and Lebrun, who were still in post—on what charge is doubtful. The Committee of Public Safety, on the other hand, had earlier sent a message to the Commune saying that the Convention would guard its ministers (which did not stop them being arrested on 2 June). Roland, however, argued with his visitors, saying he knew of no law requiring him to submit to such an authority and that they would take him only by violence. The men politely agreed to consult the Commune and some of them left.[5]

At this point in the evening, Marie-Jeanne seems to have taken leave of her senses, embarking on a frantic and quixotic series of journeys, which she describes in her memoirs as if in a film. She decided to denounce to the Convention the attempt to arrest her husband, which she considered isolated and outrageous. No doubt she was remembering her moment of triumph, but cannot have grasped what had been happening in the interim. She took a cab to the Convention, dressed in her 'morning dress with a black shawl', to veil her face. She pretended to be 'a Robespierre fan' to get in, and passed a letter through to the president, but finding it was not being read, asked someone to fetch—of all people—Vergniaud.

---

[4] See Slavin (1986), p. 87: Garat claimed it was organized by the 'men of the Café Corrazza': Gus-man, Proli, Desfieux, plus Chabot and Collot. According to Guérin (1968), I, pp. 136–43, key men included Desfieux, Proli, Dobsen, and Varlet. On Hanriot as *septembriseur*, Jones (1988), p. 353.

[5] Slavin (1986), pp. 105, 116. NB Slavin's account pp. 118–19, based on contradictory reports, while inaccurate on certain details, suggests that the 'Roland Affair' was crucial in the power struggle, which might explain why Mme Roland became a pawn.

At his wits' end himself, no doubt, Vergniaud warned her that it was most unlikely the Convention would consider her letter. Leaving a warning note at Louvet's address, she returned by cab and on foot to the rue de la Harpe, where she arrived 'dripping with sweat', to find that Roland was no longer there. Following a further inconclusive visit from the officers, he had opted for discretion, and left the flat by a back entrance via the landlord's lodging. This led into the street behind—the rue des Maçons-Sorbonne, today the rue Champollion. Marie-Jeanne set off using the same route. Guessing wrong at her first port of call, she found him in the second safe house where she looked. This must have been at the lodgings of nearby friends—probably Creuzé-Latouche, in the rue Hautefeuille, 'two minutes away'.

In the memoirs, she says simply: 'I found him there.' Was it at this meeting, or earlier in the day that Henri Agasse, Panckoucke's son-in-law, offered his help? He later wrote that the day Mme Roland was arrested, he had begged her to escape, but could only obtain her consent to her husband's going away. She would stay and face all-comers, since she 'had nothing to reproach herself with'. He called her obstinacy 'incomprehensible', since 'alas! They hated the wife as much as the husband'. Although offered a passport and a disguise, she would have none of it. However, at this hurried conference, Roland himself was evidently offered the means to escape.[6]

It was the last time Jean-Marie and Marie-Jeanne were to see each other. Rushed and uncertain, they must have agreed a provisional plan. Roland would be helped by friends to vanish, while his wife returned to their daughter in the flat. Jean-Marie Roland's escape from the city was apparently engineered by the faithful Louis Bosc (who had had a scare at his office that same morning). On 2 June, both men managed to cross the barriers and reach Sainte-Radegonde priory, Bancal's property near Montmorency, where Bosc was lodging. Roland probably stayed there a couple of weeks, long enough to hear that the Girondins had been proscribed and were under house arrest—unless like Brissot, Pétion, Buzot, Barbaroux, and others, they had been warned and escaped. Roland made no effort to contact anyone, as far as we can tell, but went north, possibly to Amiens. By 20 June, we know that he was being lodged in Rouen by his old friends the Malortie sisters (who showed great courage in the circumstances). He would effectively stay hidden there for the remaining months of his life. Very little is known about what he thought, wrote, or did between June and November.[7]

Marie-Jeanne meanwhile continued her demented odyssey through the evening of 31 May, returning once more to the Convention after ten at night, and apparently finding that everyone had gone home. Shocked at what she thought a dereliction of duty, she returned home by cab—befriending a stray dog on the way, with whom she seems to have, perhaps understandably, identified. Having gone to bed, she was aroused in the small hours of 1 June by another knock on the door.

[6] BNF MSS, naf 9533.
[7] See *Corr.*, II, Appendix K, pp. 681–2; he may have been helped by his old friend Pasquier, alerted by Mme Roland, *Mém.*, p. 40.

In her memoirs, she poses the rhetorical question 'Why did I go back home?' when it was obviously dangerous. She claims that she thought to kill her in her own home would be an atrocity her enemies would not dare commit; that to arrest her could hardly be of any interest to them, but that if the massacres began again, she would rather die and be a glorious victim, while Roland might be better able to bide his time. Besides, she did not want to endanger any of her friends. All this was written in a kind of brainstorm in the early days of her confinement, while she may have believed things might settle down.

A delegation from the *comité révolutionnaire* now ordered her to come to the Abbaye prison under arrest, and for seals to be placed on her flat. She says correctly that neither this, nor another order from the Commune, gave any legitimate motive for the arrest. Deciding resistance might do more harm than good, despite the doubtful legality of the procedure, she consented, first packing a bag for herself and sorting out clothes for Eudora. A crowd of people milled round the tiny apartment, handling (and sometimes pocketing) household goods, until 7 a.m., when she bade farewell to her tearful daughter and the distressed servants, Fleury and Lecoq, and found herself walking between two lines of armed men to a cab which drove her the short distance to St Germain. She was probably shaken, though she does not admit it, by the hostility of a few women who had gathered outside the house. Eleven-year-old Eudora was taken round to the Creuzé-Latouche family, who now looked after her for several weeks with their own children, pretending that she was their adopted daughter.[8]

There were relatively few women in the Abbaye prison, and both the concierge, Devacquerie, and his wife went out of their way to make Mme Roland's arrival reasonably comfortable, despite the risks. In a state of high exaltation that lasted for several days, she wrote that she would not exchange for the happiest days of her life the first moments she felt herself alone, in the small room hastily prepared for her. She was buoyed up at first by a feeling of completely righteous anger, which translated itself in a fury to write, as well as by a kind of relief that she could concentrate on her private love for Buzot, without any conflict of duty to her husband. Again, her tendency to view herself as an incarnation of Julie in *La Nouvelle Héloïse* seems to have bolstered her resistance—since she was convinced that she would soon be released.

Grandpré, the inspector of prisons, appointed by her husband and an obvious ally, arrived to see her at once. He urged her to petition the Convention about her arrest, which he too considered a mistake. Her letter was uncompromising, calling for the proper application of the law, such as a reason for holding her and interrogation within 24 hours. She ended it by referring to Roland as 'that irreproachable man'. 'If my crime is to have shared his severity of principle, the energy of his courage and his ardent love of liberty, I admit I am guilty and await my punishment.' Grandpré, after consulting Champagneux, returned on the morning of 2 June,

---

[8] Jacques-Antoine Creuzé-Latouche (1749–1800), deputy from Châtellerault, moderate, but not proscribed on 2 June.

and asked her to tone down the letter, and to put in a covering note to Garat, so that he would present it to the president of the Convention.[9]

This was all wasted effort of course, since 2 June was the decisive *journée* when, surrounded by a hostile crowd, as well as the National Guard, the Convention, having at first tried to march out of its chamber in the Tuileries, was forced to retreat, and ended up agreeing to the proscription of 29 Girondin deputies and the arrest of the other two ministers. Mme Roland heard the disturbances, but it was only next morning when she was given a newspaper that she realized what had happened. This explained Grandpré's anxiety (he had tried in vain to get her letter read). In the 36 hours since her arrest, the situation had completely altered. From now on, while powerless to move, she would be guilty by association with what soon turned into charges of treason and fomenting civil war.

Why were the Rolands singled out *before* the proscription of the Girondins? Mme Roland appears to have been the only person of note successfully arrested before 2 June, and that was clearly because her husband could not be found. While the couple were closely associated and personally friendly with several of the proscribed deputies, they were formally outside the political arena, and it is difficult to see how they could be charged with any crime against the Republic. Despite Roland's links with moderate opinion in Lyon, the attempt to arrest him was unconnected with the revolt of the southern city on 29 May, which was not reported in Paris until 2 June. Once it was known, he was naturally suspected of involvement. He no doubt sympathized, but there is no evidence that he contacted the insurgents, let alone that he went there. Essentially, it was a matter of retrospective guilt by association, repercussions from the supposed *bureau d'esprit public*, and having the wrong opinions and friends.[10]

It is also perhaps an early case of the power of the media. All those bitter public attacks on the Rolands had kept their names in the public eye all spring—the Brival report dated from only a few weeks earlier. Neither Marat nor Hébert had stopped attacking them in print. Some of the men responsible for the risings of 31 May and 2 June (Desfieux, Proli, and others in the Commune) seem to have had a personal vendetta against Roland for his constant criticism of the Paris authorities. However, it also seems likely that the Girondin ministers were simply identified with the Girondin deputies. The harsh line taken with Mme Roland— imprisoning her with *no option of house arrest*—suggests she was being used as a counter in the early stages of the 31 May–2 June insurrection.

---

[9] *Mém.*, pp. 45–9; Grandpré helped others, Beugnot (1959), p. 117, and was briefly imprisoned after Thermidor.

[10] Guérin (1968), I, p. 144. On the Lyon insurrection see Edmonds (1990); Hanson (2003); Hardman (1973), pp. 67–74. Lebrun escaped, but was recaptured and executed in December; Clavière committed suicide in the Conciergierie on 8 December. 'Guilt by association', Le Guin (1966), p. 113.

27

June–October 1793

'A la vie et à la mort'[1]
Prison and Flight

> Today on the throne, tomorrow in irons. That is the lot of virtue in revolutionary times.
>
> Opening lines of Mme Roland's memoirs.

Marie-Jeanne Roland had no idea how long she would be in prison, but she was confident that there was no case against her, especially as a woman. To date, there had been few serious condemnations by the Revolutionary Tribunal, designed to handle 'attacks on the unity and indivisibility of the republic'. Twelve days after her arrest, she was interrogated in the Abbaye prison, by A.-C. Louvet, a police administrator of the Commune. The questions were disquietingly loaded, but she fended them off with stonewalling answers, in particular saying that 'being only a woman', she was not involved in public affairs.[2]

On 24 June, she was suddenly freed: it had been recognized in retrospect that her arrest was, indeed, unconstitutional; but this was a cat-and-mouse manoeuvre, 'a refinement of cruelty', and she was re-arrested, on different charges, in the name of the Committee of Public Safety, as soon as she set foot on the stairs in the rue de la Harpe. She was taken to a different prison, the former convent of Sainte-Pélagie, near the Jardin des Plantes, just down the road from her own convent school. There she would remain all summer, until 31 October.

Mme Roland spent just over five months in all in prison; five months that secured her place in history, because in her 'cellule', like the one she had as a child, she had little to do but think and write. She wrote and wrote. Hardly any leading revolutionaries were able to set down at such length, so close to events, their views, judgements, and accounts of the Revolution. Brissot's memoirs, probably begun earlier, concentrate on his youth; Buzot's, Pétion's, and Barbaroux's, written on the run, are hasty and scrappy by comparison. There is nothing of the kind by Danton,

---

[1] Mme Roland to Bosc, 1 June 1793, from the Abbaye: 'Je vous embrasse cordialement; à la vie et à la mort, estime et amitié,' *Corr.*, II, pp. 469–70.

[2] *Mém.*, pp. 95–7: e.g. 'Did I not have links to traitors?' Her own version printed in *Thermomètre*, 21 June; cf. *Mém.*, pp. 375–7, and *Mém.*/Perroud (1905), II, pp. 431–3. The Revolutionary Tribunal had tried only 60 cases by 1 June 1793, with 18 death sentences. Most of the accused were acquitted.

Robespierre, Desmoulins, or Marat, or by the Girondins, such as Vergniaud, who were imprisoned.

Mme Roland also wrote letters, about thirty of which have survived. Trembling with anger, sorrow, excitement, exaltation, and despair, as the skies changed over her head, these writings track her changes of mood as she heard of outside events, over which she had no control, but which were spinning an inextricable web around her. As the civil war developed, many of her friends became prisoners or refugees accused of treason. The virtually non-existent grounds for her arrest in June hardened into charges, not unfounded of course, of 'being in contact with' persons who *by then* could be regarded as treasonous.

MATERIAL LIFE IN PRISON

In material terms, Mme Roland was subject to a Spartan regime, moderated by what friends tried to do for her. She was supposed to be kept 'au secret', meaning incommunicado, but her maid Fleury and her friend Sophie Grandchamp gained admittance almost at once. In her three weeks at the Abbaye, Mme Roland had an individual cell, 'about ten feet square' with a bed, table, and chair. Prison meals were supplemented by extras she could buy or receive from visitors. Ironically, Roland himself—another economy measure—had reduced the allowance for prisoners' keep, and when his wife tried to observe the basic regime (no chocolate for breakfast, no wine, very meagre rations) she became ill. She had to borrow money from her landlord, against funds stored in a locked desk in her apartment.[3]

In Sainte-Pélagie from 24 June, her conditions were worse at first. The ex-convent is visible on the Plan Turgot, opposite La Pitié. Sections of the eighteenth-century prison survive today in the rue du Puits de l'Hermite. She was put in a cell on the 'women's corridor' with paper-thin walls and on the top floor, where 'the heat was unbearable'. Her neighbours were 'corrupters of the young', i.e. brothel-keepers. In mid-July, thanks to Sophie Grandchamp and the concierge, Mme Bochaud, she was given a single room (not a cell) on the ground floor, with cupboards and even room for a piano. Despite some drawbacks, such as the dangerous proximity of a meeting room, the month from mid-July to mid-August was the most comfortable of her imprisonment. She wrote lyrically about how serene she felt with jasmine round the window and no jailer drawing bolts across at night.[4] She was moved back to a regular cell once a Commune official found she was getting this special treatment. By then, however, her fellow-prisoners were 'respectable women' and included Mme Pétion, so she had some companionship. In early September, some actresses from the Théâtre français arrived which sent the noise volume up. Evidently, prisoners could move about inside the prison for part of the day.[5]

---

[3] *Mém.*, pp. 54–5.   [4] Ibid., p. 183.
[5] Ibid., pp. 182–3, 190; 259 ('laughter in the next room').

In captivity, Mme Roland had two priorities—cleanliness, and the possibility of reading and writing. She often refers to her efforts to keep her cell as clean as possible. Above all she wanted writing materials and books: a remarkably Anglophile selection. With her she had brought James Thomson's *The Seasons*, 'a work I cherish for more than one reason'. She asked visitors to bring her Plutarch, David Hume's *History of England*, Sheridan's *Dictionary* to help her, and works by Shaftesbury. She particularly regretted Catharine Macaulay's ('republican') *History of England*, which she knew from a borrowed copy, probably Brissot's. We know that she was also reading Tacitus in prison.[6]

How did she obtain writing materials or conceal what she was doing from her jailers? Although she refers to subterfuge and being closely watched at times, she must have benefited from complicity. Inspector Grandpré, while unable to intervene with the judicial system, was in a position to improve her conditions, and the concierges, both at the Abbaye and at Sainte-Pelagie, were sympathetic. From them she bought a portable writing desk, pens, ink, and the notebooks of greyish paper that contain the memoirs. Above all, she could receive visitors, and a blind eye must have been turned to their comings and goings, as well as to what they carried. The *au secret* rule was a dead letter, except when someone in authority appeared.[7]

VISITORS

Mme Roland records that she saw Eudora only twice during June, accompanied by Fleury. She seems not to have seen her at all after that. 'With her blonde curls, innocent face, and her eleven years', her daughter was a target for abuse, and she feared for her if she visited the prison.[8] She also mentions 'four people' seeing her in the Abbaye: Bosc, Grandpré, Sophie Grandchamp, and Champagneux, still at the Interior ministry as Garat's right-hand man. Champagneux visited regularly during June and July, until he was arrested himself on 4 August.[9] He often stayed, 'from five till ten at night', which seems a generous dispensation, and took her small treats, pastries, and fruit.[10] Bosc, another frequent visitor was also under suspicion: he worked on after his scare on 31 May, but was sacked on 14 September. He retreated, 'disguised as a *sans-culotte*', to his lodgings at Sainte-Radegonde, but still managed a weekly visit until Mme Roland was transferred to the Conciergerie. Through his friendship with Thouin, at the Jardin des Plantes, he brought flowers to Sainte-Pélagie.[11] In the early weeks, both men smuggled out letters and sections

---

[6] Ibid., p. 50; letter to Buzot 22 June, *Corr.*, II, p. 483. *Seasons* bought for her by Roland in 1787, Kermina (1976), p. 37, still in family possession. See *Corr.* I, 17 January 1787, pp. 668–9: '*Mon bon ami*, when you want to give me a big present, buy Thomson for me: in English, and buy a translation. [...] I've marked places we can read together!'

[7] 'The tyrants spy on everything and forbid everything,' *Corr.*, II, p. 503; see Perroud 1905, p. lxii.

[8] *Mém.*, p. 180: Strangers pointed her out as the 'child of a conspirator. How well these cruel people know how to tear the heart of a mother!'

[9] Ibid., p. 183: Champagneux was arrested at Collot's request, *Corr.*, II, Appendix N, p. 719.

[10] Champagneux (1800), p. xliv.

[11] *Corr.*, II, Appendix K, pp. 682–3.

of her memoirs. It was probably through them that she communicated with her husband, since she knew he had reached Rouen, and received regular news of him.

Other visitors were part of the support system provided by Girondin families. Their networks were always rather vulnerable. Louvet's mistress, later his wife, Marguerite Denuelle, carried some messages. Vallée, a deputy from the Eure and friend of Buzot, brought Mme Roland letters from him in early July.[12] One network was based on the boyhood friendship of Brissot and Pétion. Arrested at home on 3 June, Pétion escaped to Normandy on the 25th, helped by the Goussard family. Alexandre Goussard was another childhood friend of Brissot's, and his wife, Marie-Anne-Victoire, née Goussier, brought letters from Buzot on her single visit to the Abbaye on 22 June. This 'good angel' left Paris with Mme Pétion for Normandy next day, but her sister carried on as go-between. The Goussier sisters devised an alternative name ('Sophie') for the prisoner to use.[13]

Claude-Romain Lauze-Deperret (1747–1793) a deputy from Bouches-du-Rhône and a friend of Barbaroux, was 'one of the most resolute adversaries of the Montagne, but also one of the most imprudent'.[14] Mme Roland was barely acquainted with him, but wrote to him on 5 June, asking him to help her get out of jail: 'I have a child, a family in tears, and I must not neglect any way of being restored to them.'[15] Lauze, who was not among the proscribed, did quite bravely speak up for her in the Convention on 7 June, backing Garat's effort: 'Some days ago, the minister of the Interior passed the Convention a protest from a citizeness who was taken by force from her home and sent to the Abbaye. But the letter has not been read out. This is Citoyenne Roland.' There were 'murmurs' and cries that this was nothing to do with the Convention.[16] She wrote again on 24 June, giving him her version of her interrogation, and referring to 'our friends under arrest'. It ended: 'burn this letter'. He didn't, nor did he destroy a little note telling him about her re-arrest that day—intending him to pass to the refugees in Normandy the information that she was now in Sainte-Pélagie. A third letter to Lauze in late June said, 'News from our friends is the only good thing that touches me. You have helped me to be able to experience this. Tell them that knowing of their courage and all they are capable of doing for liberty consoles me and replaces everything for me.' These letters were the only documentary evidence used to convict Mme Roland at her own trial. The last one was also cited by the public prosecutor (Fouquier-Tinville) during the Girondins' trial, with the comment that it proved Roland and his wife to be 'the main leaders of the faction and that Duperret [*sic*] was the central point of their correspondence'.[17]

---

[12] *Corr.*, II, pp. 497–8, and note.
[13] *Corr.*, II, pp. 507–10, 31 August 1793.
[14] *Corr.*, II, p. 475, Perroud's note. His name is variously given (Lauze de Perret, Du Perret, etc.).
[15] *Corr.*, II, p. 475, original in her dossier AN, W 297 dossier 227, piece 6.
[16] *Moniteur*, 8 June 1793, quoted *Corr.*, II, p. 478, note.
[17] *Corr.*, II, p. 492; *Actes,* p. 322. Lauze's reply (drafted on the back), made matters much worse: 'the whole of France will rise up and I already see civic crowns on your brow and that of your august spouse'. [!] ibid., p. 323.

Lauze-Deperret's willingness to help got him into deep trouble. It was to him that Charlotte Corday came from Caen with a letter of introduction from Barbaroux. On 12 July, Lauze escorted her to the ministry of the Interior (apparently both he and Barbaroux were unaware of her reason for coming to Paris). Corday engineered an interview with Marat on a fictional pretext next day and, as the world knows, stabbed him to death in his bath. Lauze was arrested shortly afterwards; his home was searched and seals placed on it. He had written at length, supportively—and to outside eyes very seditiously—to Mme Roland, and his fatal imprudence in failing to destroy his correspondence cost both of them dear.

Apart from political networks, Mme Roland had a number of women friends, who visited her. Her faithful friend from childhood, Soeur Sainte-Agathe (Angélique Boufflers) having retired from the no-longer-existing convent and living in poverty nearby, was one of them.[18] Helen Maria Williams also saw her:

> I visited [Mme Roland] in the prison of Sainte-Pélagie, where her soul, superior to circumstances, retained its customary serenity and she conversed with the same animated cheerfulness in her little cell as she used to do in the hotel of the minister. She had provided herself with a few books, and I found her reading Plutarch. She told me she expected to die, and the look of placid resignation with which she spoke of it convinced me that she was prepared to meet death with a firmness of manner worthy of her exalted character. When I enquired after her daughter, an only child of thirteen [*sic*] years of age, she burst into tears.

Miss Williams smuggled out some papers, but had to destroy them in panic when she was arrested herself.[19]

One visitor from the past was Henriette Cannet. She had travelled to Paris, apparently at Jean-Marie Roland's request. 'Filled with terror' on hearing of his wife's second arrest, 'he sent a person to try everything'—a plan for Henriette to exchange clothes with her and stay behind, while Marie-Jeanne escaped. Predictably, she wouldn't hear of it, saying she could not live knowing she had endangered a friend's life.[20]

The person who left the most detailed account of these months was her former friend, Sophie Grandchamp. Their relations were complicated: Sophie's memoirs hint at past differences, but she now became a valued support. Through her connection with Grandpré, Sophie could visit frequently and bend the rules. When she came hurrying to the Abbaye, Mme Roland immediately enlisted her as a courier for her memoirs: she was already writing her *Notes historiques*, 'every morning'. Aware of the dangers of writings falling into hostile hands, Sophie cautioned her against sending letters to the wrong people, a warning that was disregarded. After the move to Sainte-Pélagie, they both assumed that Mme Roland would be in prison 'until the peace'. Sophie brought paper and drawing materials, and even contrived to have the piano delivered. She remembered coming 'every other day

---

[18] Sainte-Agathe, *Corr.*, II, p. 10 and Appendix U, pp. 785–7.
[19] Williams (1794) pp. 197–8.
[20] See *Corr.*, II, p. 498, Henriette visited on 6 July. Buzot also tried to arrange her escape.

after dinner', and was able to continue her visits through the next three months, until Mme Roland's last night in Sainte-Pélagie, 30 October.

Towards the end of her imprisonment, several of her visitors were themselves in custody, or had to lie low. One final good Samaritan appeared unexpectedly. The 'Jany', to whom some of her last letters were addressed, was identified years later as Edme Mentelle (1730–1816) who taught geography at the Ecole militaire. He had benefited from Roland's patronage, acquiring one of the coveted Louvre apartments. Mentelle made contact with Mme Roland after seeing his long-time friend Brissot in prison in September. Although failing to get official permission from Fouquier-Tinville, he managed to visit 'when our friend Bosc was under threat himself. [Mme Roland] entrusted to me her memoirs, her watch, the portrait of her husband and one of herself, and I kept these precious objects, unknown even to my wife, in the lodging in the Louvre which M. Roland had granted me'.[21]

LOVE AND MARRIAGE: THE DIFFERENCE

During summer 1793 then, Mme Roland, although suffering the privations of a Paris prison, and longing for fresh air and freedom, was at the centre of an active network of well-wishers and friends, all willing to risk contacting her. By contrast, Roland, from whom she had hardly spent a night apart during the previous two years, was, as she wrote to Buzot in June, 'more captive than I am myself'. Obliged to keep a low profile, seeing hardly anyone, he was closeted in the Malortie house in central Rouen. She feared 'for his head and his sanity', but wrote that she owed him a sacrifice, in return 'for his sorrows'. 'By putting [me] on trial his enemies might be less furious against him.'[22]

Her references to Roland become colder, however, over the summer, no doubt because his letters had become painful to read: 'He is in R[ouen] near you, with old friends, well-hidden, and kindly cared for, pampered even, so I needn't worry on that score; but in a moral condition so sad and so overwhelming that if I get out of here, I will have no choice but to go to his side.'[23] In late August, 'Sophie' was writing to Buzot that 'her *old uncle* is in a horrible state of collapse. His life, although threatened, might be prolonged a long time, but [he is] weak, angry, and difficult. He finds this life torture, and is making it so to those around him.' 'He is incapable of any action [...] he has given himself up to melancholic inaction.'[24] Roland had unwisely let her know that his memoir would be harsh on Buzot for ruining his marriage. Perhaps he had even more unwisely sent her a copy. As she wrote to Mentelle later:

> Would you believe, he had actually written about it, with all the fury and false interpretations of an irritated soul who detests his rival, and wants to deliver him up to public obloquy, and it was only very recently that I managed to prevail and get these

[21] BNF MSS, naf 6241, letter to Champagneux, 1800, quoted Perroud (1896), p. 28. See Brissot (1912), p. xvi, re Mentelle: Brissot met his wife at his house. For letters to 'Jany' see *Corr.*, II, September–October 1793.

[22] *Corr.*, II, pp. 484–5.

[23] *Ibid.*, p. 498, to Buzot, 6 July 1793.   [24] *Ibid.*, p. 509, 31 August 1793.

venomous writings burned? Can you imagine how indignant their existence made me, for one thing, and for another actually enhanced the feelings whose object I saw being so unjustly slandered?'[25]

This marriage was well and truly over.

On the other hand, Mme Roland went on being committed to Roland's record in office. She stoutly defended him in an (unsent) letter to Robespierre written on 14 October: 'Robespierre, I defy you not to believe that Roland is an honest man; you may disagree with his views on this or that, but your conscience must tell you of his probity.'[26] In her 'Observations' in mid-October on Amar's act of accusation against the Girondins, she put up an extremely detailed and robust defence of her husband's ministry.

But all her previous warm affection for him seemed to have drained away. References to him in the last pages of her memoirs, written about this time, are respectful, but no more (encouraging readers to think this bleak relationship was the whole story of the marriage). Her farewell to him is written in a very different tone from that to Buzot. To Roland she wrote: 'Forgive me, respectable man, for disposing of a life I had devoted to you; your sorrows might have attached me to it, if I had been in a position to temper them; the faculty to do so has been taken from me, and you are losing but a shadow, a useless object of desperate anxieties.'[27]

To Buzot by contrast, she poured out her heart in Rousseau-esque fashion: 'I press [your letters] to my heart, I cover them with kisses.' 'Anyone who can love as we do carries with him the principle of the greatest and best actions, the prizes of the most painful sacrifices, the compensation for all ills. Adieu, my beloved.' She ends with a deist prayer:

> And you (*toi*), whom I dare not name! [...] You, whom the most terrible of passions did not prevent from respecting the barriers of virtue, will you be distressed to see me going before you to a place where we will be able to love each other without crime, where nothing will stop us being united? There all deadly prejudices, arbitrary exclusions and hatred, and all kinds of tyranny fall silent. I will wait for you there.[28]

It was only long after the tragic end of all concerned in this love triangle that the evidence came to light, but it is conclusive. Mme Roland, with a certain ruthlessness, had written the husband, to whom she was once so close, out of both her memoirs and her life. She would see neither husband or lover again and had to face her last months relying only on herself.

THE CHARGES AGAINST HER AND THE FATE OF THE GIRONDINS

After her first interrogation, Mme Roland suspected that her enemies were determined to prosecute her. Her name was bandied about in the Jacobin press—in

---

[25] *Ibid.*, p. 529.
[26] Not a plea for clemency, but a protestation of innocence, expressing criticism and a certain respect for the addressee. But Mme Roland decided Robespierre was beyond reaching. *Corr.*, II, pp. 522–6 [14 October 1793].
[27] *Mém.*, p. 342.   [28] *Corr.*, II, pp. 481, 500, *Mém.*, p. 342.

particular a notorious number of Hebert's *Père Duchesne* (20 June). This printed a fake 'interview' by 'le Père Duchesne', full of sexual innuendo. Writing as a 'Vendée general', to provoke 'this toothless old woman' into 'unbuttoning' and giving the game away ('le pot aux roses'), he claimed she confessed that her 'virtuous spouse' had 'paid an army to preach counter-revolution in the provinces', and that the Girondins were in league with the Vendéens and England. Civil war was being encouraged by 'my dear Buzot, my little Louvet, and the darling of my heart, the divine Barbaroux'.[29]

After her second arrest, Mme Roland realized that she was unlikely to be released without charge. Representatives of her local section, Beaurepaire, which was sympathetic to the Rolands (and got its knuckles rapped) had asked for reasons for her re-arrest: the Commune rejoined that it was on the 'newly-valid' grounds that she was in contact with the 'deputies under arrest'—*not* those on the run—and because her husband was 'stirring up civil war in Lyon'. Neither of these charges had any foundation.[30] Garat's attempt to intervene on her behalf was answered by Chabot:

> Citizen minister, the Committee of General Security gave as motive for the arrest of *la femme* Roland the escape by her husband, who at this very moment is fanning the flames of civil war in the *département* of Saône-et-Loire [i.e. in Lyon], and the complicity of this so-called [*prétendue*] Lucretia with her so-called virtuous husband, in a plan to pervert public opinion, through a so-called bureau of formation of the said public opinion. Since this trial will be linked to that of the grand conspiracy, Citizeness Roland will just have to wait for the general report on that, once we have saved the nation's finances by a grand plan, and thrown down the anchor of constitution concerning national education and the simplicity of the [criminal] code.[31]

She deemed this a ridiculous reply, but by late June the Convention was faced with what it described as the federalist revolt (the grand conspiracy). In Lyon, the radical city council under a pro-Chalier mayor had waged an aggressive campaign all spring against anyone identified as 'the rich'. Arrests and requisitions had alienated moderates, although 'the Jacobin municipality was no more capable than the Rolandins of solving the economic crisis'.[32] Roland's former allies were involved in the 29 May rising against Chalier—who was executed in July in horrific conditions (guillotine malfunction), turning him into a Jacobin martyr. So it was logical to imagine the ex-minister's involvement, although Mme Roland told Buzot on 22 June that she had dissuaded her husband from protesting to the Convention. The Vendée, meanwhile, was still in open revolt, while several other provincial centres were moved to protest against the *journées* of 31 May and 2 June, and the purge of the Girondins.

---

[29] Reproduced in *Mém.*/Perroud (1905), II, as Appendix, pp. 431–4; *Mém.*, pp. 375–7. Although not 'in league' with either the Vendée or England, her friends in Normandy were encouraging resistance to the purged Convention. That she was in sympathy with them is not in doubt.

[30] *Mém.*/Perroud, II, Appendix, the Commune's reply to the Beaurepaire section.

[31] Champagneux (1800), p. liiij; *Corr.*, II, pp. 490–1.

[32] Hanson (2003), p. 154, Edmonds (1990).

An army was being raised in Normandy, based on Caen where Buzot and Barbaroux had taken refuge.[33] There is no doubt that Mme Roland was wishing the rebels well, and was optimistic about their success, although she discouraged her friends from joining any army in person. She thought 'the majority of Parisians' should liberate Paris: it would be unwise to 'come marching in with battalions'. 'You will be even deadlier to [your opponents] staying where you are with perseverance, than by acts of war.' Rather they should wage a propaganda battle 'to keep people in good opinion through writings marked with the seal of truth'.[34] Had these letters been found, they might have condemned her far more obviously than the Lauze letters, but she still assumed in early July that the due process of law would be on her/their side: 'they may even drag me to the Revolutionary Tribunal, but then I would be able to defend myself, and that is why they are putting off trying the 32 [Girondins]'.[35]

However, within a week or two, the situation changed dramatically. On 13 July, a dissident army under the command of General Wimpffen was routed with hardly a shot fired at Brécourt, Pacy-sur-Eure, in Normandy. It happened on the same day, 13 July, that Charlotte Corday assassinated Marat, an event of which the immediate result was a massive popular demonstration commemorating the People's Friend and his transfer to the Pantheon. Vergniaud said of Corday, who went to her execution unflinchingly, 'She has done for us, but she has taught us how to die.' Mme Roland shed no tears for Marat, but recognized what a fateful blow this was to the Girondin cause.[36]

In the aftermath of the Brécourt debacle, Buzot, Barbaroux, Pétion, and others had fled. Buzot's house in Evreux was burnt down. The fugitives, now outlaws with only the clothes they stood up in, escaped westward to Brittany, then to Bordeaux. Mme Roland wrote on 31 August, as 'Sophie', referring to her unsuccessful attempt to get some money from Roland to help the refugees. She encouraged Buzot to think of sailing to America, in this last surviving letter to him. He took ship for Bordeaux on 20 September. The *Moniteur* of 16 October reported that 'almost all the fugitive deputies are in or near Bordeaux', and Mme Roland realized their danger, since the area had become politically hostile to them.[37] The net now tightened around the Girondin deputies still under arrest, and around herself. Although no official moves were made to put her on trial at this stage, she was anxious to finish her memoirs.

PRISON MEMOIRS

The book we now call Madame Roland's memoirs is a complicated text, with a no less complex publishing history. Existing versions depend on Perroud's 1905 edition,

---

[33] See Grall (1989). Buzot was protected by the Eure department. The deputies in Caen issued a manifesto saying: 'Being unable to fulfil our mandate, our first duty is to tell you this…we have been expelled by force,' Vatel (1872), II, p. 336.

[34] 'The majority of Parisians will open their arms to their brothers from the *départements*,' 7 July 1793., *Corr.*, II, pp. 503–4.

[35] Ibid., p. 499, 6 July 1793 and 504.

[36] On Marat and Corday, see Mazeau (2009); cf. *Mém.*, p. 184.

[37] *Corr.*, II, p. 763, Vatel (1872), I, p. xi.

based on uncensored manuscripts—the three sets of papers smuggled out of prison by Bosc, Sophie Grandchamp, and Mentelle. Instalments were copied for security, but the version now in the Bibliothèque Nationale is all in Mme Roland's handwriting. Other fragments entrusted to Champagneux and Helen Maria Williams were destroyed. Perroud thought there was an even fuller set of 'confessions', about Buzot, now lost.[38]

Mme Roland intended her writings to be published, if only after her death. She no longer believed it was a woman's place to keep silent. In this respect at least, she now parted company with Jean-Jacques Rousseau:

> If I had been able to live longer, I would have had only one temptation, to write the *Annals* of the century, and to be the [Mrs] Macaulay of my country; I was going to say the French Tacitus but that would not be modest... I can't get to sleep without reading a few paragraphs by him; it seems to me that we see things the same way, and with time, and an equally rich subject, it would not be impossible that I should express myself by imitating him.[39]

When she heard that someone in Champagneux's household had panicked and burnt her first batch of manuscripts, she wrote in despair that she would rather have been thrown on the fire herself. Her original intention was a history of the Revolution, vindicating her husband, herself, and their colleagues. The first half of the surviving text is devoted largely to the politics of 1791–1793: it occupies *c.* 150 pages in the current French edition.

The next 150 pages, entitled *Mémoires particulières*, consist of an account of Marie-Jeanne Phlipon's childhood and upbringing. Determined that 'misfortune will not overcome me', she wrote, she would describe happier times. She would also write with 'frankness for myself; and I shall not hang back from being frank about others: father, mother, friends, husband, I shall paint them all as they were or as I saw them'. This *is* obviously inspired by Rousseau and Mme Roland continues with a kind of rejection of what might be described as 'polite' writing:

> Since circumstances, political and other storms have developed the energy of my character, I will above all be frank [*franche*] without taking notice of the little scratches made along the way. I don't compose epigrams, because they suppose taking pleasure in making pinpricks of criticism, and I no longer amuse myself killing flies. But I will take pleasure in exercising justice through truth and I will state the most terrible truths in the face of those concerned, without myself being surprised or moved or angry, whatever the effect is on them.[40]

Given the circumstances in which they were written, these manuscripts are a remarkable piece of work, containing very few strikings-out or alterations by her (as distinct from her editors). They have been widely used as a historical source, and much of what she wrote can be checked against other records, in particular her correspondence. However, as with any autobiography, the narrative is the version

---

[38] BNF MSS, naf 13736; *Mém.*/Perroud (1905), introduction, for detailed analysis of the text.
[39] *Mém.*, pp. 338–9.   [40] *Mém.*, p. 202.

of herself in which Mme Roland believed, and which she wanted to oppose the caricatural representations of her in the Jacobin press.[41]

In the political sections, her preferences are undisguised, and she was putting up a case for the defence—while not shrinking from criticizing her friends. She said herself that, rather than spend her time having to combat lies, she would rather read a chapter of Montaigne, draw a flower, or play an arietta on the piano, to soften prison life.[42] Her pen-portraits are sharp and, in some cases, very biased. Allowing for that, it is *fairly* rare (but as we have seen, not unknown) for her to write something that can be disproved. Her memory for dates and political events is acute. On the other hand, she passes over some things. While fiercely rebutting the charges of holding 'conciliabules' at dinner, for example, she lets drop many examples, unintentionally revealing, about the conversations she really did have with many politicians. She passes over in silence, however, her role in keeping the accounts of the *bureau de l'esprit public*, or handling agents: Gadol does *not* get a mention.

The personal memoirs were started in the second week of August. She worked at them with redoubled vigour after 5–17 September, when Terror had been declared the order of the day, and the law of suspects was enacted. She now feared 'not to live twenty-four hours'. A the end of the month, she delivered her seventh notebook to Mentelle, before learning on 4 October that she had been cited in the accusation against Brissot and the other Girondins, and would probably stand trial.

What survives is an exceptionally rich document about her early years, but the last twenty pages or so—summarizing her courtship and marriage among other things—are quite rushed. People who meant a lot to her (Bancal and Bosc, for example) are hardly mentioned at all. Her haste partly explains why she said so little about the years 1780–1789. She ended the text by saying that the last thirteen years of her life would have provided matter for 'the fourth and most interesting part of my Memoirs'.[43] Even so, her near-silence, or downright disparaging remarks, about Roland's courtship, their marriage, and those years, are striking. I am inclined to see the memoirs as, in part, a long love-letter to Buzot—the many references to him, open and hidden, clear and coded, would have been understood by him if, as she seemed to hope, he escaped to America and read her book one day. She was particularly anxious to convey a view of her marriage as dutiful, but no more, and by September was bitterly trying to block her husband's own writing plans.

PREPARING FOR DEATH

After 5 September, Mme Roland fully expected to die soon. But how? Her greatest dread was a repeat of the September massacres. It would be better to mount the scaffold, after a trial at which she could speak her mind (or so she assumed), but she twice considered suicide. In early October, she set out to starve herself to death and wrote

---

[41] On this aspect see for example, Gelfand (1983).
[42] *Mém.*, p. 305.   [43] *Mém.*, p. 338.

'My last thoughts,' including farewells to her husband and lover. She also wrote touching goodbyes to her daughter and Fleury. By 14 October, she was in the prison infirmary (as we know from the unsent letter to Robespierre). Rejecting starvation as too difficult, she asked both Bosc and Sophie Grandchamp to procure a lethal dose of opium. Bosc, however, wrote her 'the hardest letter of my life', arguing that she would do more for the cause and her own reputation by going on trial and if necessary to the scaffold.[44] Sophie later claimed she had said the same. So Mme Roland resolved to live at least until the trial of the Girondins—to which she was summoned as a witness on 24 October. One of her wilder fantasies was that she would give evidence and take poison on the spot. Her infuriated reply to the act of accusation against them, written simply for herself but smuggled out, is a very forceful political testament.

In the event she was not called, although she was taken to the Palais de Justice for a day, saw the courtroom and the Girondin prisoners, and observed to her horror the irregularity of citing unexamined evidence, still under seals in the lodgings of the accused.[45] She was taken back to Sainte Pélagie, unheard, and the trial proceeded with denunciations of the Gironde by hostile speakers. On 29 October, with Robespierre's approval, the Convention passed a new decree, that the jury could move to judgement after three days, if they deemed 'their consciences sufficiently enlightened'. No defence witnesses were heard. The next day, death sentences were pronounced. Sophie Grandchamp witnessed her friend's despair and devastation at the news: Marie-Jeanne Roland had not expected this outcome, even hoping there would be a movement to rescue them.[46] On 31 October, all the imprisoned Girondins (including Valazé who was already dead) were guillotined, showing fortitude after this simulacrum of a trial.

Knowing she would be called soon, Mme Roland drew up a careful record of her worldly goods, leaving her father's two rings to Creuzé-Latouche and Bosc. She was particularly keen that Eudora (*la petite*) be able to keep the harp they had out on rental, and her own piano.[47] She wrote to Mentelle:

> As for me, Jany, it's all over. You know the sickness the English call *heart-breaken* [*sic*]? I am suffering from it and there is no remedy, and I have no wish to delay its effects. The fever has started, I hope it will not be very long. It's a good thing, Jany. My freedom will never be granted to me; heaven is my witness that I would devote it to my unhappy husband. But I shall not have it and things might be worse…I believe *he* [Buzot] is lost; if ever he reaches the happy land where your son is a farmer [America]…I have duties to others before him and I will never even be able to fulfil those. Adieu, dear Jany, my unique consolation![48]

The same day, Mme Roland was moved to the Conciergerie, with a brand new charge sheet: she was 'accused of conspiracy against the unity and indivisibility of the Republic and having sought to foment civil war'.

[44] *Corr.*, II, pp. 538–9.
[45] Ibid., pp. 532–3. On the legal arguments see Walzer (1974), pp. 72–5.
[46] Grandchamp, pp. 484–9.
[47] *Mém.*, p. 345, she estimated her property as worth 13–14,000 livres, although this record is inconsistent with other papers.
[48] *Mém.*, p. 345 ('Mes dernières pensées') and *Corr.*, II, pp. 529–30.

28

November 1793
The Tribunal and the Dagger

I confess to you that when reading a novel or play, I have never been keen on a minor role; I have never read the account of a single act of courage or virtue without daring to imagine myself capable of imitating it.

Marie-Jeanne to Jean-Marie Roland, 1782.

Mme Roland arrived in the Conciergerie (the 'antechamber of death') on the evening of 31 October, still under the shock of the execution of the Girondins. Two fellow-prisoners, Honoré-Jean Riouffe and Jacques-Claude, comte de Beugnot, witnessed her week-long stay here. Their often quoted testimony praising her appearance and conversation in romantic terms probably has to be treated with some caution, but remains valuable. They both agree that conditions in the Conciergerie, on the Ile de la Cité, were horrific. The Revolutionary Tribunal sat in the Great Hall on the first floor, and the prisoners were housed underneath it. During the Terror, it was notorious for the lack of light, proper sanitation or fresh air, with straw as the usual bedding, the enforced proximity of large numbers of prisoners, and the almost universal fate of a death sentence. Mme Roland herself wrote that she had now arrived in 'a filthy place: I lay without sheets on a cot which one of the prisoners lent me'.[1]

The women prisoners' quarters were separated from the men's by a grille, but they were able to speak quite freely and both witnesses talked with Mme Roland. Beugnot mentioned his surprise that most of the women took great pains over their appearance, even in these circumstances, changing their dress often, and using the fountain in the courtyard to wash their clothes in a determined effort to keep clean. It seems that Mme Roland did the same.

'Not in the first bloom of youth [she was] still very attractive with an elegant figure' (Riouffe). The memoirists disagreed about her colouring (blonde with blue eyes according to Beugnot, which is obviously wrong) but both say they could have listened to her talking for ever: 'no woman spoke with more purity, grace, and elegance'; 'her conversation had a purity and a prosody that made her language a kind of music of which the ear never tired'.[2] Both claim that she was revered and

---

[1] *Mém.*, p. 365.
[2] Riouffe (1795), p. 70, Beugnot (1959), p. 137.

respected by her fellow women prisoners. Perhaps it had something to do with her sharing her money with the needy, if that is true; perhaps too this was a way of contrasting her with Mme du Barry, who behaved very differently. However, there is no reason to think that Mme Roland departed from her habitual self-control and courtesy, at least in public. As Beugnot remarked, she revered the ancients and modelled herself on them. It is likely she was steeling herself to make a good death.

Beugnot was a political opponent, a former Feuillant, prejudiced against her before meeting her. He criticized her approach—she liked anyone who agreed with her and detested those who didn't. They argued about Louis XVI, whom she fiercely condemned. When Beugnot pointed out that he had died bravely, she replied 'Agreed, he was quite noble on the scaffold, but you shouldn't call that merit: kings are brought up from childhood to look good in public.' Their conversation if true is revealing because it suggests that she had adopted for herself a similar noble code, even more praiseworthy in her own eyes. She also told him: 'The coldness of the French people astonishes me. If I were free, and they were executing my husband, I would stab myself at the foot of the scaffold, and I am certain that when Roland learns of my death, he will put a knife through his heart.'[3]

Mme Roland was called for interrogation on 1 November (11 brumaire), before the judge, David-Delisle, and the deputy public prosecutor: a protégé of Robespierre, J.B. Fleuriot-Lescot. That session lasted three hours; the second was held next morning at eleven. She replied defensively and firmly, if not truthfully, to all the questions, denying having heard discussion of the departmental force, or having 'organized' a *bureau d'esprit public*. She declared that she did not know where Roland was, but would not tell if she did, which brought a furious scolding. Riouffe reported that she returned from the sessions with eyes red from weeping, because of the insulting insinuations. Alongside the usual loaded questions, the following exchange was apparently designed to elicit confession of a particular fondness for Barbaroux:

Asked whether among those named at previous interrogations, there were not some with whom she had had more intimate and particular relations than with others.

Replied that she and Roland had been friendly since the time of the Constituent Assembly with Brissot, Pétion, and Buzot.

Asked again, whether separately and distinctively from her husband, she did not have relations with any of those named.

Replied she knew them with Roland, and through Roland, and […] had for them the degree of esteem and attachment that each seemed to merit.

It was observed to her that she was making constantly evasive replies, and obviously intended to outrage the truth […] which she would not do if she had no liaisons contrary to the Republic; she was summoned to declare whether yes or no, she had had particular and personal relations with Barbaroux and Lauze-Deperret.[4]

---

[3] Beugnot (1959), pp. 139–40. He did.
[4] *Actes*, p. 365.

Mme Roland on coming out of this session wrote down furiously that the prosecutor had been rude, insulting, and had tried to reduce her to silence. She had turned to the clerk and told him to write down 'An accused person is answerable only for her own deeds, not those of other people. If Roland had not been refused the justice he called for for four months, he would not be absent and I would not be obliged to say anything about his whereabouts.'[5]

She realized that the letters to Lauze-Deperret were the only significant evidence against her. In her 'Notes on my trial', she rightly described this fairly innocuous correspondence as three or four notes, from early in her imprisonment, when she hoped to enlist his help; he was not a close friend, but she judged him brave enough to cooperate. Mme Roland was assigned a lawyer, Chauveau-Lagarde (who had also defended the queen, the Girondins and Charlotte Corday), but sent him away, not wanting to implicate him in her case.

Both Beugnot and Riouffe agree that when she was called to appear before the Revolutionary Tribunal a week later, Friday 8 November (18 brumaire), she took special care over her appearance. According to Sophie Grandchamp, she had kept a 'little packet' with her, which she called her 'toilette de la mort'—'my death outfit'. This consisted of 'an English-style dress of white muslin, decorated with pale yellow, and tied with a black velvet belt. She wore a bonnet style of hat, of elegant simplicity, and her hair was loose on her shoulders.'[6] Beugnot says many women crowded round to kiss her hand when she went up to the chamber.

She had already seen the Tribunal during the trial of the Girondins. In the long chamber, five judges sat at a table, and the public prosecutor had a separate desk. Against the wall stood pillars carrying busts of Brutus, Marat and Lepeletier. Either side of the presiding judge sat two assessors, wearing hats with black plumes. The jurors, twelve men drawn by lot, sat along the side wall. The accused sat opposite them: if only one person, then in a metal armchair. The public was admitted to a gallery behind a guard rail.

At Mme Roland's trial, which was brief, Fouquier-Tinville did not appear: Fleuriot-Lescot substituted for him. The only witnesses called were her servants Fleury and Lecoq, neither of whom said anything really incriminating, and the governess, Mlle Mignot, who claimed to report on several private conversations, among them that at dinner the Roland's guests had 'regretted the lifting of the siege of Lille' and had divided France up among them.[7]

The prosecutor read extracts from the Lauze-Deperret letters, which the accused acknowledged—on these grounds, she was sentenced to death for 'conspiring against the unity and indivisibility of the Republic'. Because of her notoriety, Fouquier-Tinville directed that the sentence be carried out immediately, departure scheduled for 3.30 p.m. When Mme Roland tried to read out her long-prepared defence, she got through only a few lines before being stopped. She said she was

---

[5] *Notes sur mon procès, Mém.*, pp. 364 ff.
[6] Grandchamp, p. 495; Beugnot (1959), pp. 140–1.
[7] The documents suggest heavy pressure was applied to this woman, who lived at the same address as one of the Pantheon-section activists.

being accused of 'complicity with so-called conspirators'. However, 'my friendship with some of these men predates by far the political circumstances which has made them be declared guilty': all her contacts had been private. In any case, she did not believe that the proscribed men had perverse intentions. 'If they erred, it was in good faith: they have succumbed without losing dignity, and in my eyes they are unfortunate and not guilty. If I am guilty in wishing them to be saved, I declare it in the face of the universe.' Probably it was at this point that the president said that 'this breathed federalism from start to finish', and told her she could not abuse her right to speak in order to praise the crimes of Brissot and his associates. 'The accused turned to the public and said "I call on you to witness the violence being done to me", but there were cries of "Long live the republic, and down with traitors".'[8]

The accounts of Mme Roland's last journey would force anyone's admiration. Riouffe reported that coming out of the courtroom she 'showed a certain joyfulness in her steps and made a playful [or Roman] gesture, pointing her thumb down to signify she was doomed'.[9] She was to be executed along with a prisoner called Simon-François Lamarche or Delamarche, former director of the bureau of *assignats*, with whom she shared her lunch, while doing her best to give him some backbone.[10] Both prisoners had their hair shorn before execution and were led to the open two-wheeled wooden cart with no seats, for which the normal French term is a *tombereau*—in English the word is specific to the Terror: 'a tumbril'. It would take them from the Ile de la Cité across the Pont-Neuf and westwards to the Place de la Révolution (Concorde today). They had to stand up, with their hands tied behind their backs, a sadistic refinement of discomfort, while the cart, surrounded by a detail of pike-bearers, made the laborious journey, which could last an hour and a half.

Sophie Grandchamp left her account of seeing Mme Roland as she travelled to the guillotine. At their last meeting (probably 30 October), Marie-Jeanne had asked her if she would do her one final service. Having rejected the option of suicide—reluctantly—she was determined to display her fortitude if she could. She asked Sophie to stand on the Pont-Neuf, 'near the first step, leaning on the parapet, and dressed as you are today', i.e. disguised as a laundress. So that Friday afternoon, Sophie arrived 'an hour early', with great trepidation. She recognized faces all around, probably ex-neighbours of the prisoner, and was worried about being spotted herself. When the cart at last rumbled towards her:

> [Mme Roland] looked fresh, calm and smiling; you could see that she was trying to cheer up the unfortunate [La Marche] whose pallor and despair contrasted with her confident stance and bright colour. As they approached the bridge, she searched for

---

[8] *Actes*, pp. 377 and 608; see also *Mém.*, pp. 371 ff., 'Projet de défense'.
[9] Quoted May (1970), p. 285.
[10] AN, W 294, file 228, not 'an old man' but aged 35. His dossier is so complicated it is unclear whether he was guilty or not. Beugnot (1866/1959), pp. 140–1; Grandchamp. pp. 493–7. Hearsay reports that she encouraged him by saying 'the haircut suits you', 'be polite to a lady'—plausible, but not verified.

me with her eyes; I read in them the satisfaction that she felt to see me at this last unforgettable rendezvous; as she came level with me, a movement of her eyes, accompanied by a smile, told me she was content to have her wish fulfilled.[11]

As soon as the cart was out of sight, Sophie went home, in a state of collapse. Her account has some confirmation from the historian Tissot, who was also on the bridge: Mme Roland 'wore a white dress sprigged with pink embroideries [...] A charming smile played on her lips and yet she was serious and not joking with death.'[12] The cart continued its route. By the time it reached its destination, it was five in the afternoon, and getting dark. The guillotine was set up in the middle of the square, with soldiers all around, plus the usual spectators. David's huge plaster statue of Liberty, erected on 10 August 1793, loomed over it. Mme Roland argued to the last, it is said, with the executioner, Sanson, asking him to take Lamarche first, since he was distressed, so that he would not see her death. When it was her turn, although there was apparently a sympathetic silence, one shout was heard of 'A la guillotine', and she replied, 'I'm on my way' ('*J'y vais*'), before looking at the statue. According to Mercier, she said 'O Liberty, what crimes are committed in thy name'. Another version is 'O Liberty, they have made a fool of you [*on t'a jouée*]'. Both are quite plausible.[13] She was, like some before and many after her, strapped to a plank of wood, and thrust under the blade which, one hopes, worked swiftly.

There are no graves for the victims of the guillotine. The bodies of those executed were packed into wicker baskets by the executioner's assistants, and in that year were taken to a communal burial ground, the Cimetière de la Madeleine, north of the Place de la Révolution (not the present-day Madeleine, but the grounds of a convent). Mme Roland's would have been among them. The cemetery was closed in 1794, perhaps because the large number of burials were a health risk. It is no longer visible: under the Restoration, Louis XVIII (Artois) built the Chapelle de l'Expiation on the site, dedicated to Louis XVI and Marie Antoinette, whose presumed remains were transferred to the Cathedral of Saint-Denis. In 1844, the other skeletal remains in the old cemetery were transferred to the west ossuary and then to the Paris catacombs.

Mentelle was already at Sophie's apartment that evening, when Bosc, who came to Paris every Friday night, arrived there. 'The violence of [his sobs] was almost fatal.' All three were grief-stricken. Their thoughts turned to Roland, who 'would immediately think she had died to save him'. To forestall his hearing about it in the newspapers, Bosc wrote immediately to his old friend, but it seems that this letter cannot have reached him before he took his own life, as his wife had predicted.

---

[11] Grandchamp, p. 495.   [12] Quoted *Actes*, p. 377.
[13] In *Nouveau Tableau de Paris*, quoted *Actes*, p. 378. Mme Roland had a private rhetoric about liberty of long standing: in a letter to Sophie Cannet in 1776, she had written: 'O Liberty, you are but a name to me,' expressing regret at having been born a woman, *Corr.*, NS. I, pp. 374–5.

THE DEATH OF ROLAND

Marie-Jeanne Roland's well-documented courageous death under the blade of the guillotine became the stuff of legend. She was able, like Danton after her, to go defiantly to her last rendezvous. Jean-Marie Roland's death is also well-documented, but was far more obscure and is almost forgotten. His last months must have been extremely miserable, despite being sheltered by his friends, the Malortie sisters, who were themselves not very well-off. He had not seen Eudora, whom he dearly loved, since that evening of 31 May, although he may have been able to write to her at the Creuzé-Latouche home. He certainly exchanged letters with his wife, but this correspondence is lost. It would have been a forlorn echo of their former affectionate life. From Mme Roland's letters to Buzot a sad picture emerges, rendered sadder by her coldness. Roland's attempt to persuade his wife to escape from prison, aided by Henriette Cannet, had been refused. As time went on, she seemed to become even more detached and knew he had fallen into a devastating state of depression. Reading the Paris newspapers, Roland would have learnt of the events of the summer, and then the trial and death of the Girondins at the end of October, which would further have driven him to despair.

The account of his last day comes from Champagneux, who had it from the Malorties.[14] Apparently on Sunday 10 November, he read in the newspaper (probably the local *Indicateur politique, mercantile et littéraire*) that Marie-Jeanne had been due to appear before the Revolutionary Tribunal on Friday 8 November.[15] Given the fate of the Gironde, he knew her death sentence was inevitable. His last message reads: 'I learnt that they were *going to* cut my wife's throat.' His reaction was an emotional collapse, but on recovering, he debated how best to follow her. His first instinct was to travel incognito to Paris, and present himself at the Convention, 'to astonish them into being forced to listen to some truths useful to the nation', before asking to die on the scaffold. This plan was hardly realistic, but in any case, his friends persuaded him that if he were condemned to death, his property would be forfeit and his daughter would be penniless. 'His paternal tenderness' therefore convinced him to kill himself after leaving the Malortie house, so as not to draw suspicion upon them.[16]

Accordingly, he destroyed any remaining papers—presumably including his wife's letters—and asked for a pen to write his suicide note. He embraced his friends, took his sword-stick—a gift from Bosc to defend himself back in the winter—and set out along the road to Paris, as darkness fell. He was wearing a broadcloth overcoat, a woollen jacket and breeches, a fine linen shirt, flannel undershirt, black silk hose, and his usual shoes tied with ribbons. About four leagues out of town, in the commune of Radepont, he left the road and turned into

---

[14] Champagneux (1800), p. lxxxij.   [15] Perroud (1895) for clarity on the dates.
[16] Champagneux, p. lxxxiv ff. In fact, Roland's property was both confiscated and sequestered until after Thermidor.

an avenue leading into a wood.[17] Next morning, 11 November [21 brumaire], passers-by, seeing an elderly man slumped on the raised border beside the road, at first thought he was asleep. When someone realized he was dead, the mayor, a surgeon, and a justice of the peace were called. They examined the body, and found that he had stabbed himself to death with the blade of the sword-stick. There were two wounds, one shallow, one deep. In his pockets were four documents. Two were identity cards from his Paris section (all citizens had to carry them). There was also a note which read:

> Whoever you are who finds me lying here, respect my remains: they are those of a man who died as he lived, virtuous and honest. A day will come, and it cannot be far away, when you will have a terrible judgement to make; wait for that day; then you will act in full awareness of the cause and you will recognize the reason for this advice. Would that my country could at last abhor so many crimes and return to human and social sentiments.   J.-M. Roland.

On the back, a few words are added. 'It is not fear, but *indignation* [underlined]. I left my shelter at the moment I learnt they were going to cut my wife's throat; and I do not wish to remain any longer on an earth which is covered with crimes.'[18] The fourth scrap of paper—it must have been an oversight, lost in a pocket, but a dangerous one—carried the name and address of Aimée Malortie. Aimée was consequently questioned, and arrested, but released after a few weeks, since the authorities seem to have believed only that Roland was on the way *to* Rouen, rather than having been there for months under her roof.

As it happened the *commissaires* at that time, on a mission from the Convention to the district, were Legendre and Delacroix. They were summoned to identify the body as that of the ex-minister. Champagneux recalled indignantly that Legendre was Roland's butcher, and the minister had done him several favours. However, he was now a political enemy, who proposed that Roland's corpse be displayed with a notice condemning the 'perverse minister'. The local authorities, taken aback by such fury, simply buried the body where it had been found.[19] It was a sad and lonely death, but a brave one and not lacking in dignity, for a man whose reputation was very effectively denigrated and who could even be said to have been airbrushed from most revolutionary history. It was a bitterly tragic end to a marriage that for him had been the light of his life.

---

[17] BNF MSS, naf 22422, cutting from *Revue de Rouen et de Normandie*, 1852, based on the registers in Rouen. The exact place was apparently the avenue to the chateau of Coquetot, near Bourg-Beaudouin.

[18] Originals in AN, C 278. The Malortie paper looks like a scrap from a letter, in Mme Roland's writing. See also Champagneux (1800), p. lxxxvij.

[19] AN, C278 for Legendre's report.

Epilogue and Conclusion

The period known as the Terror lasted a comparatively short time, from summer 1793 to summer 1794. But violence in many forms continued, and the European war, begun so confidently but rashly in 1792, went on with interruptions until 1815. Few of the people mentioned in this book survived until then.

The Girondins in Bordeaux spent a gruelling few months, ending in almost all their deaths. Buzot, in hiding in Saint-Emilion, received news of Marie-Jeanne Roland's execution on 13 November. To a friend he wrote: '*She* is no more. [...] The villains have murdered her. Consider if there is anything left for me to regret on earth.'[1] With Barbaroux and Pétion, he survived with difficulty until the summer of 1794. Barbaroux, having failed to kill himself, was captured and guillotined in Bordeaux on 25 June. Buzot and Pétion, vowing to 'blow their brains out', rather than be taken alive, apparently shot themselves in a cornfield in the commune of Saint-Magne. The two bodies were found 'half-consumed by animals', also on 25 June, and buried where they lay. Their papers were eventually recovered from St Emilion. Buzot's manuscript ended with a belated but touching farewell to his wife.[2]

Many of the Rolands' adversaries also perished in 1794. Hébert was executed in March 1794, with Desfieux, Cloots, and other so-called *hébertistes*. Danton and Desmoulins were executed with their associates in April, as 'Indulgents' who wanted to halt the Terror. The waters were muddied by charges of financial wrongdoing (justified in the case of Fabre d'Eglantine). Robespierre himself, with Saint-Just and his associates, was toppled by the coalition of 9 Thermidor (27 July 1794). Badly injured by a gunshot, which broke his jaw during the assault on the Hôtel de Ville, Robespierre was guillotined next day, 28 July. Earlier, on March 31, in a statement hinting at regret, although not error, he had mentioned his former friends:

> I was the friend of Pétion; when he was unmasked, I abandoned him; I had connections with Roland too: he turned traitor and I denounced him. Danton wants to take their place, and now he is in my eyes nothing more than an enemy of the *patrie*.[3]

Few leading Girondin deputies or ministers survived. Lebrun was executed, Clavière and Condorcet committed suicide in prison. Louvet de Couvray successfully escaped to Switzerland. Returning to France in 1794, he set about rehabilitating the reputation of the Girondins, before dying in 1797. The 75 deputies, who had

---

[1] *Corr.*, II, p. 765.
[2] Ibid. p. 766. Details in Vatel (1872), II, pp. 144 ff.
[3] Quoted Linton (2008), p. 59.

protested at their proscription in summer 1793, although imprisoned, had survived, following Robespierre's intervention.

The Rolands' less prominent friends—Bancal, Lanthenas, and Bosc—all outlived the Terror. Bancal was handed over to the Austrians by Dumouriez, and then exchanged for Louis XVI's daughter, Marie-Thérèse, in 1795. He retired to Clermont, married Marie Girard, and had six children. Lanthenas remained in the Convention, but lay low until after Thermidor. He had made some contribution to revolutionary policies, but was understandably haunted by the Rolands' memory, regretting the Revolution's 'innocent victims'. He died in 1799.[4]

Bosc remained below the radar and helped other Girondins. His future was briefly linked with that of Eudora Roland. In October 1793, the Creuzé-Latouche family sent her under an assumed name to Mme Godefroid, the wife of an artist. (Mme Roland, hearing of the move just before her death, had written anxiously to her new protector.)[5] Eudora had few relatives left—Dominique Roland, aged 72, was guillotined during the Lyon Terror; Jacques, aged 63, briefly imprisoned, survived to 1807, but she hardly knew him. So in December 1794, Bosc became Eudora's official guardian.[6]

Recovering her family property turned out not to be easy, and to provide some income for her, Bosc published the first edition of her mother's memoirs in spring 1795. 12,000 copies were sold, bringing in a notional 98,570 francs—but in *assignats*.[7] Complications arose, when, aged 37, Bosc fell in love with his teenage ward (or with her mother's memory). When she seemed to reciprocate, Bosc prudently sent her to stay with the Malortie sisters in Rouen in November 1795. However, Eudora changed her mind and her guardianship was transferred to Champagneux, who not only brought out the next, fuller, edition of the memoirs, but married Eudora to his second son, Pierre, on 13 December 1796. She was fifteen years and two months.[8]

Eudora eventually inherited Le Clos, as well as the Villefranche house and other family property. She had two surviving daughters, and the family has descendants to the present day. The maidservant Marguerite Fleury (who had been tried but acquitted) was kept on by the family.[9] Bosc, after spending two years in America, married his cousin Suzanne in April 1799, and, like Bancal, had six children. Although never well-off, he devoted himself to botany, under the protection of Cuvier, and ended up a member of the Institute.[10] He and Eudora finally became 'friends'.

---

[4] Dorigny (1989a) for a positive evaluation of Lanthenas's contribution.

[5] *Corr.*, II, pp. 541–2; the letter was concerned for Eudora's safety, since Mme Godefroid (unlike the Creuzé-Latouches) had a teenage son—perhaps reviving the trauma of the apprentice boy.

[6] Ibid., Appendix K, pp. 666–87, esp. pp. 674, 680. *Acte de tutelle* in BNF MSS, naf 22424.

[7] Ibid., p. 685.

[8] Papers relating to her property, BNF MSS, naf 9533, fo 133 ff.

[9] Louis Lecoq, their manservant, was guillotined in 1794 simply for working for them. Marguerite Fleury was released as 'unfit to plead', *Mém.*, p. 384, note.

[10] Died July 1828, buried at Sainte-Radegonde; *Corr.*, II, Appendix K and Rey (1901).

CONCLUSION

This double biography had two aims: first to offer a new perspective on the famous 'Mme Roland'. Instead of treating her in isolation as an exceptional woman, it has explored the crucial partnership with her husband, examining their private life before the Revolution. Secondly, it has pursued their partnership into the revolutionary years, where controversy and cliché have gathered round their names. This has meant considering their actions when Jean-Marie Roland was minister of the Interior. My hope—a difficult one—was to distinguish between what is verifiable, or fair comment, and what seems to be invented or exaggerated. I cannot claim any more than most writers to be objective: biographers are forced into close proximity with their subjects. I ended up feeling both exasperation with and admiration for the Rolands. But while not setting out to act as their defence lawyer, I think there is a case for reviewing their reputations.

THE MARRIAGE

The Roland marriage was fairly unconventional for the ancien régime. Analysing it means deconstructing some of the statements by Marie-Jeanne Roland herself in her memoirs. Over the course of the union, its internal dynamics altered several times. It would be surprising if the young Mlle Phlipon had not been overawed at first by her older, more sophisticated, and higher-status husband—playing Dorothea to his Casaubon, as it were. But the documentary evidence of the 1780s indicates that the marriage was not only one of affection and intimacy, but quickly developed into an unusually equal partnership. There must have been other examples of this kind of companionate marriage, but rarely with such a wealth of documentation. While conventional gender roles were being outwardly observed—Marie-Jeanne taking full control of the household, including the accounts—they were also being modified, with Jean-Marie not being unwilling to take on childcare, and Marie-Jeanne having an appreciable input to her husband's lectures and publications. This academic couple *avant la lettre* sat at adjoining desks, while their somewhat neglected daughter played at their feet—and caused them some heart-searching on that account.

It is also clear that they had complementary talents, but similar world-views. ('When there are two of you who think the same way, it makes you very strong.') Both had something to gain from their union. Jean-Marie Roland was a man seduced by the technology of the day and a concern for trade and industry. Yet in his writings, public or private, down-to-earth practicality coexists with what William Reddy has called 'sentimentalism'—a passionate attachment to feelings as a guide for conduct, and a view of both 'virtue' and 'esprit public' rather than calculation as a principle for living by—an attitude shared by his wife. What can be seen as a rather loveless childhood made him vulnerable to emotion in later life. His actions were often impulsive, and he several times made himself ill through overwork and worry. A self-educated idealist, he may have overestimated his own talents: he was not a particularly original thinker. However, he was a man of determined character, who under the ancien régime was not afraid to challenge his superiors or entrenched practices if he thought them wrong. An outsider with few resources, he rightly claimed to have spoken out against abuses when it was dangerous to do so. Cut off from his family, he led for many years a rather lonely bachelor life, comforted to some extent by his ability to form friendships.

His wife provided the total domestic, intellectual, and affective support lacking for most of his first forty years. Like him a devotee of virtue in the Rousseauist mode, she was soon helping him fashion his written works with her superior stylistic skills, while keeping carefully out of the limelight herself. Her own writings excel in the genre today described as 'life-writing'—letters and memoirs, composed with exceptional fluency and verve, but never intended to be published under her own name, at least until she found herself under threat of death. Only posthumously did her memoirs turn her into an outstanding figure among the women writers active in the cultural field of the late eighteenth century referred to by Carla Hesse. The anonymity on which she insisted almost all her life might strike us today as subordination to her husband's reputation, and obedience to the conventions of the time, giving him everything in return merely for domestic security.

But in fact the marriage brought many gains to the obscure and virtually poverty-stricken Mlle Phlipon: it was not negligible for someone of her background to acquire the bourgeois status which gave her self-confidence in dealing with people of different degrees of social standing. By the time the Revolution broke out, with long experience of discussing philosophy, literature, and public affairs with her husband, Marie-Jeanne Roland had acquired sufficient political nous for her letters describing the situation in Lyon to be regarded as publishable by Brissot, who was himself an experienced journalist. Intelligent and lively, she could hold her own with the men she encountered, in local and eventually national politics. One of the most significant passages of her memoirs (honest, if not exactly likeable) describes her reactions when her circle of acquaintances was enlarged by her husband's appointment. What struck her was the unexpected 'mediocrity at every level', from incompetent clerks to generals, ministers, and ambassadors:

> Never without this experience would I have believed my fellow creatures to be so lacking (*pauvre*). So it was only from this time that I acquired self-confidence: until then I was as shy (*modeste*) as a convent girl. I imagined that people who had stronger opinions than me were also cleverer. Well! I'm not surprised now that people valued me a lot [*qu'on m'aimât beaucoup*]: they felt that I had some worth and yet I always sincerely paid my respects to other people's views of themselves [*amour-propre*].[1]

This gives us a glimpse of the frustration felt by an intelligent woman when the extraordinary circumstances of the time brought her into contact with men deemed to be running the country.

As for the emotional course of the marriage, not until Marie-Jeanne's meeting with Henri Bancal in 1790 did a serious fissure appear in her loyalty to her husband.

---

[1] *Mém.* p. 162.

Even the Bancal attachment was outlived eventually, since we know Mme Roland offered to help Bancal court Helen Maria Williams. Her love for Buzot, however, requited if never consummated, was a different matter. Her approach was one of ruthless self-denial, which she sublimated into a grand Rousseauist passion. Under its spell, Mme Roland projected her current feelings about her husband—rather self-righteously, as was her way—into her account of the whole marriage in her memoirs. She proclaimed her 'filial' respect for Roland—although even that was waning in the face of his desperate jealousy—and insisted, perhaps for Buzot's benefit, that her marriage had been one of reason and duty. Historians and novelists can hardly be blamed for taking her at her word if they have not seen earlier documents. It is clear, from his collapse into despair in the last year of his life that Jean-Marie Roland was deeply dependent on his wife's support and devastated by her emotional defection. But it is a pity that clichés about the May-and-December marriage have persisted as a result, to obscure the long-term identity of a partnership full of interest in what it tells us about everyday life, parenthood, paid and unpaid work, and community of ideas. The affair with Buzot, based presumably on snatched meetings and sexual longing, is not freighted with anything like the same everyday intimacy and cultural baggage, and the only surviving letters to him, touching as they are, are naturally concerned with the desperate political circumstances of summer 1793.

Until the Revolution, the Roland couple, both of whom had rebelled against their background, he against his family's clericalism and pretentions, she against shopkeeping mentalities and her sex, had settled into their identity as a bourgeois couple of modestly comfortable means. Having been to some extent outsiders in their provincial milieux did not prevent them from contracting long-lasting friendships with kindred spirits, who had a tendency to gather round them as a kind of substitute family, most visible in their willingness to think of creating a community. But both of them derived considerable strength from their own relationship in a marriage where everything was shared. Nor can their affection for their daughter in her early years seriously be doubted. It is true however that during the Revolution, Eudora would suffer increasingly from her parents' immersion in politics, which displaced her from the centre of their lives: one is left with the image of the child in tears, as first her father slipped away in secret, and then her mother was led downstairs by soldiers in the early morning of 1 June 1793. We know that all her life Eudora was particularly attached to her father's memory. Her mother's memoirs do contain some very cool appraisals of the child, but Mme Roland's last references to her daughter are contradictory and fragmentary. She wept on Eudora's twelfth birthday, 4 October 1793, as she sat in prison, and her final letters reflect anguish, concern, and affection.

REVOLUTION

What, finally, is one to conclude of the Rolands' importance in the history of the Revolution? One aspect of Jean-Marie Roland's career sometimes rather overlooked is his modest but real participation in the municipal revolution. These people were provincials in 1789, and thought to remain so. In the conservative city of Lyon, Roland emerged as a noteworthy radical conscience in 1787–1791, offering recipes for reform, and looked up to by a slightly younger generation of local revolutionaries, such as Vitet, Champagneux, and even Chalier at first. Rarely present in person, he was certainly not a noted orator at either public or council meetings. His pamphlets made their mark, and he appears to have been a respected figure, representative of the sincere desire to make the Revolution work at local level; but like his friends, he was caught in the middle between the reactionary old order and the pressure from more radical groups. In concrete terms, he successfully negotiated the city's bail-out from debt, but was not popular enough (or too unpopular in certain milieux) to be elected to the Legislative Assembly. He continued to advise and help the city's 'moderately-radical' administration from Paris, though as far as we know played no further part in the events in the city in 1793, whatever his accusers thought. His wife, though sidelined from formal politics, observed them with interest and reported regularly to Brissot in Paris, herself becoming a kind of political journalist.

With the crucial year of 1792, we enter troubled waters. The problem with almost all revolutionary figures is that the factional politics of the time draw the biographer into taking sides. However much we might wish that Montagnards and Girondins of 1792–1793 could have sunk their differences and cooperated on constructing a republican constitution and making it work—a revolutionary undertaking if ever one was in the eighteenth century—that is not what happened. And yet in many ways what is most disconcerting about the subsequent split between Gironde and Jacobins is how much they had in common. Take the following speech for example:

> In our country, we wish to favour morality over egotism, probity over honour, principle over custom, duty over convention, the reign of reason over the tyranny of fashion, scorn for vice over scorn for misfortune, pride over insolence, greatness of spirit over vanity, love of reputation over love of money, good people over polite society, merit over display, the charms of true happiness over the staleness of pleasure, the greatness of mankind over the pettiness of noblemen, a magnanimous powerful and happy people over a frivolous, complacent and miserable people, in short we wish to replace all the vices and ridiculous aspects of the monarchy with all the virtues and miracles of the republic.[2]

These are the words of Maximilien Robespierre in February 1794, when the Rolands, Brissot, and the leading Girondins were all dead: yet they would most likely all have agreed with every word of it. Nevertheless, their quarrels are recorded day after day in speeches made in the Convention or at other venues such as the Jacobin Club, during the winter of 1792–1793. Some Girondin deputies were as determined and irresponsible in their assaults on their opponents as the fiercest members of the Montagne or the Jacobin Club (and during the spring of 1793, they made devastating strategic errors by their legalistic attacks on Marat and

---

[2] Quoted Sonenscher (1989), p. 360, my translation.

Hébert). Key elements in the quarrels were retrospective accusations: the Gironde accused the Montagne of complicity in or responsibility for the September massacres. Montagnards accused the Girondins of having voted for various degrees of clemency for Louis XVI. However, nobody on either side originally set out either to restore the monarchy or to start a civil war, let alone unleash the Terror. Robespierre had originally been an opponent of the death penalty.

This is not a book about the split. But the Rolands, through their friendship with Brissot, contracted fortuitously before the Revolution, and cemented with great commitment over time, were inevitably located on the Brissot–Girondin side of the great divide. These three people did not always think alike by any means. There is no evidence that the Rolands shared Brissot's enthusiasm for the war and some signs that their pragmatic acceptance of it was reluctant. Nor was the couple's June letter to the king at all appreciated by Brissot. But several turning-points in 1792 twisted the knots of their personal relationship ever tighter: the September massacres, Marat's hostility, Robespierre's distrust, above all the king's trial. Unfortunately the loss (destruction?) of almost all correspondence between Brissot and the Rolands after September 1792 makes it hard to see quite how the friendship evolved, but we can assume it remained close, probably making any rapprochement with Brissot's enemies out of the question, despite the intriguing approach by Romme.

A key element in the hostility to the couple, explored above at some length, was Roland's position as minister of the Interior. The opposition he faced from the Montagne in the Convention obviously arose partly from his association with Brissot and certain Girondins, partly from his ministerial functions, which, it is argued here, have been much underestimated. Throughout Roland's second term of office, there were no clear constitutional rules for the relation between the executive and legislative branches of government. In a situation fraught with problems—largely, but not exclusively because of the war—everyone was navigating without a compass. Deputies had power to legislate, but little personal responsibility. Ministers could not challenge decrees, but had to implement them, carrying very visible responsibility. There was no 'prime minister', but by his range of duties, the Interior minister seemed to be in charge of a great deal of the country's affairs, as witnessed by Roland's constant appearances in the Assembly or written messages to it.

It is ironic that he has attracted so little biographical interest, since that autumn, he was virtually never out of the limelight. As he said, 'people'—by whom he probably meant Robespierre, certain Jacobins and the Montagnard deputies—imagined he had a great deal more power (and funds) than he did. Robespierre had always been suspicious of ministers as essentially power-seekers. Roland claimed to see his task as keeping the national machinery functioning, under rules which kept shifting, and over a range of matters that almost beggar belief. His concern was to maintain the rule of law, an awkward position admittedly, since he owed his reappointment to an uprising. His chief problems came less from national policy, where there was often a degree of consensus, than from his daily contact with the French provinces and consequent battles with the Paris Commune. Dealing every day with the 83 *départements*, as he kept reminding people, meant that he saw the Parisian authorities as usurping power, using their role as the 'vanguard' to excuse various kinds of non-cooperation with the minister, who represented 'the nation', as he saw it. He was undeniably partisan therefore, in the political battles of autumn 1792. Yet from long experience, he was more familiar than many deputies with the lives of ordinary working people, and had seen the Revolution as a chance for them to escape oppression and enter 'a new creation'.

Roland is certainly open to criticism on a number of grounds. Too much involvement in detail, not enough political nous; stubborn and self-righteous, he was far from adroit, displaying naïvety several times, and not just over the *armoire de fer*. His attempts to fight his corner by sending out agents and subsidizing partisan literature, although no doubt less significant than his enemies claimed, were clumsy and vulnerable to charges of favouritism. He relied unrealistically on moral exhortation which even his allies sometimes found irritating. However, his reputation for 'virtue' was not undeserved. Unlike some of his enemies, he was completely untouched by a desire for personal gain: in that respect he was as 'incorruptible' as Robespierre. Some of the men who actually brought him down (Collot, Chabot, Desfieux, Bentabole, Fabre) later revealed themselves to have serious flaws—sadism, vindictiveness, and corruption are not too strong terms to level at them. Nor could Roland be said to cling to office: he resigned from his post—reluctantly, agreed—on the democratic grounds that he lacked support within the Convention. Thereafter, as far as can be judged, he took no active part in politics, aiming determinedly to retire to the country. The most damaging rifts within the Convention became most intense only after he had left office. The Vendée rising post-dated his resignation, as did the civil war.[3] Throughout his tenure, this rather frail near-sixty-year-old, who made more of a mark than most ministers, showed grit in doing his duty as he saw it. Without his wife at his side, he probably wouldn't have lasted as long.

One of the ironies of Mme Roland's reputation is that the daughter of a Parisian artisan—exactly the milieu from which the *sans-culottes* were drawn—should have been reviled by their representatives in terms that make her look like an aristocrat.[4] A week or so after her execution, which followed closely on those of Marie-Antoinette and of the actress and campaigner Olympe de Gouges, an anonymous article in the *Moniteur* of 19 November 1793 commented, grouping these three women together:

> La femme Roland, a would-be wit [*bel esprit*] with grand projects, a philosopher who wrote little notes [*petits billets* suggests love-letters], *queen of a moment*, surrounded by mercenary writers to whom she gave *supper, distributed favours, posts and money*, was a monster in every respect. Her *disdainful* countenance towards the people and the judges chosen by [the people], the proud stubbornness of her responses, her ironic gaiety and the firmness she paraded on her journey [to the scaffold] proved that no

[3] See Le Guin (1966), pp. 117 ff. for a robust, but by no means indulgent defence of Roland's position vis-à-vis the legislature.
[4] Cf. *DCRF*, p. 419, article 'Sansculotte'.

painful memory was troubling her. And yet she was a mother, but she had sacrificed nature by wanting to raise herself above it [nature]. The desire to be learnèd [*savante*] led her to forget the duties of her sex, and this neglect, always dangerous, finally led her to perish on the scaffold [my italics].[5]

Madame Roland was seen by certain of her opponents, rightly or wrongly, as embodying particularly feminine aspects of the old regime: entertaining, intriguing for appointments, using behind-the-scenes influence. The rhetoric of Robespierre's speech quoted above (fashion, vanity, pleasure, show, frivolity) is Rousseauist, and therefore to modern readers unmistakably gendered. The virtues are male and austere; the vices are feminine and distracting. If hostility to Jean-Marie Roland came straightforwardly from his position of power, his friendship with Brissot, and his dealings with the Paris Commune, hostility to his wife employed the words of her hero, Jean-Jacques Rousseau, to condemn her. Nobody in the eighteenth century used the word *salonnière*, but later writers have often characterized Mme Roland as primarily a political hostess. As suggested earlier, if we imagine that Jean-Marie Roland had remained unmarried, and had recruited a brother or some other male relation to act as his right-hand man (he did after all appoint Lanthenas and Champagneux without raising comment) such a person could have enjoyed his private confidence very much as his wife did: influencing appointments, and indeed dining with him. Danton, as we saw, used his friends to support him in the ministry. But a woman in such a position was almost inevitably seen as different. The only previous role-models were royal queens or mistresses.

It is perhaps worth pointing out that it was journalists such as Marat and Hébert who specifically directed this kind of rhetoric against Mme Roland. More heavyweight enemies (and what enemies!) such as Robespierre and Danton, perhaps did her the honour of treating her as a political opponent rather than simply a feminine meddler. Having met her at close quarters, they may have retained some respect for her abilities, although in the absence of any documents that has to remain a speculative idea. The few genuine eye-witness accounts we have of her presiding at the ministry table (Dumont and Genet for example) stress her discretion and political sophistication, without dwelling overmuch on her charm—a two-edged quality. The picture of Mme Roland as an Egeria for the Girondins obviously contains a substantial kernel of truth. But it has been exaggerated, starting with contemporaries and magnified further by historians. The most important point about it is that, in real terms, she did not eclipse her husband: he was co-host of those ministry dinners and their raison d'être. We know that she made a strong impression on the politicians she met, but, ironically, her husband was probably the man she could least persuade to change his mind.

The Rolands' downfall had complex causes. The moves to arrest them on 31 May had no clear legal justification, as they both rightly argued. Mme Roland

---

[5] Champagneux (1800) objected strongly both to this and to Legendre's 'epitaph' on Roland (AN, C 278). While one could expect hostility from political enemies, the *Moniteur* was supposed to be a serious publication.

was virtually the only person imprisoned before 2 June, and that on the basis of vague accusations formulated against her husband by members of the Pantheon section in May. At the time, naturally, not even her enemies were anticipating a death sentence. After 2 June, the sympathies of both Rolands were perforce with the proscribed Girondins under arrest or in flight, which made them enemies of the new majority in the Convention. The later charges that Mme Roland had been the 'soul of the conspiracy, although in prison' were unsubstantiated, as were those of her husband being involved in Lyon. But effectively, they had no way out once the uprisings against Paris were under way. The persecution of the couple, caught up in the slipstream of the Girondin proscription, was perhaps an early example of what was 'often terrifyingly arbitrary and counterproductive' about the Terror.[6] The execution of Mme Roland is sometimes described as an exercise in sadism, and there is some truth in that. Both she and her husband, in their separate ways, died heart-broken: they were weeping not only for their private life, which had fallen apart, but for their Revolution, which they saw as doing the same thing. They had not always acted wisely—though who could claim to have done so consistently in 1792–1793? Not even their worst enemy could say, however, that they lacked courage in going to their deaths.

[6] Brown (2006), p. 126.

Sources and Bibliography

See also list of abbreviations p. ix.

I MANUSCRIPT SOURCES

1. Papiers Roland
Held in Bibliothèque Nationale de France, Département des Manuscrits (BNF MSS), Nouvelles Acquisitions Françaises (naf + number). Not all have clear lists of contents. See footnotes for individual references:

naf 6238, 6239: mostly letters by Marie-Jeanne Roland.
naf 6240, 6241: mostly letters by Jean-Marie Roland.
naf 6242, 6243: mostly early papers of Jean-Marie Roland.
naf 6244: early writings of Marie-Jeanne Phlipon.
naf 7543: varia.
naf 9532: Jean-Marie Roland writings and ministry.
naf 9533, 9534: varia.
naf 13736 Marie-Jeanne Roland's memoirs.
naf 22422, 22423, 22424 varia.

2. Archives Nationales (AN)
446 AP Papiers Brissot.
C 728 Assemblée nationale.
F^7 3686/6 Rhône.
F^7 4638 Dossier Chamfort.
F^{12} 178 Lettres du ministre de l'Intérieur, relatives au commerce.
F^{12} 661 Commerce et industrie.
F^{12} 677 Manufactures.
F^{12} 725 Administration du commerce.
F^{13} 502 Ministère de l'Intérieur, correspondence, bâtiments civils.
F^{17} 1001 Instruction publique.
F^{17} 1035 Commission aux monuments.
F^{17} 1059 Beaux-Arts, musées.
F^{19} 863 Couvents.
H^1 1439 Various, ministère de l'Intérieur.
H^1 1448 Various; correspondence patriotique.
W 294/2 dossier 227 Tribunal révolutionnaire, Mme Roland.
W 294/2 dossier 228 Tribunal révolutionnaire, Simon-François Lamarche.

3. Académie de Lyon
'Aperçu des causes qui peuvent rendre une langue universelle, et observations sur celle des langues vivantes qui tend le plus à le devenir', Académie de Lyon, manuscript, MS 151.

II PRINTED SOURCES

1. Published Works by Jean-Marie Roland (by date of composition)

Perroud, C. (ed.) (1769/1913). *Voyage en France*. Valence: D'Auray and Deschizeaux.

Lettres écrites de Suisse, d'Italie, de Sicile, et de Malte, par M*** à Mlle *** à Paris en 1776, 1777 et 1778 (1780) 6 vols, 'Amsterdam'.

Perroud, C. (ed.) (1909). *Roland et Marie Phlipon, lettres d'amour (1777 à 1780)*. Paris: Alphonse Picard et fils.

Dictionnaire des Manufactures, Arts et Métiers, vol. I (1785); vol. II, (1784); vol. III (1790). Paris : Panckoucke [part of the *Encyclopédie méthodique*]. [Quotations from bound edition in the National Library of Scotland.]

Municipalité de Lyon, aperçu des travaux à entreprendre, Lyon, January 1790, no 352347, Fonds Coste, BM Lyon.

L'Avis d'un des membres du conseil général de la commune de Lyon, donné le 19 juin 1790 au sujet des finances et des dettes de Lyon : payer ou faire banqueroute : voilà tout ce qu'on nous présente en ce moment (1790) Fonds Coste, BM, Lyon, 7878.

Discours prononcé à la société centrale formée des commissaires des sociétés populaires des amis de la constitution de Lyon le 6 janvier 1791, par J.-M. Roland, BML, Fonds Coste 352352.

Adresse préliminaire de la commune de Lyon, sur la dette de la ville, sur les dettes de la ville en général et sur la nécessité de les joindre toutes à la Dette nationale, presentée à l'Assemblee Nationale le 11 mars 1791, par Jean-Marie Roland, officier municipal et François Bret, Procureur de la commune, députés extraordinaires de Lyon (1791).

Lettres et pièces intéressantes pour servir à l'histoire du Ministère de Roland, Servan et Clavière. Chez les directeurs du Cercle social (1792).

Réponse au prussien Klootz, Imprimerie du Cercle social (1792).

Compte moral, October 1792, NLS, Crawford Collection, Fr 1014, no 17.

Compte rendu par le Ministre de l'Intérieur à la Convention Nationale le 6 janvier, l'an II de l'egalité et de la République, et imprimé par ordre de la Convention, Imprimerie Nationale Exécutive du Louvre (1793).

Observations de l'ex-ministre Roland sur le rapport fait contre lui par le député Brival, Paris, 21 mai 1793.

2. Published Works by Marie-Jeanne Roland (by date of publication)

Champagneux, L.-A. (ed.) (1799–1800). *Oeuvres de J.-M. Ph. Roland* [sic], *femme de l'ex-ministre de l'intérieur*, 3 vols. Paris: Bidault (An VIII/1799–1800).

Dauban, C.A. (ed.) (1867). *Lettres en partie inédites de Mme Roland (Mlle Phlipon) aux demoiselles Cannet*, 2 vols, Paris: Plon.

Unpublished Diary of Madame Roland. A fragment, dated June 1777. Communicated by Henry Arthur Bright (1872).

Perroud, C. (ed.) (1900). *Lettres de Madame Roland*, v. I (1780–1787). Paris: Imprimerie Nationale. [*Corr*. in footnotes.]

Perroud, C. (ed.) (1902a). *Lettres de Madame Roland*, v. II (1788–1793). Paris: Imprimerie Nationale.

Perroud, C. (ed.) (1905). *Mémoires de Mme Roland*, 2 vols. Paris: Plon.

Perroud, C. (ed.) (1909). *Roland et Marie Phlipon. Lettres d'amour (1777 à 1780)*. Paris: Picard.

Perroud, C. (ed.) (1913). *Lettres de Madame Roland*, Nouvelle serie, v. I (1767–1776). Paris: Imprimerie Nationale.

Perroud, C. with Conor, M. (eds) (1915). *Lettres de Mme Roland*, Nouvelle série, v. II (1776–1780). Paris: Imprimerie Nationale. [*Corr.*, NS in footnotes.]

De Beer, G. (ed.) (1787/1937). [Madame Roland] *Voyage en Suisse 1787*. Neuchâtel: Eds de la Baconnière.

[Madame Roland]: *Une éducation bourgeoise au XVIIIe siecle*, Paris: 10:18 (1964).

De Roux, P. (ed.) (1966/1986). *Mémoires de Madame Roland*. Paris, Mercure de France. [*Mém.* in footnotes.]

(NB: There is an English edition: Barrie and Jenkins (1989). *The Memoirs of Madame Roland: a heroine of the French Revolution*, trans. Evelyn Shuckburgh, but abridged by 25%. All references here are to the French 1986 edition).

3. Other contemporary printed sources: memoirs, collected documents, etc.

Anon. (1790a). *Lettre a M. R. de la P. sur sa brochure concernant la municipalité*. BM Lyon, Fonds Coste 352348 (5 April).

Anon. (1790b). *Réponse à la lettre du sieur Roland de la Platière, par un citoyen patriote*. BM Lyon, Fonds Coste 352346.

Archives parlementaires. Recueil complet des débats législatifs et politiques des Chambres françaises, Première série 1787–1799. ed. J. Madival et E. Laurent, 82 vols (1867–1913).

Aulard, F-A. (ed.). (1889–97). *La société des Jacobins: Recueil de documents pour l'histoire du club des Jacobins*, 6 vols, Paris, NY: AMS Press.

Beugnot, J.-C. (1959). *Mémoires du comte Beugnot, 1779–1815*. [1866] R. Lacour-Gayet (ed.). Paris: Hachette.

Brissot, J.-P. (1911). *J-P. Brissot, Mémoires, 1754–1793*. 2 vols, C. Perroud (ed.), Paris: Picard.

Brissot, J.-P. (1912). *Correspondance et papiers*. C. Perroud (ed.). Paris: Mémoires et documents.

Buchez P.-J.-B. and Roux, P.-C (eds) (1833–1838). *Histoire parlementaire de la Révolution française depuis 1789 jusqu'à l'Empire*. 40 vols, Paris: Paulin.

Buzot, F.-N.-L. (1823). *Mémoires sur la Révolution française par Buzot, député à la Convention*. M. Guadet (ed.). Paris: Béchet.

Chabaud, A. (ed.) (1936). *Mémoires de Barbaroux*. Paris: Les Classiques de la Révolution française.

Desmoulins, C. (1874). *Oeuvres, recueillies et publiées d'après les textes originaux, [...] par M. Jules Clarétie*. J. Clarétie (ed.), 2 vols. Paris: Garnery. [NLS, Crawford FR 1036 (5).]

Dumont, P.-E.-L. (1832). *Souvenirs sur Mirabeau et sur les deux premières assemblées législatives*. P.L. Duval (ed.). Paris: Gosselin.

Dumouriez, C-F. (1848). *Mémoires du Général Dumouriez*. J.F. Barrière (ed.), 2 vols, Paris: Firmin Didot.

Genet, E.-C. (1900). Memoir, In: *Thomas Paine 1737–1809*. M.D. Conway (ed.), trans. F. Rabbe. Paris: Plon. [Appendix, pp.439 ff., originally written in English.]

Guillaume, J. (ed.) (1889). *Procès-verbaux du comité d'instruction publique de l'Assemblée Législative*. Paris: Collection de documents inédits sur l'histoire de France.

Louvet de Couvray, J-B., *Mémoires*. Paris [1889] F. A. Aulard (ed.); re-ed., pref. by M. Vovelle, Paris: Desjonquières (1988).

Marat, J.-P. (1995). *Œuvres complètes*. 8 vols. Brussels: Pole Nord.

Mercier, L.-S. (1972). *Tableau de Paris*. nouvelle édition. Amsterdam.

Morris, Gouverneur. (1889). *The Diary and Letters of Gouverneur Morris*. A.C. Morris (ed.), 2 vols. London: Keegan Paul.

Morris, Gouverneur. (1939). *A Diary of the French Revolution, by Gouverneur Morris (1752–1816).* B.C. Davenport (ed.), 2 vols. London: Harrap.

Riouffe, H. (1795) *Mémoires d'un détenu: pour servir à l'histoire de la tyrannie de Robespierre.* Paris: Mathel.

Robespierre, Maximilien (1910–1967). *Œuvres complètes.* M. Bouloiseau, G. Lefebvre, and A. Soboul (eds), 10 vols. Paris: Société des études robespierristes.

Savary des Bruslons, J. (1726). *Dictionnaire universel du commerce.* Amsterdam: Chez les Jansons.

Tuetey, A. (1917). *Correspondance du Ministre de l'Intérieur relative au commerce, aux subsistances et à l'administration générale.* Paris: Collection des documents inédits sur l'histoire économique de la Révolution française.

Tuetey, A. and Guiffrey, J. (eds) (1910/1971). *La commission du museum et la création du Musée du Louvre 1792–1793.* Archives de l'Art français. Paris: Nobil.

Walter G. (ed. with commentary) (1968/1986). *Actes du Tribunal révolutionnaire.* Paris: Mercure de France (1968, 2nd edn, 1986).

Williams, D. (1802/1980). *Incidents in my own life which have been thought of some importance.* P. France (ed.). Brighton: University of Sussex Library.

Williams, H.M. (1796). *Letters containing a sketch of the politics of France, from the thirty-first of May 1793, till the twenty-eighth of July 1794, and of the scenes which have passed in the prisons of Paris. By Helen Maria Williams.* Dublin: Chambers.

Young, A. (1890). *Travels in France by Arthur Young during the years 1787, 1788, 1789.* M. Betham-Edwards (ed.). London: Bell & Sons.

III SELECT BIBLIOGRAPHY OF SECONDARY WORKS

[Restricted, for space reasons, largely to works for which there is a footnote reference.]

Albert-Buisson, H. (1960). *Les quarante au temps des Lumières.* Paris: Fayard.

Alder, K. (2002). *The Measure of All Things: the seven-year odyssey that transformed the world.* London: Little, Brown.

Alger, J. (1889). *Englishmen in the French Revolution.* London: Sampson Low.

Andress, D. (1999) *French Society in Revolution 1789–99.* Manchester: Manchester University Press.

Andress, D. (2000) *Massacre at the Champ de Mars: popular dissent and the political culture in the French Revolution.* Woodbridge: Boydell/RHS.

Andress, D. (2006). *The Terror: civil war in the French revolution.* London: Abacus.

Arasse, D. (1987). *La Guillotine et l'imaginaire de la Terreur.* Paris: Flammarion.

Armenteros, Carolina, Blanning ,T., DiVanna, I. *et al.* (eds) (2008). *Historicising the French Revolution.* Newcastle: Cambridge Scholars.

Arnaud, C. (1988). *Chamfort.* Paris: Laffont.

Bacquié, F. (1927). *Les Inspecteurs des manufactures sous l'ancien regime 1689–1792.* Paris: Hachette.

Badinter, R. and Badinter, E. (1990). *Condorcet: un intellectuel en politique.* Paris: Poche.

Baker, K.M. (1975). *Condorcet: from natural philosophy to social mathematics.* Chicago: University of Chicago Press.

Baker, K.M. (1990). *Inventing the French Revolution: essays on French political culture in the eighteenth century.* Cambridge: Cambridge University Press.

Balayé, S. (1988–1992). 'La Bibliothèque nationale pendant la Révolution', in: *Histoire des bibliothèques françaises.*, D. Varry (ed.), vol. 3. Paris: Promodis, pp. 71–80.

Barnard, H.C. (1969). *Education and the French Revolution*. Cambridge: Cambridge University Press.

Bayard, F. (1997). *Vivre à Lyon sous l'ancien régime*. Paris: Perrin; Paris: Comité pour l'histoire économique et financière de la France.

Benoît, B. (ed.) (1994). *Ville et Révolution française, actes du colloque de Lyon*. Lyon: IEP/PUL.

Benoît, B. (1999). *L'identité politique de Lyon: entre violences collectives et mémoire des élites (1786–1905)*. Paris: L'Harmattan.

Bernardin, E. (1964). *Jean-Marie Roland et le ministère de l'Intérieur*. Paris: Société des études robespierristes.

Biard, M. (ed.) (2008). *Les Politiques de la Terreur*. Rennes: Presses Universitaires de Rennes.

Blanc, O. (2006). 'Cercles politiques et "salons" du début de la Révolution 1789–93'. *AHRF*, 314, 2006, Special number 'La prise de la parole publique par les femmes', pp. 63–92.

Blanning, T.C.W. (1986). *The Origins of the French Revolutionary Wars*. Harlow: Longman.

Blanning, T.C.W. (1996). *The French Revolutionary Wars: 1787–1802*. London: Edward Arnold.

Bléchet, F. (1992). 'Le vandalisme à la bibliothèque du Roi/Nationale sous la révolution', in: *Révolution française et 'vandalisme revolutionnaire'actes du colloque de Clermont-Ferrand 15–17 December 1988*, S. Bernard-Griffiths, M-C. Chemin, J. Ehrard (eds). Paris: Universitas, pp. 265–76.

Bluche, F. (1986). *Septembre 1792: logiques d'un massacre*. Paris: Laffont.

Bodinier, B., Teyssier, E., Antoine, F. *et al.* (2000). *L'Evénement le plus important de la Révolution: la vente des biens nationaux*, Paris: Société des études robespierristes.

Bois, J.-P. (2005). *Dumouriez, héros et proscrit*. Paris: Perrin.

Bonnet, J.-C. (ed.) (1988). *La Carmagnole des Muses*. Paris: Armand Colin.

Braesch, F. (1911). *La Commune du 10 août: étude sur l'histoire de Paris du 20 juin au 2 décembre 1792*. Paris: Jordan.

Brette, A. (1902). *Histoire des édifices où ont siégé les assemblées parlementaires de la Révolution française et de la première république*. Paris: Imprimerie nationale.

Brockliss, L. (1987). *French Higher Education in the seventeenth and eighteenth centuries*. Oxford: Oxford University Press.

Brockliss, L. and Jones, C. (1997). *The Medical World of Early Modern France*. Oxford: Clarendon Press.

Brose, E.D. (1998). *Technology and science in the industrializing nations 1500–1914*. Atlantic Highlands: Humanities Press.

Brouard-Arends, I. (ed.) (2003). *Lectrices de l'ancien régime*. Rennes: Presses Universitaires de Rennes.

Brouard-Arends, I. and Plagnol-Dieval, M.E. (2007). *Femmes éducatrices au siècle des lumières*. Rennes: Presses Universitaires de Rennes.

Brown, H.G. (1995). *War, Revolution and the Bureaucratic State: politics and army administration in France 1791–1799*. Oxford: Clarendon Press.

Brown, H.G. (2006). *Ending the French Revolution: violence, justice and repression from the terror to Napoleon*. Charlottesville: University of Virginia Press.

Burrows, S. (2003). The Innocence of Jacques-Pierre Brissot, *Historical Journal*, 46, 843–71.

Calemard, J. (1929). *Manon Roland chez elle*. Paris: Giraud Badin.

Campbell, P., Kaiser T., and Linton, M. (eds) (2007). *Conspiracy in the French Revolution.* Manchester: Manchester University Press.

Campbell, W.J. (2010). The origin of Citizen Genet's projected attack on Spanish Louisiana, a case-study in Girondin politics, *FHS,* 33(4), 515–44.

Carbonnier, Y. (2006). *Maisons parisiennes des Lumières.* Paris: PUPS.

Caron, P. (1935). *Les Massacres de septembre.* Paris: Maison du livre français.

Caron, P. (1950). *La Première Terreur,* I, *Les Missions du Conseil Exécutif Provisoire et de la commune de Paris.* Paris: PUF.

Chartier, R. (1969). L'Académie de Lyon au 18e siècle, in: *Nouvelles études lyonnaises,* H.J. Martin (ed.). Geneva: Droz, pp. 132–250.

Chartier, R. (1990). *Les origines culturelles de la Révolution francaise.* Paris: Seuil.

Chassagne, S. (1991). *Le Coton et ses patrons 1760–1840.* Paris: EHESS.

Chaumié, J. (1980). Les Girondins, in: *Girondins et Montagnards, Colloque 1980,* A. Soboul (ed.). Paris: Société des études robespierristes, pp. 19–60.

Chaussinand-Nogaret, G. (1985). *Madame Roland: une femme en révolution.* Paris: Seuil.

Church, C. (1981). *Revolution and Red Tape.* Oxford: Clarendon Press.

Colloque Roland (1990). = *Jean-Marie et Manon Roland, Actes du Colloque nationale de Villefranche-sur-Saône, 27–29 octobre 1989,* Union des sociétés historiques du Rhône, *Actes des journées d'étude,* 1989, vol. 6.

Conner, S. (1990). In the shadow of the guillotine and in the margins of history: English-speaking authors view women in the French Revolution, *Journal of Women's History,* 1(3), 244–60.

Conway, M.D. (1900). *Thomas Paine 1737–1805,* transl. F. Rabbe. Paris: Plon. [Appendix on Edmond-Charles Genet.]

Cornevin, M. (2002). *Liberté que de crimes on commet en ton nom: vie de Madame Roland.* Paris: Maisonneuve & Larose.

Cowans, J. (2001). *To Speak for the People: public opinion and the problem of legitimacy in the French Revolution.* London: Routledge.

Crook, M. (1996). *Elections in the French Revolution: an apprenticeship in democracy 1789–1899.* Cambridge: Cambridge University Press.

Courajod, L.C.J. (1887). *Alexandre Lenoir et le Musée des monuments français.* Paris: Champion, 3 vols.

Dalton, S. (2001). Gender and the shifting ground of revolutionary politics: the case of Madame Roland, *Canadian Journal of History/Annales Canadiennes d'histoire,* XXXVI, 259–82.

Darnton R. (1979). *The Business of Enlightenment: a publishing history of the Encyclopédie 1775–1800.* Cambridge: Harvard University Press.

Darnton, R. (1982). *The Literary Underground of the Old Regime.* Cambridge: Harvard University Press.

Darnton, R. (1984). *The Great Cat Masscacre and Other Episodes in French Cultural History.* New York: Basic Books

Daudin, G. (2005). *Commerce et prospérité: la France au XVIIIe siècle.* Paris: Presses Universitaires Paris-Sorbonne.

Daumard, A. and Furet, F. (1961). *Structures et relations sociales à Paris au XVIIIe siècle.* Paris: Armand Colin.

Daumas, M. (2004). *Le Mariage amoureux: histoire du lien conjugal sous l'ancien régime.* Paris: Armand Colin.

Dermenjian, G., Guilhamou, J., and Pied, M. (2000). *Femmes entre ombre et lumière: recherches sur la visibilite sociale XVI-XXe siècles.* Paris: Publisud.

Desan, S. (2004). *The Family on Trial in Revolutionary France*. Berkeley: University of California Press.

Desan, S. (2008). Transatlantic spaces of Revolution: the French Revolution, Sciotomanie and American Lands, *Journal of Early Modern History*, 12(6), 467–505.

Desan, S. and Merrick, J. (eds) (2009). *The Family, Gender and Law in Early Modern Europe*. University Park: Pennsylvania State University Press.

Descimon, R. and Haddad, E. (eds) (2010). *Epreuves de noblesse: les expériences nobiliaires de la robe parisienne, XVIe-XVIIIe siècles*. Paris: Les Belles Lettres.

Devance, L. (1977). Le féminisme pendant la Révolution française, *AHRF*, 49, 341–76.

Diaconoff, S. (2005). *Through the Looking-glass: women, books and sex in the French Enlightenment*. Albany: SUNY Press.

Diaz, B. (1993). "Le bonheur dans les fers", Lettres de prison de Mme Roland, juin-november 1793, in: *Expériences limites de l'épistolaire, lettres d'éxil, d'enfermement, de folie,* A. Magnan (ed.). Caen: PU Caen.

Diaz, B. (1999). Morales de la lettre: la correspondence de jeunesse de Mme Roland 1767–80, in: *Lettre et réflexion morale, la lettre miroir de l'âme,* G. Haroche-Bouzinac (ed.). Paris: Klincksieck.

Diaz, B. (2002). *L'épistolaire ou la pensée nomade*. Paris: PUF.

Diaz, B. and Siess, J. (eds) (2006). *L'épistolaire au féminin: correspondances de femmes (XVIIIe-XXe siècle)*. Caen: PU Caen.

Dix-Huitième siècle, special number 'Femmes des Lumières' (2004).

Dorigny, M. (1980). Violence et révolution: les Girondins et les massacres de septembre, in: *Girondins et Montagnards*, A. Soboul (ed.). Paris: Société des études robespierristes, 103–20.

Dorigny, M. (1981). Les Girondins et le droit de propriété, *Bulletin d'histoire économique et sociale de la Révolution*, *CTHS*, 1981–3, 15–31.

Dorigny, M. (1989a). La propagande girondine et le livre en 1792: le Bureau d'esprit public, *Dix- huitième siècle*, 21, 203–15.

Dorigny, M. (1989b). Les Girondins avant le 'fédéralisme': Paris, 'chef-lieu' de la Révolution, in: *Paris et la Révolution* (Actes du colloque de Paris I, avril 1989), M. Vovelle (ed.). Paris: Publications de la Sorbonne, pp. 285–92.

Doyle, W. (1980). *Origins of the French Revolution*. Oxford: Oxford University Press.

Doyle, W. (2002). *The Oxford History of the French Revolution*. 2nd edn. Oxford: Oxford University Press.

Edelstein, D. (2009). *The Terror of Natural Right: republicanism, the cult of nature & the French Revolution*, Chicago & London: University of Chicago Press.

Edmonds, W.D. (1990). *Jacobinism and the Revolt of Lyon 1789–1793*. Oxford: Oxford University Press.

Ellery, E. (1970). *Brissot de Warville: a study in the history of the French Revolution*. New York: Benjamin Franklin.

Fauré, C. (ed.) (1997/2010). *Encyclopédie historique et politique des femmes*. Paris: PUF ['L'action politique des femmes pendant la Révolution française', pp. 139–168].

Félix, J. (2006). *Louis XVI et Marie-Antoinette: un couple en politique*. Paris: Payot.

Les Femmes et la Révolution française. [ouvrage collectif] (1989–1991), 3 vols., Toulouse: Presses Universitaires du Mirail.

Feuga, P. (1985). *L'Hôtel de ville de Lyon: l'hôtel commun et les municipalités lyonnaises*. Lyon: Editions lyonnaises d'art et d'histoire.

Feuga, P. (1991). *Luc-Antoine Champagneux, ou le destin d'un Rolandin fidèle*. Bourgoin: Editions Lyonnaises d'art et d'histoire.

Fierro, A. and Sarazin, J-Y. (2005). *Le Paris des Lumières, d'après le plan de Turgot (1734–1739)*. Paris: Réunion des musées nationaux.

Fraser, A. (2001). *Marie Antoinette: the journey*. London: Weidenfeld & Nicolson.

Furet, F. and Ozouf, M. (eds) (1988). *Dictionnaire critique de la révolution française*. Paris: Flammarion.

Furet, F. and Ozouf, M. (eds) (1991). *La Gironde et les Girondins*. Paris: Payot.

Furet, F. and Richet, D. (1973). *La Révolution française*. Paris: Fayard.

Garden, M. (1972). *Lyon et les Lyonnais au XVIIIe siècle*. Lyon: Presses Universitaires de Lyon.

Garrier, G. (1973). *Paysans du Beaujolais et du Lyonnais 1800–1970*, 2 vols. Grenoble: PUG.

Garrioch, D. (1986). *Neighbourhood and Community in Paris 1740–1790*. Cambridge: Cambridge University Press.

Garrioch, D. (1996). *The Formation of the Parisian Bourgeoisie*. Cambridge: Harvard University Press.

Garrioch, D. (2002). *The Making of Revolutionary Paris*. Berkeley: University of California Press.

Gelfand, E.D. (1983). *Imagination in Confinement: women's writings from French prisons*. Ithaca: Cornell University Press.

Gillispie, C.C. (1980). *Science and Polity in France: the end of the ancien régime*. Princeton: Princeton University Press.

Gillispie, C.C. (2004). *Science and Polity in France: the revolutionary and Napoleonic years*. Princeton: Princeton University Press.

Godineau, D. (1988). *Citoyennes tricoteuses: les femmes du peuple à Paris pendant la Révolution française*. Aix-en-Provence: Alinea.

Godineau, D. (2003). *Les Femmes dans la société française*. Paris: Armand Colin.

Goodman, D. (1994). *The Republic of Letters: a cultural history of the French Enlightenment*. Ithaca: Cornell University Press.

Goodman, D. (2009a). *Becoming a Woman in the Age of Letters*. Ithaca: Cornell University Press.

Goodman Dena (2009b). Marriage choice and marital success: reasoning about marriage, love and happiness, in: *The Family, Gender and Law in Early Modern Europe*, S. Desan and J. Merrick, J. (eds). University Park: Pennsylvania State University Press.

Grall, J. (1989). *Girondins et Montagnards: les dessous d'une insurrection (1793)*. Rennes: Editions Ouest-France.

Grassi, M.-C. (1994). *L'Art de la lettre au temps de la Nouvelle Héloïse et du romantisme*. Geneva: Slatkine.

Greer, D. (1951). *The Incidence of the Terror during the French Revolution*. Cambridge: Harvard University Press.

Gueniffey, P. (1991). Brissot, in: *La Gironde et les Girondins*, F. Furet and M. Ozouf (eds). Paris: Payot, pp. 437–64.

Gueniffey, P. (1993). *Le Nombre et la raison: la Révolution française et les élections*. Paris: Editions de l'EHESS.

Guérin, D. (1968). *La lutte des classes sous la première république*, 2 vols. Paris: Gallimard.

Haase-Dubosc, D. and Viénot, E. (eds) (1991). *Femmes et pouvoirs sous l'ancien régime*. Paris: Rivages.

Hammersley, R. (2005). *French Revolutionaries and English Republicans: the Cordeliers Club 1790–1794*. Woodbridge: Boydell and RHS.

Hampson, N. (1974/1988). *The Life and Opinions of Maximilien Robespierre*. Oxford: Blackwell.

Hampson, N. (1978/1988). *Danton.* Oxford: Blackwell.

Hanson, P. (2003). *The Jacobin Republic Under Fire: the federalist revolt in the French Revolution.* University Park: Pennsylvania State University Press.

Hanson, P. (2009). *Contesting the French Revolution.* Oxford: Wiley-Blackwell.

Harder, M. (2008). Ex-Conventionnels and historians of the revolution, in: *Historicising the French Revolution*, Armenteros, C., Blanning,T., DiVanna, I. *et al.* (eds). Newcastle upon Tyne: Cambridge Scholars Publishing, pp. 284–307.

Hardman, J. (1973). *French Revolution Documents* II. Oxford: Blackwell.

Hardman, J. (1981). *The French Revolution: the fall of the ancien régime to the thermidorian reaction 1785–1795* (Documents of Modern History). London: Edward Arnold.

Haroche-Bouzinac, G. (1999). *Lettre et réflexion morale, la lettre miroir de l'âme.* Paris: Klincksieck.

Harris, J.R. (1998). *Industrial Espionage and Technology Transfer: Britain and France in the eighteenth century.* Aldershot: Ashgate.

Hesse, C. (2001). *The Other Enlightenment: how French women became modern.* Princeton: Princeton University Press.

Heuer, J. (2005). *The Family and the Nation: gender and citizenship in revolutionary France 1789–1830.* Ithaca: Cornell University Press.

Holmes, R. (1989). *Coleridge: early visions.* London: Hodder & Stoughton.

Horn, J. (2006). *The Path Not Taken, French Industrialization in the Age of Revolution.* Cambridge: MIT Press.

Howe, P.C. (2008). *Foreign Policy and the French Revolution, Charles-François Dumouriez, Pierre Lebrun and the Belgian Plan 1789–1793.* New York: Palgrave.

Huart, S. d' (1986). *Brissot, la Gironde au pouvoir.* Paris: Laffont.

Hubscher, R. (ed.) (1986). *Histoire d'Amiens.* Toulouse.

Hufton, O. (1971). Women in Revolution 1789–1796, *Past and Present*, 43, 90–108.

Hufton, O. (1992). *Women and the Limits of Citizenship in the French Revolution.* Toronto: Toronto University Press.

Hunt, L.A. (1978). *Revolution and Urban Politics in Provincial France: Troyes and Reims, 1786–1790.* Stanford: Stanford University Press.

Hunt, L.A. (1984/2004). *Politics, Culture and Class in the French Revolution.* Berkeley: University of California Press.

Hunt, L.A. (1992). *The Family Romance of the French Revolution.* London: Routledge.

Hunt, L.A. (2007). *Inventing Human Rights.* New York: Norton.

Jacob, M. (1997). *Scientific Culture and the Making of the Industrial West.* New York: Oxford University Press.

Jal, A. (1872). *Dictionnaire critique de biographie et d'histoire, errata et supplément d'après des documents authentiques, inédits.* Paris.

Jaurès, J. (1983). *Histoire socialiste de la Révolution française.* A. Soboul (ed.), 7 vols. Paris: Editions sociales.

Jean-Marie et Manon Roland, see *Colloque Roland.*

Johnson, C. (1993). Capitalism and the state: capital accumulation and proletarianization in the Languedocian woollens industry, in: *The Workplace Before the Factory: artisans and proletarians 1500–1800*, T.M. Saflet and L.N. Rosenband (eds). Ithaca: Cornell University Press.

Jones, C. (1990). *The Longman Companion to the French Revolution.* Harlow: Longman.

Jones, C. and Spang R. (1999). Sansculottes, in: *Consumers and Luxury: consumption and culture in Europe 1650–1850*, M. Berg and H. Clifford (eds). Manchester: Manchester University Press, pp. 37–62.

Jordan, D. (1979). *The King's Trial: the French Revolution vs Louis XVI*. Berkeley: University of California Press.

Kadane, K.A. (1963–1964). The real difference between Manon Phlipon and Mme Roland, *FHS*, 3(4), 542–9.

Kaiser, T. (2000). Who's afraid of Marie-Antoinette? Diplomacy, Austrophobia and the Queen, *French History*, 14, 241–71.

Kale, S. (2004). *French Salons: high society and political sociability from the old regime to the revolution of 1848*. Baltimore: Johns Hopkins University Press.

Kaplan, S. (1976). *Bread, Politics and Political Economy in the Reign of Louis XV*, 2 vols. The Hague: Nijhoff.

Kates, G. (1985). *The Cercle Social, the Girondins and the French Revolution*. Princeton: Princeton Universty Press.

Kawa, C. (1996). *Les ronds de cuir en Révolution: les employés du ministère de l'Intéreur sous la première République 1792–1800*. Paris: Editions du CTHS.

Kennedy, D. (2002). *Helen Maria Williams and the Age of Revolution*. Lewisburg: Bucknell University Press.

Kennedy, M. (1982). *The Jacobin Clubs in the French Revolution: the early years*. Princeton: Princeton University Press.

Kennedy, M. (1988). *The Jacobin Clubs in the French Revolution: the middle years*. Princeton: Princeton University Press.

Kermina, F. (1976). *Madame Roland ou La passion révolutionnaire*. Paris: Perrin.

Knott, S. and Taylor, B. (eds) (2005). *Women, Gender and Enlightenment*. Basingstoke: Palgrave.

Kuscinski, A. (1916–1919). *Dictionnaire des conventionnels*. Paris: F. Rieder.

Lamartine, A. de (1851). *Oeuvres complètes*. Paris: chez l'auteur: vol. XI, 'Histoire des Girondins'.

Landes, J. (1988). *Women and the Public Sphere in the Age of the French Revolution*. Ithaca: Cornell University Press.

Lapied, M. and Peyrard, C. (eds) (2003). *La Révolution française au carrefour des recherches*. Aix en Provence: Universite de Provence.

Lebrun, F. (1975). *La Vie conjugale sous l'ancien régime*. Paris: Armand Colin.

Le Corbeiller, A. (1909). La maison de Roland à Rouen, *Bulletin de la société des amis des monuments rouennais*, Rouen: Lecerf.

Lefebvre, G. (1957). *La Révolution française*. Paris: PUF.

Le Guin, C. (1966). *Roland de la Platière: a public servant in the eighteenth century*. Philadelphia: Transactions of the American Philosophical Society.

Lemay, E.H. (1987). *La Vie quotidienne des députés aux Etats Généraux en 1789*. Paris: Hachette.

Lemay, E.H. (1991). *Dictionnaire des Constituants 1789–1791*. Oxford: Voltaire Foundation.

Lemay, E.H. (2007). *Dictionnaire des Législateurs 1791–1792*. Ferney: Voltaire, Centre d'études du XVIIIe siècle.

Lenoble, M. (1908). Les inspecteurs des manufactures en France sous l'ancien régime, *Bulletin de l'inspection du travail* (online), pp.117ff.

Lévy, D., Appleby, H., and Johnson, M. (1979). *Women in Revolutionary Paris 1789–1795*. Urbana: University of Illinois Press.

Levy, M.-F. (1990). *L'Enfant, la famille et la Révolution française*. Paris: Orban.

Lewis-Beck, M.S., Hildreth, A., and Spitzer, A.B. (1991). Was there a Girondist faction in the National Convention 1792–1793? *FHS*, 15, 519–36 and 537–48, comments. [Reprinted in Furet and Ozouf (1991).]

Lilti, A. (2005). *Le Monde des salons. Sociabilité et mondanité à Paris au XVIIIe siècle.* Paris: Fayard.

Lintilhac, E. (1918). Le salon de Madame Dodun, *Révolution française*, LXXI.

Linton, M. (2001). *The Politics of Virtue in Enlightenment France.* Basingstoke: Palgrave.

Linton, M. (2008). Fatal friendships: the politics of Jacobin friendship, *FHS*, 31(1), 51–76.

Loft, L. (2002). *Passion, Politics and Philosophie: rediscovering J-P. Brissot.* Westport: Greenwood Press.

Lucas, C. (ed.) (1988). *The French Revolution and the Creation of Modern Political Culture*, vol. 2, *The Political Culture of the Revolution.* Oxford: Pergamon.

Lyon, M. (2006). *Popular Science and Public Opinion.* Manchester: Manchester University Press.

McLellan, A. (1994). *Inventing the Louvre: art, politics and the origins of the modern museum in eighteenth-century Paris.* Cambridge: Cambridge University Press.

McPhee, P. (2006). *Living the French Revolution 1789–1799.* New York: Palgrave Macmillan.

Mantel, H. (1992). *A Place of Greater Safety.* Harmondsworth: Penguin.

Margadant, J.B. (ed.) (2000). *The New Biography.* Berkeley: University of California Press.

Marion, M. (1923). *Dictionnaire des Institutions de la France.* Paris: Picard.

Martin, J.-C. (2005). *La Révolution à l'oeuvre: perspectives actuelles dans l'histoire de la révolution française.* Rennes: Presses Universitaires de Rennes.

Martin, J.-C. (2008). *La révolte brisée: femmes dans la Révolution française et l'Empire.* Paris: Armand Colin.

Mathiez, A. (ed.) (1930). *Girondins et montagnards.* Paris, Firmin Didot.

May, G. (1964). *De Jean-Jacques Rousseau à Mme Roland: essai sur la sensibilité pré-romantique et révolutionnaire.* Geneva: Droz.

May, G. (1970). *Madame Roland and the Age of Revolution.* New York: Columbia University Press.

Mazeau, G. (2009). *Le Bain de l'histoire: Charlotte Corday et l'attentat contre Marat 1793–2009.* Seyssel: Champ Vallon.

Mège, F. (1888). *Bancal des Issarts, le conventionnel.* Paris: H. Champion.

Mérat, M. (1990). Les maisons beaujolaises de Jean-Marie et Manon Roland, in: *Colloque Roland* (1990), pp. 101–14.

Michel, R. (ed.) (1993). *David contre David: actes du colloque David, Musée du Louvre*, 2 vols. Paris: Documentation française.

Minard, P. (1998). *La Fortune du colbertisme: état et industrie dans la France des Lumières.* Paris: Fayard.

Missol, L. and Perroud, C. (1896). Les Roland en Beaujolais au XVIIIe siècle, *Révolution française*, 31, 389–413.

Moore, L. (2006). *Liberty: the lives and times of six women in revolutionary France.* London: HarperPress.

O'Connor, A. (2008). The educational proposals of the French Revolution: a case study in the intellectual and cultural history of expectations, in: *Historicising the French Revolution*, Armenteros, C. *et al.* (eds). Newcastle: Cambridge Scholars, pp. 224–44.

Offen, K. (1990). The new sexual politics of the French Revolution, *FHS*, 16(4), 909–22.

Oliver, B. (2007). *From Royal to National: the Louvre Museum and the Bibliothèque National-ale*. Lexington: Lenham.

Outram, D. (1987). Le langage mâle de la vertu: women, politics and public language in the French Revolution, in: *The Social History of Language*, R. Porter and P. Burke (eds). Cambridge: Cambridge University Press.

Outram, D. (1989). *The Body in the French Revolution*. New Haven: Yale University Press.

Ozouf, M. (1991). Madame Roland, in: *La Gironde et les Girondins*, F. Furet and M. Ozouf (eds). Paris: Payot.

Palmer, R.R. (1985). *The Improvement of Humanity: education and the French Revolution*. Princeton: PUP.

Palmer, R.R. (1989). *The Year of the Terror: twelve who ruled France 1793–1794*, 3rd edn. Oxford: Oxford University Press.

Pardailhe-Galabrun, A. (1988). *La Naissance de l'intime, 3000 foyers parisiennes des XVIIe-XVIIIe siecles*. Paris: PUF.

Parker, H.T. (1979). *The Bureau of Commerce in 1781 and its Policies with Respect to French Industry*. Durham: Carolina Academic Press.

Parker, H.T. (1993). *An Administrative Bureau during the old regime 1781–1783*. Cranbury: Associated University Presses.

Pasco, A.H. (2009). *Revolutionary Love in Eighteenth- and Nineteenth-Century France*. Farnham: Ashgate.

Patrick, A. (1972). *The Men of the First French Republic: political alignments in the National Convention of 1792*. Baltimore: Johns Hopkins Press.

Peiffer, J. (1991). L'engouement des femmes pour les sciences au XVIIIe siècle, in: *Femmes et pouvoirs sous l'ancien régime*, D. Haase-Dubosc and E. Vienot (eds). Rivages.

Pellegrin, N. (2003). Lire avec des plumes ou l'art- féminin de l'extrait à la fin du XVIIIe siecle, in: *Lectrices de l'ancien régime*, I. Brouard-Arends (ed.). Rennes: Presses Universitaires de Rennes.

Perroud, C. (1895). Note critique sur les dates de l'exécution de Madame Roland et du suicide de Roland, *La Révolution française*, 29, 15–26.

Perroud, C. (1896). Jany, le dernier correspondant de Mme Roland, *La Révolution française*, 30.

Perroud, C. (1898). Brissot et les Roland, *La Révolution française*, 34, 403–22.

Perroud, C. (1899). Une amie de Mme Roland, Souvenirs inédits de Sophie Grandchamp, *La Révolution française*, 37, 65–89 and 153–70.

Perroud, C. (1902b). Un projet de Brissot pour une Association agricole, *La Révolution française*, 42, 260–5.

Perroud, C. (1909). Un ami de Mme Roland: Henri Albert Gosse, *La Révolution francaise*, 47, 481–90.

Perroud, C. (1912). Roland et la presse subventionnée, *La Révolution francaise*, 62, 206–13, 315–32, 396–420.

Perroud, C. (ed.) (1913). Un voyage de Jean-Marie Roland de la Platière, *Bulletin de la Société des Sciences et des Arts du Beaujolais*.

Perroud, C. [see also under 'Works of J.M. Roland and M.-J. Roland above, for editions].

Pinet, R. (1990). Jean-Marie Roland de la Platière et l'Académie de Villefranche, in: *Colloque Roland*.

Poirier, P. (1999). *Turgot*. Paris: Perrin.

Pommier, E. (1991). *L'Art de la liberté: doctrines et débats de la Révolution française*. Paris: Gallimard.

Pommier, E. (ed.) (1992). *Réflexions sur le Musée National 14 janvier 1793 par J. B. P. Le Brun*. Paris: Réunion des Musées nationaux.

Pope-Hennessy, U. (1917). *Madame Roland: à Study in Revolution*. London: Nisbet.

Popkin, J.D. (1990). *Revolutionary News: the press in France 1789–1799*. Durham: Duke University Press.

Poulot, D. (1997). *Musée, nation, patrimoine 1789–1815*. Paris: Gallimard.

Reddy, W. (1984). *The Rise of Market Culture: the textile trade and French society 1750–1900*. Cambridge: Cambridge University Press.

Reddy, W. (2001). *The Navigation of Feeling: a framework for the history of the emotions*. Cambridge: Cambridge University Press.

Rémond, A. (1946). *John Holker*. Paris: M. Rivière.

Rey, A. (1882). *Le naturaliste Bosc et les Girondins à St Prix, canton de Montmorency*. Pontoise: A Pâris.

Rey, A. (1901). *Le naturaliste Bosc, un Girondin herborisant*. Versailles: Bernard.

Reynolds, S. (1986) Marianne's citizens, in: *Women, State and Revolution: power and gender in Europe since 1789*, S. Reynolds (ed.). Brighton: Harvester.

Roche, D. (1978). *Le siecle des lumières en province: académies et académiciens provinciaux 1680–1789*. Geneva: Mouton.

Roche, D. (1987). *The People of Paris: an essay in popular culture in the eighteenth century*, trans. M. Evans. Berkeley: University of California Press.

Roche, D. (1988). *Les Républicains des lettres*. Paris: Fayard.

Roulston, C. (2010). *Narrating Marriage in Eighteenth-Century England and France*. Farnham: Ashgate.

Saflet, T.M. and Rosenband, L.N. (1993). *The Workplace Before the Factory: artisans and proletarians 1500–1800*. Ithaca & London: Cornell University Press.

Scott, J.W. (1996). *Only Paradoxes to Offer: French feminists and the Rights of Man*. Cambridge: Harvard University Press.

Scurr, R. (2007). *Fatal Purity: Robespierre and the French Revolution*. London: Vintage Books.

Senevas, Baron de (1938). *Une famille française du XIVe au XXe siècle*. Paris: Dumoulin.

Sewell, W.H., Jr (1988). Le citoyen/la citoyenne: activity passivity and the revolutionary concept of citizenship, in: *The French Revolution and the Creation of Modern Political Culture*, vol 2, *The Political Culture of the Revolution*, Lucas, C. (ed.), Oxford: Pergamon, pp. 105–21.

Shovlin, J. (2006). *The Political Economy of Virtue: luxury, patriotism and the origins of the French Revolution*. Ithaca: Cornell University Press.

Showalter, E. (2004). *Françoise de Graffigny, her life and works*. Oxford: SVEC.

Slavin, M. (1986). *The Making of an Insurrection: Parisian sections and the Gironde*. Cambridge: Harvard University Press.

Soboul, A. (ed.) (1980). *Actes du colloque Girondins et Montagnards*. Paris: Société des études robespierristes.

Sonenscher, M. (1989). *Work and Wages: natural law, politics and the eighteenth-century French trades*. Cambridge: Cambridge University Press.

Sonnet, M. (2003). Geneviève Randon de Malboissière et ses livres, in: Brouard-Arends, I., *Lectrices de l'ancien régime*.

Spang, R. (2000). *The Invention of the Restaurant*. Cambridge: Harvard University Press.

Sussman, G. (1982). *Selling Mother's Milk: the wetnursing business in France 1715–1914*. Urbana: University of Illinois Press.

Sutherland, D.M.G. (1985). *France 1789-1815: revolution and counter-revolution.* London: Fontana.

Sydenham, M.J. (1961). *The Girondins.* London: Athlone.

Tackett, T. (1996). *Becoming a Revolutionary: the deputies of the French National Assembly and the emergence of a revolutionary culture 1789–1790.* Princeton: Princeton University Press.

Tackett, T. (2003). *When the King Took Flight.* Cambridge: Harvard University Press.

Tarbell, I.M. (1896). *Madame Roland: à biographical study.* London: Laurence and Bullen.

Taylor, I.A. (1911). *Life of Madame Roland.* London: Hutchinson.

Terson, H. (1913). *Origine et évolution du ministère de l'intérieur.* Montpellier: Firmin et Montane.

Thépot, A. (ed.) (1985). Roland de la Platière et les patiences de l'inspection méthodique, in: *L'Ingénieur dans la société française.* Paris: Mouvement social.

Thomson, J.K.J. (1982). *Clermont-de-Lodève 1633–1789: fluctuations in the posperity of a Languedocian cloth-making town.* Cambridge: Cambridge University Press.

Tosh, J. (1999). *The Pursuit of History,* 3rd edn. Harlow: Longman-Pearson.

Traer, J.F. (1980). *Marriage and the Family in Eighteenth-century France.* Ithaca: Cornell University Press.

Trouille, M.S. (1997). *Sexual Politics in the Enlightenment: women writers read Rousseau.* Albany: SUNY Press.

Tucoo-Chala, S. (1977). *Charles-Joseph Panckoucke et la librairie française 1736–1798.* Pau: Editions Marrimpouy jeune.

Vatel, C. (1872). *Charlotte Corday et les Girondins, pièces classées et notées,* 2 vols. Paris: Plon.

Viénot, E. (2008). *La France, les femmes et le pouvoir,* II, *Les résistances de la société (XVIIe-XVIIIe siècle).* Paris: Perrin.

Vovelle, M. (ed.) (1995). *1789–1799: nouveaux chantiers d'histoire révolutionnaire, les institutions et les hommes.* Paris: Editions du CHTS.

Wahl, M. (1894). *Les premières années de la Révolution à Lyon.* Paris: Armand Colin.

Walton, C. (2009). *Policing Public Opinion in the French Revolution: the culture of calumny and the problem of free speech.* New York: Oxford University Press.

Walzer, M. (ed.) (1974). *Regicide and Revolution.* London: Cambridge University Press.

Watts, G. (1958). The Encyclopédie méthodique, *PMLA,* 73, 362–5.

Whaley, L. (2000). *Radicals: politics and republicanism in the French Revolution.* Stroud: Sutton.

Whatmore, R. (1996). Commerce, constitutions and the manners of a nation: Etienne Clavière's revolutionary political economy 1788–1793, *History of European Ideas,* XXII, 351–68.

Whatmore, R. and Livesey, J. (2000). Les fondations intellectuelles de la politique des Girondins, *AHRF,* 2000 (no 321).

Wiewiorka, A. (2010). *Maurice et Jeannette.* Paris: Fayard.

Woodward, L. (1930). *Une Anglaise, amie de la Révolution française: Helen Maria Williams,* Vol. 64. Paris: Bibliothèque de la Revue de Littérature Comparée.

Woolf, V. (1966). Mr Bennett and Mrs Brown, in: *Collected Essays,* L. Woolf (ed.). London: Hogarth, pp. 319–37.

Unpublished dissertation

Perl-Rosenthal, N. (2011). Corresponding Republics: Letter Writing and Patriot Organizing in the Atlantic Revolutions, ca. 1760–1792, unpublished PhD dissertation, Columbia University, NY.

Acknowledgements

Most of my acknowledgements are covered by the footnotes and the bibliography, and my gratitude reaches well beyond, to the many scholars who have worked on the history of eighteenth-century France and the Revolution. Because of renovation works at the Bibliothèque Nationale de France in the rue de Richelieu site, and the continuing move of documents from the Archives Nationales (CARAN) to Pierrefitte, it was not always possible to see all the desirable documents, but individual members of staff at both venues courteously did what they could to help me, as did staff at the BNF, Site François-Mitterrand. The National Library of Scotland in Edinburgh became my second home since it has many French holdings, including the Crawford collection of revolutionary documents. I am particularly grateful to the staff there for all their help over the years. The university libraries in Stirling and Edinburgh were also invaluable resources.

Many colleagues and experts on the period have helped enormously through their personal advice, or by providing comments on conference or seminar papers; if I've got things wrong it isn't their fault. I must make special mention of Nathan Perl-Rosenthal, whose dissertation was being completed at the same time as this book, and who generously let me see drafts, as well as sharing references and ideas; and also James Thomson, who kindly sent me some of his handwritten notes on the Languedoc. Oron Joffe helped me with computer advice. Peter France read drafts, made sensible comments, and suggested I improve the translations, when I'm sure he would rather have been reading Pushkin.

i

Index